Wakefield Press

Ashton's Hotel

Rhondda Harris is a retired archaeologist. She studied at Flinders University where her honours thesis on archaeology and post-contact Indigenous Adelaide was both the start of her career and the beginning of a passion for researching the history of early Adelaide.

She now works on deceased estates, sorting through the accumulations of lives. Rhondda sees this as a sort of archaeology and it is a job she loves.

Rhondda Harris moved to Adelaide in 1974, has two sons, two grandsons and a dog. Despite growing up in New South Wales, she sees Adelaide as home.

Henry Heath Glover, *William Baker Ashton*, circa 1850 [SLSA, B 11202]

Ashton's Hotel

The journal of William Baker Ashton, first governor of the Adelaide Gaol

RHONDDA HARRIS

Wakefield Press

Wakefield Press
16 Rose Street
Mile End
South Australia 5031
www.wakefieldpress.com.au

First published 2017
Reprinted 2018

Copyright © Rhondda Harris, 2017

All rights reserved. This book is copyright. Apart from
any fair dealing for the purposes of private study, research,
criticism or review, as permitted under the Copyright Act,
no part may be reproduced without written permission.
Enquiries should be addressed to the publisher.

Cover designed by Liz Nicholson, designBITE
Edited by Margot Lloyd, Wakefield Press
Typeset by Clinton Ellicott, Wakefield Press

National Library of Australia Cataloguing-in-Publication entry

Creator: Harris, Rhondda, author.
Title: Ashton's hotel: the journal of William Baker Ashton, first governor of
           the Adelaide Gaol / Rhondda Harris.
ISBN: 978 1 74305 482 6 (paperback).
Notes: Includes index.
Subjects: Ashton, William Baker, 1800–1854 – Diaries.
           Adelaide Gaol (S.A.) – History.
           Prison wardens – South Australia – Adelaide – Diaries.
           Jails – South Australia – Adelaide – History.
           South Australia – Social conditions – History.

In memory of John Hodges,
a true scientist, addicted to the wonder of it all.

And for my brother Neil, who has shown so much faith in me.

Contents

A note about words	ix
Preamble	1
Discovering the journal	3
William Ashton in early 1839	10
Adelaide in early 1839	20
The temporary gaol	39
Introduction to the governor's journal	45
The governor's journal 1839	51
The governor's journal 1840	76
The governor's journal 1841	128
The governor's journal 1842	176
The governor's journal 1843	210
The governor's journal 1844	253
The governor's journal 1845	302
Postscript	346
Notes	350
Index	364

A note about words

A number of words commonly used in early Adelaide would now be considered incorrect – words such as 'lunatic', 'tribe', and 'natives'. At that time these were not offensive words. They were, in fact, perfectly ordinary and correct words. The problem is what to do with them now.

In this book, when I quote directly from a text such as the journal itself, or from other sources such as books, letters or old newspapers, I keep true to the original and retain these words. It would seem ridiculous to do otherwise.

In my own text I have my own guidelines. For example I will use the word 'lunatic', but only in quote marks, and only when it seems important to retain the word or when a modern word would sound completely wrong. Wherever it seems appropriate or possible, I use 'mentally ill'.

In my own text, when referring to Indigenous people, I do not use the word 'native', not even in quote marks. I use the terms 'Aboriginal people' and, less often, 'Indigenous people'. The term 'Aboriginal people' has the advantage of being relatively acceptable in the present and also close to 'Aboriginal', used in early Adelaide. The word 'Indigenous' was almost never used in early Adelaide, and when it was, referred to vegetation and animals, not to people, so to me it does not seem to fit when referring to Adelaide's early years. The word Indigenous is however the currently most accepted word so I use it on occasion when it seems right to do so.

In early Adelaide, Colonel Light's parklands were almost always written as two words – 'Park Land' or 'Park land' – whereas now the usual, for a long time at least, has been one. Recently the use of two words has crept back into vogue, with as yet no consistent practice. When using source material I keep to the original form. In my own text I use my preferred modern usage, 'parklands'. It helps me with a sense of history in the present. Our parklands are still here, the same place, the very same piece of ground, as the early 'Park Land', where most events in this book took place.

The journal has an odd mix of words beginning in both upper and lower case letters within the one sentence, unusual punctuation, sometimes odd spelling and occasional mistakes. I have turned off the autocorrect and transcribed it just as it is in the original. It is an editor's nightmare but an authentic read.

Preamble

June 11 Wednesday: A Poor Woman Named Wilkinson Supposed to be Insane was found at 7½ this Morning with 2 Small Children Nearly Dead from wet and Cold at the end of the ditch Near the Gaol the Poor Children were in a Dreadful State their Arms and legs being quite Stiff from the Wet & Cold I had the Woman & Children brot into the TurnKeys lodge by a good fire and Mrs. Ashton and Mr Perry took their Wet Clothes off and put warm Blankets on them and they Soon got better . . .
- Sheriff Visited the Gaol Saw the Prisoners and Saw the poor woman & children found in the Water this Morning, wished her to Remain in the Gaol and he would Report the Circumstances to the Government her Husband was for some years in the Government Employ at the port but have left the Colony Since and this Poor woman has no home for herself or Children.

June 12 Thursday: Mrs Wilkinson Still in Gaol and her children Supplied from the Gaol Rations by order of the Sheriff.

This story is from an old journal, written in Adelaide, South Australia. The date was 1845, in the sixth year of this extraordinary journal and in the ninth year of the South Australian colony. This incident, so briefly recorded, is in itself an ordinary story, yet it hints at the far-from-ordinary character of the writer, William Baker Ashton, first governor of the Adelaide Gaol.

There are many such stories in his journal. They provide entry into the little-known underclass of early Adelaide, a world where many of the poor, the inebriates, the prostitutes, the debtors, as well as many Aboriginal people, mentally ill people, children who stole or absconded from their masters, sailors, runaway convicts, petty criminals and serious criminals, including bushrangers and murderers, were collected in the confines of the first Adelaide gaols. Some of these people escaped and were recaptured. Some were hanged. Many were transported by sea to be punished in the penal colonies of Sydney and Van Diemen's Land, out of Adelaide's sight. They were all looked after for a time by the governor of the gaol, William Ashton; his wife Charlotte; the guards and turnkeys and sometimes their wives; and by visiting officials – doctors, nurses, the protector for the Aboriginal people, the sheriff, religious ministers, and the colonial governor. It is a fascinating journal, a real treasure, and now that it is known, it is a fabulous addition to the story of early Adelaide.

Discovering the journal

I came across the journal in the State Records of South Australia at Gepps Cross.

I had been asked by the South Australian Museum to search the archives to help in the understanding of an archaeological excavation taking place within the Old Adelaide Gaol.[1] The area being dug was under the floor in what was thought to be the earliest women's cells. These had been built in 1849 at a time when a second half of the gaol was being added to the first.

The first half of the gaol had been built – to a stage where it could take at least some of the colony's prisoners – as early as December 1840. This half-gaol had then received the rest of the prisoners by the time Ashton moved into his residence there in June 1841.

The original plan had been for a gaol nearly twice the size. However, soon after construction began, a severe financial crisis in the colony showed no signs of abating and Governor Gawler was forced to essentially halve the plans for the new gaol. The original drawings and plans for the larger gaol were lost in a fire at the old Government House shortly after the new Government House was built.

It was not until 1849, long past the end of this journal and long after the next governor, Governor Grey, had left the colony, that a second half to the gaol was built. The sheriff announced its completion and listed its buildings in his 1850 report.[2] In that same year Charlotte Ashton, William's wife who had assisted him from the start, was officially appointed first matron of the gaol, to look after the special needs of the women prisoners in the new women's cells.³

The journal itself was begun in 1839, before even the first half of the gaol was built, at a time when an earlier 'old gaol' was in use. The earliest entries in the journal all refer to this earlier temporary gaol.

In my search for information about the women's cells, the archivist at Gepps Cross showed me their Department for Correctional Services index. I immediately saw references to a matron's diary (later than Charlotte's time but I thought it would be interesting), to architects' drawings of buildings at various stages of the gaol's expansion, to letters from the sheriff, registers of whippings and hangings, wood and coal supply books . . . and the governor's journal. I ordered them all.

After reading the later matron's diary, a dull repetitive account of an unchanging daily routine for the women, and also the sheriff's letters (mainly recommendations to the colonial governor for clemency for certain prisoners), I began to read the governor's journal. It occurred to me almost immediately that current historians and heritage researchers could not have read this journal. It contained material I had never seen mentioned and also facts that, had they been known, would have altered the established histories of the gaol completely.

This was particularly apparent to me in regards to the 1849 women's cells. The area being excavated was considered by all the historians to be the first cells built especially for women prisoners in the gaol. Here in his journal William Ashton was referring to dedicated women's cells being constructed as early as December 1841, when it was still a half-gaol. The cells being excavated could not have been the first!

When I checked, I found that the 1841 women's yard and cells were definitely included in the official expenditure records (for example, works completed, and wood and coal books). Somehow heritage researchers had skipped these details[4] – and had I not been researching the 1849 women's cells, supposing them to be the first, I may have missed them too.

And there was another puzzle. Though the new gaol was meant to have an inner brick wall and an outer stone wall to make it absolutely secure, Ashton talked in his journal of a 'wooden fence'. The half-gaol was indeed surrounded by an inner brick wall, with additional loose bricks stacked on top. These would fall if the wall was climbed and alert the guards. The outer wall however, though built of stone, was a partial wall only; there was a gap where the gaol was later to be extended, presumably to complete its original design. This gap was filled by a wooden fence, and though the illusion of a fully secure gaol was maintained, even up to recent historical accounts of the gaol, Ashton's journal details two escapes and a number of attempted escapes in the area of the wooden fence. It is in one of these accounts, written in December 1841, that Ashton mentioned a breach being made in the wooden fence to allow completion of a women's yard and cells. This breach and some almost comical bungling by the guards patrolling the wooden fence allowed a prisoner named John Carter, posing as a worker, to nonchalantly walk out of the gaol and not be missed until the cells were locked at night.

I have searched extensively and, apart from the expenditure records above and a brief mention in the sheriff's account of the escape, I have found only one other reference to the 1841 women's yard and cells.[5] This is a newspaper article in which the same escape incident is described. The article mentions the early women's cells being constructed at the time, the writer significantly remembering them as a westerly addition to the half-gaol of the time:

> [The prisoner Carter] had been secured in the new Gaol, to which even at that early time it had been necessary to add another ward to contain female prisoners. This ward was a westerly extension of the premises which had been erected by Colonel Gawler, the original capacity of which he considered to be sufficient, but it was not found to be so, and an enlargement was therefore commenced, and to do this the high outer wall had to be broken through.[6]

A derivative article was printed in 1919:

Another ward was added to the Gaol in Governor Grey's time for female prisoners. This ward was a westerly extension of the premises, erected by Col. Gawler, the original capacity of which he considered to be sufficient. This was not found to be so, and an enlargement was therefore commenced. To do this, the high outer wall had to be broken through. A runaway convict from New South Wales escaped during the building operations.[7]

Curiously these 1841 cells are not represented in Kingston's 1842 *Map of Adelaide* where he depicted every building built at that time. This famous map could be expected to include cells built in December 1841. This is particularly the case when it is known that Kingston was the architect for the original 'whole-gaol' and would have known of any changes at the gaol. So this was indeed a puzzle.

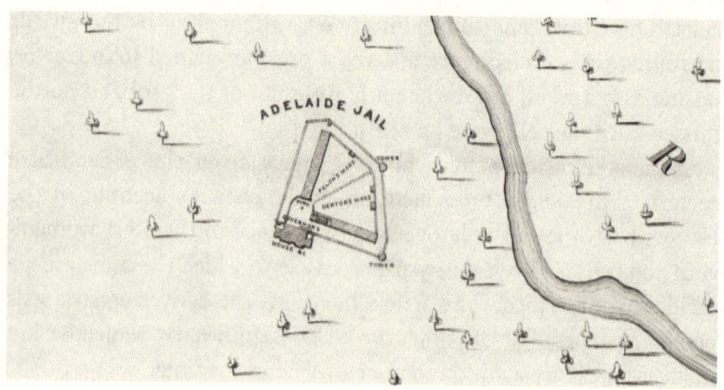

Detail from G.S. Kingston's *Map of Adelaide*, 1842
[State Library of South Australia, map820i1435207a rbr]

The answer may be simple. On its arrival in Adelaide, in July 1843, Kingston's map was lauded for its accuracy, but with a proviso:

> Mr Kingston's splendid map of Adelaide has at last arrived in town ... altogether the map gives a complete and accurate view of our city as it was at the time the work was done.[8]

The map was started in 1840 and completed and published in London.[9] When it finally arrived in Adelaide, in 1843, it included useful information or 'Memoranda' across the base of the map. These were dated 8 December 1842, hence it came to be known as 'Kingston's 1842 *Map of Adelaide*'. However, one of the items on the memoranda reads 'The present Map shews the Buildings in Adelaide on 1st January 1842'.[10] The early women's cells were still being built just a few weeks earlier, in the last part of December 1841, so perhaps it is no surprise that they were not included. It is interesting to note that despite Kingston's later insistence that even fence lines were correct up to the 1 January date, and although he used a special symbol on the map's key for 'ruinous buildings', the 'old gaol', known to still exist in an abandoned state in 1842, was not included either.[11]

So, here I sat, in the quiet of the archives, reading what felt to me like a new discovery and wondering why it had taken until now for someone to find it. I was almost hiding the journal behind my hands so no one could look over my shoulder. Much later I came across a handwritten note tucked inside the back of the journal which said 'Is this official record of the sheriff's office?' and a reply in another hand 'Presumably so'. I wondered if the journal had been lost and maybe only recently found.

Another answer to the mystery of the journal's disappearance however came before I saw these archivists' notes. I had come across files suggesting Kingston had handed over his own sketches of his whole-gaol plans to Governor Grey, under threat of not being paid for some work.[12] I was intrigued by the date of the correspondence – 17 May 1842. I sat up. These letters were written more than a year *after* the 1841 fire that had destroyed the original plans. I hoped the sketches might yet be found somewhere in the archives and asked the archivist on duty for assistance. The journal was open on my desk and for some reason she first typed the details of the governor's journal into her computer, only to look up at me in surprise.

'It's not here,' she said. 'It's not in the index'.

I answered dumbly that it had to be as I had it right in front of me. She tried another tack and found it. It was indexed incorrectly, under

'Governor's journal – Adelaide gaol', but with the dates '1939–1945', truly memorable years, but 100 years too late.

So, it was as simple as that, a clerical error, arising possibly from the move of the archives to Gepps Cross and the computerisation of the index. I had not noticed! She corrected it immediately.

I did go back to the histories, just to check if anyone had seen it. I found three researchers who had mentioned it; I was not the first. Jean Schmaal was the first. She had written an article in 1984 entitled 'Ashton's Hotel, Being a brief history of H.M. Gaol, Adelaide, SA'.[13] As part of her article she had extracted 14 quotes, referenced as 'Gaol Minute Book, State Archives'. She had obviously found it in the old archives.

The others were Malcolm Johnston (1990) a descendant of Ashton who wrote a biography, and also Max Slee (2010) who wrote about the earlier, temporary gaol.[14] These two had used the exact same excerpts, with the same errors in the diary dates that Schmaal happened to have made, but neither had seen the original. Malcolm Johnston gave Schmaal as his source for his information. Slee used the same attribution as Schmaal had, the Minute Book in the State Archives. No other researcher had come across it.

It seems clear then that it was in the old state archives and went astray, only to be found at some point, renamed 'The governor's journal' and hidden in plain sight. I had simply been lucky.

Over a period of a year I transcribed the journal, a most unusual experience of unfolding saga, not unlike a modern soapie, and with the time it took to unravel the handwriting, it was experienced by me at a similar pace. I caught myself wondering, 'What has happened to Bella? And to the reverend, what has happened to him?' I was turning to the next page and then the next, just to find out what was going on.

Part way through transcribing, a truly fortunate thing happened. I met the Ashton sisters, Rose and Maxie Ashton, descended in a direct line from Henry Hamilton Ashton, one of William and Charlotte's sons. It was a situation typical of Adelaide. I told an old friend what I had been doing and within a week received an email from her. 'Good to see you,' she wrote. 'I met up with my old friend Rose who says her great-great-grandfather was the first governor at the gaol – is this your William Ashton?'

I met with Rose as well as with her sister. I was still at the stage of hiding the journal behind my hands, however they could not have been more fascinated with what I had come across. They knew of the work of their relative Malcolm Johnston and had believed there was nothing else. They helped me finish the transcribing and encouraged me in my wish to write a book. Maxie has worked in the field of mental health and she in particular was aware of William's pioneering work at the gaol, where settlers deemed to be 'insane' were also kept. I began to feel that though this story is set in the very beginnings of the City of Adelaide, a great-great-grandfather is not so very long ago.

The copyright for the journal belongs to the South Australian Department for Corrections and many thanks go to staff in that department who were as excited as Rose and myself about the journal and have allowed us to publish it in full or in part.[15] To fulfill a promise made at that meeting a copy of the transcript will be placed in the archives for researchers of the future.

William Ashton in early 1839

The journal begins on 10 March 1839. William Ashton had arrived in Adelaide late the previous year, on 16 November 1838, following a sea voyage of exactly four months. He had been a Scotland Yard police officer and, according to his diary at the time, his daily activities had included transporting female convicts onto a ship bound for Australia and also dealing with the various crimes typical of England at the time – murder, body-snatching, theft and robbery. He had witnessed rioters protesting unemployment and well knew the overcrowding, drunkenness and poverty that were rife in London. The prisons in London were in an extremely poor state, overcrowded and with 'gaol fever' – typhus – out of control.[16]

Ashton had long hoped to emigrate to Australia with his family. His opportunity came quite suddenly when he and another officer, PC Stuart, were appointed sub-inspectors of police by Rowland Hill for the colonisation commissioners to help set up a police force in South Australia.[17] The request had come from Governor Gawler when he was still in England preparing to leave for Adelaide. The new governor of the colony had been given authority to set up a police force, so had applied to London Police for two of their best officers to assist him. This information is contained in a letter, dated 24 May 1841, written by Gawler after his later recall to London and provided by Gawler to Ashton who then kept it among his personal possessions.[18]

Ashton did not know that a police force of sorts had already been appointed and that he would instead be asked to govern a gaol when he landed in Adelaide.[19] He may not have even known there *was* a gaol.

Adelaide had begun with no plans for crime. It was envisioned as a very different city – with no convicts and equal numbers of men and women to avoid the possibilities of prostitution and crime.[20] However,

> while the new method of colonization was attracting men of such fine stamp as the early pioneers, no attempt seems to have been made . . . to check the influx of . . . undesirables from Van Diemen's Land and Botany Bay who were naturally attracted to the new colony.[21]

Although there was a constable for the marines and soon a judge, jury and court, Colonel Light had been given no instructions to include a gaol in his vision for Adelaide. Hence his maps of Adelaide contain none.

As early as 1837 runaway convicts from the eastern colonies had begun to turn up in Adelaide. They came overland, following the routes of explorers and cattlemen, and the emigrant settlers in Adelaide were feeling quite un-settled. This was not as they expected. South Australia was meant to be convict-free. Officials warned the settlers not to employ and not to trust anyone coming by land, only those arriving by sea.[22] They saw these intruders as the source of the emerging crime in Adelaide. To some extent this was understandable; some of the criminals were indeed escaped convicts, operating as 'bushrangers'; some were freed men who nonetheless had been convicts in a brutal and violent system.

The truth however was that Adelaide had begun to have its own criminals – felons, debtors, prostitutes, petty thieves, brawling drunks, and Aboriginal people breaking the new laws. When these offenders had to be leg-ironed on board the settler's ships (both the *Buffalo* and the *Tam O'Shanter* were used for this purpose) or else shackled to logs in the parklands, it became obvious that a gaol was required.

Only months after settlement began the settlers felt the want of a gaol. One settler, bothered by a drunk, wrote a letter of complaint:

I went to the Constable, Mr Coltman, who took him in charge, but having no place to confine him, he went home with him and put him to bed, he had not left him alone a few minutes before he returned to my tent . . . threatening to pull the tent down.[23]

One report suggests that a canvas prison-tent was erected:

The first prison used was a canvas tent placed under the guard of a squad of Royal Marines, who came . . . in the Buffalo with Governor Hindmarsh. The tent was pitched on the south park lands, so that it was some distance from the river.[24]

This account includes a story of 'lax' guards sending an Aboriginal prisoner to the river to get water and him taking his chance to abscond.

There may have been many such arrangements. John Wrathall Bull, who arrived in Adelaide on 2 May 1838 remembered coming across a similar scene. He had crossed the bridge from North Adelaide (now Hackney Bridge) to a place that later became Botanic Gardens. There was a tent, a log fire, prisoners chained by the legs and guards from the marines – and all were asleep. The 'sentinel' who should have been awake, was 'lying on his back, cuddling his Brown Bess, with an empty beer bottle by his side'.[25]

On the same day that Bull arrived it happened that influential colonists presented a submission to Sheriff Smart to discuss deficiencies in the judge, delays in justice and the backlog of untried prisoners. In response the sheriff held a meeting attended by 500 settlers.[26] It must have been soon afterwards that a temporary gaol was built – on the only land not marked for sale, that is, land set aside as the Adelaide 'Park Lands'. This temporary gaol was soon a shambles, the guards habitually drunk and the buildings and enclosing stakes insecure.

The leadership of the colony was also a shambles.

On 14 July 1838, the *South Australian Gazette and Colonial Register* printed a letter signed by many of the settlers farewelling Governor Hindmarsh. He had left the colony a week earlier, recalled to

London by the colonisation commissioners.[27] He was to be replaced by Governor Gawler who had already departed London but not yet arrived in Adelaide. The administration of the colony was handed over temporarily to George Milner Stephen.

Stephen's first address to the settlers was printed as a supplement to the paper. He began:

> I have first to announce with regret that there are no funds whatever in the treasury[28]

His first concern was that public servants would not be paid, his next that the marines were leaving and that the colony would be undefended:

> This province, with a population exceeding 4000 persons is abandoned to the protection of eighteen policemen, lately embodied by Governor Hindmarsh, while there are now twenty-one prisoners confined in the weather-boarded building used as a gaol, and perhaps double that number of desperate runaway convicts in the neighbourhood of the town. At the same time, as I have observed, there are no funds for the support of the force now constituting our only protection.
>
> We have happily no immediate cause to apprehend hostility from the aborigines, or our situation would indeed be deplorable.[29]

In London on that same day William Ashton was preparing to depart for Australia. Two days later, on 16 July 1838, he left England with his wife Charlotte and his three children – William James, Henry Hamilton and Thomas Mills, aged eight, five and three – along with nearly 250 passengers in a small vessel. The Ashton sisters, Rose and Maxie, living in the Adelaide area now, are descended from the second son, Henry Hamilton. They are among hundreds of descendants, many of whom still live in South Australia. Charlotte was in an advanced state of pregnancy when she boarded the ship. William's personal diary of the sea voyage records not only the difficulties Charlotte endured giving birth to their first daughter amid seasickness and rough weather, but also the behavior of some of the passengers. The ship was host to numerous elements of criminal misbehavior, with acts of stealing, fighting, drunkenness on duty, sexual crimes, and insurrection toward the captain. It was not a virtuous lot of passengers and crew – and they were all there on the *Rajasthan*, coming to add to the problems already beginning in South Australia. Ashton and Stuart were obliged to apprehend people for crimes and drunkenness before they had even arrived.

Interestingly, a ship that arrived soon after Ashton's also had hardship and disagreeable passengers. A woman wrote in her diary that 17 children including her own two had died aboard ship and that in addition there was 'so much scandal and ill-nature, and prying into each others affairs, you would hardly believe'.[30]

The diary of Ashton's sea voyage ends eight days out of Adelaide. The rest, if it was written, is not known to have survived.[31]

This sea-diary has been kept within the Ashton family and was transcribed by descendant Malcolm Johnston in *A Governor, Aye Every Inch a Governor: A biography of William Baker Ashton, the first governor of the Adelaide gaol* (published 1990 and updated in 2010). Until now however, neither he nor the family knew that Ashton had written so much more about his time in Adelaide.

While Ashton was still at sea, Gawler arrived in Adelaide. In response to public concern he almost immediately appointed a grand jury to investigate the need for a new gaol. This information is contained in letters from the sheriff in which he described the temporary gaol as 'filthy miserable and insecure'.[32] Sheriff Dutton headed a campaign to see that a substantial new gaol would be built. He suggested that once Governor Gawler selected a suitable site, they could erect

> a wall some 20 feet high to enclose a square of some extent as a preliminary step which could then be sufficiently secure to erect a gaol within its confines.[33]

The colonial secretary had replied

In answer to your letter ... I am commanded by the governor to inform you that his Excellency approves of your suggestion & will take an early opportunity to determine an eligible site.[34]

On arrival in Port Adelaide on 16 November 1838 Ashton and Stuart were to discover they were not expected and that decisions about a police force had already been made. It was to be led by Alexander Tolmer who was shortly to arrive. They were nonetheless appointed deputy inspectors of police, with the town and district of Adelaide assigned to Stuart.[35] On 11 January 1839 Ashton was offered the governorship of the gaol, an offer he accepted. His appointment was backdated to 1 January 1839.[36]

This appointment began in the temporary gaol in the parklands, renowned for easy escapes, with gaolers and prisoners alike more often drunk than sober. Ashton liked a drink himself – this is obvious from his diary while at sea – and he probably, along with society in general at the time, would have seen the consumption of liquor as very often a medical necessity. However, his experience in London and aboard ship had informed him of the pitfalls of alcohol and he immediately clamped down on liquor being available in gaol. It was often a losing battle, with gaol guards the worst offenders.

Although Dutton's idea of an enclosed square was never carried through, these discussions, immediately prior to Ashton's arrival, could well have influenced Ashton's decision to accept the governorship of what would eventually be a new gaol. It was a new position, and a much needed one in the new colony.

By the time Ashton was appointed governor of the gaol he had already spent two months employed in South Australia's new police force and would have acquainted himself fairly quickly with the main crimes already committed since the colony began. It was not a long history. The first ships had landed on Kangaroo Island less than three years since and in Holdfast Bay just a little over two years since. The first crime of any note had been in 1837 when a man named Driscoll was murdered near Encounter Bay. The Aboriginal suspect was brought to Adelaide but escaped. In March 1838 a man named

Pegler had been murdered in the parklands, killed in retribution for sitting between the wives of Aboriginal men in a drunken state. Two Aboriginal men escaped up a tree, were flushed out by settlers setting the tree alight, handed over to police and by morning had escaped. In March 1838 the captain of the *Giraffe* had been wounded with a spear as he walked along Port Road. In May 1838 Walter Bromley, at one time *ad interim* protector of the Aboriginal people, had drowned in the Torrens with suspected foul play. Several Aboriginal people had been shot, allegedly in self-defence, and dogs belonging to Aboriginal people had also been shot.[37]

It was obviously easy to escape from custody in this new colony, and obvious too that tensions between settlers and Aboriginal people sometimes ran high. Ashton may also have looked at the record of charges laid. For the year of 1838 he would have found a range of charges including felony, neglect of duty, 'absenting from fishery', suspicion of felony, 'defection from ship', illegally obtaining goods, desertion from ship, refusing to work on board ship, being disorderly and idle, assault, absconding from the gaol, stealing a pair of shoes, stealing a dog, stealing a sovereign, bringing spirits to prisoner in gaol, and debt.[38]

He would certainly have been told of the most sensational crimes so far in the colony. One of these had been against the previous sheriff, Sheriff Smart, who had survived an attempted shooting. Three men, Magee, Morgan and Scroggins had arrived overland and had shot at the sheriff when he tried to apprehend them.

> It was as early as 1838 ... Mr Smart, a Tasmanian, was appointed South Australia's first Sheriff to deal with the Vandemonians, as the runaway convicts were called ... Sheriff Smart had hardly settled into his quarters, a meagre tent on North Terrace, when he was attacked one night by three desparadoes, robbed and shot at.[39]

The criminals involved were held in the temporary gaol then tried and Magee sentenced to hang. He was hanged from a tree in the parklands in May 1838, six months before Ashton arrived. The other two were sentenced to be transported back to Van Diemen's Land.

The youngest one, Morgan, who had escaped capture for some time was later described as 'a handsome young "Vandemonian", still in his teens, whose parents had been transported to Port Arthur for sheep stealing in England'.[40]

The other crime Ashton would most certainly have been told about was the murder, in April 1838, of Mr Hallett's shepherd, James Thompson. He would have been aware that three accused Aboriginal men were now being held in the temporary gaol. He would also have known that this murder and the impending trials of the three men were causing considerable disquiet among the settlers. Ashton was not to know that a very similar situation would soon happen again. The shepherd of Mr Gilles, William Duffield, was murdered soon after Ashton took up his position as governor of the gaol. Another three Aboriginal men were arrested and placed in the temporary gaol.

At first Ashton lived in Caroline Place. Malcolm Johnston found this out from a letter written by Ashton and kept within the family. The handwriting was difficult to decipher and the best achieved was 'Caroline Place near Tordh... [or Fordh...] and Rundall Street'.[41] Caroline Place no longer exists. Fortunately it is depicted on Kingston's 1842 *Map of Adelaide*, located where the extremely grand Adelaide Arcade, connecting Rundle Mall and Grenfell Street, came to be built in 1885.

We know that William Ashton and his family were then allocated a small dwelling. In June 1839 the *Colonial Register* recorded that the government had approved the purchase of a house for the governor of the gaol. The cost was 12 pounds and expenditure was authorised for another six pounds to make it complete as a residence.[42]

The report did not give a location, however, many years later an article concerning a Mr Garlick, who had previously owned this same house, appeared in the *Register*. It provides information on how Mr Garlick had originally constructed the house and also clues to its location.

The first house built by Mr Garlick's family was situated on the south bank of the Torrens, about a hundred yards east of the Adelaide

Bridge. The material consisted of gum logs, obtained on the spot, and square blocks of turf were employed for walling up between the uprights. The rafters were secured from the pine forests where Enfield now stands, and the Reedbeds supplied the thatching material for the roof. Doors and windows were constructed from some ship's fittings. When the ground was being leveled for the floor it was discovered the house had been erected on the site of a native burial ground as a large number of skeletons were unearthed ... When settlers were ordered to vacate the park land and ordered to construct residences elsewhere Mr Garlick's home was purchased by the Government for 12 pound as a residence for the first Governor of the Gaol, who had just then arrived from England. It was convenient for this purpose, having been adjacent to a temporary small stone gaol erected near where the present Destitute Asylum buildings stand.[43]

The temporary gaol consisted of wooden structures but with one stone cell, known as the 'stone jug'. The destitute asylum buildings mentioned still exist, now part of the Migration Museum on Kintore Avenue in the city, east of Government House.

The article was written by Mr Garlick's son, when he became an architect interested in Adelaide's early colonial buildings. His mention of the discovery of the burial ground during the leveling of the ground is not surprising. This whole stretch of the riverbank where the colonists had camped contained extensive evidence of burials and occupation of the riverbank and riverbed by Aboriginal people. Another reminiscence fills out the picture:

> Native graves were common on the banks of the Torrens from Hindmarsh Bridge to the Company's Bridge [Hackney], and when the banks broke away during floods the skeletons were left exposed, whilst in the early days it was not uncommon for boys bathing to dive and bring up bones and even skulls of blacks from the bottom of the pools.[44]

Apart from this lucky description of Ashton's house, there are only a few other general indications of its location and character. One clue is contained in a note scribbled on a letter, now in the government archives. In 1841 Robert Gouger, the colonial secretary, received this letter from the sheriff. The letter was written after Ashton had moved from his hut to his new house at the new gaol. In this letter the sheriff reported that

> The Gov of the Gaol has now moved in and ... his old hut is empty for someone else to use.[45]

The note scribbled on the letter in red and in a different hand reads:

> The cottage mentioned is opposite the old Government Hut [signed] Robert Gouger.

Ashton himself gave a similar location when he wrote of the birth of Albert Gawler Ashton, the first of the Ashton children to be born in Adelaide. He 'was born in the cottage behind Government House'.[46]

Another settler happened to mention Ashton's house:

> The Private Secretary's office, a two-roomed stone cottage with a paling roof – I am talking now of early in 1840 – was at the north-eastern part of the Government Domain, and just below was the residence of the Governor of the Gaol – Old Ashton – whilst the Gaol itself was a few yards away. It was a wooden place, paled in.[47]

Throughout the first part of the journal Ashton mentions the proximity of his hut to the gaol. He first mentions 'my house ... near the Gaol' on 11 July 1839.

Adelaide in early 1839

At the start of 1839, when Adelaide as a British settlement was just over two years old, the number of emigrants reached 6000. The young colony had grown rapidly from small beginnings:

> The white population, about 500 in January 1837, increased quickly with the arrival of each new ship bringing immigrants, and by January 1838 had swelled to about 3000. The population ... doubled to 6000 by the end of that year.[48]

By March 1839, when the journal begins, there were nearly 7000 settlers in Adelaide.[49]

Estimates of the Aboriginal population at this time were considerably smaller. After the initial few settlers in 1836, the number of Europeans rapidly swamped the number of the local Kaurna. The ships just kept coming. An undated letter from a colonist back to England comments that in 1838 97 ships came into the colony and that in only the first six months of 1839 99 ships, including supply ships, had already arrived. The colonist's numbers were not completely accurate; it was even more than this. The impression that he wished to convey, however, is accurate; the number of ships arriving was gathering pace.

The disparity in the two populations was already in train. There were indications early on that the 'Adelaide Tribe' had been a much larger group of people at one time but that their numbers were already much reduced; smallpox had done its damage, this deadly and disfiguring disease passing across the country from the eastern colonies, from Aboriginal group to Aboriginal group, before the settlers in South Australia had even landed. It had wiped out an unknowable number of Aboriginal people, including most of a generation. In 1842 John Gell wrote:

> About ten years ago they caught the smallpox (*nguya*) from the eastern tribes it probably came from Sydney. They have no remedy against it but the *ngaya palti*, or small pox song, which they learnt from the eastern tribes.[50]

John Adams, who arrived on the *Buffalo* and was therefore one of the first to arrive in the colony, recalled a kangaroo hunt with an Aboriginal man and a boy aged about 15:

> The lad who went with us was about the only boy about that age in the Adelaide Tribe, all that generation appears to have been taken off by smallpox, all the survivors were very much marked – we learnt this from the white men.[51]

The white men he referred to were whalers who had lived with Aboriginal women on Kangaroo Island for a number of years prior to Adelaide's settlement and who made themselves useful interpreting and providing information for the new settlers in Adelaide. Wyatt, who arrived in Adelaide in February 1837 and was *ad interim* protector of the Aboriginal people from 1837 to 1839, estimated that in the early years of Adelaide 'the Adelaide tribe ... varied from 150 to nearly 300 at one time'.[52] By 1839 Wyatt had had a lot to do with Aboriginal people in Adelaide. He had set up a 'Location' for them in 1838 and in June 1838 he reported that 87 'Adelaide Tribe' people, both adults and children, were living in the huts at his Location in the parklands and an estimated 200 were in the 'neighbourhood'.[53]

Of interest to Ashton, of course, was the size of the criminal population in Adelaide in early 1839. The closest numbers I can find are for 1 December 1838. A newspaper reported that at that time there were over 20 prisoners being held in the temporary gaol, fitted for nine at the most, and the number of desperado criminals hiding in the hills was estimated at twice that number. There were also 13 or 14 out on bail awaiting trial.[54]

At the beginning of 1839 Adelaide had barely begun. Colonel Light, founder and first surveyor general, had declared the site for the city only two years earlier, on 29 December 1836. It had been an unusual decision, the city not adjacent to the incoming ships, but rather inland, 13 kms east of the landing place, next to quite a small river. Most of the population of settlers now camped or lived in huts along the city stretch of the river. This had its advantages, as everyone was there together, close to the river where they could swim, collect water and wash clothes. Although the preliminary sections of land were surveyed and chosen as early as March 1837, and sold in November the same year, many settlers kept living on the 'Park Land' – for that was what Colonel Light now called it – where water was easier to obtain.

Light's choice was much affected by landform. Adelaide is exceedingly flat. The plain stretches inland until a rise just before the city, and flattens out again. It is then further inland that the arc of foothills and famous Adelaide Hills begin. The geologist Selby wrote that

> [Light] chose a site for the city on the Para Fault scarp, which was the first piece of flood-free rising ground inland from the coastal plain.[55]

He went on to write that this obvious advantage, plus the presence of the river itself and its bordering forest of abundant trees and wildlife, meant that it should have been no surprise that the site had already been chosen by the Kauna people. It seems the Kaurna were not in the vicinity when Colonel Light struck camp; they are not mentioned, though the evidence of their usual presence – campfires, cooking stones, burnt-out hollow trees, flaked stone, even their wurlies – would have been apparent. It may have been that it was summer, a time of year the Aboriginal people left the area, or they may simply have been watching from afar.

The river was not as we know it now. Colonel Light's 1837 map of the city clearly shows an intricately braided stream within a relatively wide riverbed, the whole width of the trench deeply gouged, with the edges of the bank steep and high. Now, filled bank to bank, it is the Torrens Lake: then it was a trickle so small that people would 'step across the "Torrens" without knowing it',[56] or else they could not even cross, it was such a torrent:

> Of course, the tiny little Torrens all but vanishes in such a sun ... There are, however, several pretty good holes which have too much water in them to be entirely exhausted by the sun's heat, and it was on account of these waterholes that the town was placed [on this site].[57]

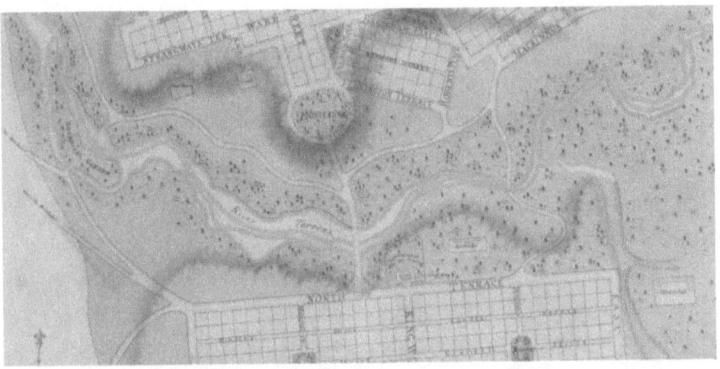

Detail from Colonel William Light's map showing the Torrens River, *Plan of the city of Adelaide, South Australia*, 1837
[State Library of South Australia, zmp sm 00301216]

Reverend Blacket, who wrote a history of Adelaide 70 years after settlement began, provides a wonderful description of the earliest colonial river bank settlement, much of which still existed when Ashton arrived.

> One who came to the colony in the early days and published his reminiscences at 'Home' thus describes the temporary settlement on the banks of the Torrens: 'The huts were scattered about without any attempt at regularity or uniformity. Every man had built his house on the spot where whim or choice pointed out, or where material

was easiest got; the consequence was that a collection of as primitive looking wigwams as can well be imagined soon lined the banks of the Torrens – some of them facing the east, some the west; in fact every point of the compass might have claimed one or more facing it.

They stood just as though a mad bull had been playing his mad antics among them, and had tossed them hither and thither. . . .

Here and there in the encampment that we have described there was some little attempt at order. It was only natural that emigrants who came out in the same ship would desire to pitch their tents or build their huts together, so in the settlement on the banks of the Torrens there was a 'Buffalo Row' and a 'Coromandel Row.' Evidently the immigrants who had come by the *Buffalo* and the *Coromandel* had pitched their tents or built their houses in a line together. 'Buffalo Row' stood near the Adelaide Gaol, 'Coromandel Row' a little eastward.[58]

The gaol referred to here we now call the Old Adelaide Gaol but at the time of this early settlement it was not yet built.

Another colonist, Finlayson, recalled that he and his wife lived for six weeks among others from their ship, in a dwelling made from cloth and hairpins. They had walked from Port Misery (Port Adelaide) to set up camp in the settlement by the river:

> [There] was nothing much to look at in town but stunted peppermint trees and surveyors pegs, here and there. Outside fronting what is now the jail but nearer to North Terrace was a row of reed huts, dignified with the name of Buffalo Row . . . between that and the River Torrens, & what a miserable river, were a number of tents and non-descript huts . . . bowers and tents were erected near together without any attempt at regularity . . . no one directed or found fault with us, in building we followed our own sweet will . . . it was truly amusing to look at the various styles of architecture exhibited all around us, – as our materials were of the simplest kinds – cloth of all kinds – interspersed with ti-tree and reeds – this was gypsying and never was a gypsy camp more picturesque than was the encampment of the 'John Renwick' at the end of the summer of 1837.[59]

Although the streets had been pegged, the city was not yet cleared:

> At that time it resembled an extensive Gypsy encampment. Not the semblance of a street existed on the land; although all the main streets had been laid down on the plan. It was in fact an extensive woodland, with here a solitary tent and there clusters of erratic habitations. There were canvas tents, tarpaulin tents, wurleys made of branches, log huts, packing case villas and a few veritable wooden cottages.[60]

As a child Chittleborough lived in this 'first settlement ... on the banks of the River Torrens'. More specifically he lived in Buffalo Row.[61]

There is evidence in the sheriff's letters that some huts remained in this colonial camp at least until the end of 1841, despite numerous attempts to evict the settlers living in them.[62] The condition of even the government-built huts was extremely poor:

> The structures in Emigration Square, Coromandel Row and Buffalo Row ... freely admit ... the extreme heat of the day and the cold winds of night, and in rainy weather like the present, are just preferable to the open air.[63]

Emigrants continued to arrive and live in these huts throughout 1839. Molineux who became a guard at both the temporary and the new gaols arrived in January 1839 and he lived with his family in Buffalo Row.[64] The settler Flavell landed in Port Adelaide in January 1839 and went to live in Emigration Square. He recalled that

> When we got to the Park Lands a lot of natives were camped near the river. The greater number of them were young ones, and all in Nature's clothes ... We went to live in Immigration-square.[65]

A letter dated 3 April 1839 described Emigration Square:

> As you approach Adelaide from Holdfast Bay, the first place that comes into view is Emigration Square, the four sides of which are bounded by wooden houses brought from England ... The square is supplied with a good well.[66]

The accommodation was basic, wooden huts set on bricks, each hut containing up to two families, one each end, in a space 'not exceeding 10 feet.'[67] An infirmary had been built in the centre of the square.

> Mr Fischer, the resident Commissioner, took immigrants under his special care and erected about 50 wooden cottages, called 'Immigration Square', for their use on the Parkland, west of the promulgation of Hindley Street.[68]

In July 1839 the government ordered the superintendent of police and his officers prepare a general list of the population 'from the Governor to the occupier of the humblest wattle and daub hut in the park lands'. This was to become the start of the 1841 census, the first official census for the colony. The tally for Buffalo Row was 48 males and 54 females, for Coromandel Row, 19 and 19, and for Emigration Square 134 and 138.[69] It is not certain to which months of 1839–1841 these numbers apply but in any event the count illustrates that in 1839 settlers continued to live in the parklands.

A painting by Anne Gliddon, published in London in 1839, depicts huts in the parkland across from Trinity Church.

Adelaide had, as well, been expanding beyond the parklands. Settlers began to camp or build on their allotments in the city. Hotels in Hindley Street thrived and lodging houses were receiving settlers, including in Caroline Place, where Ashton first lived.

During 1839 many of those living in Emigration Square were employed in work gangs felling trees and grubbing stumps to form the city streets. The government ordered that all settlers residing in the city help by felling and grubbing out the trees in the street in front of their allotments in return for the firewood and building timber so gained.[70]

A settler who arrived in April 1839 described the town:

> Most of the older buildings of the town are mere cottages built of clay – for temporary shelter from the sun and rain; but now the numerous handsome brick and stone edifices lately erected or in the

Adelaide in early 1839

Anne Gliddon, *Part of North Terrace, South Adelaide, South Australia [picture]/drawn in stone by Anne Gliddon from a sketch in the possession of Saml. Dendy Esqr*, 1839
[National Library of Australia, PIC Drawer 1741 #S1184/nla.obj-135763710]

course of erection, prove that our thriving colonists are looking upon this place as a home ... crowds of emigrants are arriving daily ... have your packing cases made with hinges, so that they may be converted into cupboards when you arrive.[71]

Special surveys had now mapped places beyond Adelaide, places such as Mount Barker and Port Lincoln. Roads were connecting the close areas such as the Para River to the city. A road line was surveyed from Adelaide to Encounter Bay. Menge, a geologist and mineralogist, noticed the considerable expansion of the settled areas. In 1839 he wrote that areas he had reported on in the previous year, at Mount Lofty, Mount Barker and Onkaparinga, had begun to be built on.[72]

Outsiders from the eastern colonies were also coming into Adelaide. In March 1839 news was sent ahead that a second large herd of cattle would soon be arriving.⁷³ Adelaide was beginning to reach out in 1839 and others were reaching in.

Not everyone was happy. A letter home to England published in *The Times* complained bitterly:

> The colony continues in an uproar. The officials are quarreling amongst themselves while the emigrants are starving. It is true the land is allotted; but the officials here hold so many of the best pieces of land, that no further progress has been made.⁷⁴

The editor of the paper heartily disagreed with this complaint, saying that far from starving, workers in the colony were commanding high wages. The quarrel referred to was a public brawl between Gouger and Fisher, a fight that the editor considered long past.

Another letter, a suicide note printed in the paper, expressed regret:

> Ambition was the lure which brought me here – would that I had been content to join my dear parents in the wilds of America – then would I have been happy; but here, without the sweet counsel of some judicious friend, and wanting all manner of soothing kindness, I have felt truly miserable. How short-sighted I was to come without sufficient capital to settle down here! But I was a stranger to the enormous expense of conveyance from the Port here, as well as the difficulty of securing warehouse room to any extent.⁷⁵

This man left the goods he had brought with him by ship, including 40,000 slates, a considerable amount of timber and numerous household items to be sold at auction to pay his debts.

For those still living in the parklands, life was changing. Rubbish was piling up. Brick-making, allowed in the parklands since settlement, was already banned as it polluted the river and the air.⁷⁶ Hides soaking upstream for processing in a tannery befouled the water in the town.⁷⁷ Cattle and sheep were butchered close to the water and dogs were buried there or dumped in the river. Many trees had already been destroyed:

> [T]rees on the Park Land are daily being destroyed by parties occupying dwellings thereon, both by cutting them down and employing Aborigines to lop off their branches.[78]

Chittleborough explained:

> The trees and scrub along the river were cut down for fuel and other purposes, and the pebbles and gravel carted away for paving and building. Consequently ... the banks ... were gradually washed away and deposited in the bottom of the deep holes.[79]

To curb these excesses and also to 'remove all nuisances' a 'Keeper of the Park Land' soon needed to be appointed.[80]

A description of the city just prior to Ashton's arrival provides an impression of the Adelaide that greeted Ashton and his family. The writer was James Hawker who had arrived in October 1838 on the same ship as Governor Gawler. He described his entrance into Adelaide after walking from Glenelg:

> The reality completely staggered us. Instead of the stone or brick buildings we expected to see, were wooden ones, interspersed with tents, a stone or brick being quite a curiosity. ... I had been requested by the Governor to look at Government House, and report to him what kind of building it was. We were ... astonished at the architectural appearance of the vice-regal residence. It was a hut, with slabs of wood for the sides, and the interstices were filled with clay and then whitewashed; the roof was of reeds. There were three rooms in the main building, and two small rooms attached with separate entrance. After having viewed Government House we determined to look for the River Torrens. Some of us had sketches showing the barque City of Adelaide at anchor opposite to Government House.... we came to a watercourse in which was a miserable dribbling current with an occasional waterhole. Any number of fallen trees blocked the bed of the river, and here and there were patches of ti-tree growing ... 'That's the Torrens' was the general exclamation ...[81]

Hawker returned to Glenelg and after his report on the small size of Government House, Governor Gawler decided to stay in Glenelg for a while longer.[82]

In 1839 Aboriginal people continued to live in their traditional camps in the new 'Park Land' among the settlers, but were an increasingly visible presence in the city as well, wandering in Hindley Street, the main street at the time. One settler described the situation as he saw it:

> There are numbers of natives regularly about the town. I have seen a great many quite naked: but they are now for the most part, supplied with a covering of some kind, either a blanket, wool shirt, or cast-off clothes. They are civil and simple ... upon the whole, a fine set of fellows, and capable of being brought into a state of civilization and usefulness if properly managed.[83]

John Adams, who lived in Buffalo Row, recalled a degree of contact and trust between the two populations:

> Whilst on the Park Lands and when we were few in number the natives mustered pretty strong at times. I once saw about 500 assembled on the flat on the North Adelaide side, and it was there they held their corroborees and their fights when other tribes visited. ... On one occasion we saw a tribe come by the hill of North Adelaide ... they appeared much surprised to see white men camped ... The women belonging to the tribe about Adelaide came creeping about the huts and wanted us to go and shoot them. They were much frightened until one of their protectors came and allayed their fears; but they kept about the huts for some time.[84]

The settlers were not always considered so useful and sometimes it was said out loud that they were not welcome,

> I remember once a native woman, saying to some of the arrivals, 'You go to England, that is your country; this our country'.[85]

Chittleborough remembered a happy childhood:

> In the early days the natives were very plentiful, and the camp of the Adelaide Tribe was always on the Torrens ... We children were almost brought up with the natives and all the boys knew the language of the Adelaide tribe.[86]

One of three sisters who arrived in December 1838 remembered:

> On the way to town, when we reached the river, near where the Gaol is, we came across two iron stores kept by the brothers Beck, and about them the blacks were congregated in their hundreds. Still I had no apprehension of them and though I lived among them many years I never had any trouble with them.[87]

A number of experiments by the government in relation to the Aboriginal people had already failed by the time Ashton arrived in Adelaide. An early Aboriginal Location, set up by Walter Bromley in 1837 on an island in the Torrens, had been spectacularly unsuccessful, and at the time Ashton arrived, late in 1838, a new Location of 12 huts and a school within the current Bonython Park, set up by William Wyatt, had also proved to be unsuitable and was hardly used. In early 1839, in the first months after Ashton's arrival, a more substantial Location was built across on the north side of the river. In the same newspaper that Ashton's appointment as governor of the gaol was announced, tenders were called for one of the dwellings at this new Location, the third attempt at a Location or place for the Aboriginal people in the parklands.[88]

Two German missionaries, Teichelmann and Schurmann, arrived a month before Ashton, when Wyatt still had his 'old Location'. Schurmann described

> what the government has done for the natives; as compensation for what has been taken from them. First a protector has been appointed who is to represent them to the government ... [second] because all the wildlife has been driven away in the vicinity of Adelaide [it] apportions some rusks [biscuits] to the natives, but not enough for them to live on... [third] a small piece of park or government land

has been fenced off for the aborigines and several huts of split boards built on it as well as a schoolhouse and a storeroom ... these houses it is rumoured, are to be moved to another site, but whether one foot of land will be set aside as property for the natives is extremely doubtful.[89]

Schurmann wrote that, at that time, '200 souls' of the 'Tandanye-tribe' lived in the immediate area along with 'strangers' from the 'Ramony (English Encounter Bay) tribe' who 'immediately take on the local dialect'.

[S]trangers, by name Ramony, are coming here to say that gradually (purro purro) many more would be coming. A few days ago a woman from the Murray was here who told us that there were many black men and women there who gradually intended to come.[90]

It was to be the beginning of an influx of Aboriginal groups into Adelaide. Wyatt later spoke of it. He stated that, as he understood it, some groups from outside Adelaide, such as those from Goolwa and Encounter Bay, had always visited, but that within a few years, other groups had arrived.[91] Some of these groups were traditional enemies of the Adelaide people and in the coming years a number of battles between different Aboriginal groups were staged in Adelaide. In early 1839 only a small number of outside groups were known by the settlers to visit Adelaide.

The settler MacPherson reflected on the situation:

I arrived (in 1839) when but little change had taken place in the number of the natives or their customs. The tribe inhabiting the plains and hills adjacent to Adelaide was called the Adelaide Tribe; to the South were the Encounter Bay, Lower Murray, Big Murray and Mount Barker tribes. These tribes alternately were trying to expel the Adelaide tribe for the object of enjoying the better food bestowed on them by the whites, nevertheless the Adelaide tribe kept possession of their territory and general peace was brought about by the Protector of Aborigines, Mr Moorhouse, and they severally kept their own boundaries except when on friendly visits.[92]

He mentions Matthew Moorhouse, who arrived in June 1839 to replace Wyatt. Moorhouse was to have a lot to do with William Ashton when Moorhouse presided over the next Aboriginal Location on the north side of the river. In early 1839, though, this new Location was yet to be built. Schurmann, who was temporarily living in Wyatt's old Location, wrote in his diary that the new Location was to be in 'a place where the natives' name ... is *Piltawodly* ... or possuma hausen'.[93] He wondered if the new protector, Matthew Moorhouse, would allow this name to be retained. There is no evidence that Moorhouse did retain the name, and it was not until recently, in 1998, when Schurmann's letter was finally translated from German into English by the Lutheran Archives in Adelaide, that the name Piltawodli was recovered as the name for this particular Aboriginal Location.[94]

There is no map of the new Aboriginal Location as it was in late 1839, however the general area of this Location, overseen by Matthew Moorhouse and run day-to-day by the missionaries, is depicted in Kingston's 1842 *Map of Adelaide*.

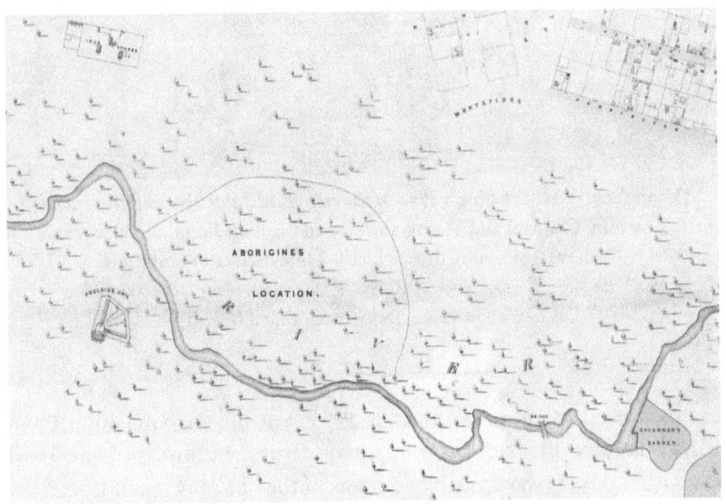

Detail from G.S. Kingston's *Map of Adelaide*, 1842
[State Library of South Australia, map820i1435207a rbr]

There is also no surviving map for Wyatt's old Location on the south side of the river, showing how it looked in 1838 and 1839. A map drawn much later however, by Freeling in 1849, does depict an unnamed structure, probably a fence surrounding what appears from other written descriptions to have been the remains of the old Aboriginal Location.⁹⁵ This old Location was the place where most of the colonists, including Ashton, would meet on 10 October 1839 to join the funeral procession for Colonel Light. His body was taken from his home across the road in Thebarton, via the old Location to its burial place in Light Square.⁹⁶ It was also the landmark later named as near to where the new gaol was to be built.⁹⁷

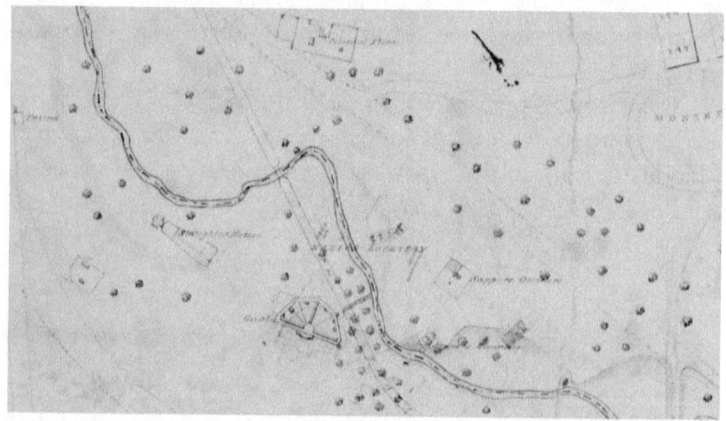

Detail from A.H. Freeling's *Plan of the city of Adelaide showing town acres*, drawn by Counsel and Young and signed Captain Freeling, Surveyor General, originally drawn in 1849 but with later additions
[State Records, Gepps Cross, GRG35/585 Maps – Surveyor General's Office, Lands and Survey Department Unit 5 Item 41]

By 1849 the gaol no longer looked as it did in Kingston's map; it had doubled in size. The unnamed feature southwest of the 1840 slaughterhouse is the probable remains of the old Aboriginal Location. Before the slaughterhouse was built, the old Location was the nearest landmark, south of the river, to the proposed new gaol.

Not long after Ashton arrived something happened that saddened the settlers and underlined the extreme fragility of the new colony. On 26 January 1839 fire destroyed the hut of Mr Fisher, along with the adjacent survey office and Colonel Light's hut, all in the colonial camp in the parklands. Although the survey maps were saved, possessions destroyed included Colonel Light's journal of the previous 30 years and a folder of his paintings.

> The whole of this awful and distressing scene did not occupy the space of half an hour.[98]

Colonel Light moved to a house in Thebarton, but he was not to live much longer. Looked after by Maria Gandy he spent his last months a very ill young man. A Mrs Amey, who arrived as a teenager in December 1838, was later to record her memories of Colonel Light's hut in the parklands, and the fire. She also remembered his funeral:

> Colonel Light and Sir James Hurtle Fisher had a place on the parklands. It was made of all sorts of things, and the partitions were of canvas and hession. I remember seeing it burned down. The fire was started I believe by one of the girls placing a candle near a partition. . . . I saw Colonel Light many times, and spoke with him. He appeared every inch a gentleman, and had a lofty bearing. I went to his funeral – he was buried in Light Square . . . I saw the coffin put in the ground.[99]

The situation in relation to prisoners and crime in 1839 was beginning to change from the minor crimes and petty criminals that had disturbed the first of the settlers. When the colony had been new drunken sailors were the typical offenders. They had been kept restrained in irons on board the *Buffalo*, then, when the *Buffalo* sailed to Sydney in June 1837 the worst offenders had gone with her. Captain Mitchell of the *Tam O'Shanter* was ordered to take care of the remaining two prisoners with the help of three marines.[100] As the number of prisoners inevitably grew, *ad hoc* arrangements of leg irons attached to logs and tents to shelter the prisoners were made.

Before the *Buffalo* had sailed, Adelaide had had its very first 'gaol delivery' (despite there being no gaol). Those who had been charged and held on the *Buffalo* were brought to trial. The crimes had been numerous but not yet considered dire. James Hoare stole a flitch of bacon from the colonial store, James Gordon was brought before the bar for burglary, and Thomas Oakley for stealing from the store at Holdfast Bay. Other charges were against sailors for drunkenness, riot and escape.[101] Sentences included imprisonment and fines and, in the case of James Gordon, seven years transportation.

Transportation was a curious punishment, known about but I believe little recognised as part of South Australia's early history. South Australia had been founded without convicts and was proud of this special status. All South Australian emigrants were free and came to be considered as of a purer mettle than those residing in the penal colonies, now the eastern states. It seems however that this had nothing to do with an objection to transportation *per se*, as when it came to its own criminals South Australia did exactly the same as Britain had done: transported its worst as convicts to the established penal colonies of either New South Wales or Van Diemen's Land. Some were immediately taken from Sydney on to Norfolk Island. If escaped convicts from the eastern colonies committed crimes in South Australia they were sentenced and determinedly sent back. However, increasingly it was South Australia's own colonists that were transported away.

A small booklet by Graham Jaurnay provides an excellent though incomplete list of names and ships used for those who were transported from South Australia, this information gleaned from various sources.[102] One of the special aspects of Ashton's journal is that it details prisoners taken by Ashton to the port for transportation and describes each of these occasions, sometimes in detail. It was one of Ashton's duties to undertake this task. The most shocking revelations in the journal in this respect concern a number of Aboriginal people sentenced to be transported. Each was later pardoned by His Excellency, the governor. Perhaps he recognised the deep injustice of this situation, however the fact that such sentences existed is now hard to comprehend.

There was considerable feeling about the exclusiveness of South Australia. An article in the Launceston *Advertiser* put the argument for keeping South Australia free of convicts. It was written by Thomas Horton James who, as well as living in Adelaide for six months, had experienced the penal colonies, and had then returned to England. The language is strong, agreeing with an old philosophy that wherever you plant convicts you will 'spoil the plantation' and lauding those who saved South Australia from such a fate. The writer of the article imagines the thoughts of those on the eastern coast towards the inhabitants of Adelaide:

> The settlers of the old colonies may jeer at what they no doubt term the ignorance and prejudice of the purer province, and point at their own prosperity and success as proof of their doctrine that no new colony can do without convicts: but after long experience in New South Wales and Van Diemen's Land . . . [I] can contemplate at a distance the leper-like ghastliness and deformity of convict society in those colonies . . . the friends of South Australia may congratulate themselves . . . that the moral virus of contamination is for ever excluded from their shores. . . . There are no huge barracks in Adelaide, full of wicked and condemned men – no female factories or penitentiaries – no enormous jails and permanent gibbets in the public streets: here are no poor-houses . . . nor lunatic asylums . . . Nothing of this kind.[103]

The increasing visibility of escaping prisoners in Adelaide and the obvious need for a more secure gaol was not comparable to the horror in the penal colonies, nonetheless it was a new situation to come to terms with in South Australia.

Adelaide, in early 1839, was a social experiment with high hopes and precarious possibilities, a society curious about but conflicted in its relationship with the Indigenous people already here and afraid that moral contamination would creep in from the east. For Aboriginal people the change to their lives when the settlers turned up to take over was immense, unfathomable even. William and his family had certainly emigrated to a very interesting place at a very interesting time.

Ashton had arrived in a settlement where the gaol he was asked to govern was much maligned. It was a settlement still beginning that had already quite a history: where the river was polluted; the early settlers' first habitations were being dismantled; where many of the trees in the parklands had been cut down; and where Aboriginal people were being corralled into one, albeit shifting, place. There was also a financial collapse looming, right when a new Government House and a substantial new gaol were being contemplated. There was great pressure on the government but also great pressure on the small temporary gaol, reflecting as it did the society it was in. Inside this gaol, not only was the number of felons increasing but also the number of debtors – and it was seriously overcrowded.

The temporary gaol

Mr. Ashton, first governor of the gaol, had two 'hotels'. The first was a little wooden building, surrounded by a low paling fence, built to accommodate eight prisoners, and often holding as many as 30. More prisoners escaped than could be effectively secured, even with the aid of armed guards. The second was ... the most imposing architectural landmark in South Australia – more substantial and impressive by far than Government House.[104]

Of interest, particularly to archaeologists and historians, is the long-lost knowledge of the location of the temporary gaol. Because of the vague nature of the archival descriptions and the need to piece together small fragments of information from many unrelated sources, it has taken some deciphering to get an archival answer to this question.

Max Slee was the first to put together archival clues to come up with a suggested location. His suggested location for the temporary gaol is the northeast corner of the current Government House enclosure, extending into the current footpath and road of Kintore Avenue. His conclusion is not totally convincing based on his sources. However, with the introduction of Trove, the National Library of Australia's digitised collection, including historic newspapers, it has now been possible to find many more fragments of information, so that at least the general vicinity suggested by Slee appears to have been confirmed.

Apart from these now numerous fragments of information, there are three longer historical descriptions that, when understood, confirm this as the approximate location of the early gaol. The first description is an account of a walk along the Torrens River in 1842. The writer, who called himself the 'Loiterer', placed each building in order in the landscape as he walked along. Although the temporary gaol was no longer in use by 1842 it was still in existence in a deserted state and luckily the writer included it in his description.

The 'Loiterer' begins at a bridge built across the Torrens and walks along the south side of the river. His account is extremely hard to understand, pompous and packed with literary and philosophical asides, so this is a simplified account. Walking east he first notes that the new gaol and Trinity Church are over his shoulder behind him. He walks along the bank and soon passes the Government Gardens in a stringybark enclosure, then, on a rise above the river, comes across the new Government House in another stringybark enclosure. He notes that the original Government House burnt down but that it had been located in this same enclosure with the new Government House. We know from other sources that this enclosure protruded out from the current boundary, straddling what became King William Road. He continues on his walk. East of the new Government House he comes across the old gaol full of spiders, then Mr Frome's house and the police barracks.[105] Kingston's 1842 *Map of Adelaide* shows the area where he walked.

The old gaol did not remain abandoned. It was mentioned again in August 1845:

> His Excellency the Governor, in compliance with your request ... authorises ... for the repair of the two cottages, originally forming part of the old Gaol, now occupied by two married men of the Detachment of Royal Sappers and Miners.[106]

Several later maps (1849, 1851 and 1865) show buildings depicted in this spot.[107]

The second description is a reminiscence and refers to a few years earlier, in 1838, a time when the temporary gaol and also the first

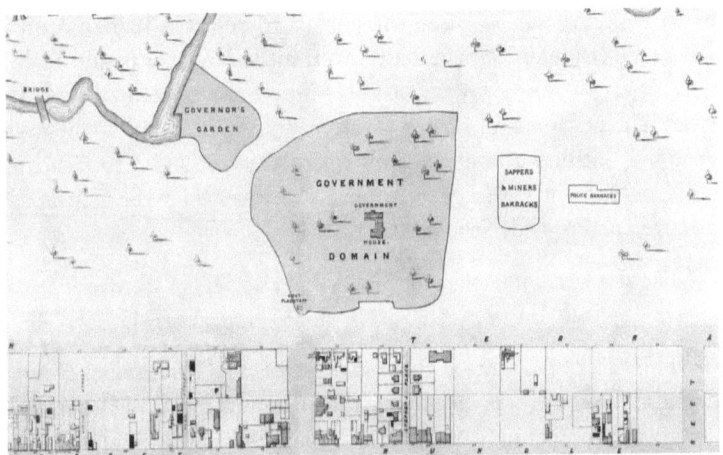

Detail from G.S. Kingston's *Map of Adelaide* showing where the 'Loiterer' walked, 1842 [State Library of South Australia, map820i1435207a rbr]

Government House were still in use. This memory belonged to the settler named Hawker who came to South Australia with Governor Gawler. On 17 October, after staying awhile in Glenelg, Governor Gawler proceeded to the city amid great fanfare, to take up residence in the vice-regal hut. Tents were brought up to Adelaide for many of his party, including Hawker, to set up nearby. Hawker described the scene:

> Government Residence was then located near about where the Government Offices are in the present Government House and from it the ground sloped gradually down to the flat, where the Rotunda now stands, by the Torrens.[108]

In the same description he mentioned the gaol:

> Looking towards [the first] Government House, our tents were all pitched to the left, and about 60 yards behind them was the Gaol.[109]

So here we potentially have the location of the gaol. We know that the new Government House was built close enough to the old Government House to be in the same enclosure; the 'Loiterer' alerted us to this. We can also see the enclosure depicted in Kingston's 1842 map. In addition, the old Government House was said to be north-west of the new one, on the edge of the slope down to the river. The new one, for obvious reasons, was built higher up on level ground.[110] Still, without knowing where Hawker stood to face the old Government House we are none the wiser. Hawker continued however, and provided the necessary clue:

> The site where [the old gaol] stood, and also part of where our tents were erected, has been removed by stone being quarried . . .[111]

This places the tents at the back edge of the Government House domain. This area was indeed quarried and now forms the slope and parade ground behind Government House. With the tents being to the left of the old hut it seems Hawker was looking east from the vicinity of the rotunda, along the rear of the Government House domain, past the old hut to the gaol. The 'stringybark enclosure' for Government House, as described by the 'Loiterer' in 1842, did not exist in 1838; Hawker wrote that in 1838 the grounds were heavily wooded and that it was not yet 'fenced around'.

In some maps there is a triangular cluster of buildings depicted in or just down-slope of the northeast corner of the new Government House domain and it is this cluster that is thought to be the remains or later uses of the old gaol.

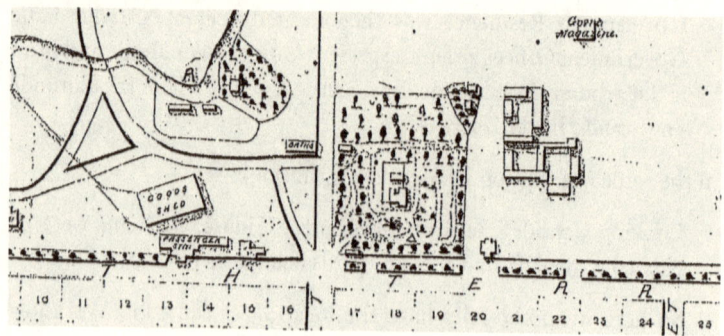

Detail from surveyors' map of Adelaide, 1865
[Adelaide City Council Archives J/42]

The third passage is another reminiscence, this time written by ex-Commissioner of Police Tolmer, who had been a contemporary of Ashton's. As an older man in 1882 Tolmer described the position of the old gaol. He was thinking back to 1840 when he first lived next door in the police barracks.

The passage makes sense only when it is realised that when Tolmer uses the Aboriginal Location as a landmark he was not, as you might expect, referring to the Location that existed at the time the old gaol was operating. This would have been Piltawodli, and it is definitely not Piltawodli that he meant here. Instead he was thinking of the 'Native School Establishment' that began in 1845, after Piltawodli was closed. By then the gaol buildings were still there, but not still used as a gaol. The clue to confirm this is the mention of the teacher, Mr Ross. Mr Ross had never taught at the Piltawodli school, north of the river. The missionaries had been the only teachers there. However, in 1846 Mr Ross was employed to teach at this new establishment in what became Kintore Avenue, and his wife was employed to look after the girls.[112] Tolmer wrote:

> Looking west from my front door, about two chains distant were the sappers and miners' barracks. . . . Adjoining the sappers and miners' barracks was the native location . . . At this establishment native children were taught to read and write, and the girls to sew, under the superintendence of Mr and Mrs Ross. A short distance from the latter stood the gaol, which consisted only of a small stone building, and another built of wood, the whole enclosed by a paling fence. In these insecure buildings murderers and the very worst characters were incarcerated under the charge of the late Mr Ashton, the governor, assisted by a limited number of guards. Mr Ashton himself lived in a small pise hovel on the banks of the Torrens . . .[113]

The layout can be seen in Freeling's 1849 map. Maps were sometimes added to rather than redrawn and this is the case with Freeling's 1849 map. This makes for a busy map with the barracks and the SA Institute included as later changes. The original captions from 1849 show the relative positions of the first police barracks, the

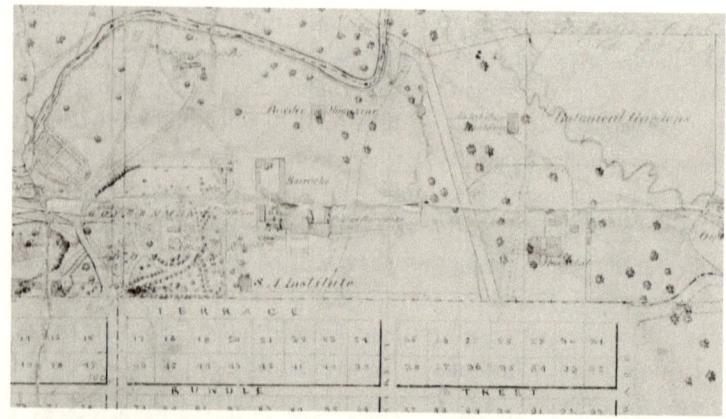

Detail from A.H. Freeling's *Plan of the city of Adelaide showing town acres*, drawn by Counsel and Young and signed Captain Freeling, Surveyor General, originally drawn in 1849 but with later additions
[State Records, Gepps Cross, GRG35/585 Maps – Surveyor General's Office, Lands and Survey Department Unit 5 Item 41]

1845 'native school' and the unnamed triangular cluster. Two chains, mentioned in the description, equates roughly to 40 metres.

Working out the positions of previous buildings from archival information can be difficult in Adelaide. Landmarks used as reference points have sometimes changed position, maybe several times. The Aboriginal Location for example had five different sites in the parklands at different times. The police barracks had two different sites, its first near the old gaol then its second, from 1913, near the new gaol. Add to this the fact that many crucial documents including, presumably, maps were lost to history in both Colonel Light's fire in 1839 and in a fire at old Government House in 1841, and it is not surprising that difficulties occur.

Introduction to the governor's journal

The journal spans almost seven years, from 10 March 1839 until the end of December 1845. It starts in the small temporary gaol, to which William was appointed in January 1839. The gaol was in chaos, filled with prisoners who had been waiting a long time to be tried – and there was as yet no list ready for the courts. At the end of January 1839 the *Southern Australian* expressed its outrage:

> We have no words to express sufficiently the disgust with which we have noticed in the *Gazette* the postponement of these Sessions. Nine months have elapsed since a jail delivery was held in the Province, and our gaol, a filthy hovel in which the dog of a Christian ought not to be confined, has long been unhealthily crowded with wretched inmates, men whom the noble Constitution of the mother country looks upon as innocent until their guilt has been proved. Gracious heaven! Do we not live in a British Colony, and one which is accounted to be the especial repository of an Englishman's boasted priviledge?[114]

In March 1839, a gaol delivery was finally held. Newspapers covering this event quoted warnings from the court that justice would be difficult as witnesses were now hard to find. Nonetheless a court hearing to assess the fate of what was now almost a year's intake of accused criminals, both prisoners in the gaol and those on bail, 'about 40 in all', was underway. The outcome of the trials was that *all* the accused received a verdict of 'not guilty', for the reasons that the offences were trivial, the offenders in grave cases had escaped, or witnesses could not be found.[115]

It had been a farce. There were now only nine prisoners left in the gaol: those not yet ready for trial. It was suddenly a comparatively quiet place and there was time to begin the journal.

The journal is a single, bound book. The cover is inscribed 'Minute Book No. 1' however it has come to be indexed in the archives as 'The governor's journal', a more apt description of its contents.[116]

Most of the journal was written by Ashton, however at times there is a change of hand. Sometimes the handwriting is clearly different, sometimes the difference is not so clear. The clearest indication of when it is Ashton's handwriting is his characteristic use of spelling and sentence structure. For example he often uses 'brot' whereas others always used 'brought', he uses only occasional punctuation, and he has a markedly more liberal use of capitalised words. His use of capitals is expressive. A capital does not denote a proper noun, not even necessarily an ordinary noun, rather it indicates the important words for that particular sentence: that is, where the emphasis lies. When it is Ashton's handwriting you can hear him talk.

The beginning of the journal is written by others and is more of a minute book, a daily account – as officially intended – and is sometimes tedious. However, as Ashton takes it over it gradually becomes a journal, and though never as personal as a personal diary might be, it begins to contain passion and pride, and sometimes humour, in the exercise of what William Ashton clearly saw as his life's work, his own very important contribution to the colony. There is no question that the temporary gaol and then the new gaol were awful places to be incarcerated, however, at the risk of overusing the word 'compassion' in relation to the governor, the journal shows that he had this quality, and it is this evidence of his humanity that helps make the journal such an interesting read.

Except for the first entry to mark its beginning, the days when no 'occurrences' were recorded have been omitted. In the actual journal these entries have simply the date, the day of the week and 'None', followed by the number of prisoners for that day.

Introduction to the governor's journal

The number at the end of each entry is the occupancy that day and at the end of each month is a tally. Occasionally words or parts of words in the journal have been replaced by an ellipsis (. . .) as they were simply too hard to read.

The governor's journal

The governor's journal 1839

The journal begins with little to say, except for the daily numbers in the gaol, the names of those brought in, those discharged and the monthly tally. Fluctuating daily tallies without any explanation show that not all these movements in and out of the gaol were noted, at least not in the journal.

There were many slow days. We find out however, right at the beginning of the journal, that convicts from the east were still absconding to South Australia and that the gaol held debtors as well as felons. In the early days debt had been rare, occurring only when a person was addicted to alcohol; anyone else was seen to be able to get ahead.[117] However as the financial collapse of the colony took hold, debt became a more common condition for anyone, even for some of the most prominent citizens of Adelaide. As this journal progresses there are some surprising entries of this kind.

Typically debtors were simply brought into gaol by the sheriff at the behest of the creditor and charged, 'at the suit of' the person owed. Sometimes the creditor brought the debtor in. The debtor was then the responsibility of the gaol. On 26 July 1838 the sheriff had been told by the governor of the colony that

> until an Act is passed for the purpose of compelling Creditors to support Debtors confined at their suit, you are authorized to supply them with moderate rations.[118]

We also find out in this first part of the journal that special care was taken by the visiting doctor to protect the health of prisoners with, in the case of the prisoner Packman, port wine and fresh meat ordered to be supplied daily.

1839 Daily Occurrences   *No. of Prisoners in the Gaol Each Day*

March 10 Sunday: None   9

March 12 Tuesday: 4 PCs from the Gaol back to their duty on the Town.   10

March 19 Tuesday: Hateley and Birmingham PCs brought in a man named Chas Festwell happened to be an absentee from V.D Land who said he had come to this Colony in the Lady Emma.   8

March 21 Thursday: Chas Festwell brought in on 19th was taken away by Birmingham and discharged.   6

March 25 Monday: Isaac Henry brought to the Gaol for debt by Thos Jones Sheriff's Officer.   6

March 31   130

April 2 Tuesday: The prisoners rec'd biscuits instead of bread supplied by Mr. Stuckey.   5

There is a gap here with no more entries until 8 May.

May 8 Wednesday: Mr Cotter ordered Packman to have a Gill of Port Wine per diem, and ¾ lb of fresh meat daily, to commence on Monday last.   14

Not noted in the journal, perhaps because of the gap in the entries, was an incident that later resulted in George Pfeiffer being briefly confined in the gaol. His crime was to pass spirits over the fence. Ashton had placed a sign at the front gate warning against giving spirits to prisoners. Pfieffer had gone to the back fence to evade the sign. The incident was reported in the paper thus:

> Under the judicious management of Mr Ashton the gaol has become what it ought to be, a place of punishment. Formerly it was quite usual for prisoners to convert the prison into a drinking shop and there was not the least difficulty in procuring liquor and enjoying it with their visitors. During the last week Mr Ashton secured the conviction of one party for conveying spirits into the prison.[119]

It was also reported that William Hollyer was committed for fraud and Henry Taylor for assaulting and attempting to stab the sub-inspector of police. Interestingly the reporter commented that this intention by Taylor

> certainly would have been accomplished, but for the prompt interference of Mr Ashton, the Governor of the Gaol.[120]

Ashton was certainly working hard and was being praised for his efforts. In a colony where the newspapers could be, and often were, scathing in their criticism of officials, this was quite an achievement.

During this time a new judge was appointed. On introducing him to his post, His Excellency the Governor was reported to tell Judge Cooper that he could take comfort in the knowledge that, among the criminals in the colony, very few were working emigrants. These particular members of the British working classes could not be 'more respectable, better disposed or more orderly', and, he said, would give him very little to do:

> It is true that our gaol was lately full, but our gaol is a very small one, and its prisoners... [are mostly] runaway sailors or escaped convicts from other colonies.[121]

His Excellency mentioned sailors and convicts. The group not mentioned by him is the Aboriginal prisoners. It seems that all these groups – sailors, runaway convicts and Aboriginal people – were considered differently in Adelaide: they were not part of the emigrant population. The yardstick of success in the crime statistics was a low number of criminals among the accepted emigrant citizens of Adelaide. The sentiment continued and a year later it was still being said that:

> Among the *real colonists* of South Australia, it may almost be said that crime does not exist.[122]

This belief in the exclusiveness of the emigrants and the priority of their rights as citizens of the new colony was clearly reflected in newspaper debates. Sailors would soon leave; convicts had no place; and Aboriginal people were said to have lost their rights to the land. The 'true' owners were seen to be those who came and 'did something' with the land. Many were adamant that because the settlers tilled the soil they now had a right to it, and that because the Aboriginal people had not done so they had forfeited their rights; they had had their chance and had not taken it.[123]

Other settlers believed the Aboriginal people did rightfully own the land and felt sorry for the effects the settlers had had. They listened to Wyatt who observed that Aboriginal people had a notion of land ownership that had nothing to do with tilling the soil. These questions were hotly discussed in the newspapers, with a passion that has not since been matched, and it is one of the questions of history as to why the voices of compassion, logic and scientific observation in this debate became more and more muffled over time. Even Wyatt was at heart a committed colonist and believed that the only course was to bring the Aboriginal people into the 'true interests of the colony'.[124]

The journal continues:

May 9 Thursday: Two natives named 'Peter' and 'Williamy' brought in for the murder of Mr Gilles shepherd. The Hon: Mr G.M. Hall, his Excellency's Private Secretary came to the Gaol to see them. 15

May 10 Friday: Mr Wigley came at 1 PM and took evidence against 'Peter & Williamy' for the murder of Mr. Gilles Shepherd. The prisoner Packman continues very ill. At 8PM Mr. Howard the Col'l. Chaplain visited him. 15

May 13 Monday: His Honor the Judge, accompanied by the Sheriff, visited the Gaol at 11½ A.M. 19

May 14 Tuesday: The Hon: The Adv: General (Mr Bernard) visited the Gaol. 19

May 17 Friday: His Honor the Judge accompanied by Mr Wyatt Protector of Aborigines came to the Gaol respecting the Native Prisoners - Packman continues very ill. 16

May 18 Saturday: Mr Cotter was called at 12½ A.M. to attend the prisoner Packman who was much worse than yesterday. 16

May 21 Tuesday: The Sessions commenced this day Hollyer and Rob't Wilson were tried & found Guilty Packman and Peter the Native still ill. 16

May 22 Wednesday: Three Natives for the Murder of Mr Gilles Shepherd were tried this day - Yerr-i-Cha, otherwise known as 'George' was found guilty, the other Two were Acquitted. P.C. Hateley brought in a Man named Pendergras, an absentee from V.D. Land and Supposed to have committed a Murder there. 17

May 23 Thursday: Henry Packman was tried, found Guilty & Sentenced to 14 days Imprisonment - 'Tam O'Shanter', & 'Tommy Roundhead' & 'Bob' were tried for the Murder of James Thompson 'Tommy Roundhead' was found Guilty the other Two were Acquitted of the Murder. - John Wilson was ordered by the Court to enter into his own Bail to appear next Sessions. 14

May 24 Friday: No Court Sat this day. 15

May 25 Saturday: Mr. Williams of the Gov't Stores did not supply the rations for the Gaol, because the order was not signed by Mr. Stephens, Col'l Secretary. 16

May 26 Sunday: Dismissed Warren the Turnkey for allowing Tommy Roundhead one of the Natives found Guilty of the Murder of James Thompson, Shepherd to Mr. Hallett, to get the irons from his legs during the time of duty thus very nearly Making his Escape. 16

May 27 Monday: His Honor the Judge Sentenced W'm Hollyer to be transported for life for Forgery - and Rob't Wilson to 7 yrs transportation stealing £35. Mr. McDougal Guilty of a Libel on Hon. J.M. Stephens. 15

May 28 Tuesday: The Sessions ended this day - The other Indictment against Mr McDougal put off until next Sessions. 15

May 29 Wednesday: Sam Thickness brought in for not having paid a fine of £10 for an Assault on 2 Sailors some time ago. 14

May 30 Thursday: Sam Thickness paid his fine of £10 and was discharged. 15

May 31 Friday: The last Sentence of the law was carried into effect at 8 o'Clock this Morning on the Park Land near the Iron Stores on Yerr i Cha, otherwise George for the Murder of William Duffel shepherd to Mr Gilles - and Wang Nucha otherwise 'Tommy Roundhead' for the Murder of James Thomson Shepherd to Mr Hallett. They were taken from the Gaol to the place of Execution in a single horse Cart - After hanging One hour their bodies were brought to the Gaol, & buried near the gate on the right hand side as you enter the yard. 14

<u>454</u>

Despite the slow start, a lot has now begun to happen. We are introduced to the imprisonment of Aboriginal people, to the practice of transportation of prisoners to the penal colonies, and to the first hangings of Aboriginal people in Adelaide. The gaol was also busy with official visitors and a number of prisoners' trials had taken place. Ashton was again praised, this time by the judge, for efficiency in providing lists to the court and ensuring all the prisoners arrived at the court without escaping.[125]

The temporary gaol received numerous officials – the sheriff; the colonial secretary; the advocate general; His Honour, the judge; Mr

Williams, who was the colonial storekeeper; Mr Wyatt, the current protector; Mr Howard, the colonial chaplain; and Mr Cotter, the physician. It becomes clear later in the journal that Ashton welcomed the input of these officials and that he routinely followed their advice and directions. He always called on the doctor and the protector for instructions on the care of sick or Aboriginal prisoners.

A look at the judge's comments in opening the above trials of Aboriginal prisoners and the subsequent hangings of two of them provides a window into the feelings running high in Adelaide at the time. It was the first sitting of the criminal court, and prominent citizens had been newly appointed to the jury. In reference to the two instances of murder of shepherds by Aboriginal people now to consider, the judge warned members of the jury against retaliation:

> In small communities, like our own, political differences will arise . . . it becomes us to shew every indulgence . . . if you suffer your minds to be influenced by your prejudices, it will be impossible for you to do your duties . . . while I express grief at those painful circumstances, I cannot but think that there is some consolation, in that these murders appear to have been committed by isolated individuals: nothing like combination among the natives for the destruction of the white population appears to have taken place . . . I do trust, that nothing like a feeling of revenge exists in your minds. I altogether deny that the natives are, as a body, cruel or treacherous, experience has proved the contrary.[126]

The judge however felt on trial himself, mindful of the unrest in the settler community. In reference to the trial for the murder of William Duffield, shepherd to Mr Gilles, the judge's fears and recommendations were clear:

> I think that now is the time for making an example among them – we should check these crimes in the bud . . . I do earnestly hope, that in mercy to the other natives, you will do your duty on this occasion, for if the guilty escape punishment, the poor fellows will be hunted and shot like wild dogs . . . I need not tell you of the fearful excitement

that has existed in the minds of the colonists, such feelings only remain in abeyance, they only await the result of these trials, to see whether through the law they receive that protection which they have an undoubted right to expect from the law: if they do not receive it, I fear they will take the law in their own hands, and the consequences must be dreadful.[127]

Despite no direct evidence of guilt against the three accused in this case, he pointed out that in England there is not always direct evidence either. He was certain in himself of the guilt of the accused and commented that they, the jury, were unfortunately hampered by not being able to accept as direct evidence the testimony of Aboriginal witnesses (this was not allowed under British law as without a belief in God or seemingly in any supreme being, Aboriginal people were not considered able to swear on God's oath). The jury returned a verdict of guilty against Aboriginal man Yerr-I-Cha for the murder of William Duffield and acquitted the other two Aboriginal prisoners. Yerr-I-Cha was sentenced to hang.

In the case of the murder of James Thompson, Mr Hallett's shepherd, the jury found Aboriginal man Tommy Roundhead guilty and two other Aboriginal prisoners not. He too was sentenced to hang.

At around the same time as these judgements Governor Gawler was trying in his own way to smooth over any difficult relationships between the settlers and the Aboriginal people. To celebrate the Queen's Birthday he hosted a 'Dinner for the Aborigines' at Government House, 'a festival for the natives such as they have never had before in their entire history'.[128] Mrs Gawler, the new governor's wife, described it in a letter to her sister in Derby:

> [W]e had a meeting of the blacks on our domain by previous notice ... at 12 o'clock the interpreter (Cronck), and Dr. Wyatt, the pro-tem Protector, went to their settlement and paraded them down, the men dressed in new woollen shirts, and the women as well as they could.
>
> They were formed in a ring and the Governor addressed them.[129]

It was an important speech for the Governor. He assured the Aboriginal people that they would be protected by British law. He exhorted them to be friendly, to work, build huts, wear clothes and live like the white men. He then regaled them with beef and pudding and presented them with a pewter plate each, embellished with an image of Queen Victoria one side and letters of the alphabet on the other. Along with other principal settlers, Ashton attended this gathering. The occasion was written up in the paper, including the names of Ashton and other colonists present.[130]

The hangings of the two Aboriginal men were not the first in the colony. Magee, who had fired on Sheriff Smart, had been hanged from a large tree in the parklands, witnessed by a crowd of settlers. The hangman botched the hanging and fled, only to be retrieved and forced to finish his grisly task.[131]

This time the hangings were in the same place, near the colonial store, however a free-standing wooden scaffold was erected to avoid a repeat of the earlier disaster. Again the crowds watched. The colonial store (sometimes called the iron store) was north of the river and, at the time of the hangings, the Aboriginal Location was the Piltawodli site nearby. A reporter wrote that:

> [O]n passing the native huts immediately after the execution, we found the women and children and many of the men lamenting, in a most piteous manner.[132]

Another wrote of the lead-up to the hangings:

> The wagon in which the prisoners were conveyed was surrounded by a numerous and armed body of police ... When crossing the river they began to talk with the interpreter ... apparently about the natives, whose encampments were in view. We understand that on the preceding night they expressed a desire to be given up to their own people for interment. This ... proves that they were quite aware of the situation in which they were placed ... [Afterwards] the bodies were taken down, placed in the coffins ... and conveyed to the jail, where, in accordance with the sentence, they were buried.[133]

A settler wrote home of many wonderful new sights he had seen in Adelaide, then:

> I am sorry however at having to say that I have witnessed the death of two natives who have been hanged for the willful murder of two shepherds. They did not belong to what is called the Adelaide tribe. And they were the first that have been brought to punishment. It was indeed an affecting sight. They had a regular trial by jury through their interpreter.[134]

The journal records that on 31 May 1839 the two Aboriginal men were buried in the grounds of the temporary gaol 'near the gate on the right hand side as you enter the yard'. This is the only record known of this highly specific and important information.

The next part of the journal describes problems with staff at the gaol and contains the first mention of the stone building in the temporary gaol. This stone building, known as the 'stone jug', is mentioned in later reminiscences but with no dates. Here we have a date.

The journal also makes mention of *lascars*, the name for sailors from the Indian subcontinent. Sailors and ships were now coming from many places in the world.

June 2 Sunday: Drubill Drawbridge commenced duty as a Turnkey in the place of Warren discharged this day week.   11

June 5 Wednesday: Packman discharged.   11

June 10 Monday: Discovered a large Hole made through the Wall in the Stone Gaol at the East End – Supposed to have been the work of Pendergras & Hollyer, Double-Ironed Pendergras.   10

June 13 Thursday: Took the prisoner Swift to the Judge's residence to be bailed – His Honor refused to bail him.   10

June 16 Sunday: Drawbridge Reported himself sick, and did not come on Night duty.   10

June 19 Wednesday: Drawbridge returned to duty.   9

June 20 Thursday: Seven Lascars were Sent here by Mr Wigley, R Magistrate for the Night to give Evidence against the Capt. and Mate of the Ship Planter for having Assaulted the Lascars – They received 14 lb Biscuit ¼ lb Tea 1 lb Sugar.   16

June 21 Friday: The 7 Lascars left the Gaol – 10 Sailors brought in from the Katherine Stuart Forbes.   35

June 22 Saturday: Williams the Turnkey left and Thomas Owen was engaged in his place.   21

June 23 Sunday: The Lascars had two of the Gaol Rugs.   21

June 27 Thursday: Drawbridge Reported himself Sick last Night.   20

June 28 Friday: Went to Drawbridge's Lodgings could not See him; found him at Bailey's Sydney Hotel, drunk & lying before the Fire – Dismissed him when he confessed he had not been sick, but drunk since Monday. About 10 A.M. a woman named Eliz. Bunkin was brought to the Gaol by P.C. Pollard who said that she had attempted to drown herself: her husband Came subsequently to the Gaol and she was delivered up to him.   21

June 30 Sunday: Thomas Perry Came on duty as Turnkey in the place of Drawbridge who left on the 26th Instant.   21

    422

July 4 Thursday: A man named John Barry was fined £5 for having in his possession about 5 Gallons of Gin – He was Sent to the Gaol by Mr. Wigley R.M. but immediately paid his fine & was discharged not having been in the Gaol more than 10 minutes. – About 6½ P.M. a fire broke out in the house of John Kennedy one of the Gaol Guards on the Park Land wh. Destroyed the House & the greater portion of his effects.   24

July 6 Saturday, P.C. James was brought to the Gaol by P.C. Halford, charged with being drunk and disorderly in the Streets of Adelaide at 8¼ P.M. 24

July 7 Sunday: Pendigras attempted to escape. 24

July 10 Wednesday: At 12¾ A.M. caught Perry and Marra loitering at the fire for 20 min: without their Guns. 25

July 11 Thursday: Jeremiah Swift made his Escape from Kennedy Whilst down at my house at Work near the Gaol at 11 A.M. 13

Escapes, especially from the flimsy buildings of the temporary gaol, were a constant problem, made easier when guards were drunk. Ashton appears to have been vigilant with both prisoners and his staff. He made no particular judgement on his warders, gaoler and turnkeys but did take a stand to dismiss or suspend them for drunkenness.

Elizabeth Bunkin, mentioned in this section for being brought to gaol for attempting to drown herself, died later in the year when she cut her own throat.

> The deceased had shown symptoms of a deranged state of mind for some time past, which induced her husband, who holds an appointment in the Customs House at Port Adelaide, to watch her narrowly.[135]

Elizabeth was one of many considered mentally ill who were to pass through the gaol in Ashton's time.

The journal continues with various incidents. Several prisoners who had escaped are found and returned, and two prisoners are taken to the port to be transported.

July 17 Wednesday: The Sessions Commenced. 13

July 18 Thursday: Mr. G.M. Stephens tried for Perjury and Acquitted – Sessions Ended – Took James Pendigras an Absentee from V.D.L. & placed him on board the Lady Emma at Holdfast Bay, & left him in the Custody of P.S. Halford to go to Launceston. 11

July 26 Friday: G. Hall Esq. Came to the Gaol to see Flatt confined for Debt. 11

July 27 Saturday: A prisoner named James Moran under confinement to find bail Not to leave the Colony made his Escape from the Gaol at 9 A.M. Without being seen by the Turnkey or Norris the Policeman on duty. - Owen the Turnkey was dismissed by the Sheriff, and Norris removed from the Gaol duty. 13

July 30 Tuesday: Edw'd Moss came on duty as Turnkey in place of Owen dismissed. 12

490

August 1 Thursday: James Evans who made his escape the latter end of Dec'r last, was Returned to the Gaol by P.C. Williams from the Port. 12

August 2 Friday: Myself & P.C. Hately took James Moran who made his Escape from the Gaol on Saturday last in Morphett Street at 3 P.M. 13

August 5 Monday: John Scott was discharged by the Magistrate & taken to the Hospital. 13

August 10 Saturday: Thos. Thomas was put on the bar for abusive language to the Gaoler & disorderly conduct in the Gaol. 11

August 11 Sunday: The prisoner Thomas broke the lock to pieces, and got the bar off - put him in a pair of x leg irons. 11

August 12 Monday: Jeremiah Swift who made his Escape July 11 was taken at 10 P.M. Yesternight, I brought from the Port this day. 12

August 13 Tuesday: Mr Insp'r Sheard made a charge against P.C. Hateley for having Rec'd £5 from the prisoner Swift on Thursday last, and not having taken him into Custody - Mrs Swift refused to give Evidence either for or against her husband - P.C. Hately resigned his Situation. 11

August 16 Friday: His Ex. The Gov'r accompanied by Mr Geo. Hall came to the Gaol to see Bob.   11

August 19 Monday: Moss the Turnkey has been the Worse for Liquor for the last two Nights - Suspended for one week.   11

August 25 Sunday: Moss the Turnkey Came on duty last night, having been suspended 1 week.   11

August 26 Monday: The Police (xcepting Kennedy) left the Gaol duty and a new Gaol Guard appointed unconnected with the Police   11

August 31 Saturday: Patience Neblett bailed out for Felony.   12

363

September 1 Sunday: Took Rob't Wilson & W'm Hollyer to the Port and placed them on board the Ship Charlotte at 7 A.M. to be taken to V.D. Land.   12

September 5 Thursday: John Dutton was brought in on the Coroner's Warrant for Manslaughter by P.S. Edwards from Encounter Bay.   11

September 8 Sunday: The New Guard commenced duty at the Gaol - John Kennedy & Arthur Travers came on at 8 A.M. & H'y Pitman and Edw'd Molineux came in at 1 P.M.   12

The journal contains many entries about the turnkey John Kennedy. Not made public until after his daughter's death was that Kennedy was a former convict from Van Diemen's land. He had arrived in Adelaide on the schooner *Tamar* from Launceston in 1838. In his will Kennedy left his estate to his daughter for her life, then if she had no children, on her death, half to his sister who was the wife of the employer he had robbed in England. The estate was re-allocated and in the search for descendants of his sister in England the story came to light. The claims of descendants were verified by the court by matching the convict's signature to the gaol warder's signature.[136]

The journal also contains many entries concerning the guard Molineux. Molineux worked in both the old and new gaols. He was often drunk and often ill. In 1905 the *Register* interviewed his son:

> I came here in January, 1839, at the age of six and a half years . . . For the first year we lived in Buffalo Row, on the rise opposite where the Adelaide Gaol now stands. During that time my father was very ill indeed . . . so . . . had to take the position of guard and turnkey at the Adelaide Gaol. The Adelaide Gaol was then behind Government House. In my father's time the notorious Stagg was hanged.[137]

Instead of other people's vague descriptions that Buffalo Row was near the gaol or in one case 'in the place the Gaol now is', we have here the more credible evidence of a man who as a child actually lived in Buffalo Row and who would have been extremely familiar with the locations of Buffalo Row in relation to the gaol, and in fact to both the gaols. His description fits closely with that of Chittleborough, also a child when he lived at Buffalo Row. Chittleborough described it as 'between where the gaol and the slaughterhouse now stand'.[138] They probably played together. Without Ashton's journal we would know little to fill out the story of Molineux.

Buffalo Row and Coromandel Row were iconic parts of early Adelaide and are a story on their own. They deserve a brief diversion.

Chittleborourough was a favourite with journalists and spoke of Buffalo Row many times:

> [T]he whole of our family (consisting of father, mother, and five children) tramped the seven miles from the bay to the river, near where the Adelaide Gaol now stands. There we camped . . . until father built a primitive reed hut with a sod chimney alongside other similar places . . . to which was given the name of Buffalo Row.[139]
>
> Some months after the building of Buffalo row the ship Coromandel arrived, bringing some small wooden houses. These were erected, in continuation of our row, toward Colonel Light's camp . . . These two rows of dwellings were the first settlement of immigrants in the colony before there was any land surveyed that they could occupy.[140]

Buffalo Row was on an open piece of land, where the olive plantation now is, and nearly opposite the slaughterhouse. It stood about 50 yards from the south bank of the little gully that runs from the back of the Gaol past the slaughterhouse. The row extended in an easterly direction toward the survey camp, and all the huts faced north.[141]

Passengers on the *Buffalo*, especially the children, were true pioneers living an adventure. Those on the *Coromandel* were not so eager to arrive. Thos Cotter, sent on board the *Coromandel* by Gouger, described the many difficulties of landing at Glenelg and the passengers' panic at rumours that the site for the town was less than ideal. He reported to Gouger:

> [T]hey flocked around me on my appearance on deck asking 'What would become of us? What should we do? For we had been taken from our comfortable homes in England and out with our wives and children to a barren wilderness to starve.[142]

Back to the journal:

September 16 Monday: Four Sailors belonging to Mr. Hack were brought to the Gaol by the Police, Remained a short time, were taken away again by the Police, and did not Return - Came to the Gaol about Noon. 17

September 20 Friday: The Rev. C. B. Howard came to the Gaol. 11

September 22 Sunday: At 9½ A.M. a man named Geo: Atkins came running to the Gaol in a dreadful State of madness and Said that persons were following to shoot him - Sent for Dr. Nash Col'l Surgeon who came and Saw him; I allowed him to remain in the Gaol. 11

September 23 Monday: Geo: Atkins the Same as Yesterday: Saw Mr. Hall his Exc: private Sec'y respecting him. 12

September 24 Tuesday: Geo: Atkins Remains in the Same State - Dr. Nash Came, Saw him & ordered his Removal to the Hospital. 14

September 30 Monday: About 2 O'Clock this Morn'g Mr Smith, David Chambers & James Green attempted to Escape from the Stone building, by removing a board from the Ceiling & taking some Battens from the Roof - they were detected by the Guard. 11

357

October 1 Tuesday: Expected the before mentioned prisoners to make another attempt to Escape but they did not & the night passed off quietly. 17

October 2 Wednesday: The above named Three prisoners Still in Irons. 17

October 3 Thursday: Mr. Moorhouse the Protector of the Aborigines Came to the Gaol to see 'Bob' the Native - This is the 4th visit Mr. M. has made to him. - Received from Gov't House 6 Testaments and 24 Tracts for the use of the Prisoners in the Gaol. 13

While dealing with another attempt at escape, visits by the protector and requirements of the reverend, Ashton and Dr Nash had also to deal with the 'dreadful State of madness' of Geo Atkins. The gaol was to an extent a refuge for such people. In this instance Ashton called in assistance and the man was taken to the hospital, however there would come to be many more mentally ill people admitted to the gaol, some not for any crime but specifically with lunacy as the charge. There was little option. There was as yet no asylum, only private arrangements of dubious quality or else doctors treating people as best as they could outside the gaol. In 1841 when there was still no asylum, it was reported that 'there are no fewer than seven insane persons at this present time under the care of the Colonial Surgeon at Emigration Square.'[143] When the first official asylum, a cottage in Parkside, was opened in 1846, 12 mentally ill people from the gaol were placed there. However when the asylum was full the gaol took the overflow, a situation that did not end until 1852 when the Adelaide Asylum opened.

The journal is a critical resource in this regard, tracking some of the early practices thought to be treatments that, though seen as appalling today, were believed in utterly and carried out with good intent. Ashton showed a great deal of compassion for the 'lunatics' in his care, typically noting in his journal what sort of day each had had and whether there was any improvement in their state.

Having to accommodate the mentally ill caused him endless logistical problems with never enough space to keep people separated and calm. He had to allow them to be looked after by other prisoners, usually debtors, or if they were women, by other women prisoners. This did not always work, especially with the women. The 'lunatics' were often exceedingly noisy and in an effort to keep the peace Ashton allowed all sorts of combinations of sleeping arrangements such as letting them or other prisoners sleep in the guards' quarters or later the chapel – just so everyone could get some sleep. He monitored these people closely, called in medical help whenever someone became worse, and appears to have had endless patience.

Many times he called in the protector, as we can see here with Bob. Tippa Warr-icha, known as 'Bob', was one of the accused in the murder of James Thompson. He had been acquitted after awaiting trial in the gaol for almost a year. At the end of his trial he was tried and acquitted of stealing sheep but then found guilty of throwing a spear at a policeman in the course of the arrest regarding James Thompson. He was now serving a sentence of 12 months imprisonment with hard labour for that offence.

Reverend C.B. Howard was to become a regular visitor to the gaol. Ashton made a note of all his visits, monotonously, almost every Sunday.

October 8 Tuesday: A man named Jacob Evans was killed at the Stone Quarry a little below the Gaol by the ground falling in on him at about 1½ P.M. his corpse was brought to the Gaol, & the Coroner held an Inquest on it at 5 in the Afternoon - the body was removed at 12½ A.M. on October 9th.   14

October 10 Thursday: Attended Col'l Light's funeral.   15

October 13 Sunday: Chas. Davis came on duty as one of the Gaol Guards at 8 o'Clock last night in the Stead of Henry Pittman Resigned. 19

October 15 Tuesday: 5 persons brought in at 10 A.M. charged with assaulting the Police – one of the party named Davridge had his head Cut by the Police – Sent for Dr. Nash who came & dressed the wound – they were too drunk to be taken before the Magistrate. 23

October 26 Saturday: I Went to Mt Barker at 2 P.M. 26

October 28 Monday: Returned from Mt Barker at 7 P.M. 25

October 29 Tuesday: Moss the Turnkey came on duty on Saturday, Sunday & Monday nights, at 8 A.M. the worse for Liquor. 25

605

November 2 Saturday: Moss the Turnkey Resigned and John H. Kennedy came on duty at 8 P.M. as Turnkey to the Gaol in his place. A prisoner named John Ratcliffe attempted to make his escape from the Officers when going for the Rations near the Government Stores – Turnkey Kennedy was in charge. 23

November 4 Monday: The Sessions commenced this day. 26

November 5 Tuesday: At the court all day. 26

November 6 Wednesday: At the Court all day. 27

November 7 Thursday: The Sessions terminated. 25

November 9 Saturday: The Officers of the Gaol received Fresh Meat in the room of [to replace] Salt. 25

November 13 Wednesday: Rec'd from the Stores a bag of biscuit which they said weighed 72 lbs. but we found there were only 60 lbs. 26

November 15 Friday: Kezziah Plough made her escape from the Gaol at 3 P.M. by pulling down two of the palings in the Women's Yard – she went to the Town & was seen by Moss the late Turnkey who gave information at the Gaol and Travers went & brought her back. The Judge admitted D. Chambers to Bail in £40. 25

November 16 Saturday: Took the pay list to his Excellency the Gov'r who signed it – the Biscuits Rec'd from the Stores were not good. 26

November 17 Sunday: A prisoner named Mr Brown made his escape about 4 P.M. by removing a thin board at the back of the privy & scaling the fence behind the Stone Building. 27

November 18 Monday: Obliged to take the child of Kezziah Plough from her owing to her ill treatment of it. Mr Wright had it all night. 28

November 19 Tuesday: David Chambers was brought to the Gaol charged with Stealing a Box of Cigars – came to the Gaol at 5 P.M. and made his escape by forcing a board in the privy at 6 P.M. 27

Along with all the notable colonists of Adelaide, Ashton attended Colonel Light's funeral. A large number of officials gathered at the old Aboriginal Location, in the parklands opposite Thebarton, to join the funeral procession from Light's home in Thebarton to Light Square.[144]

The everyday incidents of the gaol had continued – three more escapes and one attempted escape, drunkenness among the staff, replacing staff, and making decisions about the welfare of people in his care, in this case for the child of Kezziah Plough. Kezziah was described in the newspaper:

> Kaziah Plough, a miserable-looking girl, apparently not in her senses pleaded guilty to stealing two fowls ... and not guilty to a charge of stealing a bonnet and veil.[145]

She was found guilty of larceny and sentenced to transportation for seven years.[146]

Ashton paid particular attention to the amount and quality of food for the prisoners and always objected if the suppliers fell short. He was famously a large man who liked his food and was especially fond of Christmas fare. Many of his Christmas entries mention special Christmas food for the prisoners.

November 23 Saturday: A man named Harding a Servant to Mr Kaynes together with his Horse were drowned in the Torrens below the Gaol at about 4 P.M.   23

November 24 Sunday: Bob and Brown were at the River to day Searching for the body of the Man who was drowned yesterday, but without Success. Davis one of the Gaol Guards was absent last night from his duty: came on this Ev'g at 8 P.M. and Stated that he had been too ill to come on duty.   23

November 25 Monday: Rec'd 1 Cwt of Flour and 56 lbs of Rice from the Gov't Stores, they not having any Biscuit there or Potatoes which the Prisoners could or would eat.   23

November 26 Tuesday: The prisoners with the exception of Bob and the Woman refused to take the rice which was served to them.   23

November 29 Friday: Took the 9 Prisoners under Sentence for Transportation to the Port, and put them on board the Ship Kate for Sydney, left the Gaol with them at 11 A.M. - the body of the Man Harding who was drowned last Saturday was found this Morn'g and brought to the Gaol on which an Inquest was held in the Evening.   24

November 30 Saturday: The Rev'd C. B. Howard came and addressed the Prisoners last Ev'g for the first time since my Appointment.   16

<u>732</u>

December 1 Sunday: Gave Davis leave of absence.   13

December 5 Thursday: Took the Prisoners to the River, and formed a bridge over the Torrens just below the Gaol - Capt'n Bull accompanied us.   13

December 6 Friday: Sent James Knowles to the Infirmary by the order of Dr. Nash, but there being no vacant bed he was brought back.   14

December 7 Saturday: Sent James Knowles to the Infirmary where he was taken in - Perry the TurnKey came on duty a little the worse for Liquor but was allowed to do duty.   13

December 10 Tuesday: Lennon went home Sick.   16

December 13 Friday: Went up to the Tiers with Mr Inspector Sheard & others to look for Chambers and Brown. Searched Bishop's house wherein we expected to find them, but it was in vain. We left Adelaide at 12½ A.M. & returned at 1 P.M.   15

December 14 Saturday: Sent Mr. Williams Six pairs of Handcuffs to go to Port Lincoln.   16

December 20 Friday: Went up to the near Tiers accompanied by Mr Edwards, Serg't Halford etc - took Chambers & Brown about Midnight - Conveyed them immediately to Crafers & brought them into the Gaol about 7½ this Inst. We left Adelaide for the Tiers at 9¼ last night.   19

December 25 Wednesday: Three prisoners named Brown, Collins, and Thos. Murphy Made their Escape through the Hole in the Stone Gaol at 3¾ P.M. Brown & Collins I retook about 2 miles from the Gaol - Murphy escaped altogether.   22

December 30 Monday: Four Natives brought in Charged with Stealing Potatoes from Mr Abbott's N. Adelaide.   32

572

Accounts of the fate of Harding who 'together with his Horse were drowned in the Torrens below the Gaol' combine to confirm the general location of the temporary gaol and Ashton's hut.

> Last Saturday . . . a man on horseback was crossing the Torrens at the ford opposite Government House, when the horse lost its footing.[147]

[While] crossing the Torrens at a fordable part of it near the stone quarries at Government House ... the deceased and his horse accidentally fell.[148]

[T]he Ford above the river Torrens, a little above the house of the Governor of the Gaol, should be secured by some kind of fence in order to prevent accidents in future.[149]

The 'Tiers' mentioned in the journal are the low foothills in Beaumont behind Burnside. A 'native track' existed from the city area, through the southwest parklands along what became 'The Road to Beaumont', a vestige of it now Beaumont Road (re-aligned but the name remains), through the wattle-covered land that became Glenside Hospital, then through to the Tiers and beyond.[150] It was probably this track that was used by Ashton and his party. It was a well-trodden track, long used by Aboriginal people and now also the most common route for settlers trekking into the hills.[151] German settlers used it to walk through to their early settlement of Hahndorf and foresters used it to gain access to the newly located stringybark forests near Mount Lofty. These forests provided splittable and easily sawn timber to the settlers for the first time, at last solving the problem for settlers of building fences.[152] It simultaneously created a problem for Aboriginal people, as the new fences blocked their access to traditional grounds. The Tiers, near Gleeson's place, formed a narrow pass, a favourite haunt for bushrangers and a place where Aboriginal people were often seen walking.

It was now the end of 1839. It was very hot. A woman who arrived on Christmas Day 1839 described it:

The weather was so hot it was almost insupportable and not a blade of grass or anything green except the gum trees to be seen ... [We were] occupied in ... washing and sweeping dust off ourselves.[153]

Much had been achieved in the colony during 1839 but there was still much to do:

Many pressing requirements of a very expensive character still remain. ... works at the New Port ... A city gaol, a new immigrant depot, and an infirmary. The present substitutes for the three last mentioned buildings are not only discreditable to the province, most inconvenient and insufficient, but they actually entail a heavy burthen of expense... In the instance of the gaol, respectable persons confined for debt are crowded in a small space with felons of the worst description, and all are kept in, not by walls, but by a multiplication of sentries, creating a very expensive gaol establishment. Five prisoners escaped from the gaol during the past year, of whom, however, four were retaken at a considerable expense, of course, of time and labour.

Aborigines. ... There have ... been erected, in connexion with this department, two houses for German missionaries, a schoolmaster's residence, and five neat cottages for the natives at Adelaide, and a house for a missionary at Encounter Bay; a large sized building for a school house and hospital are also in course of construction in Adelaide. ...

Police ... [must deal with convicts who] accompanying overland parties, found their way to South Australia ... Two-thirds of the prisoners in our jail has invariably consisted of them. One half of the remaining third has usually been composed of runaway sailors ... [need for a more efficient police force for these] and further, to control the ill-informed and sometimes very law-less natives ... Connected with the police are the keepers of the park lands in Adelaide. This body was instituted at a period when very serious depradations were being extensively committed ... six men at first were absolutely necessary to give a decided check to the evil ...

Three years and a half ago the spot on which we are standing was a desert to Europeans. Now we are surrounded by a populous, and to a considerable extent, handsome city. Our principal streets are lined with well-filled warehouses and shops, and crowded by all the attendants of active traffic. Handsome and substantial buildings are to be seen on every side ... Our Port ... is now filled with large shipping from Europe, India and the neighbouring colonies. The swamp is traversed by a substantial road ... the neighbourhood of the capital is studded with numerous and populous suburbs and villages ... flocks and herds of cattle from New South Wales, following each other in countless succession, already cover a tract of two hundred miles in length, and their enterprising proprietors are even now seriously contemplating a noble attempt at geographical discovery. The aborigines have been kept under humane control, and considerable, though ... as yet unsatisfactory, efforts have been made toward their civilization.[154]

A report on criminal statistics for South Australia for 1839 found that there had been 60 cases for the year of 1839 in a population of 7000, and concluded:

The state of the criminal calendar speaks favourably for the moral condition of our population.

It went on to say:

[T]he Court of Resident Magistrates acted powerfully to repress minor misdemeanours.[155]

A report in 1843, looking back on the statistics for 1839, wrote:

Of the prisoners in 1839, several were natives charged with murder, which shews a large amount of that species of crime. It seemed an outburst of native feelings on the country being taken possession of by the white men and their stock, and before the former properly knew the power of the white and his weapons. The instances of this crime have been more rare since that period. ... The number transported does not so much indicate the greatness of the crimes committed as the determination of his Honor Judge Cooper to rid the colony of lawless men previously convicted, who at this time, came from the other colonies as sailors, and with stock, by sea, and overland ... the Emigrants only forming a fifth of the whole.[156]

The governor's journal 1840

In January 1840 the *South Australian Register* printed the following:

> There are at present 35 prisoners confined, of which 25 are awaiting their trials at the next gaol delivery; and not withstanding all the care and attention of the governor of the prison, Mr Ashton, we should say the number is too great to be crowded in the limited space the present gaol affords – to say nothing of a certain degree of injustice which distant intervals between criminal sessions inflict – at least upon the innocent.[157]

The newspaper was taking a wide view; the journal however concentrated on the pressing everyday issues of running a gaol:

January 5 Sunday: Neither Perry nor Molineux Came to their duty last night: Perry Sent Word by Lennon that he was intoxicated and not fit to come: Wright the Gaoler Went to the house of Molineux who Said that he was in company with Perry And was in a like State - I remained in the Gaol all Night - This Ev'g at 8 o'Clock they returned to their duty. 28

January 9 Thursday: Went with P.S. Halford to the Tiers after Murphy, but did not Capture him. Left Adelaide at 1 A.M. & ret'd at 7 A.M. 28

January 10 Friday: William Brown cut his Irons off, & got over the fence, was re-taken and chained to the Shed where the Turnkeys sit. 30

January 11 Saturday: Chas. Davis was dismissed for Suffering Brown to get over the fence & not firing at him when ordered to do so by the Gaoler & Turnkey Kennedy. 31

January 17 Friday: The Sheriff & Mr. Moorhouse Came & discharged Bob the Native. 36

January 20 Monday: Myself, Wright, Perry, Kennedy, Travers, Molineux, Lennon & Wylie were Sworn in as Constables of the Gaol by the Hon: The Col'l Sect'y at his Office. 35

January 30 Thursday: About 11 P.M. a prisoner named Michael Edmond, charged with Felony made his escape from the Wooden building having Removed a board thereof. Kennedy, Lennon and Wylie [unfinished entry] 32

January 31 Friday: David Chambers made his Escape by getting over the Fence near the Gate whilst the Turnkey was called to another part of the Gaol. 31

Not yet mentioned in the journal was a measure about to be introduced to help stop the escapes:

> I have the honor to request that you will immediately ascertain if any quantity of red and yellow cloth can be procured in the Colony for the purpose of making Gaol clothing ... if these colours cannot be obtained whether any two other very opposite and glaring colours can be procured.[158]

The journal continues with considerable drama for Ashton. He had to deal with the death and burial of a prisoner in his care; with an intoxicated couple brought into the gaol with their children; the holding, execution and burial of the newly condemned bushrangers and another escape attempt. The insecure state of the gaol and the violent behavior of the bushrangers required them to be held in the police barracks next door and extra police constables, sappers and miners to be called in.

February 1 Saturday: At 12¼ this Morn'g one of the Gentlemen belonging to Mr Gleeson, was brought to the Gaol by 6 P.Cs viz: D..., Norris, Maxwell, Bootes & two others, Charged with being Drunk in Hindley St. He was placed in the Wooden Building & at 5 A.M. was found to be dead. I Sent for Dr. Nash who came & having examined him Said that he had been dead some time: there were no marks of violence on his person – An Inquest Sat on the body (Mr. Nicolls Coroner) at 2 P.M. & the jury returned the Verdict of 'Died by the Visitation Of God whilst in a State of intoxication.' Mr. Bell made a Shell For the body And brought it to the Gaol at 7½ P.M. – the Corpse was locked up in the Engine House for the Night. 27

February 2 Sunday: His Excellency was good enough to allow the deceased Gentleman to be interred on the Park Land, and wished me to point out a Spot to Ram Sham, which I did, About Midway between the Gaol and the S.A Company's Station. Ram Sham & 5 other Gentlemen dug a Grave about 5½ feet deep. And buried the body about Noon this day. 25

February 4 Tuesday: A Man & Woman with their two Small Children Charged with being Drunk were locked up All Night. 27

February 5 Wednesday: Insp'r Shaw took four Men in the Tiers Supposed to be bushrangers: – Mr. Inman Superintendent of Police Sent over two P.C.s to do duty at the Gaol. His Excellency & Mr. Gouger Said I should have as many Men as Guards as I wished. 29

February 7 Friday: David Chambers was retaken and brought to the Gaol by the Police of the Port. He was ironed – he broke a part of the fence down, – we then Hand-Cuffed him behind & chained him to a large log in the yard. 30

February 8 Saturday: Hughes and Curran committed for Trial for a Robbery at Mr. Pffender's & also for Shooting at Mrs Pffender. 31

February 11 Tuesday: David Chambers cut his Irons off, & got under the floor in the Wooden building at 1½ P.M. - Went on board the Rajasthan. 33

February 12 Wednesday: Fox connected with Hughes & Curran was taken by Insp'r Edwards & brought to the Gaol. 36

February 14 Friday: Went with Mr. Gouger the Col'l Sect'y to arrange respecting the Iron Store at the back of Beck's in reference to the Prisoners being removed there. 37

February 15 Saturday: Curran, Hughes & Chambers were removed from the Gaol to the Horse Barracks & left in Charge of the Police there for a few days in Consequence of the dreadful threat used by Curran - Mr. Inman & the Sheriff were here, and I was obliged to Request the assistance of the Sappers & Miners. 38

February 16 Sunday: Dined on board the Rajasthan with Stuart & Shaw. 39

February 25 Tuesday: Wright the Gaoler Very ill, Dr Nash came & bled him. 41

February 26 Wednesday: Wright Still ill - Mr. Mann came to See Several Prisoners. 39

February 27 Thursday: A Small portion of the Wooden building was parted off for the use of Debtors, into wh. Mr Symonds A Debtor Refused to go. At 10¾ P.M. found him lying in the yard before the fire, & was obliged to use force to get him inside for the Night. Mr. Fleming another debtor asked my permission to Sleep a night or two longer in the Office as he Expected to be liberated in a few days, to which request I acceded. 42

1046

March 3 Tuesday: The Sessions commenced - Murphy & Campbell attempted an escape from the Wooden Building, but I detected them, and Ordered them to be chained to the Turnkey's Shed for the Remainder of the Night. 48

March 4 Wednesday: At the Sessions all day. 48

March 5 Thursday: Pye found Guilty - Death. 41

March 6 Friday: Hughes, Curren & Fox tried on one Indictment and found Guilty. 40

March 7 Saturday: Hughes, Curren & Fox tried on another Indictment, for Shooting at Mrs Pffender with intent to Murder her, found Guilty & Sentence of Death was passed on them by his Honor Judge Cooper. 38

March 9 Monday: Brown & Collins tried and found Guilty of Highway Robbery, and Sentence of Death recorded against them – This was the last day of Sessions. 39

March 10 Tuesday: Mr Dawbiney was sworn in as Gaoler by the Hon'ble the Col'l Sect'y in the room of Mr. Wright appointed Sup't. of the Prison Working party – Mr Dawbiney's appointment to bear date March 9 1840. 42

March 11 Wednesday: Two prisoners named Glanville and Williams Suspected of Horse Stealing were Sent to the Gaol from the Police Stables where they had been detained a few days. 38

March 15 Sunday: called the Sheriff out of Church by the Wish of Mr Phillips who Stated that he thought Curren & Hughes had not had Sufficient notice of their Execution which was Appointed to take place the next Morn'g. The Sheriff Said he would See His Excellency on the Subject when the Service was concluded – Accompanied by Mr. Moore went in Search of a Sailor named Quinn who had Engaged to Execute the Four condemned criminals – Saw Quinn who refused – went to various places in Search of an Executioner & at last found a Man at 2 A.M. on March 16, who agreed to perform the melancholy duty & whom I brought home and detained until the necessary time. 37

March 16 Monday: The last Sentence of the law was Carried into Effect on Hughes and Curran at the Police Barracks near the Gaol at 8½ A.M. Their bodies were cut down at 9½ A.M. & immediately Conveyed to the Gaol, in the Yard of which close to the Fence, & adjoining the Graves of the Two Natives who were Executed May 31 1839 they were interred. Hughes's conduct was outrageous & disgusting – Pye & Fox who were ordered for Execution with them & who had been removed to the Mounted Police barracks the previous Evening were respited by his Excellency at 7½ A.M.

and ordered to be transported for Life. They were escorted from the barracks to the Gaol at 10½ A.M. A great number of persons assembled to witness the Executions who conducted themselves with the utmost decorum, but were evidently disgusted with the violent & revolting conduct of Hughes. 37

Curran and Hughes now lay in graves next to those of the two Aboriginal prisoners. The bushrangers had finally been caught when they held up the hotel at Crafers. It was not a dramatic shoot-out with police, rather they had pointed their guns at Mrs Crafer, demanded drinks all round and in the next few hours become so intoxicated that when the tip-off came they were easily apprehended by troopers sent in to get them. Fox was picked up later by police. He was found quietly carrying a theodolite, hiding among a party of surveyors.[159] Fox was charged, along with Curran and Hughes, with robbery and shooting at the Pffenders. It was revealed in the trial that Fox had been an unwilling accomplice, much affected by drink, who had tried to hand back stolen clothes while the robbery was still in progress. He was sentenced to hang, however mercy was recommended and his sentence was commuted to transportation for life.

Bushrangers had been actively pursuing 'highway' robbery, donning masks and holding up people in the Gawler area where the Pffenders lived.[160] They also operated along the Para River, in the foothill Tiers, and in a patch of extremely dark forest, now the innocuous and relatively treeless suburb of Blackforest, holding up people on the road from the bay.[161]

Years later, a newspaper remembered the confinement of the bushrangers in the police barracks where they were taken to foil their plans to escape from the temporary gaol:

> The authorities having reason to expect a rescue, Curran and his mates were confined in a string room at the horse-police barracks ... At this time, Mr A Tolmer was Chief Inspector of Police.[162]

Tolmer is recorded to have said the executions took place at the temporary gaol:

> It was in this old gaol that George Hughes, Henry Curran, and James Fox were executed.[163]

This is incorrect. Both the newspaper reports of the day and Ashton's journal clearly place the executions as occurring at the police barracks.[164] It was also only Curran and Hughes that were executed. Tolmer himself, on the next page of his book, stated that:

> On the morning of the execution ... three coffins were brought, and placed in one of the barrack-rooms: but before the hour fixed upon ... Fox was reprieved, and the sentence of death commuted to transportation for life.[165]

Looking at Tolmer's original manuscript, to check his intention, it becomes clear that he did not write that the hangings of Curran and Hughes took place at the old gaol; this was added in blue pencil in a different hand. Nor did he include Fox as one of those hanged.[166]

The execution of Curran and Hughes was later credited with having saved the colony from the curse of bushrangers.[167] It was an event long remembered:

> Yes Curren and Hughes were hung in the courtyard of the Barracks. Ugh! A horrible sight. I saw the execution, and the scene is fresh in my memory. Hughes, who had told some of the troopers that he intended to die 'game', came on the scaffold smoking a short pipe, and shortly after kicked his shoes off towards the crowd who were gathered around. He said he did this to make an old woman a liar, because she had told him years previously that he would die with his shoes on. He was so violent on the scaffold, kicking the executioner when he attempted to fix the rope that an assistant had to be called in to hold the desperate villain's legs whIle the hangman did his work.[168]

A post-script to this incident was a later newspaper report of a skeleton, presumed by at least one reader to be that of a buried bushranger, that was discovered by workers digging alongside Kintore Avenue to plant trees. This occurred in 1892:

A sensational discovery of human remains took place on Monday. Some men employed by the Superintendent of Public Buildings were digging holes for the purpose of planting trees on the Government House side of the road which runs past the Institute when one of their number, sinking in front of the gardener's house, rooted up some human bones. The department was apprised of the circumstances and the work was stopped to allow of an inspection being made ... The result of the examination was that the skeleton of a man was taken from the hole. All portions of the skeleton were perfect and indicated that the man was at least 6 ft high. The corpse had to all appearances been buried in a coffin, which had decayed with the exception of the knots of the wood. The only clothing left was part of a pair of boots and a belt. Enquiries are being made with the object of ascertaining the identity of the body.[169]

In reference to the discovery of human remains made on Monday at the rear of the Police Barracks the following communication from Mr. Hiram Mildred will be read with interest: – 'I am of opinion that the remains of another, if not two more persons, are in the neighborhood. I believe Magee was buried there. Hughes and Curran, who were hanged, were buried there, and I have no doubt the skeleton found is that of one of the three bodies.[170]

If these were in fact the remains of a condemned bushranger buried in the old gaol, Ashton's journal indicates that the remains of the two hanged Aboriginal prisoners would also be alongside. The skeleton may of course have belonged to another – it was not unknown for settlers to fall down wells or to be buried in the parklands. Ashton's journal itself records that a prisoner who died in the gaol was buried in the parklands.

However the fact that the skeleton was found in front of the gardener's house is extremely interesting, as a year later, in 1893, this gardener's house is mentioned again. A journalist was describing an old photograph of the area, which was on public display at an exhibition:

Ascending from the parade-ground by the winding track one reaches what was once known as the 'Destitute-road' but is now seen under a more smiling aspect as 'Kintore-avenue ... Regular travellers from North Adelaide across the parade-ground will notice how much this road has been altered for the better. Instead of a rough limestone track, wet and sodden in winter, we have now a capital footpath, handsome trees, and a well-kept road, while the ancient cottage at the north-eastern corner of Government House domain has been removed and in its stead there is a neat iron residence for the head gardener with a green lawn in front.[171]

The gardener's cottage appears on a map in 1916, within a cut-off north-east corner of Government House domain.[172] The 'ancient cottage at the north-eastern corner of Government House domain' that the gardener's cottage replaced may well have been, at one stage, part of the old gaol.[173]

March 18 Wednesday: PC Dunn came on duty at 12 at Night, intoxicated - Dr Chambers was playing this Ev'g with one of the Mounted P.Cs, at their Barracks, who had a loaded Pistol in his hand, which went off, & wounded another PC in the thigh. 37

March 21 Saturday: 'Capt'n. Jack' a Native brot to the Gaol the irons in wh. Williamy a Native Escaped a Short time ago. 34

March 24 Tuesday: Three men and a Native Woman of V.D. Land were brought to the Gaol having been Committed by Mr. Smith the Resident Magistrate at Port Lincoln for Sheep Stealing - These are the first prisoners we have had Sent to the Gaol from Port Lincoln. 39

March 25 Wednesday: John Downing who was tried & Sentenced to 7 years Transportation for Robbing his Master Mr Lazarus - was this day pardoned by His Excellency - I restored him to Mr Lazarus about 4 P.M. 39

The 'Black Wars' in Tasmania, during which the Aboriginal people there were almost exterminated, took place throughout the years 1828–1832, ending four years before the *Buffalo* landed in Adelaide. A small group of Tasmanian Aboriginal people is known to have been taken to and to have died on the ill-fated Wybelena Mission on Flinders Island in the Bass Strait and others are known to have ended up on Kangaroo Island living with European sealers and whalers.[174] Here in Ashton's journal is mention of an Aboriginal woman from Van Diemen's Land who was as far from Tasmania as Port Lincoln and was now incarcerated in the Adelaide gaol for stealing sheep.

The Masters and Servants Disputes Act applied in South Australia. Any servant such as John Downing, who absconded, stole, or proved lax in their duties as a servant could be imprisoned. This was clearly set out as a warning for emigrants as early as 1837.[175]

'Captain Jack', who returned the irons Williamy had been wearing when he escaped, was well known to the settlers. Also known as Kadlitpinna he lived at times in one of the huts in the Aboriginal Location. In later years he was to become a particular acquaintance of William Cawthorne, a young settler intrigued by the Aboriginal people in early Adelaide.[176] His likeness was painted by George French Angas.[177]

March 27 Friday: Mr Symonds the debtor was disch'd. 42

March 28 Saturday: Mr Wright the Gaoler Remov'd from the Gaol, and Mr Dawbiney the New Gaoler Removed in - John Whitehouse a Prisoner Escaped from Mr. Dawbiney whilst assisting him to Remove from Caroline Place to the Gaol at 4½ P.M. 44

March 30 Monday: The Prison Working party Commenced Work this Morn'g, in their prison dresses, on the other Side of the Wooden Bridge over the Torrens in charge of their Superintendant - Eleven in Number. 44

1229

April 2 Thursday: Johnson was ordered by me not to go with the Working Party for the present owing to the ill State of his health - This was Sanctioned by the Hon: Col'l Sect'y but to Cook & Wash for his Comrades. 39

April 4 Saturday: Rec'd instructions from the Hon: the Col'l Sect'y to put the Prisoners under Sentence of Transportation on board of the Mary Ridgeway on Monday Morning. 42

April 6 Monday: Left the Gaol at 8¼ A.M. with the following Prisoners: - W'm Brown, Jeremiah Collins, James Pye, James Fox, Patrick Mullins, David Chambers and Edward Myers - and put them on board the Mary Ridgeway at Port Adelaide, where I left them in charge of Serg't Lorimer and 3 PCs appointed to guard them to Sydney, at 10¼ A.M. On my return to Town called on Travers one of the Guards who appeared very ill. 44

April 7 Tuesday: Glanville cut his Irons through in 3 different places, put others on him. 35

April 10 Friday: The Hon: The Col'l Sect'y Swore in as Constables for the Gaol Guard David Downing & Geo. Robertson - to commence their duty on Sunday Next. 35

April 11 Saturday: Took James Foscett to the Office of the Col'l Sect'y but he did not Swear him in he requested however that he should be brought to him again on Monday & meantime to act as Gaol Guard. Read the Rules to the New Men and ordered them to commence duty as follows: with Kennedy, Wyley, Robertson and Foscett, with Perry at 8 P.M. Molineux, Lennon and Downing. Changed the Guns at the Stores this Afternoon. 38

April 12 Sunday: Wyley, Robertson & Foscett came on duty at 8 A.M. Travers Still Sick. Gave Vansteine and Fielder two of the Working party a pair of new shoes each their others being torn. 37

April 13 Monday: Mr. Insp'r Sheard Kindly promised to take Travers on the Police he not being strong enough for the Gaol duty. Foscett not Sworn in, the Hon: Col'l Sect'y being engaged. 39

April 14 Tuesday: Foscett sworn in by the Hon: The Col'l Sect'y at his Office. 36

April 15 Wednesday: Wyley Sick at home – Murphy belonging to the P.W.P. replaced himself. 35

April 16 Thursday: Williamy the Native was bailed by Mr. Moorhouse to appear next Sessions. 34

April 17 Friday: Good Friday. The P.W.P. did not go to work. Wyley Ret'd to his duty. 35

April 18 Saturday: Wyley & Lennon had a quarrel in the Gaol Guard last Evening. At 7¼ this Morn'g Wyley came to my House & threatened to leave if I did not discharge Lennon forthwith. I told him he was at liberty to leave by giving me the week's notice. A man named Pat'k Doherty was taken, Supposed to be concerned in Horse Stealing with Glanville & Williams. Mr Edwards wished him to remain at the Police Barracks Which I allowed on the grounds that he might give evidence against his Comrades. 33

During the early part of 1840, the idea of building a high wall around the existing prison was still being floated:

> Mr Ashton's vigilance will never be to much avail as long as he has neither the means of properly securing, classifying or working the prisoners. A remedy for some of these deficiencies is shortly to be applied: and we trust a substantial and sufficiently high wall around the prison buildings will be amongst the first public works undertaken.[178]

The important people in Adelaide were becoming extremely concerned:

> The Gentlemen of the Grand Jury ... have visited Her Majesty's gaol. ... aware, that on several occasions criminals have broken out from the jail, and that the safety of the prisoners depends entirely on the guarded sentries who have to be continually on guard without the fence. They find that the prisoners are in a fearfully crowded state, and that no classification of them can be effected. ... The erection of an efficient gaol is of such importance ... that it should take precedence of all other public buildings.[179]

On 18 April 1840, on the day Ashton was busy sorting out problems with Wylie and Lennon, the *South Australian Register* announced that a brand new gaol would be built on a different site:

> [T]he Government has at last determined on the erection of a new jail, to be erected near the site of the old native location. . . . not . . . a moment too soon – the inefficiency [*sic*] state of the building at present used as a prison having been long and justly complained of.[180]

On 25 April 1840:

> The plans and specifications for the construction of a jail near the site of the old aborigines' location will be ready for inspection.[181]

The plans had been drawn up by George Kingston, who had in the early years been deputy surveyor general but was now in private practice as an architect. His plans were grand. They depicted a half-octagon-shaped outer stone wall, and within that, adjoining yards radiating from a central arc such that the outer edge of the yards formed an inner wall parallel to the outer, thus a double wall. The sentries could parade between the walls and the whole would be secure, anyone who escaped the inner wall had the guards and the outer stone wall to still contend with.

I have found no record of the reasons for the change of plan from a square outer high wall enclosing a collection of prison buildings, however because decisions about a new Government House were also being made, the change of location at least may simply have been a wish by Governor Gawler not to have the new gaol as his next door neighbor. Others have speculated that in regards to the shape, Kingston was strongly influenced by new prison designs throughout the world, where surveillance of prisoners from a central point with radiating yards and cells was in vogue.[182]

Nowhere in the journal did Ashton complain about conditions at the temporary gaol, nor did he comment on the building or design of the new gaol, not even to say it was happening. This was despite the interest and controversy in the community. He appears to have simply accommodated to each change, focused on the everyday, and reserved his thoughts and emotions for the welfare of the prisoners. This is an odd thing to say, as he was involved in an enterprise where people were hanged, transported, or incarcerated. Nonetheless his essential care for his prisoners permeates the journal.

In May 1840 the sheriff, C.B. Newenham, came to write an audit of the buildings being used in the gaol for the previous quarter. Two wooden buildings, the governor of the gaol's office and the gaoler's house, were said to be in good repair. A stone building for male prisoners had no comment on its condition. Wooden buildings for male and female prisoners and a small room portioned off within a wooden building for debtors to sleep in were all in 'a very insecure state'. No rent was paid for any of the buildings. The sheriff also wrote a list of workers, and that each received both wages and rations. Those listed were Mr Wright and Mr Dawbiney, gaolers who received 1/12 each per week; Perry and Kennedy, turnkeys who received 1/7 each per week; and Molineux, Travers, Davis, Lennon and Wylie, guards who received 1/5 each per week.[183]

The next section of the journal, as I have divided it, begins on 19 April 1840, the day that bushrangers Gofton and Broadrib were apprehended by police for horse stealing. It ends on 13 June 1840, with the escape of Gofton from the gaol.

There were many incidents recorded in this period. This was not surprising as the temporary gaol was now seriously overcrowded, with up to 57 prisoners a day.

April 19 Sunday: Two men named Gofton & Broadrib were taken into Custody by the Horse Police for Stealing & Killing Cattle near the Reed beds - Broadrib was brought to the Gaol & Gofton was detained at the Barracks. 35

April 20 Monday: Went out with Mr. Insp'r Sheard in search of Fenton concerned with Gofton and Broadrib round the Reed beds. 35

April 21 Tuesday: William Kay the Maniac was taken up by the Horse Police for being Drunk and disorderly; he was retained at the Barracks all night by my wish - The Police took Gofton to the Gaol and took Broadrib to the Barracks. 39

April 22 Wednesday: Broadrib still at the Barracks: Thompson did not go to work being Sick. 40

April 24 Friday: Geo: D... was discharged, his fine having been remitted by his Excellency. 38

April 26 Sunday: Williams a Prisoner very ill Sent for Mr. Nash at 11 A.M. not at home - again at 5½ P.M. not at home - Sent Mr Dawbiney to Mr Wyatt, & on the way to that Gentleman he met Mr. Nash who came immediately to the Gaol - Removed Williams from the Stone to the Wooden building - Found Thompson & Murphy playing at Cards: Cautioned them. 36

April 27 Monday: Lennon Sick & did not come on duty at 8 P.M. James Williams Sick of a Fever - placed him in the Women's Ward. Campbell Slept with him to watch etc - Sally the Native Slept in the Debtors Room. 36

April 28 Tuesday: Lennon came on duty at 8 P.M. Ja's Williams continues very ill - ordered Wine and Sago by Mr Nash. 35

April 30 Thursday: At 2¾ A.M. a person of respectable appearance who gave his name Peters was brought to the Gaol very much intoxicated & was placed in the Wooden Building - Shortly afterwards Flynn and Mulholland Stripped him of his Coat, Waistcoat, Shoes and Cravat but being discovered by Perry they restored them to his person. Two men came at 6½ P.M. & Emptied the Privy. 37

<u>1118</u>

May 3 Sunday: Mr Dawbiney took a pack of Cards from Murphy and others. 37

May 5 Tuesday: Vansteine used a great deal of abusive Language about a bed, which he Said he had never had since he had been in the Gaol - Went into the Room in which he Sleeps & found that he had Two Beds, and 4 or 5 Rugs, the prison allowance being two rugs: others had as many as 6 & 7. Murphy knocked Vansteine down for his conduct. 34

May 7 Thursday: Murphy violently assaulted David Kerr in the Gaol Yard without any cause whatever, & used abusive Language to Mr Dawbiney when he interfered. I advised Kerr to charge him with the Assault before the Magistrate, but he declined doing so. 43

May 9 Saturday: Rev'd C.B. Howard came to see Williams. Wyley left Gaol duty at 12 Noon. 44

May 10 Sunday: Bassett who was engaged in the place of Wyley did not come on duty but Jim one of the P.W.P. guards did it for him. 46

May 11 Monday: Bassett too ill to take his duty - Engaged a man named Rogers in his Stead. W'm Kay alias Yorke the Maniac was brought to the Gaol in a state of intoxication - he created a great disturbance & Several times Struck at me with a large Stick - he pulled down portions of the fence & broke Some of the boarding in the Wooden Building. Murphy, Ryan, Green, Wilson & Scott behaved extremely well, & contributed greatly to prevent the effusion of blood. 47

May 12 Tuesday: Capt'n Smythe formerly Superintendent of the Mounted Police, but at present one of the Magistrates of the Port Philip District came to the Gaol to See the Prisoners Supposed to be Absentees from that place & Sydney - he Recognized Smith and said that he did not believe he was a Convict & should not have apprehended him in this District & further as he had Worked in Port Philip for a long time, & also for himself, there were persons connected with the force who would have known him had he come from Sydney. Thos. Rodgers Came on duty at 8 A.M. as Gaol Guard in the place of Wyley. 46

May 13 Wednesday: W'm Jackson was brought to the Gaol having been committed from Port Lincoln by the Res't Magistrate there for 3 months to hard Labour as a Rogue and Vagabond. His Excellency Ret'd from Port Lincoln. 44

May 17 Sunday: A woman named Ann Gardner bought Some Spirits in a Ginger Beer bottle to her husband who is a Prisoner - Perry took it from her - I cautioned her not to Attempt the like again, and having a young family at the Port I did not detain her. 53

May 19 Tuesday: A person named Manifold brought in from Port Lincoln for Slaying a new born Male Child (un-named) Committed for trial by Matthew Smith Esq'r R Magistrate.   56

May 21 Thursday: The Hon. The Col'l Sect'y allowed me two extra Guards for the Gaol, in Consequence of its insecure State & the great number of Prisoners - John Bassett & Thos. Lampard were accordingly Sworn in as Gaol Guards by the Hon: Col'l Sect'y. Bassett came at 8 P.M.   53

May 22 Friday: Lampard came on duty 8 A.M.   52

May 23 Saturday: Whitewashed Buildings of Gaol.   51

May 24 Sunday: Rev. C.B. Howard accompanied by Mr H. Calton who read Prayers & preached to the Prisoners commenced a regular Service at the Gaol. The Prisoners behaved well, and were Extremely Attentive. Whitehouse who made his Escape March 28 1840 was re-taken by P.C. Burns in S Adelaide & was brought to the Gaol at 7¼ P.M.   37

May 25 Monday: The Queen's birthday Kept.   37

May 30 Saturday: At 4 P.M. Thos. Wainwright (in Gaol for Felony) made his Escape as is Supposed over the fence near the Gaoler's House without the Gaoler & Turnkey knowing ought of the Matter. Robertson perceived him a Short distance from the Gaol, followed and Captured him after being Absent from the Gaol about 20 min.   55

May 31 Sunday: Rev'd C.B. Howard & Mr. H. Calton came & performed Divine Service at 3 P.M.   57

                                     <u>1484</u>

June 3 Wednesday: Whitehouse who made his Escape March 28th 1840, & was re-taken on 24th Ultimo was taken before the Magistrate (Mr Wigley) by whom he was discharged – It appeared that he could not be made to complete the term of his Sentence at the Sessions in March last, viz. 8 months Hard Labour in consequence

The governor's journal 1840

of the Gaoler having lost Sight of him after he had taken him from the Gaol. 50

June 5 Friday: Foscett & Rogers Gaol Guards were sick last Night. Mr. Insp'r Stuart Sent me a P.C. from 10 to 12 P.M. & one P.C. from 12 to 6 A.M. 57

June 6 Saturday: PCs as Yesterday. 51

June 7 Sunday: Rogers came on duty at 8 A.M. Mr. Calton & the Sheriff came to the Gaol - Divine Service was performed. 52

June 8 Monday: Jones the Sheriff's Officer being out of Town, the Sheriff sent for me and asked me if I would assist a person of the name of John Ormrod, at the Suit of his Son W.H. Newenham which I did at 4 P.M. 54

June 10 Wednesday: I served a copy of a writ on Mr. Fitzpatrick a debtor at 1 P.M. at the Suit of John Walker. 53

June 13 Saturday: John Gofton committed for Trial with Broadrib for Stealing & Slaughtering Some Cattle, made his Escape at 5½ P.M. by scaling the fence near the privy - he was fired at by Robertson but without effect. Mr. Tolmer and Several of the Mounted Police went in different directions in Search of him - I reported his Escape, & afterwards in company with Mr. Inspector Stuart went to Several Houses in the hope of detecting him - We could discover no traces of him. Best the Butcher in Hindley St. was in deep conversation with him during the day, & on Enquiry he also was missing & could not be heard of. 55

There had been a few escapes but the escape of Gofton was a major problem and quickly took up Ashton's attention.

The *Southern Australian* told the story:

> On last Saturday evening, John Gafton [*sic*], who was committed some weeks ago on a charge of cattle stealing, contrived to effect his escape from the jail by climbing over the fence in an obscure part of the prison yard. The guard on the outside observed someone in

the act of climbing over and immediately fired his piece at him, but without effect. An alarm was given, and the guard went in immediate pursuit of him; but . . . [Gofton] has succeeded in eluding all attempts to re-capture him. No blame whatever attaches to to Mr. Ashton, the Governor of the Jail . . . The diligence, of both Mr. Ashton and the Police, in their attempts to re-capture him, are deserving of the highest praise.[184]

The saga of Gofton continued well after his escape. It included a police and Aboriginal tracker hunt, the finding of his mutilated body and the subsequent hanging of another man, Stagg for the murder of the escaped Gofton. It is a truly awful tale.

Among the incidents recorded in this period is a brief mention of a man named Manifold, brought in from Port Lincoln for 'slaying a newborn'. This was not quite as it seems. Although 'slaying' was the official description, the offence was rather one of serious malpractice: too much violence employed by a young doctor called in to assist midwives with a long and difficult birth. The case was later abandoned, thought unlikely to lead to a longer sentence than the time already spent awaiting trial.[185]

The population of Adelaide city, the area bounded by the parklands, was now enough to legislate to form a city council. Rates collected could help pay for the new gaol.[186] Three major discussions took place at the earliest planning meetings: Kingston's architectural plans were laid on the table and builders urged to tender;[187] Kingston was commissioned to draw an official map of the city area, depicting all the buildings so that rates could be charged;[188] and slaughtering of animals was regulated.[189]

Once the Adelaide Council had begun in November 1840 a site for a slaughterhouse was decided. It was 'on the southern bank of the Torrens, near to the site of the old botanic gardens'.[190] A reserve for a botanical garden had been set aside by Colonel Light in 1837 – it is depicted in his plan as an island in the Torrens (see detail from Colonel Light's *Plan of the city of Adelaide* on page 23). By 1840 the river passed only north of the island, and so this piece of land became part of what is now Bonython Park. In fact, another version of Colonel Light's 1837 plan already depicts the southern side of the 'island' as a dry channel.[191] Kingston later described the original 'Botanic Gardens Reserve', allocated by Light as 'on the southern side of the river extending eastward from Thebarton in the direction of the gaol'.[192] It was at one time used as a garden, 'Allen's Garden', described in 1838 as a 'low swampy piece of land to the west of the township, [that] has formerly been flooded'.[193] Although Colonel Light wrote the name 'Botanical Garden' on the island it seems to have referred to the sometimes marshy, sometimes dry channel as well.

The slaughterhouse finally came to be built just as the new gaol was finished, in December 1840. The slaughterhouse was a major and imposing landmark, and had it been built earlier, the site for the proposed new gaol would have been described as 'near the slaughterhouse'. As it happened, the nearest reference point on the same side of the river was the old Aboriginal Location. In July 1840 the tender for building the new gaol was granted to builders Borrow and Goodier and Kingston met with them to lay out the footings.

The next section of the journal is relatively uneventful. It fills out a little the details of the visit to Adelaide by Dr Ullathorne, the Roman Catholic Vicar General of Australia at the time. Ullathorne's autobiography and letters highlighted an attitude in Adelaide against the Catholic Church. He wrote that Governor Gawler objected to him as a 'papist' and refused him use of a building, utilised by other faiths, to preach. Adelaide had only a small number of Catholics: less than 50. It was only the offer of premises by a protestant business owner, appalled at Gawler's treatment of Ullathorne, that allowed him to hold services.[194] Ashton's journal provides the additional information that Dr Ullathorne visited a sick Catholic prisoner and conducted 'divine service' for the Catholic prisoners in the gaol.

June 14 Sunday: Mr H. Calton came to the Gaol and performed Divine Service at 3 P.M.   62

June 15 Monday: Received fro the Gov't Stores 5 Great Coats for the use of the Turnkeys & Guards. 65

June 16 Tuesday: Mullins who was fined £5 for an Assault, or one Months Imprisonment with Hard Labour refused to go out to work having had his Arm broken recently - On examination by Mr. Nash, Such appeared to be the case, & to have been badly Set. 64

June 19 Friday: Littlewood alias Jones, & Clark were taken to the Mounted Police Barracks for the Night - Sent one of my Guards there. 48

June 20 Saturday: Jones & Clark were taken to the Port, & placed under the charge of the Police there. 49

June 21 Sunday: Mr. Calton came, but performed no Service in consequence of the great Wet. 46

June 22 Monday: Gaol Guard Lampard Sick. 46

June 24 Wednesday: Lampard returned to his duty. Sent to the Port by P.C. Mason 2 Mattresses and a Lamp with a lock for the use of Littlewood & Clark at the wish of Mr. Stuart. 47

June 25 Thursday: Halloran charged with Sheep Stealing was placed in Irons having offered the Guard Robertson £10 to connive at his Escape. 45

June 27 Saturday: Thompson, Jones & Fielder belonging to A.PWP Were discharged last Ev'g at 4½ P.M by order of the Sheriff & then the PWP ret'd from work at 4½ P.M. this Ev'g. Some of them were the worse for Liquor & the prisoner Flynn was quite drunk - He created a great disturbance in the Gaol, fighting with the Prisoner Hall etc I had gone to Mr. Phillip's to request the attendance on Rollands a Sick Prisoner of the Roman Catholic Vicar General of Australia (Dr. Ullathorne) who has been on a visit to this Colony from Sydney the last few weeks. 49

June 28 Sunday: Mr H. Calton came at 3½ P.M. divine Service was performed. Foscett the Gaol Guard sick. 48

June 29 Monday: Dr. Ullathorne the Vicar General came to see Rollands. 49

June 30 Tuesday: Dr Ullathorne visited Rollands. His Honor the Judge called at the Gaol – I was at home at dinner. 49

<u>1557</u>

July 1 Wednesday: Removed Rollands who continues very ill, to the Women's Ward – I went & had an interview with the Judge. 46

July 2 Thursday: Mr. Nash ordered Rollands some Sago & ½ pint of Wine per diem. 47

July 3 Friday: Went to the Port & put on board the 'Thirteen' bound to Port Philip. W'm Clarke alias Brig'r Cross & James Littlewood absentees from that province who had been removed to the Sir Cha's McCarthy hulk at the Port June 20th last: left them in charge of Two of the Horse Police at 4 P.M, & ret'd home at 7 P.M. 48

July 4 Saturday: Henry the Native made his Escape by getting over the fence near the Gaoler's House, with an Iron on his leg: Kennedy the Turnkey Saw him about 2½ A.M. but not from that time until 4 A.M. during wh. he made his Escape. Dr Ullathorne came. 48

July 5 Sunday: Mr H. Calton came to the Gaol as also did Dr Ullathorne – each held divine Service at different hours, according to the forms of their Respective Churches. 45

July 6 Monday: One of the P.W.P Guards came to do the day duty at the Gaol in place of Foscett Still Sick. 43

July 7 Tuesday: Dr. Nash came to the Gaol – The Sessions Commenced today – at the Court House. 47

July 8 Wednesday: At the Sessions all day. 50

July 9 Thursday: Dr. Nash called & reported Rollands as capable of taking his Trial tomorrow. At the Court all day. 48

July 10 Friday: Rollands conveyed to the Court House in a Cart – At the Court all day. 47

July 11 Saturday: Dr. Nash visited the Gaol – at the Court all day. 48

July 12 Sunday: Rev' C.B. Howard Came, and at 3 P.M. performed divine Service. 48

July 13 Monday: John Crafter came on duty as Gaol Guard in the place of James Foscett who resigned on Saturday on account of ill health. The P.W.P. commenced Supplying the Gaol with Water in the place of the Water Cart supply. 49

July 14 Tuesday: Mr. Nash came to the Gaol - Rollands Improving in health - Sally a Native of V.D. Land discharged by his Honor the Judge. 48

July 16 Thursday: W'm Kay, alias Yorke the Maniac was brought in last Night at 11 P.M. he was exceedingly outrageous and broke 10 panes of Glass in the Wooden building. 44

July 18 Saturday: Mulholland & Scott Sentenced to 18mo: Imprisonment, but Not Hard Labour. Appointed Wardsmen: viz: Scott of the Wooden Building & Mulholland of the Stone Building. 44

July 19 Sunday: Rev'd C.B. Howard & Mr H. Calton Came & performed divine Service at 3 P.M. 45

July 20 Monday: The following Prisoners went to work on the Roads: Vansteine, Flynn, Johnson, Campbell, Holloway, Patton, Shepherd, Kelly, Theile, Williams, Hall, Halse, Lancaster & Breynard. 53

July 24 Friday: Gave Mr Dawbiney leave of absence for the day to Shoot etc 43

July 25 Saturday: William Kay was brought to the Gaol at 11½ P.M. ... Drunk. He was Handcuffed and had the Leg Bar on and Stopped by the fire all Night. 48

July 26 Sunday: The Rev.d Mr. H. Howard and Mr. Calton Came to the Gaol we had divine Service at 3 P.M. 47

After this period of relative quiet, with Gofton still at large but police ever closer to tracking him down, events suddenly took a turn. Gofton was found. However, he was dead.

July 27 Monday: The Body of John Gofton was found near the River Para he has been Shot Through the Head - and Joseph Stagg was brought to the Gaol Charged on the Suspicion of having Murdered the Said John Gofton. - Mr. Insp'r Tolmer Sent the Horse Police to fetch Stagg to the Barracks, but as he was locked up for the Night I thought it much better to let him Stop where he was. 47

July 28 Tuesday: Joseph Stagg brought in last Ev'g for the Murder of John Gofton was not taken before the Res't Magistrate, but taken before the Coroner & Jury who were Sitting at the Australian Arms on the body of Gofton. I attended the Inquest all day. 45

July 29 Wednesday: Mr. Newenham Clerk of the Supreme Court Came to the Gaol this Morn'g. At 10 A.M. and took the Affadavits of Glanville, Smith and Williams the Supposed Absentees from the other Colony. At 10 I attended the Adjourned Inquest on the body of John Gofton with the prisoner Stagg until 3 P.M. Attended Maj'r O'Hallorans Office & reported Lomas & T. . . of the Mounted Police as being in a State of Intoxication when the former brought a Prisoner to the Gaol and the latter came from Mr. Insp'r Tolmer for Jos. Stagg on Monday 27th Instant. 44

July 30 Thursday: The Coroner's Inquest ret'd a Verdict this Aft'n at 4½ of Wilful Murder against Joseph Stagg. 46

July 31 Friday: AT 1 P.M. His Ex: the Gov'r accompanied by the Hon: the Acting Col'l Secretary & A.M. Mundy Esq'r Private-Sect'y to His Ex: inspected the Gaol, the Prisoners, the Office and books and expressed his Satisfaction at the orderly conduct of the men, the general appearance of the place, and the creditable State of the Accounts etc. The Sheriff & myself received His Ex: & conducted him over the buildings. 48

1423

August 1 Saturday: At 11½ A.M. took Smith, Glanville & Williams before his Honor the Judge upon a Habeas: Charged on Suspicion of being Absentees from the other Colonies - they were discharged by his Honor, as he Considered there was Not Sufficient Evidence to detain them. Doherty (Another Absentee) was taken there by the Police who has been confined at the Barracks of the Mounted Police, but still under my charge was also discharged by the Hon: The Advocate General by a written Mem: to me to that effect. Eleanora Rau comm'd for Trial for concealing the birth of her female child was admitted to Bail by the Res't Mag: - her bail being 8/- Hon: The Acting Col'l Sect' and the Sheriff. Taken from the Court & delivered by me at the Sheriff's House. 50

August 2 Sunday: Mr. H. Calton Came and we had divine Service at 3 P.M. His Excellency Sent 4 Bibles for the use of the Prisoners in the Gaol etc – 2 Men Names Hamilton Bailey and Charles T... was brot to the Gaol by the Police Very Drunk, they Created a Great Disturbance and Tore the Gaolers Coat to pieces – & Also Robertsons one of the Guards Coat. 44

August 3 Monday: Glanville, Smith & Williams who were discharged by his Honor the Judge on Saturday last were brought to the Gaol as Escaped Convicts etc, by two of the Port Philip Police. The two Men who created Such disturbance last Ev'g – were fined 5/- each for being drunk & 30/- each for damages done to the Clothes of the Gaoler & Robertson the Guard. 52

August 4 Tuesday: Finnigan an Escaped Convict was brought in by the Mounted Police – Smith alias Coyle and Finnigan alias Edwards were taken to the Court by the officers of the Port Philip Police & Remanded until to-morrow. Elise Sophia Leigard was taken from the Gaol by Mr. Insp'r Tolmer and put on board a Ship bound to Port Philip. 46

August 5 Wednesday – Mr. Insp'r Stuart sent me a P.C. from 8 last night to 6 this Morn'g in Consequence of One of My Guards being Sick. A Man Named Joseph Hatfield was taken into Custody for felony and was Kept at the Barracks he being a friend of Stagg's. 48

August 6 Thursday: Glanville, Smith, Williams and Finigan were ordered to be detained by the Res't Magistrate, in order to their being Sent to Port Philip – I went & Saw the Hon: the Acting Col'l Sect'y (Mr Hall) relative to their being Sent away Immediately, who took instant Steps to forward them by the Ship 'Dauntless' on the following Morn'g – Consequently all things were arranged to this End – Mr. Stuart Sent Me an extra P.C. and Mr. Tolmer three of the Mounted P.C. who Arm'd in Mr Dawbiney's house all night as Some fears were Entertained of an outbreak, from their Known Violent Conduct – The night passed off without their making any attempt to Escape. 46

August 7 Friday: Came to the Gaol this Morn'g at 6 o'Clock, proceeded at 7 to the Port with the undermentioned Prisoners: William Glanville, James Williams, John Smith alias Michael Coyle, William Edwards alias John Finnigan and Patrick Doherty in the Police Cart, and a Horse & Cart Engaged at McDonald's Stables at the back of the Southern X. Arrived at the Port at 9½ A.M. Immediately placed the Prisoners with the two Port Philip Officers on board the Ship Dauntless, Weighing Anchor to proceed to Port Philip - Returned at 2 and reported particulars to the Sheriff. 47

August 8 Saturday: At 5 P.M. Mr. Kelly one of the P.W.P. returned from work very much intoxicated & commenced quarrelling & fighting with Vansteine & several of the other Prisoners - I called Cohen one of the P.W.P. Guards into the Gaol, in order that he might Witness the State in which Kelly Was, Who told me that he had been 'brought in quite Sober'. 47

August 9 Sunday: Mr. Calton Came at 3 P.M. we had divine Service etc. 43

August 10 Monday: Reported Kelly's Drunken State to the Sheriff, this Morn'g - Locked a Man & Woman up at 9½ P.M. for indecently Exposing their persons in the Park lands, near the Gaol. 48

August 11 Tuesday: The Man and Woman As above was taken before the Magistrate and the Man was fined £5 - and the Woman £2 - for indecently exposing their Persons. 47

August 13 Thursday: Joseph Stagg was this day taken to the Res't Mag: Court, & remanded until to-morrow. 42

August 14 Friday: Stagg again taken before the Court, and remanded until tomorrow. 42

August 15 Saturday: At 12½ Noon took the four undermentioned Prisoners to the Port, and placed them under the Escort of 2 P.C.s on board the 'Christina' for Sydney. Charles Staples, John Jones, W'm Rollands, Geo: Hall Conveyed to the Port in the Police Bullock drag, and Horse & Cart. 43

August 17 Monday: Mr. Freeman brought to the Gaol for Debt. 46

August 18 Tuesday: Mr. Goldfinch brought to the Gaol for debt - James Thomson convicted of being drunk at the Port, was committed to Hard Labour for 3 days in default of payment of a fine of 5/- & also for having been convicted of the like offence before - In consequence of an injury Sustained in the hand, Thomson was not Sent on the P.W.P. 46

August 19 Wednesday: The P.W.P. refused to receive the Meat supplied - Sent at 4 P.M. to the Sheriff, who came immediately to the Gaol accompanied by Mr Dumbleton from whom the Meat had been procured - he pronounced the whole as good & Such as no respectable Gentlemen would refuse to have served at his own table - At 5 P.M. offered them the Meat again - all refused to take it, & Steel was very Insolent. 44

August 20 Thursday: At 1 A.M. Mr Kenneth Campbell was brought in for debt. At 6 this Morn'g the P.W.P were called by TurnKey Perry when Steel made use of the most disgusting language to him. Lancaster, Bates & Packman refused to go to Work - Steel refused to join the P.W.P in the Afternoon because I would not give him Meat he having Refused it yesterday. Job Baker brought in for debt but was discharged at 6½ P.M. August 20. Stagg was this day taken before the Res't Mag: Remanded until Monday August 24th 1840. Mr. Best, who had absconded from his Bail & against whom a true bill for Felony was found last Sessions, Was Captured, & detained at the Mounted P. Barracks in consequence of Stagg being confined in the Gaol for Murder, with whom Best is Supposed to have connexions. 45

August 21 Friday: Called up this Morn'g to the Gaol at 7 A.M. in consequence of a disturbance between Scott and the Turnkey Perry - on Enquiry found there was nothing worthy of my interference. Scott having been appointed Wardsman, and receiving Rations as Such, I punished him by the Stoppage of his extra rations. Edw'd Pavelin brought to the Gaol under Arrest for debt. 44

August 22 Saturday: The P.W.P. received their Meat Excepting Packman who refused to go to work, & consequently was not supplied with Meat. Went to the 'Bay' last night in company with Mr Andrews with a writ to apprehend Jos: Lonsdale late Livery Stable Keeper in the Town, for debt. After waiting for some time he ascertained from the Chief Officer of the Lalla Rookh that the Christina had passed down on the opposite side of the Gulph about 2½ P.M. 44

August 23 Sunday: Mr. Calton Came at 3 P.M. we had divine Service. 45

August 24 Monday: Joseph Stagg was taken before the Magistrate and Remanded to the 27th. - I took William Best before His Honor the Judge who Committed him on his Warrant a True Bill having been found against in July last for Stealing a Bullock the Property of William Rogers. 49

August 25 Tuesday: Took the Prisoner Matthew Gardener to the Port to See his wife who was found Dead before the fire this Morning At 6½ left the Gaol at 2½ P.M. and Returned with him at 6½ P.M. 50

August 26 Wednesday: John Wrathall Bull was brot to the Gaol by Thomas Jones Sheriffs Officer for Debt. 48

August 27 Thursday: Stagg was taken before the Res't Magistrate & fully Committed on the charge of Murder of Gofton - Gardiner's Wife was buried this day, he was allowed to attend the funeral in charge of Molineux the Guard. 48

August 28 Friday: Mr. Dawbiney the Gaoler discharged a man named John Wilson who was committed for one Month to H. Labour in default of the payment of £6 - 6, for the Sum of £5 through mistake. Rations drawn on Friday for the 1st time. 48

August 30 Sunday: Mr. Howard and Mr. Calton Came at 3 P.M. We had divine Service. 50

August 31 Monday: Waited on his Honor the Judge, and the Adv. General to arrange respecting the Sessions. 50

September 1 Tuesday: Sessions commenced - Kerr, Halloran & Smith were tried for Sheep Stealing at Port Lincoln - Kerr & Halloran found Guilty Sentence deferred. Smith Acquitted. 49

September 2 Wednesday: Eleanora Rau was Sentenced to 12 mo: Imprisonment with Hard Labour for concealing the birth of her Child - Halloran & Kerr Sentenced to Transportation for Life, also Gibson, and Sentence of 'Death Recorded' against Hawkshaw for Burglary. The Sessions terminated this Ev'g at 5 P.M. 50

September 3 Thursday: Mr. Fleming in for Debt was discharged this Day by order of the Sheriff. 47

An extensive search for Gofton had been undertaken when he escaped, and at the last had concentrated on the Para River where 'some suspicious characters were lurking about'.[195] The *Southern Australian* using similar interesting language had earlier reported that 'three or four people were skulking in the neighbourhood under very suspicious circumstances'.[196] A day before Gofton was found, a woman was offered a large value coin for bread for someone 'lost in the bush'. She became suspicious and called in the Mounted Police.

Police and Aboriginal trackers, already in the area, followed footprints they had been thinking for a while were those of Gofton, through swampland near the mouth of the Para. These led them to a 'miserable hut', roughly put together from swamp bush. Inside they found Gofton alone and quite dead, shot through the head, and with no gun to be found. Police Inspector Tolmer was brought in to examine the scene and declared a second set of footprints as those of Gofton's friend Stagg. The size of the prints and evidence of a peculiar walking gait convinced him. Sergeant Lomas then apprehended Stagg at the Buffalo Head in Hindley Street and the shoes Stagg was wearing seemed to match the prints in the mud.[197]

The details of the discovery of Gofton's body and Stagg's possible involvement differ in almost every newspaper account. Stagg himself denied being there and was never to confess.

> It is said he trembled when charged with the murder, but preserved the most dogged silence.[198]

He did however speak when he accompanied Ashton to view the body:

> Mr Ashton, Governor of the Jail, knew John Gofton; who was under his charge, and made his escape from jail on the 13th June, 1840. Saw the body of the deceased and identified it; saw it in the presence of the prisoner, and prisoner himself said 'that is Gofton poor fellow, sure enough'.[199]

He also spoke at the inquest, accounting for his movements the previous days. The coroner did not believe him and brought in his finding against him. The day before the body was found, Stagg was in town visiting a Mrs Watts who was in the gaol. Daubiney the gaoler's son, then aged 11, gave evidence that he had seen him there. He was one of many and varied characters both willingly and unwillingly providing conflicting accounts of Stagg's whereabouts in the days before Gofton was found. The body had been brought to town and a great many of the people of Adelaide had turned up at the Australian Arms. The *Southern Australian* reported:

> The room was crowded, and the greatest interest was manifested in watching the proceedings.[200]

The paper expressed the general feelings of the settlers:

> Without prejudicing the case, we hope that the enquiry will tend ... to the breaking up of the gang of desperadoes, who have infested the colony for some time past, and committed their depredations with impunity.[201]

The journal shows that it was not until immediately after attending the inquest that Ashton had a chance to lodge a complaint against Lomas for being intoxicated when he brought Stagg into the gaol. He also lodged a complaint of intoxication against the man sent by Tolmer to then transfer Stagg from the gaol to the police barracks. Ashton had not complied with the request. He was not going to lose his prisoner now.

In his *Reminiscences* Tolmer told a strange tale of a much later confession by Sergeant Lomas, in which Lomas said that it was he that had killed Gofton, finding him alone in the hut. Lomas had by then been dismissed and had left the colony, but had returned to confess. He had spent time in a 'lunatic asylum' and Tolmer dismissed his confession as 'pure fiction, caused by a disordered mind'.[202]

Stagg's was not the only sensational case to interest the people of Adelaide. A young woman, Eleanora Rau, who was brought into the gaol on suspicion of having killed her newborn child near the German village of Klemzig, also excited much attention. The infant was found floating in the Torrens by boys playing on the bank. Damage to the child's throat and medical opinion that the child had been born alive led to a coroner's verdict of murder by persons unknown. Among the local German community suspicion fell on Eleanora Rau. Dr Nash confirmed she had been recently delivered of a child, a claim she at first denied, however later she asked to tell her story to Pastor Kavel.

She told Kavel that she had hidden her pregnancy, even from her mother. This seems hard to comprehend except that with the voluminous fashions of the day, with petticoats and dresses, and coverall shifts, it was achieved. She gave birth, she said, during the daytime but in a very dark room next to a room where her family used to live. After gasping to take a breath and not having uttered a cry, the infant had expired in her arms. She told Kavel she never had a thought to kill the child. Her mother had been outside milking the cows and she insisted she would have told her had the child lived. However she now took her chance and hid the baby under a tree to bury when she could. The father of the child happened by, knowing she was ill, and on seeking his advice he told her not to tell another soul, asked for the child's body to be given to him and left. He later told her he had placed the corpse in the water. When police, and later the court, questioned him he denied he was the father or involved with her in any way though he said he knew her. She explained to Kavel that he was 19 and frightened he would hang. She thought the reported damage to the infant's throat may have occurred on a snag in the river or from being retrieved by the boys; she knew nothing of it. Eleanora was charged with being an accessory to murder and with concealing a birth. When it came to court she alone was charged with murder; the young man called only as a witness. The court dismissed the charge. She admitted the lesser charge of concealing the birth of her child, and was granted bail. She was later sentenced to 12 months gaol with hard labour.[203]

These accounts of Joseph Stagg and Eleanora Rau are from newspaper reports. Ashton rarely wrote any comment on prisoners or provided detail of crimes. His entries typically are understated, with only some exceptions. He generally noted only enough to record the person in gaol and the reason, also any incident involving the prisoner that occurred within the gaol and any action he or his guards were required to take in relation to them. His is an official account yet, at the same time, an oddly human account.

Ashton had a lot to worry about during this time. The gaol had many difficult prisoners and chaos was never far away. Not only did he have to deal with Stagg and Best, an associate of Stagg's, he also had a number of escaped convicts. They were dealt with swiftly, however, with Ashton assisting their transport to the boats that returned them to the eastern shores.

The gaol was inundated with debtors, including well-known and influential men. John Wrathall Bull was one such. He is well known in history for his popular books and articles on his own experiences in the early colony.[204] One curious aspect of Bull's writings, in the light of this journal, is that nowhere did he mention his own time in gaol, nor did he record the whereabouts of the old gaol, when it seems he was in a position to know everything about it. He does tell the story of coming across a tent used to hold prisoners.[205] This must have been soon after his arrival in Adelaide. He also writes about the old gaol but only in a tale of supplying information that helped Stuart and Ashton apprehend some villains in the Tiers, saying that on his way to the police station he 'had called at the Old Gaol, to let [Mr Ashton] know that he had got information that would give him great pleasure'.[206]

Although Ashton's handwriting is similar to some of the others who occasionally filled in the minute book, it is clear that the person writing the entries now changes. Instead of a generous scrawl and story-like style, the coming section has neat tiny writing and a formal style. It begins in a much less interesting way and threatens to be tedious. As it goes on however it does provide a different perspective on life at the gaol, on the prisoners, on the doctor's treatments and on Ashton, who was never so observant of himself.

September 4 Friday: John Devnell - Butcher - (under arrest for Debt) was this day discharged by Order of the Sheriff. - (left at ¼ past 5 p.m)

About ¼ past 7 p.m. alarmed by a sudden Report of Fire Arms at a short distance below the Gaol at the N.E. Angle - Mr. Daubiney

& 2 of the Guards immediately went off to try to discover the parties who had so improperly acted - but returned after having sought in various directions without success. 45

September 6 Sunday: At 3 P.M. Mr. Henry Calton Came to the Gaol - and read the Evening Prayers and Psalms for the day - and gave a short address to about 30 of the Prisoners etc in the Wood Prison. At ¼ past 6 P.M. 'Lampard', one of the Guard - feeling very unwell was permitted to leave Duty. 44

September 7 Monday: 'Lampard' (the Guard) still ill & unable to attend the Gaol this Morning.
At ½ past 11 - Job Baker - brought to the Gaol under arrest for Debt: At ½ past 4 p.m. Isaac Sladden brought in - under an arrest for Debt. Mr Daubiney - the Gaoler - unable to move out of the House from acute suffering in the Ancle Joint - 44

September 8 Tuesday: 'Lampard' (the Guard) returned to his duty this Morning - but still very unwell.
- At ¼ past 1 pm. David Sheibeners brought to the Gaol by Thos. Jones - under arrest for Debt.
- At 2 p.m. 'Lampard' the Guard (who had sent Dr. Nash's Assistant this Morning - and had taken some Medicine -) was allowed (being still very ill) to go home to his residence - being unequal to duty - Mr Daubiney the Gaoler still suffering from the attack in the Ancle Joints - and otherwise unwell & unable to leave the House. 45

Daubiney and Lampard were both ill and so were a number of the prisoners. This is perhaps why Ashton handed over the writing of the minute book. He was also busy, not only with felons, but with debtors continuing to be brought in. With 46 prisoners crowding out the temporary gaol, four of the debtors, including John Wrathall Bull were moved over at the end of each day to sleep in the new gaol, by then almost built.

September 9 Wednesday: 'Lampard' (the Guard) came on duty again this Morning - rather better than yesterday tho' still weak: Last night 4 of the Debtors - namely Messrs 'Campbell' 'Bull' 'Sladden' & Scheibeney' were allowed to Sleep in the New Prison: Mr Daubiney much worse this morning & suffering the most acute pain: continued ill thro' the day.   46

This is the first mention in the journal of the new gaol. It was not yet finished and not yet even declared a gaol. The builders had achieved much in only a few months. Having won the tender in July 1840 Borrow and Goodier had entered a time of complete upheaval. They had dug the footings and made all their preparations, and then the rules had shifted. Governor Gawler, worried about the cost, decided to halve the size of the gaol. Borrow and Goodier were forced to adjust, to fill in surplus trenches and change what they were in the process of doing.[207] In spite of this they had now built the revised plan to a stage where at least some of the debtors could be taken there to sleep, relieving the pressure on the temporary gaol. The writer with the neat hand continues:

September 10 Thursday: Lampard 'the Guard' nearly recovered - Mr Daubiney still very ill - and - unable still to leave the House.   45

September 11 Friday: Mr Daubiney rather better to=day but still unable to leave the House: Dr. Nash's assistant visited the Gaol.[208]   45

September 12 (Saturday) Mr Daubiney continues unable to leave the House altho' gradually improving in Health. - Dr. Nash visited the Gaol to=day - & prescribed for 3 patients: 45

September 13 Sunday: Mr Daubiney Still unable to leave the House: The Rev'd Mr. Farrell recently arrived from England was expected to perform divine Service in the Gaol this Afternoon - The Forms & the Desk were placed in the Wood Prison & the Books carried over ready for the Service - but owing to the extremely boisterous State of the Weather - and the violence of the Rain - the Rev'd Gentleman was unable to come.   45

September 14 Monday: Mr Daubiney Still unable to attend to active duty - although steadily improving in Health. Isaac Sladden (under arrest for Debt) was realeased by Order of the Sheriff - about ½ past 5 p.m. - this day.   46

September 15 Tuesday: Mr Daubiney was this day able with the assistance of his Stick to get out into the Prison Yard and the Garden 3 or 4 times. - He was bled by Mr. Slater in the Aft'n - and Seems now generally amending in Health:

A number of very ill=looking fellows from the Tiers etc called outside the Prison=Yard this Aft'n to see Donovan: Mr. Sullivan: Peter Smith & others of the Overlanders - but they were narrowly Watched - and towards Sun=Set went away - About ½ past 7 p.m: the Wife of Edw'd Green with an Infant in her Arms - came to the lower End of the Wood Prison - and made much disturbance with her lamentations & the Cries of the Infant. - A Small Sum of Money was collected, among the prisoners, for her present assistance - a Cup of Tea was made for her, and given to her by 'Kennedy' and at length she was induced to depart quietly. 46

September 16 Wednesday: Mr. Daubiney was to=day able to be about the Yard & to attend to various duties in the Prison - tho' still obliged to derive support from his Stick. - The Police having taken away 'Joseph Stagg's' - 3 pairs of Shoes - which were Required in Evidence on his approaching Trial - he was Yesterday Supplied with a pair of the Government Shoes. 48

September 17 Thursday: Mr Daubiney better: Dr. Nash Visited the Gaol and went round with Mr. Ashton to inspect the Prisoners generally - He prescribed for 4 patients and directed that James Bailey should be cupped: In the Afternoon Mr. Slater attended for the purpose but Bailey absolutely refused to submit to the operation -. Williams and Kelly were ordered to go to Work being no longer sick. 47

September 20 Sunday: The Rev'd Mr. Farrell, (accompanied by Mr Sheriff Newenham) came to the Gaol at 3 p.m. and performed Divine Service. 44

September 21 Monday: This morning at 10 - 'Joseph Webb' (a Journeyman Tailor in the employ of Mr. Pearce) residing in North ... Currie Street - came to the Gaol to ask for the return of his Gun - which Mr. Ashton had detained from him Yesterday - 'Webb' had at ½ past 11 A.M. on Sunday 20th Instant - fired off his Gun on the Park Lands immediately below the N.E. Angle of the

Gaol - on which one of the Guards was ordered to secure
the offender & bring him up to the Office which was done -
and Mr. Ashton then shewed him the impropriety of Such
conduct, particularly at a Spot so contiguous to the Gaol -
'Webb' having this Morning expressed his Sorrow for the
Offence - and promised not to forget himself again in such
a manner his Gun was returned to him - Mr. Ashton having
previously satisfied himself that Webb was possessed of a good
Character.

At ½ past 11 to=day Mr. Ashton read to the Prisoner 'David Kerr'
an extract from the Government Letter in which His Excellency
had ordered to be communicated, the mitigation of 'Kerr's'
Sentence - from Transport'n for Life - down to 7 Years Tranp't
with Hard Labour in this Colony. The Prisoner received the
welcome Intelligence with much thankfulness - and his Irons
were immed'y taken off - He was Supplied with a P.W.P Dress
and ordered to join them tomorrow.

Mr. Ashton also read from the Same Letter the extract
announcing to the Prisoner 'Joseph Hawkshaw' His Excy's
mitigation of the Sentence of 'Death' - as recorded against
him - to Transportation for Ten Years.   44

September 24 Thursday: The P.W. Party - this afternoon, completed
the Fence around the Debtor's Prison.
Number of Posts used 27: Rails 69 (& 64): Palings 427.   46

September 25 Friday: Benj'n King - (under arrest for Debt) was this-
Day discharged by Order of [unfinished entry]   46

September 27 Sunday: At 3 p.m. the Rev'd Mr. Farrell Came to the Gaol
& performed Divine Service in the Wood Prison: At 4 p.m. Dr.
Nash Visited the Gaol & prescribed for Mr. K. Campbell & for
Mr. Daubiney.   45

September 29 Tuesday: At 5p.m: a Fight occurred in a detachment of
the P.W Party (who were at work near the Police office on the
Park Lands) between the Prisoners 'Shepherd' & 'Packman'.
It appears that 'Shepherd' had been teazing 'Packman', who

under strong excitement threw his Spade with much Violence at 'Shepherd' - who then Struck Packman a severe blow or two in the face - on which the latter ran off - He was pursued by the Guard and finding him gaining ground upon him - 'Packman' pelted the Guard with pieces of Lime=Stone - & threw himself down by a Tree - Notice was brought to the Gaol - and Mr. Ashton went down and secured Packman and brought him up to the Gaol - where he was hand=cuffed as he was very violent - and quite incapable of controlling himself. He seemed to be under the influence of liquor - and was a long before he came=to from a State of half=Stupor, half=Fit, in which he laid on a Mattress near the Gate. - About ½ past 8 P.M., his Handcuffs were Removed and he was placed in the Solitary Room in the Wood Prison where he remained quiet thro' the Night. 46

It was now 29 September 1840. This happens to be a date recorded by Sergeant McLean, who had arrived in the colony a little over two months earlier. He started work with the mounted police on this date. It was a memorable night. He was stationed in the barracks standing guard over a man who had been arrested on a vessel in the port dressed as a woman. On the same day a French vessel had sailed off with sheep and other unlawful cargo before the captain had thought better of outrunning a pursuit and returned to the port. The crew were now detained in Captain Fergusen's iron store in Waymouth Street to await the judge's decision.[209] So, on this one night prisoners were detained not only in the old gaol, but also in the police barracks and in the iron stores, as well as still presumably the four debtors sleeping in the new gaol!

The gaol is also mentioned during this time in government correspondence. The subject of discussion was rations for prison guards – rations that supplemented their income:

Having submitted for the Governor's consideration a Memorial addressed to His Excellency by the Gaoler Turnkeys and Guards of the Prison, I am instructed to request that you will inform those persons respectively that in consideration of the character of their duties His Excellency will allow the ration of Spirits to be issued to them as heretofore until the 31st December.[210]

You will therefore issue 7 Gills of Spirits per week to each of the persons above mentioned during the remainder of the current year.[211]

So liquor was part of the guards' rations, a situation not unlike that of nurses in Florence Nightingale's time who were also paid in liquor.

Someone other than Ashton continued to write the journal until 1 December 1840. During this time a steady stream of transportations took place and Ashton saw all of these prisoners safely off. The sheriff also was busy, petitioning the governor for mercy on the harshest sentences and making practical arrangements for transport ships and for carts to deliver the prisoners to the ships.[212]

November saw the trial of Stagg and his hanging for the murder of Gofton, the sixth hanging in the colony and the first to take place at the new gaol. Temporary gallows were built outside the front entrance while the new gaol was still under construction. The sheriff made the arrangements:

> I have the satisfaction to remark that everything passed off in the most orderly manner. The culprit made no confession.[213]

Before ascending the scaffold Stagg wished to speak with the commissioner for police. Tolmer later recalled:

> Upon perceiving me, he at once said, 'Mr Tolmer, I did not shoot Gofton: but I deserve to die'. He showed wonderful nerve to the last ... and ... died without a struggle.[214]

The newspaper concurred:

> On the scaffold, Stagg seemed calm and collected. His countenance betrayed little or no emotion; and though he was quite conscious of the awful position he had occupied, yet he showed no symptoms of that intense bodily terror which many criminals on the scaffold exhibit. ... He expressed contrition for his sinful course of life, but maintained his innocence of murder to the last.

A large concourse of people assembled to witness the execution, and a strong body of horse and foot police were stationed around the scaffold. After hanging the usual time, the body was cut down, and afterwards interred in the court-yard of the new jail.[215]

The journal includes a detail not recorded elsewhere – that Stagg was buried 'in the right hand Ward in the far corner'. The official list simply records that Stagg was 'Buried in the gaol'.[216] Later in the journal there are further mentions of Stagg's grave. The first adds a possible hint as to its location. It refers to a stillborn child of a prisoner who delivered in the gaol.

This Child was Buried Near Stagg – at the west-end of the grave Just at the parapet of the wall.[217]

They would have been buried between the walls, and the 'parapet of the wall' likely refers to the castellated rim of the tower that forms the easternmost corner of the gaol. Another mention refers to an Aboriginal prisoner named Ngarbi. The journal states that he is also buried near Stagg.[218] The official list says only 'An Aboriginal. Body buried in the Gaol'.[219] The locations of many of the graves in the gaol are not known as the earlier graves were unmarked – it was not until 1862 that initials of the condemned and the date of execution were routinely marked on the wall next to each grave.

September 30 (Wednesday) William Morgan (who some time back was connected with 'Magee' in this Colony - who was executed for Shooting at Mr Sheriff 'Smart') was this day brought in by P.C. Naughton - on a Warrant from the Police Magistrate at Port Philip - charged on Suspicion of being connected with Wilson & Green now in the Gaol awaiting their Trial for Horse= Stealing. 46

Dr. Nash attended to see 'Morgan' - who required Surgical assistance for the Stump of his Right Arm - which had been shot off by the Port Philip Police when Morgan was trying to escape from them: Dr. Nash also prescribed for 3 other patients.

October 1 Thursday: At 6¾ p.m. 'James Wood', a Labouring Man was brought to the Gaol by the Servant of W.R. Wigley Esq'r charged with lurking about the premises of that Gentleman and refusing to give any account of himself - A Note was sent to Geo Stevenson Esq'r by 'Woods' - and that Gentleman wrote to Mr. Ashton that he would be answerable for his appearance at the Court on Friday Morning. Mr. Wigley being satisfied with the pledge - about ½ past 8pm, the Man was allowed to depart to his Home. 46

October 3 Saturday: At ½ past 8 a.m. - Joseph Bennett was brought to the Gaol for Debt at the suit of Mr. Stuckey - At 1 p.m. police Constable 'Hinch' brought in a dead Sheep which he had taken from Will'm Moss (a prisoner in the Jail under charge of Stealing the Same) last night at 9 - in Hindley St. - The Prisoner Moss was carrying the Sheep in a Bag - the Head was off & the Sheep opened - but the Skin not taken off - & the Prisoner would give no account of it - Under the direction of Mr. Ashton the Sheep was skinned & dressed - the Skin given to P.C. 'Hinch' - & the Flesh was divided among the various Prisoners in the Gaol - At ¼ past 5 - on the return of the P.W.Party - it was noticed that several of them were the worse for Liquor - especially Vansteine & Flynn - From their outrageous Conduct when locked up - they were obliged to be removed from the other prisoners & put in Irons in the Yard - Late at night when they had become calmer - Mr. Ashton allowed them to return to the Ward. 48

October 4 Sunday: At 3 p.m. The Rev'd Mr. Farrell attended and performed Divine Service in the Wood Prison. 48

October 5 Monday: Reported to the Sheriff (by Letter) the disgraceful state of the P.W.Party on their return from Work on Sat'y last - 6 pairs of Leg Irons were brought in this Morning - on the return of the Police from Port Philip - Dr. Nash's assistant attended to see 'Johnson' - and 'Morgan'. 52

October 6 The P.W Party commenced working at 6 a.m. this day - & returned at 8 for Breakfast. - At 3½ PM Peter Shanks brought to the Gaol for Debt - by Thos. Jones at suit of Charles Beck.: Dr. Nash attended at the Gaol - prescribed for 'Steel' and ' Johnson', visited Mr. Campbell - saw 'Quinn' whom he said must Keep quiet - but would not need medicine.   53

October 7 Wednesday: Mr. Slater came to the Gaol at ½ past 9 a.m. having been sent for to visit 'Quinn' - He found him suffering from a high state of Inflammation caused by contusions on the thigh etc - Mr. Slater bled him, ordered poultices to be applied etc - and gave orders that he be Kept as quiet as possible.   54

October 8 Thursday: At ½ past 10 AM read to the Prisoner 'George Halloran' that His Excell'y could not mitigate his Sentence as the Judge did not recommend such a course Read also to the Prisoner Edw'd Alf'd Lister - that His Excellency had consented to allow him to work out at the Rate of 2/6d per Diem - the amount of the Fine of £2; Lister did accordingly this day join in the P.W. Party with that view = At 2p.m. The Town Visited with a perfect Hurricane of Winds and the Dust was so excessive that with great difficulty the Guards could see across the Prison Yard - Every vigilance was used by the Gaoler - Turnkey - & Guards on & off Duty - at the period of the Gale which continued nearly ½ an Hour   54

October 9 Friday: Dr. Nash visited the Gaol & prescribed for Quinn - Steel - Mr. Campbell - & others. - This day completed the first Week of Mr. Edwards' serving the Prison with meat = The meat supplied was all Fore Quarters and furnished in the proportions of Beef 203½ lbs: Mutton 13½ lbs together 217 lbs whereas, had it been furnished in terms of the Contract, it ought to have been alternately in Fore & Hind Quarters - & in the proportions of Beef 152 lbs: Mutton 65 lbs, together 217 lbs.

The Meat generally was not of the prime quality supplied by the previous Contractor & was furnished exceedingly closely in Weight.   57

October 10 Saturday: At ½ past 5 p.m. considerable disturbance was created in the Gaol by the violent conduct of 'George Scott' who was much excited by Liquor - He had been sent out to the Iron Stores to procure Sundry Supplies - in the charge of 'Lampard' the Guard - and on their return both were much the worse for Liquor - They had been seen in 'Morphett St' during the time they were absent from the Gaol - After much violent resistance on the part of Scott - he allowed Mr. Ashton to puts Hand Cuffs on him - 'Bailey & Shepherd' aided by several others of the P.W.Party prevented the Guards & TurnKey from putting the Cuffs on 'Scott' - & they repeatedly struck 'Perry' - 'Lennon' & 'Downing' while they were endeavouring to do their Duty - Several of the P.W.Party were much excited by liquor on their return from Work in the Aft'n: _ & in the Evening Mr A found concealed among the P.W.Party's Tools in the Engine House 4 Bottles of Spirits which he secured by putting a different padlock on the Door of the Engine Ho:

About 8 p.m. 'Scott' having with the assistance of some of the other prisoners taken off his Hand Cuffs - handed them out to Mr Daubiney thro' the Prison Window - & was afterwards quite peacable. 57

October 11 Sunday: At 11 A.M. Mr. A went to the Engine House - removed the 4 Bottles of Spirits, which were there secreted by the P.W.Party's Guards - replaced the usual Padlock on the Door - and brought the Spirits to the Office.

Reported by Letter to the Sheriff the disgraceful 'Row' of Saturday - the discovery of the Spirits etc - and received directions to attend for the investigation of the Affair at the Office of the Sheriff at 9. tomorrow Morning:

At 3 p.m. the Rev'd Mr. Howard visited the Gaol and performed a Divine Service in the Wood Prison. 55

October 12 Monday: At 9 - attended at the Sherriff's Office - when myself - Mr. Wright - & the 3 Guards of the P.W.Party were present-: The 3 Guards were discharged from their situations: and the Gaol Guard 'Lampard' was also dismissed from his - in consequence of his being Drunk himself and allowing the Prisoner 'Scott', while in his charge, to get drunk also - 3 of the Police attended the P.W.Party this day as Guards -

At 3 p.m. Sent 'Kennedy' to the Police Office to see a prisoner there who had given his name 'Baker' - charged with Stealing a quarter of Mutton. - Kennedy identified him as 'Michael Edmonds' who escaped from the Gaol on the 30th Jan'y last. 'Bath' one of the late Guards of the P.W.Party was this day engaged by me as Gaol Guard - in the room of 'Lampard' discharged. 55

October 13 Tuesday: The Prisoner 'Bailey' was this day taken up to the Court House - fined £1 - for assaulting the Turnkey - or 1 Week to Hard Labour 'Michael Edmonds' alias Hy Baker identified by Mr. Ashton as the person who escaped from Gaol 30th Jan'y last was this day 'brought to the Gaol.' 52

October 14 Wednesday: 'Bailey', this morning, paid his Fine and was discharged. This day being the Opening of the New Port the P.W.Party were allowed a Holiday - and his Excellency granted a Bottle of Porter - between each two of the P.W.Party. 52

The prisoners of the Inside party were also allowed ½ pint of Draught Porter each: All Hands conducted themselves with greatest propriety thro' the Day.

October 15 Thursday: W'm Edwards - brought to the Gaol by Thos. Jones (Sheriffs' Officer) under arrest for Debt. 53

October 17 Saturday: 'South' one of the new Guards of the P.W. Party refused to take 'Shepherd' out with the Party this aft'n alledging that 'Shepherd' had attempted to escape when down at the River for Water with the 'Party'. 56

October 18 Sunday: 'Molineux' one of the Gaol Guards did not come on duty this morning having sent word that he was ill = At 3p.m. The Rev'd Mr. Farrell (accompanied by the Sheriff) - visited the Gaol and performed Divine Service in ... Wood Prison. 55

October 19 Monday: 'Molineux' returned to duty this Morning.

10¼ am. Alexander Rollason brought to the Gaol for Debt by Thos. Jones (Sheriffs' Officer) - at the suit of John Stuckey.

At 8pm. 'George Robertson', one of the Gaol Guards did not come on duty - being taken ill - He was unable to send word to the Gaol. - A P.C. on duty from 12 to 6. 56

October 20 Tuesday: 'George Robertson' better this morning: Arthur Baker alias Michael Edmonds who escaped from this Gaol in Jan'y last - was this Day fully committed for Trial on a charge of Stealing some Mutton;

At 8 p.m. 'George Robertson' returned on Duty: - At 8¼ pm a Sudden Report of Fire Arms immediately below the Fence at the Northern side of the Yard caused some excitement. Two Of the Mounted Police immediately Sallied out on their Horses &

scoured the ParkLands below the Gaol, but did not succeed in capturing any person: The Wardsmen 'Scott & Mullholland' in the course of the Night emptied the Privy in the Gaol Yard.   55

October 21 Wednesday: Dr. Nash visited the Gaol - & prescribed for Mrs Watts: E.Rau: Kelly: Green: Blackford: Lister: Rollason: 55

October 22 Thursday: Mr. Ashton this day paid 'Scott' & 'Mulholland' the £1- each arranged with them for Tuesday Night's Work -
At ½ past 10 p.m. found 'Rogers' one of the Gaol Guards fast asleep while on duty outside the prison on a Log. -
Mr Slater - Dr Nash's assistant visited the Sick in the Gaol.   55

October 23 Friday: His Excellency having been pleased to remit the remainder of Mary Watt's Sentence - she was this day released - and Mr. Ashton received her into his own Service for a time, to give her an opportunity of obtaining a Character to fit her for any other situation.   55

October 24 Saturday: Mr. Ashton being absent on important business - The Wages of the Guards etc were paid by Mr Daubiney.   54

Wright, and then briefly another, continue writing the entries until 4 November 1840. It is the most tedious section of the journal to read, without its usual intrigue. I have included it for the sake of a complete record, however for those more interested in Ashton's account, it can easily be skipped.

October 25 Sunday: Dr. Nash visited the Gaol - & prescribed for Wilson - Vansteine & Mr Rollason - : directed that Hornabrook & Kelly should continue their former medicine: Ordered that David Kerr be Supplied with Vegetables & Lime=Juice - to remove a scorbutic attack: - At ½ past 12 - Mr. Anstey of North Terrace Sent a Message to require some person to go to his House to bring a Man to the Gaol - We referred him to the Police Office - as it belonged to that department - no one being able to leave duty at the Gaol. 'Cragan' one of the Gaol Guards - having had his House burnt down last Night - did not come on duty this Morning having received permission to that effect from Mr Daubiney - At 3 p.m. Mr. Sheriff Newenham came to the Gaol and performed Divine

Service in the Wood Prison: At 5 p.m.: Thos. Jones Sheriff's Officer brought to the Gaol one Bryce Thompson (Baker) late of Rundle St. whom he had apprehended on his journey overland for Port Phillip: Thompson was charged with Stealing a Horse, Cart and Halter rope - the property of John Allen and Two Writs for Theft were lodged against him: Mr Ashton out on very pressing duty all day - returned at 6 p.m. 55

October 26 Monday: At ¼ to 8 p.m: 'David Downing' - one of the Gaol Guards - Sent word that he was too ill to leave his Home - & he consequently did not come on duty. 63

October 27 Tuesday: Dr. Nash visited the Gaol at 3 p.m. and prescribed for David Kerr: Hornabrook: Smith: & Mr Rollason. - 'David Downing' Gaol Guard not able to come on duty to=night - Molineux, Gaol Guard - , did not come on duty 'til ½ past 8 - 1 Policeman doing night duty, in room of D Downing - 62

October 28 Wednesday: Mr. Ashton attended, yesterday & this day the Board of Inquiry - held at the Col'l Secretary's Old Office - in the matter of Dr. Litchfield - v= Mr. Gouger. - David Downing Still too ill to come on Duty - a P.C. supplied his place. 64

October 29 Thursday: David Downing sent to the Gaol a Certificate of his Illness - signed by Dr. Mayo - 1 P.C. on night duty. 64

October 30 Friday: His Excellency having been pleased to remit the remainder of the term of Hard Labour allotted to 'Edward Halse' the communication was read to him - and on returning his Clothes of the P.W. Party - he was released. 1 P.C. on night duty. 60

October 31 Saturday: Mr. Slater visited the Sick Prisoners in the Gaol: - His Excellency having remitted the remainder of the Sentence on 'Shepherd' & 'Steele' they returned their P.W. Party Clothes & were, this Evening, released. About 6 p.m: 'Kennedy' the TurnKey brought to the Office a Bottle of Spirits which he had, after considerable resistance, taken from the Guard, 'Bassett' - whom he charged with attempting to introduce the Spirits for one of the Prisoners in the Wood Prison. 1 P.Con. N't duty. 59

November 1 Sunday: The Sheriff came to the Gaol at 3 p.m. - & performed Divine Service in the Wood Prison. 2 P.C. on duty in room of Downing and Bassett. The latter [incomplete entry] 57

November 2 Monday: Mr. Ashton waited on the Governor - & delivered in Lists of the Prisoners for Trial at the Sessions: Dr. Nash visited the Gaol & prescribed for the Prisoners: 'Vaughan, Kerr, Smith and Mr. Rollason': Mr. Freeman - under arrest for Debt - was this day discharged on all the 5 Suits - 'Bassett' the Guard suspended for One Week from Oct 31st to Nov 6th & to lose One Weeks pay and Rations (for his bad conduct). 2 P.C. on duty. 57

November 3 Tuesday: The Sessions Commenced this day. Mr Ashton with Perry at the Court House. 10 Prisoners sent up. Mr. Nixon call'd Respecting Gibsons character. 2 P.C.s doing night duty in the room of D Downing - ill and J Bassett suspended. 58

Ashton starts writing the journal again:

November 4 Wednesday: At the Sessions all day. 57

November 5 Thursday: At the Sessions all day - Dr Nash Came to the Gaol. 55

November 6 Friday: Bryce Thompson Was this day Acquitted of the felony and was brot back to the Gaol for debt. At the Sessions all day. 52

November 7 Saturday: At the Sessions all day William Best got Drunk and Could not take his trial this day he was Sent to the Police Station for the Night. 49

November 8 Sunday: Bassett Returned to duty this day he having been Suspended for One Week. The Rev'd Mr. Howard performed Divine Service. Dr. Nash Came to the Gaol. 48

November 9 Monday: At the Sessions all day Wilson & Green tried this day and found Guilty of Horse Stealing and Sentenced to Transportation for life. 47

November 10 Tuesday: Dr Nash Visited the Gaol No Sessions this day. 50

November 11 Wednesday: At the Sessions all day Staggs trial for Murder Commenced. Dr. Nash Call'd at the Gaol. The Court Sat later this day. 50

November 12 Thursday: Staggs trial Still on this day Halloran and Gibsons Sentences Mitigated to 7 years in this Colony with Hard Labour. 50

November 13 Friday: Stagg was this day found Guilty of the Murder of John Gofton was Sentenced to be Executed on Monday Next the 16th Inst - Cragon One of the Guards was Absent from duty all Night. William Best was Acquitted of felony and brought to Gaol for debt - The Sessions ended this day. 57

November 14 Saturday: The Sheriff Visited they Debtors to hear a Complaint against Mr Dawbiney the Gaoler - Cragon was Sent from the Police Barracks Drunk he having been Sent as Guard over Stagg. 50

November 15 Sunday: Went in the Bush this Morning at 5 A.M. with Capt'n Litchfield about Stagg - Returned about 12 Noon - At 9 P.M. Several Prisoners under Sentence of Transportation Cut their Irons off with a View of Making Their Escape from the Gaol Sent for Mr. Frome who Came with Six of the Mounted Police I Stay'd at the Gaol all Night. 50

November 16 Monday: At 6 A.M. had foot Irons put on the prisoners - at 4½ P.M. left the Gaol with the following Prisoners for Sydney & took them to the New Port and put them on board the Ship Dorset at 6½ P.M. and left them in Charge of the Police Constables Names of the Prisoners - John Wilson - Edward Green - Peter Smith - William D. Seawood - Joseph Hawkshaw - Thomas Flannery - William McSawley - Philip Le Boulangere - Edward Little - And William Morgan Returned to Town at 10½ PM. 53

November 17 Tuesday: Searched the Stone Building found Several Files - Knives etc 43

Briefly, another writer, with an occasional entry by Ashton:

November 18 Wednesday: At 4 OC'k this Morn'g Mr. Ashton Removed Joseph Stagg from the Mounted Police Barracks to the new

Gaol (Building) where At 8 OC'k he was Executed The Rev'd Mr. Howard and the Rev'd Mr. Farrell Attended him The Horse & Foot Police - the Sherriff, Mr. Ashton etc was present The Body was Afterwards Buried in the Right Hand Ward in the far Corner. 43

November 19 Thursday: The Sherriff Visited the Gaol. Downing Returned to duty he having been Sick for Some time. 44

November 20 Friday: Dr. Nash Attended the Gaol Joseph Barnett a Debtor was this day discharged by Order of the Sheriff. 44

November 21 Saturday: 13 Debtors Received Rations by Order of His Excellency. 44

November 22 Sunday: Mr. Duthy a Debtor was discharged this day at 3P.M. 44

November 23 Monday: At 7A.M. Packman One of the Prison Working Party Made his Escape from the Guard down at the water. William Johnson was this day discharged by Order of His Excellency. 46

November 24 Tuesday: Dr. Nash Visited the Gaol. 44

November 25 Wednesday: Dr. Nash visited the Gaol. 43

November 26 Thursday: Dr. Nash Came to the Gaol - Smith & Edmonds was discharged. 43

November 27 Friday: Received No Vinegar or Soap from the Stores this day. 41

November 28 Saturday: Mr. Dawbiney went In the Country with Mr. Duthy for a day or 2. 42

November 29 Sunday: The Sheriff Came And we had divine Service in the Gaol at 3 P.M. 42

Ashton again – his next sentence uses 'they' which appears to be his own new plural form of the word 'the'.

November 30 Monday: Mr. Fisher Visited they Debtors this day. Mr. Dawbiney still in the Country John Kelly was this day discharged by Order of His Excellency. 42

December 1 Tuesday: Mr. Dawbiney the Gaoler Returned at 2 P.M. from the Country - Bassett the Guard Did Not Come on duty last Night had a P.C. on duty all night at the Gaol Bassett being Sick. Mr. Ashton Visited the New Gaol about the fence. 41.

December 2 Wednesday - Bassett Came on Duty this Night - Went to WalkerVille in the Evening. 41

December 3 Thursday - Dawbiney attended the Resident Magistrates Court about a Person Selling Spirits in the Tiers. 41

December 4 Friday: Downing Made Use of improper Language to Perry when told to Guard the out side fence of the Debtors Yard. 41

December 5 Saturday: Went to Mr. Garretts and he gave Me Goldfinch to Discharge - went to Mr. Hardy he was not at home nor the Sheriff either At 8P.M. Saw the Sheriff and he told me to Discharge Goldfinch which I did. 42

December 6 Sunday: The Rev Mr. Farrell Came at 3 P.M. we had divine Service. 41

December 7 Monday: At 9 P.M. Kelly and Bull 2 Debtors used Threatening and Abusive Language to Perry the TurnKey. I Spoke to them and they were very Violent etc - Bull Swearing he would Never Sleep in the Place again if Perry was not Discharged from the Gaol. 41

December 8 Tuesday: Went with the Sheriff to the New Gaol. The Sheriff Visited The Gaol this morning and Dr. Nash this afternoon. 42

December 9 Wednesday: Hall - Alias Packman who Made his Escape from the Road Guard on the 23rd Nov 1840 was this day retaken and brot back to the Gaol by P.C. More. At 5½ P.M. He had nothing on but the Shoes belonging to Government when brot to the Gaol - he was put in Irons. 43

December 10 Thursday: Sarah Ann Best was discharged She having been in a Month - Packman Still in Irons. 44

December 11 Friday - took Packman before the Resident Magistrate and he was Committed to take his trial for Escaping from the Guard and Also for Stealing the Government Clothes. 45

December 12 Saturday: Dr. Nash visited the Gaol. 46

December 13 Sunday - Went to the Port with Mr. Insp'r Sheard in the Police Cart Returned Home at 1 P.M. The Rev'd Mr. Howard Came & we had divine Service at 3½ P.M. 46

December 15 Tuesday: C...cliffe & C... was discharged by order of His Excellency - William Wells and William Abbott brot in for Debt by Jones and Perry and L... Attended the Resident Magistrates Court about an Assault Case. 49

December 16 Wednesday: ... in for Debt was Discharged by order of the Sheriff Mr. De Horne Paid me £1-10- as part of the Sheriffs Poundage etc which I gave to the Sheriff. 50

December 18 Friday: South the Road Guard Reported to me that the Other Guards left they Prisoners Several times to go and get drunk I Mentioned it to the Sheriff (Wright being at home with his wife Very Ill) the Sheriff Ordered them to attend his office in the Morning. - About 11½ P.M. during the heavy Rain and Very dark the Native Named 'Jemmy' Made his Escape from the Gaol he got out of the Wooden Building between the Irons Bars - leaving his Clothes behind And then over the fence with one Iron on his Right leg. 49

December 19 Saturday: went to the Sheriffs this Morning at 9 A.M. with the Road Guards they were Cautioned etc Samual Selby - and Thomas Bland, & Tristram Bath was Sworn in as Guards at the Gaol by the Hon'ble the Colonial Secretary - Selby Came on duty at 8 P.M. with Perry & Bland to Come on duty at 8 O Clock to Morrow Morning. 47

December 20 Sunday: Dawbiney the Gaoler was taken Very Ill at 4 OC'k this Morning Dr. Nash was Sent for & went down to Mr. Smarts with Mr Wilson about Kenneth Campbell - the Sheriff Came at 3 P.M. we had Divine Service. 47

December 21 Monday: Dawbiney Still Very Ill Dr. Nash Came to the Gaol - Palmer used Abusive Language to Dr. Nash. Campbell & A.N. Rollison Debtors were discharged by order of the Sheriff. 48

December 22 Tuesday: Dawbiney Still Very Ill Dr. Nash Call'd and Saw him. 46

December 23 Wednesday: Dawbiney Still Very Ill Dr. Nash Came to him this Morning and again in the Afternoon William York was ordered this day to find Bail to Keep the Peace & he was Allowed to Remain at the Police Station for a day or two - Received Orders to Remove the Debtors to the New Gaol to Morrow Morning. 47

December 24 Thursday: At 5 O C'k this Morning Took 12 Debtors to the New Gaol left them in Charge of Perry the TurnKey & Robertson the Guard. 46

December 25 Friday: Several of the Prisoners were Fighting in the Gaol this Afternoon - the Prisoners had a Pint of Porter and a Pound of Meat each etc 45

December 26 Saturday: Dawbiney Still Very Ill Dr. Nash Came & Saw him. 45

December 27 Sunday: We had No Service in the Gaol this day. 45

December 28 Monday: They Prison Working Party did not go out to work in Consequence of the heavy Rain Dawbiney Still Ill. 45

December 29 Tuesday: They Prison Working party did not go to Work this Morning in Consequence of the Rain They went to work in the Afternoon - Dawbiney Still Ill. 46

December 30 Wednesday: Several of the Working Party did not go out to work before Breakfast this Morning - Dawbiney Still Ill - At 11 A.M. Took William Wells a Debtor before his Honor the Judge - Wells was Afterwards Discharged by Order of the Sheriff. 45

December 31 Thursday: Dawbiney Still Sick. 16 Sailors was brot to the Gaol for Refusing to do their duty on board Ship - At the New Port. 60

In November the debtors had written a group letter via the editor of the *South Australian Register* to the governor of the colony, asking to be released. They asked for bail for debtors, as had recently been legislated in Britain, so they could return to their families. Because they had come alone to South Australia their wives now had no extended family support to help them through.[220] The debtors were not released as they had wished, however the day before Christmas 12 debtors were moved from 'their former miserable lodgings' to the much better conditions at the new gaol, where as time went by they were allowed their own furniture, lamps and books.[221] They were able to pay extra for a private room.[222] There was in fact considerable community sympathy for debtors, who were often previously wealthy men. An early twentieth-century historian wrote:

> In 1841 there was a debtor's department ... well filled owing to the commercial calamities occasioned by the dishonouring of Col. Gawler's bills. Not withstanding the inability of these inmates of the Gaol to pay their creditors, they could always find money for newspapers and other luxuries. The newsrunner for The Independent always found many customers at the Gaol. He records his surprise at seeing the debtors living as though in fairly comfortable circumstances. One in particular – a bogus bank manager – had a well-furnished room, with reading desk and other conveniences.[223]

The new gaol would soon become known to everyone in town as Ashton's Hotel. Governor Gawler took pity on the debtors allowing them to draw rations rather than rely on their families to provide for them. A letter to one of the newspapers objected to this, citing not only the cost of rations but also 'the expense of jailors, and the cost of the splendid mansion in which they are now lodged'. This writer urged creditors to accept that the law would soon change; notice the misery they were causing the debtors; take note of the cost to everyone via the public purse; and release the debtors imprisoned at their suits.[224]

The governor's journal 1841

The first quarter of 1841 saw a last rush of escapes from the temporary gaol and the eventual move of almost all the prisoners to the new gaol.

> Removed altogether from the Old Gaol to the New Gaol except Mrs Dawbiney who stayed at the Old Gaol with Mary Rhodes.[225]

The sheriff was busy organising beds and stretchers and dismantling useful building materials from the old gaol.[226]

January 1 Friday: Dawbiney Still Sick - Edwards the Debtor Discharged. 60

January 2 Saturday: Abraham Adams brot in for Debt left at the New Gaol - Dawbiney Still Sick - A Woman Named Marg't Morris was brought to the Gaol for being Drunk & Exposing her Person in the Streets - brought in at 11½ A.M. & Made her Escape from the Womans Yard at 1½ P.M. I had but one Guard on duty with Kennedy at the time. 61

January 3 Sunday: No Service in the Gaol this day the Woman who Made her Escape Yesterday was Retaken about 12 Noon this day by the Police and the Police detained her at the Police Station for Me. - Dawbiney the Gaoler went into the Country for a few days in Consequence of being in Ill health. 61

January 4 Monday: The 6 Sailors belonging to the Helen Thompson was discharged by Order of the Resident Magistrate the Capt'n Paying £1- each in Room of £4 each as they was first fined. - Tully in for Debt was discharged this Day by order of the Sheriff. 63

January 5 Tuesday: Dawbiney in the Country the Rev'd Mr. Howard Call'd to see Mr. Bull. 53

January 6 Wednesday: Alex'r Rollason in for Debt was discharged by Order of the Sheriff - Took Shanks the Debtor was taken to the Resident Magistrates Court Relative to a Suit of ... - Dawbiney in the Country - Dr. Nash Call'd at the Gaol. 53

January 7 Thursday: Dr. Nash Came to the Gaol - Dawbiney Still in the Country. 53

January 9 Saturday: Went at 5 A.M. to the Reed Beds to See Dawbiney, brought him home with Me. - The Prisoner Conway Committed for Trial was let out of the Yard by Mistake (by the Guard Bassett) with the Native Party - he Ran away from the Guard At the Water he was Retaken by the Horse Police Near the Companys Station and brought back to Gaol etc he was put in Irons. - I have Had a P.C. on duty at the Gaol Since the 1st January 1841 - in Consequence of having So Many Prisoners in the Gaol and 4 of Them at the New Gaol with the Debtors. 54

January 10 Sunday: One of the Road Guard Came on Duty at the Gaol this Day. Dr. Nash came to the Gaol Mr. Howard Came at 3½ P.M. and we had divine Service. 54

No entries were made 11–29 January 1841. It is easy to tell that they were not made rather than removed as the original journal is a bound book.

January 30 Saturday: The Prisoner Johnson Committed for felony was put on the Bar & Confined in the Building lately the Debtors Place for delivering to the Women Prisoners a disgraceful Print & Note. 45

January 31 Sunday: Johnson as above - and Kept on bread and water - at 7 this Evening Johnson Begged Pardon and promised Not to do the like again. I ordered the Bar to be taken off and he was put with they Other Prisoners. 45

February 2 Tuesday: Removed they Debtors into the Other Yard at the New Gaol. John Stuckey was brot to the Gaol by Jones the Sheriffs Officer for Debt. 49

February 4 Thursday - Owen Jones was brot to Gaol for Debt. 50

February 5 Friday: Scott who Made his Escape a Short Time ago was retaken by Mr. Insp'r Tolmer at the Bay & lodged him in the Station House. George Martin was brot to the Gaol for Debt. 55

February 6 Saturday: Abraham Adams and William Abbott Debtors were Dis'd Mr. R. Sayers was brot to the Gaol for Debt. 57

February 7 Sunday: Mr. Fleming Came to the Gaol and we had divine Service at 3 P.M. 54

February 10 Wednesday: did not go to the New Gaol this day Sent the Gaoler. 56

February 11 Thursday: Dr. Nash Came to the Gaol and Said the Prisoner Campbell was to go Out to work. The Sheriff Visited the Gaol & at 5½ P.M. Campbell went Out to Work after dinner. 56

February 12 Friday: John Wilson was Comm'd for Shooting at a Police Constable last Night - etc - And George Dare was Committed on Suspicion of having Set fire to George Whites House - both Prisoners was Sent to the New Gaol and Confined there. 58

February 13 Saturday: At 7½ P.M. Joseph Storey a Prisoner under a Fine for an Assault etc Made his Escape whilst the Gaoler and Turnkey was Locking they other Prisoners up for the Night - Supposed to have got over the fence near the Office - Reported to the Police. 59

February 14 Sunday - The Sheriff Came to the Gaol and we had divine Service at 3 P.M. 58

February 16 Tuesday - Eleanora Rau was discharged by Order of His Excellency and Charlotte Hay was discharged by Order of the Resident Magistrate Marra was taken on Wrights Party but I had him to do duty at New Gaol for a few days in Consequence of having Several Prisoners there Committed for Trial. 62

February 17 Wednesday - Stuckey Debtor was Discharged - and John Rogers was brot to the Gaol for Debt by Jones Sheriffs Officer. 61

February 19 Friday: Bland the Guard was Sent to the New Gaol with Mulholland (a Prisoner) and let the Prisoner get Drunk and brought Spirits into the Gaol for other Prisoners there. Consequence was that the Prisoners got fighting and Created a Great disturbance that I was obliged to Send for 2 of the Mounted Police and take Vaughan & Mulholland down to the New Gaol and left them there. 58

February 20 Saturday: Bland the Guard was this day discharged for letting the Prisoner Mulholland get Drunk yesterday. 58

February 21 Sunday: - Marra Came on duty this day in the Place of Bland discharged Yesterday. Wright Lent Me a New Man of his for a few days. Mr. Fleming Came we had divine Service. 57

February 23 Tuesday: The Sheriff Came and brot the discharge for Hornabrook Pardoned by His Excellency at 6 P.M. 57

February 25 Thursday - 2 Prisoners Named George Worthington and David Wright Made their Escape from the Yard at 6 A.M. whilst Bassett was letting the P.W.Party out of the lower Gate to go for water. A Very Great Neglect was on the part of Bassett for letting Both be asleep at the time. 2 Debtors was brot to the Gaol by Jones Named George White & Mrs Springbott. At 3 P.M. I in Company of 4 of the Mounted Police & 4 of the Foot Police took 16 Prisoners that Stand Committed for Trial & one Native Boy down to the new Gaol and left them in the Charge of Perry the Turnkey. 60

February 27 Saturday: Mr. Bull in for Debt was discharged by order of the Sheriff. John Basset was discharged as Gaol Guard for Neglect of Duty in Allowing 2 Prisoners to Escape on the 25th And for Not Obeying Orders given to him - at the New Gaol with the Sheriff. 59

February 28 Sunday - No divine Service. 57

March 1 Monday – Saw His Excellency gave Mr Hall, 56 of the Printed lists Prisoners for Trial and went to the Judge and left him the lists. 57

March 2 Tuesday: the Sessions Continued at the Court all day Only the Grand Jury Sat. 54

March 3 Wednesday: at the Sessions all Day. Mr. Mc was dis'd by Order of the Court. 54

March 4 Thursday: John Rogers in for Debt was discharged. At the Sessions all day. 48

March 5 Friday: At the Sessions all day. 45

March 6 Saturday: At the Sessions All day John Wilson was Tried and Convicted for Shooting at P.C. Kunrilt Death was Recorded against him he Ironed in the New Gaol. 45

March 8 Monday: At the Sessions all Day. 46

March 9 Tuesday: the Sessions ended this day George Dare was tried this Day the trial lasted from 9 A.M. to 6 P.M. he was Acquitted. 42

March 12 Friday: Removed altogether from the Old Gaol to the New Gaol except Mrs Dawbiney who stayed at the Old Gaol with Mary Rhodes. 44

Mary Rhodes was a 'respectable looking woman' who had stolen a dress and a handkerchief.[227] Just as William's wife Charlotte assisted at the gaol, so too, apparently, did Mrs Daubiney, the gaoler's wife. The sheriff wrote to Gawler's private secretary officially winding up the old gaol:

> I beg to report to His Excellency ... that I have now removed all the Prisoners to the New Gaol there are now 44 confined there. Mr Ashton has the keys to the Old Gaol ready to deliver to any person appointed to take charge.[228]

Ashton had finally vacated the old gaol and it was soon abandoned and totally empty:

[T]here is now nothing to remind us of the means to which Governor Ashton resorted to charm his subjects into obedience. . . . that Indian juggler [Ashton] was never more successful in alluring . . . snakes from their hiding places, and teaching them to sit on their tails, and dance to his music . . . impressing on them that 'I am monarch of all I survey/My right – there is none to dispute' – until restored to liberty by the tardy process of the law – sent to the penal colonies . . . or conveyed to the neighbouring barracks, where they mounted the scaffold.[229]

Before Ashton joined the prisoners and staff at the new gaol however he was to be away.

March 13 Saturday: Received leave to go to Sydney with they 4 Prisoners Under Sentence of Transportation Mr. Bohr to Act for me while away. 45

The writer of the journal changes of course, Bohr standing in for William until he returns from Sydney on 12 May 1841. Bohr's entries are quite different – minimal – which is unfortunate as this period marks the beginnings of the new gaol. During this time, however, we first hear of Bella, brought in for being drunk and disorderly. Bohr at first records her simply as 'Bella', in keeping with the fact that she was well known, then later as 'Bella Anderson'. We are to become extremely familiar with Bella (Isabella) Anderson in the remainder of the journal, as her mental health deteriorates into insanity and Ashton demonstrates extraordinary compassion toward her.

March 14 Sunday: John Bohr took up charge of the Gaol from Mr. Ashton untill his Return from Sydney. 44

March 15 Monday: the prisoner Thompson was Discharged by Mr Dobney his time being up The four Convicts were leg bolted Namely John Wilson, William Jonston, Charles Drury and Alex'r Gordon. 44

March 16 At 10 A.M. P.C. More took William Vaughan from this to the Magistrates Court for Examination

At 2 P.M. Doctor Nash attended the Gaol

At ½ past 2 P.M. P.C. More brought William Vaughan here he being Committed to Stand his trial at the next Sessions. 43

March 17 Wednesday: Doctor Nash visited the Gaol

At 3 P.M. Mr. Ashton accompanied by In'r Shaw and four of the Mounted Police took the following Convicts from the Gaol to the Port for the purpose of putting them on board the Brig Bart bound for Sydney John Wilson, Alex'r Gordon, William Jonston and Charles Drury, Returned to the Convicts four Rugs and four Blankets According to the Requisition of Mr. Ashton, a crate of Irons, on Wilson 9½ lbs Johnston 4 lb Drury 6 lb Gordon 5 lb. Lyman off Duty leave being granted by Mr. Ashton. 43

March 18 Thursday: James Lyman Gaol Guard unable to do his duty on account of him and Geo Robinson Quarrelling and Fighting Yesterday Ordered by the Sheriff to be fined each a Week's Pay. Doctor Nash attended the Gaol at 1 P.M. At ½ past 3 P.M. Mr. McBeth was brought here by Thos Jones Sheriff's Officer under a Debt of £200 and £6-6-0 Costs.

At 4 P.M. John Cooper was brought here under a Charge of Assaulting two P.C one Months Instant. A Fine of £5 £1-5-6 Costs. 41

March 19 Friday: Doctor Nash attended the Gaol at 3 P.M. A Native Woman Named Warriaetti was Committed for 14 days Hard Labour John Mills was discharged at 3P.M. 42

Saturday March 20th 1841

At ½ past 11 AM William Collings was brought here by one of the Horse Police Remanded Untill Tuesday. At ½ past 12 pm William A Native was brought here by P. Constable More Remanded untill Monday. William Braly taken up to Magistrates in Place of P.C. More has not returned. 43

Sunday March 21st 1841

At ½ past 3 pm. Mr. Howard performed Divine Service Leamin o[ff] Duty. 42

Monday 22nd

At 10 AM P.C. More Brought William A Native from this to the Magistrates Court he being Discharged
At 10 AM P.C More Brought McLean from this to the Magistrates Court he being Committed for Trial
At 2 pm Andrew Baker was brought here by P.C. Norris he being remanded untill Tuesday next
Leamin off Duty being Sick, Prisoner Gordon Sick.   43

Tuesday 23rd

At 10 AM Collins and Baker was brought up to the Magistrates Court for Trial by P.C. More
At 1 pm William Collins was remanded until Friday next brought here by P.C. More.
At ½ past 1 PM Taimy A Native was discharged having Served his time - Returned his Prison Clothes
At 2 pm Doctor Nash Visited the Gaol. Leamin Sick the Prisoner Gordon Sick.   43

Wednesday 24th

At 12 am Doctor Nash's Assistant Atten'd the Gaol
Leamin Sick, Gordon Sick, nothing more particular.   41

Thursday 25th 1841

At 11 A.M. John Bohr took up Mr. Arthur to the Magistrates Court to bear Witness to a Note Returned at 2 pm
T.H. Packman was Sent from the Prison Working Party by order of Mr. . . . Superintendent Refusing to Work
At 1 pm Doctor Nash attended the Gaol, Gordon Sick.   40

Friday 26th

At 12 a.m. Doctor Nash Visited the Gaol to find that T.H. Packman is in good health At 1pm T.H. Packman Sent to the Solitary Cell for Refusing to Work
The Prisoner Collins was brought up to the Magistrates Court for trial by P.C. Norris.
The Prisoner Henry . . . Discharged having Served his time.
At 3 pm The Prisoner Collins was brought here by P.C. More Remanded. At 5 pm Mr. Moorhouse Attended Warriatti the Native Woman.   40

Saturday 27th

At 11 AM Hart and Hawkins was Discharged by Order of the Sheriff At 2PM Doctor Nash attended the Gaol M . . . and Gordon Sick. 39

Sunday 28th

At 2PM Doctor Nash attended the Gaol. M. . . and Gordon Sick. 37

Monday 29th

At 10 AM Flynn and Campbell was discharged by order of the Sheriff. At 11AM The Prisoner Collins was brought up to the Magistrates Court by P.C. Sanders of the Mounted force on a Further Examination At 3 PM Collins was brought back from the Magistrates Court by one of the Mounted Police. At 11 PM Mr. James Arthur was Discharged from Gaol by order of the Sheriff. 37

Tuesday March 30th 1841

At 12 AM Mary Davey was brought here by P.C. Chanter Remanded untill March 31, at ½ past 3 PM. Peter Sidd and Hugh Lynch was brought here by one of the Mounted Police Remanded untill April 1st Doctor Nash attended. Collins and Gordon Sick T.H. Packman liberated from Solitary confinement. 37

Wednesday March 31st

A 11 AM Mary Davey was brought to the Magistrates by P.C. Chanter for Examination, at ½ past 1 PM. Doctor Nash attended, Gordon, M. . ., Quigley and Collins Sick. At 6pm Mrs Story was brought here by P.C. Chanter Charged with Stealing A Bonnet one Months Hard Labour. 38

Thursday April 1st 1841

At 8 AM Warriatto A Native Woman Was Discharged from Gaol having her time Served At 11 AM Hugh Lynch and Peter Sidd was brought up to the Magistrates Court by P.C. Herbert. At 4PM Story and Thos. Fogarty was brought here by three of the Mounted Police Remanded untill Friday Next Doctor Nash attended the Gaol Quigley and Gordon Sick. Story was removed. 37

Friday April 2nd

At 11 AM The Prisoners Hugh Lynch Thos. Fogarty and Joseph Story was brought up to the Magistrates Court by four of the Mounted Police. The Prisoners Joseph Story and Thos. Fogarty has been Remanded untill the 9th of April. At 4 pm ? Mamagelle was brought here by the P.C. More Sentenced Two Months hard Labour. At 5 PM William Best was discharged from Gaol by order of the Sheriff, Doctor Nash Attended Quigley and Gordon Sick At 11 PM Mr Finson was brought here by Capt. Litchfield he being to Suit Mr. Edw'd Stephens. 39

Saturday April 3rd 1841

At 2 P.M. David Kerr was Discharged from Gaol by order of the Sheriff. At 4 P.M. Thos. Putland was brought here by P.C. Wright Remanded until Monday At 4 P.M. Henry Manly James Meecham James Boyce Alex'r Gilmore and Bella are Sentenced to a Weeks hard Labour for being Drunk and Disorderly. - At 4. PM Doctor Nash Attended. 44

Sunday: April 4th

At 3 PM Mr. Fleming performed divine Service. 43

Monday April 5th

At 11 AM Fogarty Story and Collins was brought up the Magistrates Court for Examination by the Mounted Police. At 3 PM the Prisoners Story and Collins was brought here by two of the Mounted Police. Remanded untill Tuesday Next At 3 pm Mr. Charles Hopkins was brought here by Thos. Jones at the Suit of Henry Medcalf Debt £50 and Cost At 3 PM Mr William Frank was brought here by Mr Thos. Jones at the Suit of Mr. Thos. Gepp debt £94-12-11 and £1-0-0 for the writ besides Sheriffs Poundage Doctor Nash attended. 44

Tuesday April 6th.

At 11 AM The Prisoners Collins and Story was brought up to the Magistrates Court by two of the Mounted Police for an Examination. At 3 pm The Prisoners Story Collins Maitland and Jenkins were brought here by three of the Mounted Police Remanded untill Wednesday Next Doctor Nash attended the

Gaol's Sick Gordon Vaughan Collins Maitland and Story. At 4 PM Margaret Morris was brought here by one of the Police Sentenced to one Weeks Hard Labour. 47

Wednesday April 7th
At 11 AM The Prisoners Story Collins Maitland and Jenkins were brought up to the Magistrates Court by four of the Mounted Police. At ¼ past 4 pm the Prisoners Story Collins Maitland Jenkins was brought here by the Mounted Police remanded until Saturday next
Tristan Bath Gaol Guard Sick
Prisoners Sick Jordan Drawbridge and Collins. 47

Thursday: April 8th
At 2 PM Doctor Nash Attended the Gaol, Sick Jordan Drawbridge and Collins. 47

Friday April 9th
The Road party Not at Work being Good Friday. 42

Saturday April 10th
At 9 AM The Prisoners Manly Meehan Boyce Gilmour and Bella was dischargeḍ their time being expired. At 1 PM Mamgela was put into Solitary Confinement by Will'm Daubiney Gaoler he refusing to work. At 2 pm The Prisoners Story Maitland Collins Jenkins, Worthington Lynch and Putland are remanded untill Monday Week. 47
At ½ past 2 pm the Prisoner Patrick McGrath was Committed for Six Weeks hard labour or a Fine of £4-0-6. At 8 pm Robert Fisher was brought here by Thomas Jones Sheriff's Officer for Debt of £29-4-10. 50

[In margin]
At 11 AM The Prisoners Story Collins Maitland & Putland, Jenkins & Lynch, were brought up to the Magistrate's Court for an Examination by the Mounted Police.

Sunday April 11th
At 8 AM Mamgalle was Released from Solitary Confinement by Will'm Daubiney Gaoler. 45

Monday April 12th

The Road Party did not Work on this Day it being observed as a Holiday, by order of the Governor in Honour of the Birth of a Princess Royal of Great Britain. At 12 AM Doctor Nash attended. 45

Tuesday April 13 1841

At 8 AM Marg Morris was Discharged from Gaol She having her time Served. 45

Wednesday: 14th

At 8 PM Mr. Will'm Finks was Discharged from Gaol by order of the Sheriff. 44

Thursday 15th

At 11 AM. Mr Rob't Lyon Milne was brought here by Thos. Jones Sheriffs Officer at the Suit of Mr Geo. Smith £3,610-15-5 and Sheriffs Poundage and Officers fees
At 11 AM James Allen was brought here by one of the Mounted Police Remanded until Monday Next
At 11 AM Mr F... left the Gaol accompanied by Mr. Dalton on Condition to Return this Evening by order of the Sheriff. At 8 PM John Henry Theakston was brought here by Thos. Jones Sheriffs officer at the Suit of Johan Solomon & Emanuel Solomon for Debt of £20-15-0 Together with Sheriffs poundage. 46

Friday 16th

At 12 AM Bella Anderson was brought here by one of the Police She being Committed for One Month unless She Shall Sooner Pay Three Separate fines of Five Shillings each together with the Costs of Conviction Amounting to 10 Shillings At 6 P.M. Mr. Crisp was brought here by Thos. Jones Sheriffs Officer for Debt at the Suit of the Bank of Australia £194-10-0 and £1-1-0 for the Writ beside Sheriffs Poundage. 48

Saturday 17th

At 1 AM Midnight Mr. Crisp Discharged by order of the Sheriff. 48

Sunday April 18th 1841

At 8 AM Cooper was Discharged his time being Up At 11 AM Packman was put in to Solitary Confinement by Will'm

Dawbiney Gaoler for destroying his Shirts At ½ past 3 PM Mr. Howard performed Divine Service. 47

Monday April 19th

At 11 AM Joseph Story Collins Jenkins Maitland Worthington, Lynch Putland and Allen was brought up to the Magistrates Court For Examination

At 3 pm the Above Prisoners Were brought back And Remanded Untill Next Monday

At 3 pm Will'm York and Elisha Cooper was brought here by PC. More. York Remanded until Tuesday Next. Elisha Cooper A Fine of £2-0-0 together With Costs of £1-5-6 or one Month at Hard Labour the Prisoner Packman was liberated from S'y Confinement by Will'm Dawbiney Gaoler At 5 pm Mrs Emma Garratt was brought here by Thos. Jones Sheriffs Officer by Virtue of a Writ to find Bail £1100

At 9 AM Will'm Wright was brought here by Thos. Jones Sheriffs Officer for Debt at the Suit of Will'm Williams for the Sum of £142-15-0 49

Tuesday 20th

At 7 AM George Davis was brought here by one of the Police Sentenced Fourteen days Hard Labour

At 11 AM Sam'l Allen was brought up to the Magistrates Court by one of the Mounted Police. 51

Wednesday April 21st

At 4 pm John Baker was brought here by P.C. Kerby Sentenced One Month hard labour and A Fine of £6-5-6. 51

Thursday April 22nd 1841

At 11 AM Will'm York was brought up to the Magistrates Court for trial by P.C. More

At 3 PM Mr J.H. Thickstones was discharged from Gaol by order of the Sheriff. Doctor Nash Attended the Gaol this day. Selby Gaol Guard taken Sick. Sent Word ¼ before 8 PM. 51

Friday April 23rd

At 1 PM Mrs Garrett was brought up to the Magistrates Court by Thos. Jones Sheriffs Officer by order of the Sheriff, was brought back at ½ past 3 pm by Thos. Jones Sheriffs Officer. 49

Saturday April 24th

At 2 pm the Prisoner Charles Morris was brought here by One of the Police he being Committed for Felony by the Resident Magistrate. 50

Sunday April 25

Nothing particular during the day. 50

Monday April 26th

At 11 AM the Prisoners Story Lynch, Putland, Maitland - Worthington, Jenkins and Collins were brought up the Magistrates Court by the Mounted Police, they being remanded untill this day. At 12 AM A Native by the Name of William was brought here by P.C. More Remanded untill May 10th. At 3 pm James Edwin Palmer and Joseph Glass was brought here by the Mounted Police, remanded until the 29th. At 3 am Jenkins King, Worthington and Worthington Remanded until the 29th. Joseph Story Will'm Collings Will'm Maitland Hugh Lynch and John Putland, Remanded until the 10th May

At 8 PM George White was brought here by Thos. Jones Sheriffs Officer for Debt at the Suit of John ... and Giles Abbott £79-9-4 & £1-1-0 for Costs besides Sheriffs Poundage. 54

Tuesday April 27th 1841

At 4 AM No. 1 Cell was broken open by the Prisoners Namely Story, Worthington, Putland, Lynch, Maitland and Jenkins. At 4 AM Story and Worthington were put in Irons, and in Solitary, At 7 AM Putland, Lynch, Maitland and Jenkins were Put in Irons. At 11 Emma Garratt was brought up to the Magistrates Court by Thos. Jones Sheriffs Officer by the Sheriffs authority. At 12 AM the Irons were taken off Lynch, Jenkins and Maitland by order of the Sheriff. At ½ past 3 PM Francis King was brought down by P.C. Norris - untill he Shall find Bail - At 4 P.M. Mr Charles Hopkins was Discharged by order of the Sheriff Doctor Nash attended. 55

This incident of the cell being 'broken open' appears to have been quite understated by Bohr. It was the first attempt by prisoners to escape from the new gaol, and as such, held great public interest. The *Chronicle* described it more dramatically:

On Tuesday morning, the 27th ult, between three and four o'clock, a most daring attempt was made by Storey and five other felons to effect their escape, by removing the brick and stone immediately below their guard bedstead, thus clearing a sufficient space to admit of their passing from the wards to the inner walls, when no other opposition but that of a guard was in their way. The design was fortunately frustrated in time by the vigilance of Mr Kennedy, turnkey, who instantly gave alarm to Mr Daubiney, the gaoler, who, with the assistance of the guards, immediately secured the ruffians, and put them in irons, not without some blood being spilt. Too much praise cannot be bestowed upon the guards for having prevented, by their intrepidity and courage, the escape of such ruffians.[230]

This newspaper's description of 'inner walls' where 'no other opposition but that of a guard was in their way' clearly refers to the 'space between the walls'. A wooden fence that joined the loose ends of the outer stone wall, had been finished just weeks earlier, however it required a constant guard.[231] A letter written by the sheriff at a later time mentions this 'cross fence'. The letter is to Captain Sturt and was in relation to a builder's quote for another much longer fence, proposed to mark the perimeter of the gaol.[232] This refers to the original perimeter, before the building size was halved. The almost mirror-image space next to the half-gaol was still within the gaol's allocated land. The sheriff writes:

> There is no necessity at present for fencing in the outside limits of the Gaol. It would however add somewhat to its security as the means of preventing the Public coming up to the wooden cross fence to communicate with the Guards.

The existence of a wooden cross-fence suggests that it was always the intention, at a future time, to complete the original whole-plan for the gaol, to make the quarter-octagon a half-octagon again. This did eventually happen, but not yet.

Bohr continued:

Wednesday April 28th

Nothing particular during the day. 54

Thursday April 29th

At 11 AM the Prisoners Worthington, Jenkins Glass and Palmer were brought up to Magistrates Court by four of the Mounted Police for Examination. At 11 AM Mrs Emma Garratt was brought up to the Magistrates Court by T. Jones Sheriffs Officer

At 2 PM the Prisoners Worthington and Jenkins were Committed Glass and Palmer Remanded

At 8 PM Gilbert McNicols was brought here by Thos. Jones Sheriffs Officer, at the Suit of Alexander Frazer for £56-0-0. 56

Friday April 30

At 11 AM Mrs Garrett was brought to the Magistrates Court by the Acting Governor of the Gaol Sentenced

At 3 PM. Mr. Story was discharged from Gaol his time being up. At 4 PM John Keating was brought here by one of the Police Sentenced one Month. 57

Saturday May 1st 1841

At 3 PM Mrs Emma Garratt gave bail to appear before the Resident Magistrate – Charged with a Conspiracy with Intent to Defraud.

At 4 PM Mrs Emma Garratt gave Bail to the Sheriff for £1100 Discharged by authority. 56

Sunday May 2nd

At ½ past 3 PM Mr Howard performed Divine Service in the Gaol. 55

Monday 3rd

At 10 AM George Davies was discharged from Gaol his time being Up The Prisoners Joseph Glass and Edwin Palmer was brought up to the Magistrates Court by two of the Mounted Police. Joseph Glass Committed for trial Edwin Palmer Discharged from the Magistrates Court. 55

Tuesday May 4th.

At 8PM James Arthur was brought here by Thos. Jones Sheriffs Officer at the Suit of Sam'l Crabb for the Sum of 115-12-0. 54

Thursday May 5th

Nothing particular occurred during the day. 54

Friday May 7th

At ½ past 12 PM King was brought up to the Magistrates Court by P.C. Norris to give Bail to Stand his trial at the Next Sessions. At 11 PM Frederick Maitland, Scott was brought here by Thos. Jones Sheriffs Officer at the Suit of Charles Gooch for £41-15 Levy £52-13-6 and £1-1-0 for the Suit besides Sheriffs Poundage. 55

Saturday May 8th 1841

Nothing particular Occurred during the day. 54

Monday: May 10th

At 11 AM the Prisoners Collins, Maitland, Lynch, Putland, Story, Jack: A Native and Williamy A Native ... brought up to the Magistrates Court for Examination, by the Mounted Police
At 12 AM The Prisoner Williamy is Remanded Untill the 24th of May. Jack is Discharged.
At 1 PM John H... was brought here by Thos. Jones Sheriffs Officer for Debt at the Suit of Edw'd Stephens for 46-3-Shillings and £1-0-0 for the Suit besides Sheriffs poundage At 3 PM Story, Collins, Maitland and Putland were brought here by the Mounted Police Remanded until the 17th of May. Hugh Lynch Committed to Stand his trial at the Next Sessions. At 3 PM Mulholland and Mary Rhodes was Discharged by order of the Sheriff. 55

Tuesday May 11th

At ½ past 11 AM Mr Will'm Finks was brought here by Thos. Jones Sheriffs Officer, at the Suit of Mr. Stephens for £68-13-0 and £1-0-0 for Suit besides Sheriffs Poundage. At 3 PM James Reading was brought by one of the Port Police Const's for one Month to hard labour by Capt. Lipson. 54

Wednesday May 12

Nothing particular during the day. 55

Thursday May 13

Nothing particular during the day. 55

[In margin]
Mr Ashton Governor of the Gaol Returned from Sydney - May the 12th 1841

At last Ashton returned and resumed the journal. While he was away, there had been the first attempt at escape from the new gaol but also problems with water and with undesirables hanging about in the huts in the immediate vicinity.[233] Water was being carried by the Prisoner Working Party from stagnant pools in the river over rough ground, resulting in spills and damage to the casks. It was poor quality water, suited only for the cistern and for washing clothes. The sheriff had suggested an alternative source:

> On the site of the late Col. Lights house there is a Well which previously to the fires yielded most excellent water in abundance. Were this well now cleaned out, fenced around, and placed in charge of the Gaol Dept an ample supply would be obtained. There is a gradual descent to the Gaol from this well, which would facilitate carriage.[234]

This suggestion was not taken up – nonetheless the description provides another small piece of the picture of the new gaol set within what had been the colonial camp. In April 1841 the sheriff suggested that the 'discreditable huts' that had been put up by the government (probably Buffalo Row and Coromandel Row) be finally dismantled for firewood for use in the gaol.[235]

On Ashton's return from Sydney there was a new governor of the colony. Governor George Grey had arrived only a few days earlier on 10 May 1841. Grey's official proclamation announced that he was the new governor and that all appointed government officials and all inhabitants had now to take their directions from him.[236] As 'Captain' Grey he had visited Adelaide from the Swan colony (now Perth) and had seemed to support Governor Gawler's ideas for South Australia, however, on finding that England was refusing to pay the bills, he publicly denounced Gawler and what he viewed as his extravagances. One of these was the new gaol.

Governor Grey was to become a one-man razor gang, extremely unpopular. He stopped all activity on public works including the gaol and announced that none of the creditors still owed money by the government could be paid until money came through from England. He challenged the costings put forward by the builders of the gaol, sought to ruin their reputations, and precipitated a lengthy legal battle that brought the firm of Borrow and Goodier to its financial knees. With three major building projects, the new gaol, the new Government House and the new facilities at the port, and no money arriving from England to pay for it all, Grey was in trouble, and along with him all of the inhabitants of the colony.

Grey's cost-cutting was breathtaking in its scale. Over almost the whole of 1841 he scrutinised every single area of government expenditure, no matter how small, and slashed ruthlessly, cutting officials' wages – sometimes in half – and axing complete jobs, mostly those of the lowliest clerks. Where workers had received rations along with a wage, the ration component was stopped and the wage was reduced as well. Where two books to write in were ordered one would now suffice. Government Farm on the Sturt was sold.[237]

There was a long-running battle of words with Thos Gilbert, keeper of the government stores, whom Grey derided as having no ability even to add up. Reading the archives for this period is a real eye-opener. He replaced all workers at the colonial store with rationed poor emigrants and cut out the entire department dealing with scab in sheep. The magistrate's salary was cut from 600 to 400 pound per annum; the colonial chaplain's by 50 pound per annum. When Ashton moved to the new gaol, previous advantages to himself and the turnkeys such as rations of wood and coal were disallowed or wages reduced to cover the supply.[238]

In answer to the sheriff's request to buy two cottages near the gaol for guards, the reply was no. There was no money. Grey suggested that one guard could be sacked when the Insolvent Bill came through, and that the supervisor of the work party could have a room in the gaol so the other guard could also be sacked. The prisoner working party was then dispensed with and prison guards replaced with military guards. The jobs of the colonial architect, the government engineer and Finniss the deputy surveyor were dispensed with. Grey even directed the postmaster general to delay the mail rather than use another cart.[239]

May 14 Friday: I took Charge of the Gaol and Mr. Borr returned to his Police Duty. 53

May 15 Saturday: White & Spring...tt (Debtors) was discharged by order of the Sheriff. Mr S.B. Garratt was brot to Gaol for debt by Thomas Jones Sheriffs Officer. 56

May 16 Sunday: we had divine Service in the New Gaol – The Rev'd Mr. Howard Attended Visitors the Sheriff, Mr. S..., Mr. Drew - Mrs Howard & 2 Daughters Service at 3 P.M. 54

May 17 Monday: Mr. Garratt in for Debt was Discharged by order of the Sheriff - I took him to the Sheriff to Serve the Bail Bond etc at 7 P.M. 53

May 21 Friday: McNichols a debtor was discharged by order of the Sheriff. 51

May 22 Saturday: Owen Jones a debtor was discharged by order of the Sheriff - Scott & Gordon was Discharged by order of His Excellency. 54

May 23 Sunday: Mr. Fleming Visited the Gaol at 3 P.M. Divine Service. 57

May 26 Wednesday: The Sheriff Call'd. 48

May 29 Saturday: ...ers & Fisher 2 Debtors was discharged and Also Charlotte Hay. 47

May 30 Sunday - Mr. Fleming Came and we had Divine Service at 3 P.M. 43

May 31 Monday: Capt'n Walker was brot to the Gaol for Debt by Jones The Sheriffs Officer. 43

June 1 Tuesday: A Quarrel & fight took place between W Dawbiney the Gaoler and Mr Shanks the Debtor - in the Debtors Yard. At 9 P.M. Perry Sent for Me all was quiet on my arrival at the Gaol. 43

June 2 Wednesday: Inquired into the Above Circumstances and found that the Gaoler & the Debtor was Both to Blame The Sheriff did Not Wish Me to interfere any more in the Matter.   43

June 5 Saturday: 8 Sailors belonging to the Lady Emma Committed for One & Two Months each to Hard Labour.   51

June 6 Sunday: Mr. Fleming Came and we had divine Service at 3 P.M. Nearly all out of the felons yard Attended but only One Debtor Attended.   50

June 7 Monday: I took Mr. McPherson to the Magistrates Court he was Bailed to Keep the Peace etc his Bail was Mr. Stevenson & Capt'n Finnis.   50

June 10 Thursday: Mr. Freeman was brot in for Debt.   49

June 11 Friday: Mr. Freeman was Dis'd by order of the Sheriff.   48

June 13 Sunday: the Rev'd Mr. Howard Came to the Gaol divine Service at 3 P.M. White & Shanks debtors fighting & Creating a Disturbance At 2¾ P.M. Scott a debtor Wanted to Send for 2 Bottles of Brandy which was Refused & he was Very Abusive & Violent at 6 P.M. 49

June 14 Monday: Charles Catchlove was brought in for Debt at 6½ P.M. by Jones Sheriffs Officer.   49

June 15 Tuesday: Edward Catchlove was brought in for Debt by Jones Sheriffs Officer - F.M. Scott a Debtor was discharged by order of the Sheriff.   51

June 17 Thursday: A Man Named Thos. Murray on Suspicion of Murder was Remanded from Wednesday last for a Week Mr. Insp'r Stuart wished him to Remain at the Police Station Allowed.   52

June 19 Saturday - A Man Named Kirby who was brot in on a Warrant for Selling Spirits - without a Licence and fined £4-0-6 or 14 Days Imprisonment - Paid the Money this Afternoon & was discharged.   52

June 20 Sunday - Mr. Fleming Attended and we had divine Service at 3 P.M.   57

June 23 Wednesday: The Prisoner Murray on Suspicion of Murder was Remanded until Monday Next Still at Police Office. 49

June 25 Friday: At 4 O Clock this Afternoon Shanks a Debtor was Drunk Creating a disturbance and Using Very Abusive Language to Capt'n Walker and also to Me So Much So that I was obliged to have him Confined in his Sleeping Room. At the Same Time Mr. G...e Came to the Debtors Yard to See Capt'n Martin & Walker when Arthur a Debtor was Very Abusive to him and Mr. G Struck him We had Some trouble to prevent them fighting which we did by Mr. G. leaving the Gaol. 52

June 26 Saturday: Shanks was Confined in his Room 7½ this Morning when the Gaoler told the Turnkey to let him out without My Knowledge I have Stoped Shanks Rations for one Week. Mr. W.H. Newenham was down to the Gaol About they debtors. 53

June 27 Sunday: No person attended to perform divine Service. 53

June 28 Monday: At the Judges all the Morning about the Debtors – had 7 of the Act for Debtors Sent Me from Mess'rs Thomas's Printing Office. 53

June 29 Tuesday: W.A. Chatfield brot in by Jones for Debt. 57

June 30 Wednesday: Paid the fine of Mr. Williams into the Resident Magistrates Court. 51

On 11 June 1841, the Ashton family moved from their hut near the old gaol into the residence that was part of the fabric of the new gaol. William and Charlotte now had five children: William James, 10; Henry Hamilton, 8; Thomas Mills, 6; Victoria Hannah Ritchie, born on the *Rajasthan* and not yet 3; and Albert Gawler, still an infant. Ashton made no mention of this move in the journal. However a sheriff's letter provides the date:

> The Gov of the Gaol has now moved in [and] his old hut is empty for someone else to use.[240]

On 14 June 1841 Sheriff Newenham wrote again to the colonial secretary, concerned that the new act regulating the sale of liquor would have repercussions for the gaol. There had long been problems with visitors and guards illicitly supplying ordinary prisoners, but this new act would affect the debtors:

> [B]y XLI clause it is enacted that no keeper of a Gaol Shall suffer any wine or spirituous liquors to be brought into such a building under penalty of £5 . . .
>
> It is customary in all Prisons to allow a Debtor to use wine and spirituous liquors in moderation – and acting on this the Gov of the Gaol has been in the habit of allowing the Debtors to send for small supplies when they require such, he feels however that he is not justified in so doing in face of this act And the question arises now whether wine and spirituous liquors shall be wholly excluded from the Gaol, or whether there shall be a New Act authorizing their introduction in the case of Debtors, the present arrangement of the Gaol, where out of the 15 debtors confined, 12 are receiving Govt. Rations I am of opinion that [it] would be advisable to exclude all wine & spirits, for if the Debtors are without the means of supplying themselves with food, they cannot be supposed to be able to afford those unnecessary articles.
>
> One difficulty only would here arise which is that occasionally a respectable Prisoner not drawing rations may be in confinement who would require wine, and it might perhaps be thought an act of severity to not allow him a supply.[241]

On 22 June 1841 the Insolvent Debtors Act was finally passed. A letter from a group of debtors, asking that this happen, had been printed on 2 June. The opinion of the paper was that such a law would allow 'the poor imprisoned debtors, some of whom have been in gaol nearly 12 months, while their wives and families have been reduced almost to beggary, [to] have at least a prospect of release'.[242]

With the passing of the act, procedures for recovering debt were at last put in place and all debtors could now be bailed on sureties being provided to their creditors. No longer was the fate of a debtor up to the creditor. Now only those debtors who refused to pay, who failed to pay by a set time, or intended to defend their charge, would stay in gaol for any length of time. However, even though sympathy was now officially leaning in support of the debtors, not everyone agreed.

In September 1841 a sketch in the *Adelaide Independent*, accompanied by doggerel, described both sides of the story:

> DEBTOR   I'm very sorry Mr Gripe,
> So long a yarn to spin,
> But truly now there's no such thing
> As getting money in.
> You know I might be out of cash, Yet be an honest man,
> And be assur'd good Mr. Gripe,
> I'll pay you when I can.
>
> CREDITOR   Don't talk to me of Poverty,
> My even temper ruffling;
> Pay what you owe, you shabby rogue,
> And lay aside your shuffling.
> Now if you don't produce the Cash
> You'll very soon be knock'd up
> 'Hard up' indeed you vagabond
> Full soon I'll have you locked up.[243]

As a group, the debtors had publicly made a number of complaints and even Ashton had at one time thought they had gone too far. This was before he had gone to Sydney and new rules had required him to fix a notice in the new gaol, reducing visiting hours. The debtors, signing as 'Justitia' complained to the *South Australian Register*. Ashton replied:

> I am the last person desirous of figuring in print ... But as I have reason to believe that my conduct as Governor of Her Majesty's Gaol of Adelaide has always been such as to meet the approval of the authorities and merit the thanks of these gentlemen who have been unfortunate enough to be placed under my charge, I am unwilling

that any imputation of a wish to curtail the comforts and privileges of the debtors should remain uncontradicted. It has always been my desire to provide comfort, as far as lay in my power, even to my own inconvenience, of those gentlemen, and I have only acted under authority in limiting the time for visitors at the new gaol, though I am bound to say that I consider the indulgence most ample, and extending over many hours beyond the time allowed to the visiting of debtors in any other prison in the world. JUSTITIA may perhaps understand me when I say that it is possible to accommodate a person in ninety-nine cases but forbid him the one-hundreth [*sic*] (which, without doubt, would prove injurious to him) and make him your bitter, although little regarded enemy. *Verbum sat!*

I am, Gentlemen,

Your most obedient servant,

W. B. Ashton

Governor of the Gaol.[244]

Verbum sat is an abbreviation of *verbum sapienti sat est*, a concluding remark with the meaning 'a word to the wise is sufficient', or 'enough said'.

The next few days at the gaol see more of the debtors discharged. In fact most entries for the next few months concern the debtors.

July 2 Friday: Hillier (Debtor) was Discharged by Order of the Supreme Court - & Aldridge Dis'd he having Served his 4 Months. 57

July 3 Saturday - Capt'n Mr Wright (Debtor) was Discharged by Order of the Supreme Court. 49

July 4 Sunday: Mr. Fleming Came and we had divine Service at 3 P.M. 48

July 6 Tuesday: Edward & Charles Catchlove (Debtors) was discharged by Order of the Supreme Court. 49

July 7 Wednesday: George White (a Debtor) was discharged by order of the Supreme Court - Packman was Discharged. - Mr. Newman Came to the Gaol and gave me an Undertaking to Pay the fine for the 8 Sailors belonging to the Lady Emma & five of them whose time was Out on Monday last was Discharged. 47

July 9 Friday: Mr B...th (Debtor) was Discharged by order of the Sheriff - David Sh... Debtor was Dis'd by order of the Supreme Court - Doubell Drawbridge in for Felony was Pardoned & Dis'd. 39

July 10 Saturday: it was Reported to Me that the Pistol that Kennedy was Allowed to have whilst on duty - had been Stolen from the Room near the Gates during the time he was gone over to the Stores for The Rations yesterday - I Sent Perry to Search Kennedys House and Perry and Kennedy went & Searched all the Guards Houses but Could Not find the Pistol the Guards of Road Party Houses was also Searched I gave the description to the Police offering 10s/- Reward. 37

July 11 Sunday: 7 A.M. Searched all in the felon's Yard the Rooms Bedding etc for the Pistol also Perrys House and Dawbineys - we had divine Service at 3½ P.M. Mr. Fleming Attended. 37

July 12 Monday: Capt'n John Walker (Debtor) was discharged by order of the Supreme Court. 37

July 13 Tuesday: they Emigrants began the draining Round the Gaol. 35

July 15 Thursday: Received from the Store 2 Tables - 6 Chairs and 2 Small Book Presses for the Use of the Office - they did belong to the Cattle Brand Office. 34

July 17 Saturday: Charles Powell was brot in for Debt by Jones Sheriffs Officer. 33

July 18 Sunday: Divine Service at 3 P.M. Mr. Fleming attended. 32

July 19 Monday: A Man Came in to See Mr My... a Debtor brought in a Bottle of Brandy Perry the TurnKey took it from him & detained it & he was Cautioned not to bring any more into the Gaol Mr Boucher was in with Mr My... who told Me that he Mr. B. was Ill & that the Brandy was for him I told him he Might Come into the Office and have Some but I would not let the Spirits into the Yard etc he Came to the Office & did have Some. 33

July 20 Tuesday: His Excellency, Capt'n Frome - & the Sheriff Visited the Gaol in the Afternoon. 33

July 21 Wednesday: The Sheriff and his Laidy Call at the Gaol at 4½ P.M. 34

July 22 Thursday: Received an Order from the Judge to take Arthur to the Insolvent Court. 35

July 23 Friday: Took Arthur to Insolvent Court at 12 Noon his Case was put off to Friday 30th Instant. 35

July 24 Saturday - Receiving from the Colonial Secretarys Officer a Reading Desk for the Chapel. 35

July 25 Sunday: Divine Service at 3¼ P.M. Mr. Fleming attended. 35

July 26 Monday: Dr. Litchfield brot in for Debt by Jones Sheriffs Officer. 36

July 27 Tuesday: The Sheriff called at the Gaol Dr. Litchfield was Dis'd by Supreme Court. 37

July 29 Thursday: I.L. Crabb (Debtor) was dis'd by order of the Supreme Court. - Mr. Ha... Came to the Gaol and brot me the Judges Order to take to the Court to Morrow Morning. The following Debtors - James Arthur - Boyce Thompson - Peter Shanks and William Alfred Chatfield at 10 A.M. 36

July 30 Friday: Took to the Insolvent Court this day the following Debtors - James Arthur - Boyce Thompson - Peter Shanks - and William Alfred Chatfield Peter Shanks was Dischargd by the Court - They other 3 was Remanded. At the Court from 10 A.M. till 5P.M. 35

July 31 Saturday: Dawbiney the Gaoler and Downing one of the Guards left the Gaol duty. 36

August 1 Sunday: Removed into My New Office this Morning at a ¼ past 2 P.M. The Rev'd Mr. Benson the Catholic Priest Came to the Gaol 3 of the Prisoners was with him in the Chapel for a Short time - Viz Vaughan, Story, & Lynch - At 3 OC'k. P.M. Mr. Fleming Came and we had divine Service. 36

August 3 Tuesday: The Session Commenced This Day at the Court all day. 38

August 4 Wednesday: At the Sessions all day. 36
August 5 Thursday: At the Sessions all day. 38
August 6 Friday: At the Court all day Hugh Lynch was Admitted in his Own Bail to Appear Next Sessions. 38
August 7 Saturday: At the Court untill 12 O Clk Mid Night with Storys Case. 36
August 8 Sunday: Bella Anderson was Discharged having been a Week in Solitary Confinement. 3 P.M. the Rev'd Mr Benson the Catholic Priest Came to the Gaol - 3½ P.M. The Rev'd Mr. Howard Attended we had divine Service. 31
August 9 Monday: The Sessions Ended this Day Mrs Garratt & the two others where the last They was the last tried. 33
August 10 Tuesday: J.H. Theakston brot in for Debt. 34
August 11 Wednesday: At the Court all day with J.H. Theakston a Debtor taken up by order of the Court as a Witness in the Case of Hopkins & Metcalfe. 34
August 12 Thursday: H.J. Theakston was discharged by order of the Supreme Court he having found Bail. 34

On 12 August 1841 the *Adelaide Independent* published a satirical piece on Ashton. It was part of a series of *Pen and Ink Sketches of High and Low in South Australia*. The sketch was cartoon-like, a line drawing of Ashton in profile, and it came with a written description signed 'Timothy Short'. In a later edition the sketcher outed himself as Nathaniel Hailes, the publisher of the paper. In doing so he sketched himself, short in stature with ridiculously short legs and divulged where he could be found on his customary walk home:

> It would be no mis-fortune to anyone if a chance blow should cut the career of Timothy Short.[245]

So, his humour is a bit odd and it is hard to know what to make of his comments on Ashton. The sketch was used for the cover of Malcolm Johnston's 1990 *A Governor, Aye Every Inch a Governor: A biography of William Baker Ashton, the first governor of the Adelaide gaol*. 'A Governor, ay every inch a governor' is the caption on the sketch, and Short explains that in his opinion Ashton is the only true governor in the colony. This is because, despite a council of officials, he is 'not encumbered . . . with the apparent check'.

> His influence is immediately felt by all his subjects, the affairs of every one of whom are intimately known to him . . . our hero makes a gaol his habitation for the benefit of his fellow creatures . . . his firm yet elastic step, the sunny twinkle of his eye, the jaunty cock of his hat, and the swing of his walking-stick, seem to denote in him the only man in the Colony who can contemplate a prison with complacency . . . may he spend the remainder of his life in prison.[246]

Nathaniel Haile's sketch of William Ashton, *Adelaide Independent*, inserted after p. 8, drawn under the pseudonym of 'Timothy Short', 12 August 1841.
[State Library of South Australia collection, William Baker Ashton B 15998/4]

Though he describes Ashton as a 'great burley man' this sketch suggests that in 1841 Ashton was yet to become the exceedingly wide man depicted in Glover's paintings (see front and back covers and facing title page). Johnston estimated that he reached 23 stone (146 kg) by the time he died and that when it came to removing his body from his upstairs bedroom at the gaol he had to be lowered out the window to the ground.[247] The walking stick that he always used, depicted here, is still treasured within the family.

August 15 Sunday - No Person Attended to perform divine Service this day at the Gaol - the Rev'd Mr. Benson Came in the Afternoon and Saw Story.   33

August 16 Monday: took the Description of they Prisoners Under Sentence of Transportation to the Colonial Secretarys Office.   33

August 17 Tuesday - William Samuel Fooks Was Committed for Trial for Stealing 270 Ewes the Property of Garratt and Hearn - and 2 Natives was brought in for felony Remanded for a Week.   36

August 19 Thursday: Arthur, Thompson and Chatfield (Debtors) was taken up to the Insolvent Court Chatfield & Thompson was discharged Arthur Sent back to the 16th Sept. 1841 - Prettyjohn - Garratt - & Crispe brot in for Debt.   40

August 20 Friday: Johns (a Debtor) was taken to the Insolvents Court & was discharged.   41

August 22 Sunday: Mr. Fleming & the Rev'd Mr. Benson attended at the Gaol at 3 P.M. Divine Service.   39

August 24 Tuesday: left the Gaol at 7 O C'k this Morning for the Port - with the following Prisoners Vaughan - Irving - McLean - Worthington, Story, Holdsworth, Aldridge, Parkinson and put them on board the Ship William for Sydney under the Charge of Wright and Dawbiney. The Ship left the Port at 4 P.M. -
Kell & White was brot in for Debt - Finke (Debtor) was dis'd by Order of the Supreme Court having found Bail.   43

August 27 Friday: took Mr. Milne a debtor to Insolvent Court he was Remanded to the 17th Sept'r Mr. Crabb (out on Bail) was Discharged by the Court – Thos. Smith Kell was discharged by Order of the Supreme Court he having found Bail. 32

August 28 Saturday: The Sheriff Call'd. 32

August 29 Sunday: The Rev'd Mr. Benson and Mr. Fleming Attended at the Gaol divine Service. 32

August 31 Tuesday: Mr. Crispe Debtor was Discharged by Order of the Sheriff. 32

September 1 Wednesday: William W...ey brot in for Debt – by Jones etc. William Roach brot in on Suspicion of having Murdered a Native Remanded. 33

September 3 Friday: Thomas White a debtor was discharged by order of the Supreme Court he having found Bail. 31

September 4 Saturday: The Sheriff & Mr. Jackson Call'd at the Gaol I went to Walkerville to Mr Wrights About the Book for Prisoners Moneys. 30

September 5 Sunday: The Rev'd Mr. Farrell & Mr. Benson Attended at the Gaol divine Service at 3½ P.M. 30

September 6 Monday: 2 Women Committed for 1 Week Solitary Confinement in default of Paying 10s/- each. 33

September 7 Tuesday: Charlotte Story one of the Above Women Paid her fine and was discharged. 33

September 11 Saturday: The Sheriff Capt'n Frome and Mr. Nixon Visited the Gaol. 31

September 12 Sunday: Mary Smith was discharged having been in Solitary Confinement One Week. – Mr. Fleming attended divine Service at 3½ P.M. 31

September 14 Tuesday: Went to the Port etc Mary Ann Collins was Committed for Trial for felony – Isaac Breaker was brot in for Debt at 11 P.M. Jones etc 32

September 15 Wednesday: 2 Prisoners was Remanded for a Month on Suspicion of Horse Stealing by Major O'Halloran J.P. 3 Sailors was Sent down to the Port with the Mounted Police at 8½ P.M. to be Put on board the Christina by Order of Capt'n Lipson. 34

September 16 Thursday: took Arthur the Debtor to the Insolvent Court he was Remanded to the 20th Inst W...ey the Debtor was discharged by order of the Sheriff. 31

September 17 Friday: Fawcett the Debtor was taken to the Insolvent Court Remanded for a fortnight took him the Court without a written order. 30

September 18 Saturday: Frederick Maitland Scott was brot in for Debt by Jones Sheriffs Officer. 31

September 19 Sunday: Mr. Fleming & Mr. Benson Attended at the Gaol we had divine Service. At 3¼ P.M. Mr Norman attempted to take a Pint of Brandy into the debtors Yard. 31

September 20 Monday: James Arthur was taken to the Insolvent Court and was Sent back time not Mentioned The Sheriff Visited Gaol the Prisoner Nunan was Very Abusive to him Garratt & Arthur (Debtors) Quarrelled about which was the Most honest of the two. 31

September 21 Tuesday: Charles Wills brot in by Jones for Debt and 6 Prisoners brought in for felony. 38

September 22 Wednesday: 6 Prisoners brot for felony - I was at the Inquest held of Rob't Dodds. 41

September 23 Thursday: at the Inquest this day. Mr Milner's Man was Stoped in bringing Spirits to the Gaol took & locked him up in the Police Station all Night. I found he had a Very large family and that he attempted to bring the Small Quantity of Spirits into Mr M who was unwell and therefore I did not Press the Charge Against Him and the Resident Magistrate discharged him. 42

September 24 Friday: Took Prettyjohn to the Insolvent Court he was Remanded for a Week. Mr...ble brot in for Debt. 43

September 25 Saturday: Mr W.A. Poulden brot to the Gaol by Jones for Debt His Honor the Judge Call'd at the Gaol this Afternoon. 42

September 26 Sunday: Mr. Fleming attended at 3 P.M. Divine Service. 42

September 27 Monday: Commenced the New Rules Relative to Visitors to felons & debtors. 43

September 28 Tuesday: The Sheriff Visited the Gaol at 6¾ A.M. 3 Prisoners Committed for Trial this day for felony. 46

September 29 Wednesday: F.M. Scott (Debtor) was discharged by order of the Supreme Court he having found Bail. 41

September 30 Thursday: York a Prisoner Committed for Trial was taken Very Ill Sent for Dr Nash who Came & bled him at 9½ P.M. last Night. 46

October 1 Friday: Prettyjohn a Debtor was taken to the Insolvent Court and was discharged. Charles Powell – Out on Bail for Debt – was Committed to Gaol for one Month by His Honor the Judge. 47

October 2 Saturday: W.A. Poulden (debtor) was discharged at 11 P.M. by order of the Sheriff. 46

October 3 Sunday: No divine Service in the Gaol this day. 45

The number of debtors was still high, however hope was literally on the horizon. At a farewell dinner for Edward John Eyre before he departed Adelaide to explore the interior, Governor Grey made a hopeful speech. The paper's comment was not about Eyre. Instead:

> The most interesting passage in the Governor's speech undoubtedly is 'I believe the worst is now gone by, and I doubt not but that the next ship will bring intelligence that our pecuniary difficulties are over'. May the next ship speedily arrive, and may this anticipation be fully realised![248]

In his speech to the 'Gentlemen of the Grand Jury' in the Supreme Court on 3 August 1841, Judge Cooper also spoke of change in the colony:

> After an interval of anxious expectation, the welcome intelligence has at length arrived, that all the engagements, whether by bills or otherwise, made by his late Excellency [the previous Governor, Gawler] with public creditors, will be fully provided for in England.[249]

The judge praised the patience of the creditors and had a good word for gentlemen who had formed a society for the relief of the poor. He also praised the ordinary emigrants as, in his opinion, despite difficult times, there had been no increase in crime. Of those on his list 15 were either sailors or runaway convicts 'leaving only seventeen properly belonging to the emigrant population'. The implication is of course that if you take out those you might expect to be criminals there is hardly anyone left. It is interesting to read then, the list of charges. Embezzlement; cheating and defrauding; and receiving stolen property – all forms of indirect stealing – and the rest for more ordinary stealing – of coins, 'trowsers', a coat, a shawl, some baby linen, and a gun. Two on his list were for more than stealing – they had compounded their stealing offences by escaping from the old gaol. So, of the emigrants going to gaol at this time, the overwhelmingly number were debtors and thieves

Most of those in gaol were men, however a number of women's names are in the journal as well. They were soon to be joined by a newcomer, Sarah Fleming.

October 4 Monday: Sarah Fleming was this Day Committed for Trial for Attempting to Murder her Child. 45

The story of Sarah Fleming is an incredibly sad one, again a case of concealing a pregnancy, and this time a failed attempt at killing her infant. The circumstances were extremely distressing, with the newborn found inside a privy of a vacant house in Gilbert Street near South Terrace. A passing policeman heard 'groaning' and when he investigated, lifted a large stone from the lid, broke down the seat and pulled the infant out. It had been placed in a corner of the privy box with a piece of sacking on top.

The reaction of the public was instant. One objected to her being sent to hospital, alongside worthy patients, believing she had 'forfeited all claim to sympathy, protection, and medical aid'. Another responded on the contrary, that she was deserving of pity and help, having suffered 'under the febrile excitement, usually following parturition'.[250] Dr O'Hea who took charge of the infant, whilst shocked and horrified when he visited the privy, nonetheless took pity and cautioned her to be careful what she said. He cared for the child in the six hours it took to return it to a natural heat. A policeman who attended her told her, when she asked his advice on her case, that she must tell the truth, that 'hers was a very heinous crime in the sight of God and that most probably she would be hung for it'.[251]

Dr Nash already knew Sarah Fleming. She had called on him when she had pains in her side. Dr Nash told the Enquiry he had suspected she was 'in the family way', however when she declined, and had answered his question of whether she was married, with a 'no', he had treated her as a dropsical patient. Now suspecting her to be the mother of this infant, she again denied, however with the authority to now examine her, he confirmed that she had given birth.[252]

The journal continues:

October 5 Tuesday: The 2 Men on Suspicion of Horse Stealing was discharged by the Commissioner of Police. 44

October 6 Wednesday: 6 Sailors Committed this day for One Month each by the Resident Magistrate - Isaac Breaker (Debtor) was discharged by Order of the Sheriff. 48

October 9 Saturday: Commenced Serving they Prisoners with Bread Supplied by Mr Starkey in Stead of Biscuits. Received from him 170 lbs of Bread.

I Received information this Afternoon that the Prisoner Charles Morris - who had been Appointed Wardsman in the Debtors Yard had taken a 10 pound note from Mr. Garratts Room a few days ago I inquired into the Case and found that Mr. Garratt and Arthur had Made the Matter up and Mr. Garratt had Signed a paper to that effect and had received £8 out of the £10 back I therefore had Morris Removed from the Debtors yard to the felons Side and there to Remain the other part of his Sentence. - Fook found 10s/- note. 49

October 10 Sunday - Mr Fleming attended for divine Service at 11 A.M. The Colonial Surgeon was Sent for to see Morgan a Prisoner and found him Suffering from the Stopage of Water Came at 6¼ P.M. 48

October 11 Monday: Went to the Port and took my Son W.J. Ashton and left him on board the Hawk Capt'n Brown going to Launceston. 48

[In margin]
the Guard Robertson and Sarah Fleming in the Tower

October 12 Tuesday: the Sheriff Call'd at the Gaol this Morning at 9 O Clk. 48

October 13 Wednesday: The Sheriff Call'd at the Gaol and Read the Answer to Morgans Petition. 48

October 14 Thursday - Charles Wills a (Debtor) Discharged by order of the Sheriff. 48

October 17 Sunday - Mr. Howard Came to the Gaol - divine Service. At 3 P.M. Mr. Howard was Very Unwell and Obliged to leave the Gaol. 50

October 18 Monday: by the Port Philip Papers I See that Dawbiney and Wright lost 3 of the Prisoners they took from here in the William whilst at Port Philip. 50

October 20 Wednesday: 3 Prisoners brot to the Gaol by the Police Supposed to be Runaways from the Other Colonies - the Sheriff Called at the Gaol in the Evening. 53

October 23 Saturday: The Honon'ble The Colonial Secretary ordered the Prisoners to have the 2nd Bread and to Allow Them ¼ or ½ lb Rice a day. 53

October 24 Sunday: Divine Service at 11 OC'k A.M. Mr Fleming Attended. 53

October 25 Monday: Received an Order from the Commiss'r of Police for the following 6 Prisoners to be taken to the Police office. Viz - Peasley - Morgan - Carter - Brown - Dwyer - & Green - in

> Gaol on Suspicion of being Runaways and Stealing Horses. - They where Remanded again untill to Morrow Morning.   54

[In margin]
His Excellency Capt'n Frome & Mr Nixon
Visited the Gaol this Afternoon Relative to a
Yard for the Women.

This is the first mention in the journal of a yard for the women. Although the temporary gaol had had a yard and a wooden building for women, the new gaol had none. It had been sacrificed when the size of the planned gaol had been halved. With only two yards, one for felons and one for debtors, the women had no dedicated space. Instead they slept in the small rooms otherwise used for solitary confinement. This row of cells opened into the space between the walls, the area that the guards patrolled, and the women used this space in the day.[253] The correspondence between the sheriff and the colonial secretary, who received and wrote letters on behalf of and at the behest of Governor Grey, shows that this situation was unsatisfactory from the sheriff's point of view as the guards were fraternising with the women. The sheriff wanted a 'separate enclosure made for the Females in order to remedy the evil'.[254] Grey was equally unimpressed but wanted the cheaper option of dismissing the offending guards.[255] However, when the financial situation briefly promised to ease, Grey agreed to the yard and building began.

October 26 Tuesday: Peter Sinclair was brought to Gaol for Debt by Jones Sheriffs Officer - Received an order from Capt'n Lipson for the 6 Sailors belonging to the Daniel Wheeler to be Sent on board Ship Sent down Accordingly by 2 of the Mounted Police at 2½ P.M.   50

[In margin]
About 16 Hundred of Bricks have been
taken from the Gaol by order of Capt'n
Frome at different Times.

October 28 Thursday: The Soldiers Commenced Duty at the Gaol this Morning at 11 A.M. The Sheriff & one of Officers Came to the Gaol. Armstrong - Wardsman in the Debtors Yard was Removed to the Felons Yard in Consequence of his Abusive Language to Molineux the TurnKey. 50

October 30 Saturday: the following Guards was discharged from the Gaol in Consequence of the Military doing duty at the Gaol. Viz - Robertson - Bath - Selby - & Marra. 51

October 31 Sunday: the Rev'd Mr. Benson Attended this day 8 Male & 2 Female Prisoners Attended him - Mr. Fleming Came at 3½ P.M. divine Service. 51

November 1 Monday: The Sheriff told me to Keep Bath the Guard on at the Gaol till after the Sessions. - Charles Powell Insolvent, Sent to Gaol for 1 Month by His Honor the Judge was discharged this Morning having been in Gaol a Month - William Kay alias Yorke was put in Solitary Confinement for Insulting the Sentry and threatening him on his duty - also taking Stones Threatening and Shaking his fist in My face etc and when in the Cell Swore he would break the Windows I therefore had him HandCuffed behind Dr Nash Came & Saw him. 52

November 2 Tuesday: None. Yorke Still in Solitary Confinement. 51

November 3 Wednesday: 3 Prisoners was Discharged. - The Sessions Commenced this day at the Court till 7½ P.M. Hunt & Horder Sentenced to Transportation for life. 51

November 4 Thursday: At the Sessions All day Sturgess was found Guilty of the Manslaughter of Williams and Sentenced to Transportation for Life. 48

November 5 Friday: at the Sessions All Day. 46

November 6 Saturday: At the Sessions All Day. Mr P. Haywood brot to the Gaol for Debt by Jones Sheriffs Officer. 45

November 7 Sunday: Mr. Howard & Fleming and Mr. Benson Attended Divine Service at 3½ P.M. 42

November 8 Monday - at the Sessions all day. 42

November 9 Tuesday: At the Sessions all day. The Sessions under this Day Roach was Ordered to be Detained till Next Sessions - Fooks was Aquitted but Ordered to find Bail to Appear Next Sessions. 40

November 10 Wednesday - None - Both the Guard was Discharged this day. 40

November 12 Friday: R.L. Milne went to the Insolvent Court Yesterday and was Sent back for a fortnight. 41

November 13 Saturday: the Sheriff & Colonial Storekeeper Came to the Gaol at 9 A.M. and Condemned a quantity of Old Stores. 41

November 14 Sunday: 2½ P.M. Daniel Gibson was taken Much Worse Sent for Dr. Nash - who Came and Saw him and Ordered him to have only light food - Mr. Benson & Mr.Fleming Attended divine Service at 3½ P.M.
A Man Named Thomas Smallacombe was brot to Gaol Committed for Trial by the J.P's of Mount Barker at 9 P.M. by the Mounted Police. 42

November 18 Thursday: An officer from The Barracks Visited the Guard on duty at the Gaol at 4 P.M. 42

November 19 Friday: at the Gaol all day 2 of the Officers Visited the Guards at the Gaol this After Noon. 42

November 20 Saturday: the female Prisoners Made a Remark as one of the Officers was going Round to Visit the Guards about his Dress - being like what Dr. Nash wore but it Appears that it was not done to insult him. 44

November 21 Sunday: Mr. Benson Came at 2½ P.M. and the Rev'd Mr. Howard at 3½ P.M. divine Service. 44

November 23 Tuesday: James Arthur, a Debtor was taken to the Insolvent Court and Remanded to the 25th The Sheriff Call'd at the Gaol this After Noon. 45

November 24 Wednesday: Mr. S. Fooks was taken before the Judge this day and Bailed to appear Next Session. 44

November 25 Thursday: James Arthur was taken to the Insolvent Court. After the Judge had heard his Case he Sentenced him to

18 Months Imprisonment from the Date of his Arrest at the Suit of Mr. Crabb at Port Adelaide the 4th May 1841 - R.L. Milne was Also taken to the Court & Was Sent back etc no time was Mentioned for his Next hearing. 43

November 26 Friday: S.B. Garratt taken to the Insolvent Court this Day and was Discharged Out of Custody by the Court - the Sheriff Visited the Gaol this Afternoon and told Horder that his Sentence was Commuted to 10 years Transportation Also Collins to 15 Years Transportation. 44

November 27 Saturday: Henry Pettman (Debtor) was Discharged by Order of the Insolvent Court he having found Bail. 43

November 28 Sunday: Mr. Fleming & Mr. Benson Attended divine Service at 3 P.M. 42

November 29 Monday: Received the £24 from Mr. Barratt as the Fine For the Six Sailors belonging to the Daniel Wheeler and which Sum I Paid to Mr. Phipson Clerk to the Resident Magistrate Peter Hughes was this Day taken to the Commis'r of Police to give Evidence about the Other Runaway Convicts and was Detained at the Police Barracks but Still Considered as My Prisoner and Rations Allowed him there. 43

November 30 Thursday: At the Gaol all day. 42

December 1 Wednesday: Saw Capt'n Butler about Allowing of 2 of the Soldiers off duty to Attend divine Service on the Sundays with they Prisoners William Rains brot to Gaol for Debt. 42

December 2 Thursday: 2 Men & One Woman brought in under Remand The Sheriff Visited the Gaol this Afternoon. 42

December 3 Friday: The Prisoner Wilson was taken and Kept at the Police Office. Sarah Reynolds was back to Gaol for Debt - Capt'n Litchford Came and Saw Casey about the Robbery at Barracks. 45

December 4 Saturday: Sarah Reynolds in for Debt was Discharged by order of the Insolvent Court She having found Bail. 46

December 5 Sunday: in Consequence of Information I Received I expected that they Prisoners Would Make a Rush on me in the Chapel this Afternoon for the purpose of Several of Them to Make their Escape Capt'n Litchfield Insp'r of Police with 6 P.C.

was in My house during divine Service Morgan Made a move but not being followed by any of they other Prisoners Nothing took Place. Dr. Duncan, Mr. Fleming & Mr. Benson Attended divine Service at 3½ P.M. - Daniel Gibson was Much Worse this evening he had Several fits. 44

December 7 Tuesday: Capt'n Symers in for Debt was discharged this day by Order of the Insolvent Court he having found Bail. 44

December 8 Wednesday: Smallacombe - Committed for Trial was this day Admitted to Bail by his Honor the Judge - Rains a Debtor was Discharged by order of the Sheriff. 43

December 9 Thursday: They Workmen began about the Yard for female Prisoners My Son William Returned this Day from Launceston with Capt'n Brown - the Sheriff and one of the Officer of the 96 Visited the Gaol. 44

December 10 Friday: William a Native was brought to Gaol for indecently exposing his Person Sentence to 3 days imprisonment. 44

December 12 Sunday: Mr. Fleming Mr. Brown & the Sheriff Attended the Gaol divine Service etc at 3½ P.M.
A Serg't & 2 P.C.s was in attendance in Case the Prisoners Attempted Any thing in the Chapel - but All was Quiet. Gibson was much worse this day. 44

December 13 Monday: Gibson Still Is sick had him Removed to the Room below the Womens Place. 44

December 14 Tuesday: Several large Boys Very much Illtreated my little Boy down by the River About 6 OC'k P.M. Lennon Caught one and he begged My Boys Pardon. 45

A number of incidents are mentioned in the journal for early December 1841.

Firstly, that a plan by the prisoners, to rush Ashton in the chapel was discovered and foiled. It had been a good plan. When prisoners went through the gates from their yards, to be escorted into the chapel, they were past the first hurdle of escape, and to overwhelm the jailors in the chapel would have given them a chance.[256]

Secondly, 'They Workmen began about the Yard for female Prisoners'.

Thirdly, Ashton wrote about his own children, showing pride in 'My Son William' who had travelled to Van Diemen's Land with only the ship's captain to look after him and had now safely returned; and his tender concern for 'my little Boy', probably Thomas, who was 'Very much Ill-treated' by 'Several large Boys' while playing at the river. Ashton's particular mention of Lennon appears to mark his sincere gratitude for the guard's quick and protective action in rescuing his little son from the bullies.

And lastly, there was a brief mention that an Aboriginal man was brought into the gaol 'for indecently exposing his person'. This last is not as it sounds. This particular 'offence' was reported in the *Adelaide Examiner* and the paper explained what actually happened:

> Mr Smith Kell stated that he had been stationed at a particular part of the river by the Commissioner of Police, to prevent people bathing, that the defendant would persist in going into the water, and on Kell interfering, defendant struck him, and with the assistance of three native women, compelled him to extend his full length on the ground, and this was the grievance he complained of, and sought re-dress for the assault.
>
> The Magistrate did not see how he could deal with it as an assault, for he knew not what right Kell had to interfere with people going into the water.
>
> Mr Kell said he was only acting in obedience to orders he had received from Major O'Halloran.
>
> Mr Wigley said that he would send prisoner to prison for three days for indecently exposing his person.[257]

The real story is not of indecent exposure but of stopping the Aboriginal people swimming in the river. The full article is worthy of study. It contains hints at the complexity and character of relationships between Aboriginal people and white settlers in the colonised territory of early Adelaide. It includes racially derogatory language from the reporter and complicated reactions by Williamy, the old and nearly blind defendant, including sheer terror at expecting to die, offering the services of his wives as bribes, wailing and clinging to the protector, relief at the leniency of the sentence, and promising that when he got out of gaol he would present his head to Mr Kell to be hit several times (his custom).

The council had, since earlier in the year, described bathing in the river by 'Natives and others' as a 'serious evil' and had wished the police to take action.[258] Following the court case it tabled a list of 'nuisance' activities that included 'bathing in the River Torrens between first creek and the aborigines location'.[259] This long stretch of river, fronting the whole of North Terrace, was traditionally a place of intense Kaurna activity.[260] With the influx into Adelaide of other Aboriginal groups this intensity had only increased. The river was polluted but, of course, the settlers were to blame for this, with their felling of trees for wood, the consequent breaking down of the riverbank and the resulting erosion by floods.[261] There was also the everday pollution of washing clothes in the river, a small brewery on the bank, brick making and cattle slaughtering. Some settlers were quick to blame 'the hundreds of natives that infest the parklands',[262] complaining that the river was 'full of them . . . not . . . to the improvement of the water, which all the inhabitants who have not wells are obliged to drink'.[263]

The plan to rush Ashton in the chapel on 5 December 1841 had not worked, but the next plan to escape, by a prisoner named Carter, did.

December 16 Thursday: A Prisoner Named John Carter - on Suspicion of being a Runaway from Sydney Made his Escape from the felons Yard about 7 OC'k A.M. by getting over the Wall near the first Tower went Round between the Walls past the Sentry at the back and went out where the fence is pulled down for the female Yard - He was not Mist untill lock up time Every Part of the Gaol was Searched Molineux Came on duty at 8 P.M. and told us that a Man had past through the fence in the Morning as above described. Information was given to the Police. They Prisoners Refused the Meat this day and threw the Beef into the Yard - Dr Nash Saw the Meat & Said it was Very good.   46

December 17 Friday: the Sheriff Call'd at the Gaol this Morning & then Afternoon about the escape of Carter. This evening I went with Capt'n Litchfield and 2 P.C.s to Several places in Search of Carter having Received Information that he was in the Town we Could not meet with him.   49

December 18 Saturday: the Sheriff and one of the Officers of the 96 Met at the Gaol to enquire about Carters escape. The Soldier - Molineux - and Several Witnesses where examined and their Statements taken down for the information of His Excellency the Governor.   49

December 19 Sunday: had 2 of the Soldiers in My house No Police Attended Mr. Howard & Mr. Benson Came Divine Service at 3½ P.M.   49

December 20 Monday: I had Morgan - Dwyer - Brown - Green - Peasley - & Thompson Runaway Convicts - put in Irons about 4½ OC'k P.M. a dreadful Storm bust, we was in total Darkness for 20 Minutes & then had the Prisoners locked up. Morgan & Dwyer - broke their Irons.   48

December 21 Tuesday: The Sheriff Call'd at the Gaol this Afternoon. - Peasley & Green broke their Irons.   48

[In margin in red]
Molineux the Guard was Suspend by order
of His Excellency for the escape of Carter.

December 22 Wednesday: about 10 OC'k of this Morning one of the bed in No 2 Cell in the felons Yard was found to be on fire. Some of the Prisoners Must have put Some fire there whilst the Cell was being Cleaned out - I had the fire taken out of the Kitchen and Made one or two Prisoners Cook for all.   48

[In margin in red]
Robinson came on duty this Morning in
place of Molineux Suspended.

December 23 Thursday: Received Orders for they Prisoners Under Sentence of Transportation to be put on Board the Brig Emma for Sydney at 6 P.M. to Morrow Ev'g they Prisoners was told they would leave the Gaol at 2 P.M.   48

December 24 Friday: had all they Prisoners Irons examined Several fresh Pairs put on. At 3 P.M. left the Gaol in 2 Vans from Chambers Insp'rs Tolmer & Litchfield and 8 of the Mounted Police after leaving the Gaol about 4 Hundred Yards the Wheel of one Van broke I Sent 9 Prisoners back to be Kept in the TurnKeys lodge Guarded by the Police Soldiers and went on with the others to the Port and Sent Mr. Chambers back for they Prisoners left at the Gaol and he arrived at the Port about 7 P.M. with Prisoners and 6 Police. The Brig was not Ready to Receive them they was put in the Police Station for the Night in Charge of the Police and Soldiers the Sheriff was down I left the Port at 10 Oc'k P.M.   48

December 25 Saturday - Christmas day, went to the port at 12 OC'k Noon to put they Prisoners on Board found the Ship not Ready put them on Board at 5½ P.M. and left them in Charge of the Police & Military all Safe Came home with Insp'r Litchfield at 8½ P.M.   29

December 26 Sunday: Mr. Fleming & Mr. Benson attended divine Service at 3½ P.M. About the Same time the Chimney in my Kitchen was on fire Put Out by Perry the TurnKey.   29

December 27 Monday: Reported to the Sheriff putting the Prisoners on Board on the 25th - 4 fresh Prisoners in.   33

[In margin in red]
Fleming brot in for Debt.

December 28 Tuesday: A Prisoner Named Daniel Gibson a Man of Colone Died at 7 OC'k this evening he had been Ill Several Months and had been Very Ill for 6 or 8 Weeks Past and had been Attended Night and Day by 2 Prisoners Named Stone - & Ballard he was Supplied with every thing he wished for Dr. Nash Saw him Nearly every day Mr. Howard & Mr. Fleming Visited him Several Times. I Saw the Sheriff About him. I ordered a Shell for him to Mr. Ross.   32

December 29 Wednesday: Mr. Ross the Government Undertaker brought a Coffin to the Gaol at 6½ A.M. And the Body of Gibson that Died Yesterday was put in. At 12 OC'k Noon Mr. Ross Removed the Body from the Gaol for the purpose of Interring the Same. - No Inquest was held on the body - Edward Molineux Guard that was Suspended on the 21st Inst for the Escape of John Carter Came on duty again having been Suspended for One Week. - George Robertson that had been lent to me for that time went back to his duty on the Park Land. 35

December 30 Thursday - Francis Henry a Debtor was Very Bad - (Quite Mad) Sent for Dr. Nash who Came and bled him Ballard and Armstrong was with him All Night. 34

December 31 Friday: the Sheriff Visited the Gaol this Afternoon. 34

The escape of Carter was investigated thoroughly. Interviews connected with the investigation take up many pages of government records.[264] Molineux was blamed, however it was a daring, well-executed escape, carried out with flair, made possible by the architecture of an unfinished gaol. Having negotiated the inner wall and having dressed as a carpenter, Carter had mingled with the workmen, chatted affably, then casually walked away. All guards who saw him commented that they had not seen him before, that he was not one of theirs. Molineux who saw him at a distance of 70 yards did not recognise him and 'supposed he was going to the Cottages at the rear of the gaol'.[265] Anyone could have been fooled.

Curiously I have not been able to find any newspaper account of this first-ever successful escape from the new gaol, that is, not until four months later, in April 1842, when there is the briefest of articles. It simply reports that John Carter was committed for trial after his recapture, having been found on a stolen horse. The newspaper records that at the trial Ashton and Tolmer explained the earlier events leading up to this point of time:

> Having found his way to this province, [he] was taken by the police, and lodged in the new gaol, from which he contrived to make his escape, and then stole the horse alluded to.[266]

This is all that was reported about the escape. The paper also records that Carter was returned to gaol to await his trial and that when his case came to court a technicality disallowed a conviction and he was instead ordered to be delivered back to New South Wales.

Carter's reappearance in the gaol, his court appearance and his subsequent departure on the *Dorset* are recorded in the journal,[267] however there appears to be no further mention of Carter's escape in the newspapers for another 30 years. At that time a series of articles on 'Early Experiences of Colonial Life' appeared in the paper, posthumously printed from stories John Wrathall Bull had written and which had been circulated among his family. One of these articles describes the escape and Carter's use of the chaos during the building of the women's cells. It also, importantly, describes the location of the women's yard, as being 'a westerly extension of the premises' as they were at the time.[268]

Bull described Carter's escape in great detail and another person, possibly a descendant (the initials are M.J.B.), later produced a shortened, more readable version of the same:

> For coolness and daring nothing in the criminal history of South Australia has equalled the escape from the Adelaide Gaol of a man named Carter. He was a convict of New South Wales and was the first man to get away from the prison in the north-west parklands . . . The prisoners were given brooms with which to clean out their cells. These had exceptionally long handles . . . [he used these to climb over the wall].
>
> The prisoner had dressed . . . in a pair of carpenter's overalls and cap. With pencil and paper in hand, he boldly approached a guard, passed the time of day, and said he had been sent to measure the sentry boxes . . . made a cursory examination . . . bade the warder good day and walked off in the direction of the city. – 'M.J.B.' Macclesfield.[269]

The year had ended with Ashton missing out on most of Christmas Day as he was making sure the prisoners to be transported were safely aboard the *Emma*. The few days left in the year had brought the death of a prisoner who had long been ill and attention to another, a debtor, who was 'Quite Mad'. Again, selected prisoners were assigned the care of sick and needy prisoners.

The governor's journal 1842

The Population of South Australia on 1st January 1842 was estimated at from 16,000 to 18,000 souls of all ages, of whom 6,500 to 7,000 might be regarded as dwelling in the City of Adelaide.[270]

The most recent count, the census printed in September 1841, had shown that more than 600 of Adelaide's inhabitants were living in the parklands and the rest in huts and hotels spread across the grid of both the city and North Adelaide, with a concentration in the northwest quarter of the city around Hindley Street. The villages of Hindmarsh, Bowden, Thebarton, Prospect and Walkerville had been settled and now had a combined population that more than matched the city.[271]

The Great Eastern (toll) Road now extended to Glen Osmond, and the road to Port Adelaide had been properly built through the last section of swamp and sand at the Port River end. There was even a public library in Hindley Street, called the Adelaide Circulating Library, where seven featured books plus '1,000 Popular Novels, Romances, and Periodicals' could be borrowed.[272]

The financial crisis had bitten hard. The *Southern Australian* recalled the time:

> [At] the commencement of 1842, we find it characterized by extreme monetary depression, trade of every kind was stagnant, and confidence between man and man nearly destroyed ... there were 1700 emigrants, including women and children, out of employment

and depending on Government for their support, and the population appeared to be reduced to a state of utter despondency.[273]

Adelaide's financial woes were supposed to have ended, but for most people they had not. There was

> A great accumulation of individual debt; – an almost universal inability to meet engagements; – an almost universal cessation of credit . . .; – a degree of individual distress and privation much deeper and more extensive than the silent fortitude and endurance of the sufferers allows to be apparent; – and, last and most fatal, an extreme scarcity of money; in truth, with fixed capital, great in amount, but unavailable in use.[274]

Cash was precious and difficult to keep safe. A savings bank that allowed small deposits had solved some of the problem of theft from houses in town, however those new in town were extremely vulnerable. A well-organised band of thieves was at the ready:

> [the gang] keep sentry day and night to pounce upon any unfortunate hard-working man who may have just arrived from the bush, and deprive him of the produce of his hard earnings.[275]

Most of the government accounts had by now been paid but significantly not that of Borrow and Goodier, the builders of the new gaol. Grey had stubbornly resisted, disputed the costings, and refused to allow a trial by jury. The public was pleading with Grey to sort out the long-running dispute, as many working people connected with the building firm were owed and suffering. Just this one resolution, they insisted, would affect the whole population of emigrants.[276]

In the next part of the journal the parade of debtors in and out of the gaol continues, the turnover faster due to the new insolvency law. Each one of these cases of debt is a human tragedy but no details are given, only names. However we read that Sarah Fleming, who we do know something about, is pardoned and returned to her father. There is no more written of her story except for a note in the margin of the journal, added later, that in 1856 she was back in gaol under a different surname, charged with a felony.

In the next part of the journal we also read that three children were imprisoned. The first child mentioned, George Newcombe, was 13 years old and charged with a felony. In the gaol he was treated well and put in with the debtors, rather than with the adult felons. He was offered no similar sympathy by the press however. Under the heading 'Juvenile Depravity' he was strongly suspected by them of being a member of a gang of thieves. Caught stealing two loaves of bread he had said in court in his defence that both his parents had died aboard the ship out and that his guardian in Adelaide had two days since departed the colony, leaving him to starve. The magistrate had remanded him in gaol for two weeks so his story could be checked.[277]

The second of the children mentioned was seven-year-old Emma Dalton. She had been asked by a woman, who resided in 'a house of ill-fame', to steal a ring for her from the couple who had taken Emma in. The child admitted to the charge. The woman, Mary Godwin, denied receiving the ring, though she had it in her possession, and both were found not guilty.[278] While Emma had been in gaol awaiting trial, Ashton had the little girl looked after by the guard in his room in the tower. After her acquittal, when the magistrate asked Ashton to keep her in the gaol for a few days as she had no friends and nowhere else to go, Ashton sent her to 'Mrs Kennedy's', presumably the wife of Kennedy the guard.

The third child, Thomas Wickham, had been found guilty of absconding from his master. In court he claimed he had been poorly treated and given only dry bread for his supper so had run away. His master, Mr T Williams Esq., begged to differ, saying 'the boy was a very bad one'. The magistrate tried for an apology and return however the master refused to have him back, suggesting a small punishment first. Thomas was sentenced to three days solitary confinement in the gaol as 'an example to other boys [to] shew them they could not do just as they liked when in service, or run away and leave their master's property unprotected'.[279] A few of the solitary cells still partially exist. They are extremely small with barely any light.

Later in the year more children were gaoled, including Mary Brown who Ashton was allowed to take into his house with Mrs

Ashton to keep her from the other prisoners; and an Aboriginal boy who was released each morning to the Location school with specially made light leg irons.[280]

During the first half of 1842 there are several incidents of note written in the journal. One is an entry that suggests Aboriginal male prisoners were chained together within the gaol. Many prisoners were routinely ironed within the gaol: this entry, however, reads as though the Aboriginal men, who were always put in together, were chained to each other.

> Mr. Moorhouse Call at the Gaol and Saw the Native the Sick Native had Some Meat and his Chain taken off from the others So that he may walk about a little.[281]

Another entry concerns a woman brought into a solitary cell with her six-week-old infant. After one night Dr Nash ordered that she be put with the other women in their yard, and also that she receive extra food. It does not say who initiated this action, however it was Ashton's practice to call in the doctor, sheriff or protector whenever he considered things were not as they should be. He had no authority to change the nature of a sentence but it seems he could implement the advice of these three officials, and always did.

Another was the sad story of a difficult birth and its aftermath. Both Mrs Ashton and a nurse assisted the 22-year-old prisoner Sarah Green when she was ill and then when she was in labour. The baby was eventually stillborn. The tiny body was buried within the gaol, at the western end of the grave of Stagg, who had been the first to hang and be buried at the new gaol.

Yet another incident of note is that we are about to find out that John Carter, the escapee, has been recaptured and returned to gaol.

January 1 Saturday: Henry Much better.   34

January 2 Sunday: Mr. Fleming & Mr. Benson Attended at 3½ P.M. divine Service.   34

January 4 Tuesday: Dr. Nash Came. Henry Much better.   35

January 6 Thursday: brot Holbrook and Bryden a Shirt each they having none to change themselfs. 34

January 8 Saturday: The Sheriff Visited the Gaol this Afternoon – His Excellency Pardoned Sarah Fleming Sentenced to 2 Yrs Imprisonment for Attempting to Kill her Child And She was discharged at 7 OC'k P.M. and given up to her Father. 33

[In margin]
Afterwards (in 1856) Committed for 12 mo.
for forgery as Sarah B...

January 9 Sunday: Mr. Fleming & Mr. Benson Attended the Gaol divine Service... 34

January 10 Monday: the Sentry had a Woman with him at 8 P.M. Sitting by the Wooden fence. My Perry Spoke to him and he Used Very Abusive Language to him he was Reported to his Officer. 34

January 11 Tuesday: Francis Henry was discharged being in Gaol for Debt By order of the Sheriff. 34

January 12 Wednesday: Yorke & Patch in the Felons Yard was Striped and fighting at 10½ OC'k this Morning I had them brought out and put in Separate Cells. 34

January 13 Thursday: Patch (Soldier) was discharged at 7½ this Morning and taken away by 3 Soldiers – Yorke was Kept in the Cell untill 9 OC'k this Morning for fighting in the Yard Yesterday. 33

January 14 Friday: Over at the Stores Nearly all day getting the Rations for the Quarters Supply Robert L Milner was to gone up to the Insolvent Court but I received a Letter from His Honor stating that he was unwell and not to take Milner up. 32

January 15 Saturday: Saw the Sheriff about Patch the Soldier not Coming on duty at the Gaol he having threatened to Shoot Lennon. 32

January 16 Sunday: the Rev'd Mr. Howard & Mr. Benson Attended at the Gaol divine Service at 3½ P.M. 32

January 18 Tuesday: Peter Came to the Gaol this Morning and brought Matthew Gardiner Discharged His Excellency having been pleased to Pardon him. 33

January 20 Thursday: Rob't Conner was discharged this Morning he having been in Gaol for 2 months for Selling Spirits without a License - R. L. Milner was taken to the Insolvent Court and was Remanded to find Bail. 34

January 23 Sunday: Mr Fleming & Mr. Benson Attended at the Gaol Divine Service at 3½ P.M. 34

January 27 Thursday: a Boy Named George Newcombe 13 years of age was Sent to Gaol Remanded for a fortnight - I put him in Debtors Yard. 33

January 29 Saturday: a Prisoner named Patrick Connor was brought to Gaol Committed for Trial for Shooting & wounding a Native at Port Lincoln Committed by Mr. McDonald Resident Magistrate Edward Gibson was this day Pardoned by His Excellency and discharged. 32

January 30 Sunday: the Rev'd Mr. Farrell & Mr. Benson Attended at the Gaol divine Service at 3½P.M. 31

January 31 Monday: Joseph Barrett was brought to Gaol for Debt. 33

February 1 Tuesday: 5 Prisoners brought in together Remanded for felony. 38

February 2 Wednesday: a Large Stone was found under the Bed of Samuel Thomas at 9 P.M. 40

February 3 Thursday: Hall - Armstrong - Nunan - where [were] discharged this Morning they having Served their 6 Months. 40

February 4 Friday: Henry Pittman out on Bail for Debt was Sent back this day to Gaol Remanded by the Insolvent Court. 35

Change of handwriting.

February 6 Sunday: Mr. Fleming Attended divine Service at 3½ P.M. Mr. Benson did not attend. 37

February 7 Monday: a Woman named Eliz'th Owens was Sentenced by the Resident Magistrate to 14 days Solitary Confinement for an Assault. 30

February 8 Tuesday: John Carter that Made his escape from the Gaol a Short time ago was retaken and brot back to Gaol by Serg't Halford at 10½ OC'k A.M. His Excellency - the Sheriff - Mr. Kennedy and Capt. Frome Came down to the Gaol they did not Come inside Went to the Port and took Capt'n Alex'r Drysdall of the King Henry for Debt brot him to town at 11½ P.M. 41

February 9 Wednesday: the Sheriff Visited the Gaol this Morning. 43

February 11 Friday: Henry Pettman was taken to the Insolvent Court and was Sentenced to 5 Months Imprisonment to Commence from the 20th Nov'r 1842 [should read 1841] the day of his arrest - I took Capt'n Drysdale to the Bush Tavern at 10 OC'k P.M. to a Meeting of his Creditors by leave of the Sheriff brot him back to Gaol at 5 P.M. 41

February 12 Saturday: I took Capt'n Drysdale to the Port by leave of the Sheriff at 6 OC'k A.M. brot him back to Gaol at 10 A.M. he was Discharged at 1 P.M. by order of the Sheriff Mess'rs Andrews and Frew having Bailed him. 40

February 13 Sunday: the Rev'd Mr. Howard Mr. Fleming & Mr. Benson Attended at the Gaol divine Service at 3½ P.M. 37

February 14 Monday: John Kitsby was brot to Gaol for Debt - by Mr Bean. 38

February 15 Tuesday: Capt'n. Alex'r Drysdale brot to Gaol for Debt - by W.B. Ashton. The Sheriff Sent an Order for the Discharge of Francis Jolley who have been Some days in Solitary Confinement for an Assault. 39

February 17 Thursday: F.M. Scott was brot to Gaol for forgery - Mess'rs Frew & Andrews Rendered Capt'n Drysdale on Bail for Debt. 39

The governor's journal 1842

February 19 Saturday: I took Mr. C S. Driver in Custody for Debt at the Suit of Samuel Myles for the Sum of £460 - He was Bailed at the Same time by the Sheriff. 38

February 20 Sunday: Eliz'th Owens - was disc'd having been in Solitary Confinement 14 days - George Green was also discharged having been in Gaol 2 Months for Selling Spirits without a License - Mr. Fleming and Mr. Benson Attended divine Service at 3½ P.M. 38

February 21 Monday: Took Capt'n Drysdale to the R Magistrates Court - he was discharged on all the C...'s by order of the Sheriff. 36

February 22 Tuesday: William Regan was brot to Gaol for Debt by Jones William Hallack was brought to Gaol for Debt by W.B. Ashton. 37

February 23 Wednesday: Went to the Port in the Afternoon. 37

February 24 Thursday: Hughes & Johnson was Committed for Trial. 36

February 25 Friday: Hallack in for Debt was Discharged by order of the Insolvent Court having found Bail. 37

February 27 Sunday: Mr. Fleming & Mr. Benson Attended at the Gaol Divine Service at 3½ P.M. 36

Ashton's handwriting again:

March 2 Wednesday: John Bond was fined £10 or to be imprisoned untill the fine be Paid. 38

March 3 Thursday: the Sheriff Visited the Gaol this day - I was unwell at home all day. 38

March 4 Friday: a little Girl named Emma Dalton aged 10 years was this day Committed for Trial for felony Sent her Down to the Tower with Mr Kennedy. A Boy was also Sentenced to 3 days Solitary Confinement for absconding from the Service of Mr. Thomas Williams J.P. 44

March 5 Saturday: Received 50 printed lists of Prisoners for Trial. 44

March 6 Sunday: Mr. Fleming & Mr. Benson - Attended divine Service at 3½ P.M. 43

March 7 Monday: Round with the Printed lists for Prisoners for Trial. 42

March 8 Tuesday: the Sessions Commenced this day At the Court all day No Prisoners Tried. Several Bills found. 40

March 9 Wednesday: at the Sessions all day. 40

March 10 Thursday: Sessions. 36

March 11 Friday - Sessions. 35

March 12 Saturday: Sessions all day James Ilbury out on Bail for Cattle Stealing was tried this day found Guilty and Sentenced to be Transported for life. 37

March 13 Sunday: the Rev'd Mr Howard and Mr. Benson Attended divine Service at 3½ P.M. 36

March 14 Monday: At the Sessions all day Emma Dalton aged 10 years was acquitted for felony His Honor wished Me to bring her back to Gaol for a few days She having no friends and no place to go - Sent her to Mrs Kennedys. 36

March 15 Tuesday: Sessions. 34

March 16 Wednesday: W.S Fooks was this day tried for Sheep Stealing and Acquitted the Trial lasted untill 11 OC'k at night. 30

March 17 Thursday: to up to the Court F.M Scott. - J. A Hughes whose Trials was put off to Next Sessions - Johnson's Trial was fixed for Monday Next - Thos. Bush who was Sentenced on the 15th to 7 years Transportation was this day Sentenced to 12 Months Hard Labour - The Court was then adjourned to Monday Next. 28

March 20 Sunday: Mr. Fleming & Mr. Benson Attended at the Gaol Divine Service at 3½ P.M. 27

March 21 Monday: At the Sessions all day Johnson was tried for Uttering forged Notes he was Acquitted the One Charge and Remanded to Next Sessions on the Others - Can have Bail - The Sessions ended this Day. 26

March 23 Wednesday: the Sheriff Visited the Gaol - Mr. Dutton Call'd and Wished to See over the Gaol which I allowed. 27

The governor's journal 1842

March 24 Thursday: James Arthur was brought to Gaol for Debt by Jones Sheriffs Officer. 27

March 25 Friday: Good Friday. 27

March 27 Sunday: the Rev'd Mr Howard Mr. Fleming & Mr. Benson Attended at the Gaol divine Service at 3½ P.M. 27

March 28 Monday: the Sheriff Visited the Gaol. 27

April 1 Friday: John Carter in Gaol As a Runaway Convict was taken before the Resident Magistrate & Major OHalloran I Attended and he was ordered to be Sent to V D Land. John Kitsby (a Debtor) out on Bail was this Day Sentenced to 3 Months Imprisonment at the Suit of George Bean - from the Insolvent Court his time to be dated from the 14th Feb'y 1842 - The Sheriff the Rev Mr. Howard and the Rev Mr. Farrell Came to the Gaol to See Mr. Milner (Sick) a Debtor. 34

April 3 Sunday: Mr Fleming & Mr. Benson Attended the Gaol divine Service at 3½ P.M. 35

April 4 Monday - James Arthur in for Debt was This Day Discharged by Order of the Insolvent Court he having found Bail. - Mary Godwin Sentenced to 9 days Solitary Confinement was discharged at 6P.M. James Quigley fined 15/- for Being Drunk was this day Sentenced to 7 days Solitary Confinement. 36

A change of hand.

April 5 Tuesday: Elisha Cooper's Sentence was commuted by H: Ex'y from Transportation for Life - to 15 Years. 35

April 6 Wednesday: John Rogers' Sentence commuted by H: Ex'y - from Transportation for 7 Years to - 12 Mo. Imprisonment with Hard Labor in this Colony. 35

April 7 Thos. Freeman Surrendered himself at the Gaol, for Debt: Will'm Wright, brought to the Gaol for Debt by Mr. Ashton:
James Ilberry's Sentence of Transportation for Life for Cattle= Stealing - was this day by His Ex'y's clemency - commuted to

One Year's Imprisonment with Hard Labour - in this Colony. The Sheriff visited the Gaol to announce the Remission. 37

April 8 Friday: Mr. Ashton left the Gaol this Morning at 7 o'clock - in charge of the following Prisoners who were conveyed by Bullock Drays to the Port - and then put on Board the Brig 'Dorset' - (Capt'n Welsh) to be conveyed to Hobart Town - V. D. Land, namely -

'Samuel Thomas	Thomas Quinn
'Ja's McGouveran	Elisha Cooper
'Thos. Wilson	James Riley
'Ja's McKenzie	Patrick Kelly
'George Lowe	John Carter a runaway Convict
'Henry Thos. Hoadley	

The Ship got under weigh at 4 p.m. when Mr. Ashton left the Port - About 6 p.m. His Excell'y: Capt'n Frome: and the Sheriff visited the Gaol - when His Excell'y was graciously pleased to Pardon the following Prisoners

viz: 'Cornelius Stone' Sentenced to 12 Mo's H.L. and 'John Ballard' - under sentence of Transportation for 7 Years: on the occasion of the official announcement of the Birth of the 'Prince of Wales'

A Man named James Thompson, was this day brought in, charged as a Run=away Convict - Joseph Mitchell was brought in - under Fine of 5/- for Drunkenness - or 3 days Solitary Confinement - & in default of payment - was duly locked up. 39

April 10 Sunday: James Quigley & Joseph Mitchell was this day discharged: having been in Solitary Confinement
Mr. Fleming Attended divine Service at 3½ P.M. 29

Ashton re-commences writing.

April 11 Monday: At home All Day. 27

April 13 Wednesday: Mr. Freeman a Debtor was Discharged by Order of the Insolvent Court having found Bail At home All Day Very Ill with a Cold. 30

April 14 Thursday: John Wright in for Debt was This Day Discharged by order of the Insolvent Court having found Bail. I at house all day Ill. 28

April 16 Saturday: A Soldier (Prisoner) was Sent Down to be Detained in the Guard Room inside of the Gaol. 27

April 17 Sunday: Dr Nash was Sent for for Mr. Milner the Dr Told him that there was No Occasion to have Sent for him. - Mr. Fleming Attended and Mr. Benson divine Service at 3½ P.M. 27

April 18 Monday: 2 Women and a Girl was Committed for Trial with 2 Men for highway Robbery - and a Man for an Attempt to Murder. 33

April 20 Wednesday: R.L. Milner was this Day Sentenced to 14 Calendar Months Imprisonment at the Suit of Mr. Smyth of Sydney to be dated from the 15th April 1841. 33

April 22 Friday: the Sheriff Visited the Gaol this Afternoon in Company with Dr. Nash. 33

April 23 Saturday: Jane Tr... (with a Young Child) was this day Sentenced to one Month Solitary Confinement. 34

April 24 Sunday: Dr. Nash Came to the Gaol & Saw Jane Tr... in Solitary Confinement for One Month and Ordered her to be Removed to the Womens Ward in Consequence of her Young Child (6 weeks old) and to be Allowed More to eat than is Allowed in Solitary Confinement. She was Removed. The Rev'd Mr Howard and Mr. Benson Attended the Gaol Yesterday Afternoon divine Service at 3½ P.M. 34

April 28 Thursday: Charles Huon was brot to Gaol for Debt. 35

April 30 Saturday: John Newington was brot to Gaol for Debt. 38

May 1 Sunday: in Company with Inspector Litchfield I took Mrs Hoadley to the Port and put her on Board the Emma for Hobart Town - following her Husband Transported from here last Sessions. 36

[In the margin in red]
Lennon was Sick from this day.

May 4 Wednesday: Mr. Williamson was Sentenced to a Months Solitary Confine't. Serg't Clark of the 96 R. Sent down this day 30 lbs of Candles for the Oil used in the Guard Room in the Gaol he Sent Some a Short time ago.   42

May 6 Friday – Regan a debtor was this day taken to the Insolvent Court and Remanded to Monday the 9th Inst. –   43

May 7 Saturday – Baker in Gaol for Shooting at Mr. Pearce was admitted to Bail by the Resident Magistrate.   41

May 8 Sunday: Mr. Fleming and Mr. Benson Attended the Gaol Yesterday Afternoon divine Service at 3½ P.M.   41

May 9 Monday: Regan a Debtor was taken to the Insolvent Court this day and was Remanded.   39

May 12 Thursday: The Sheriff Visited the Gaol Isaac Nonmus a Debtor was discharged by order of the Insolvent Court having found Bail.   39

May 14 Saturday: K... a Debtor was discharged this day having Served his 3 Months as he was Sentenced by the Insolvent Court. – Sarah Green was taken Very Ill at 11 P.M. Mrs Ashton was with her About an hour – She was Better.   38

May 15 Sunday: Mr Fleming & Mr Benson Attended the Gaol divine Service at 3½ P.M. Sarah Green a little better this day.   37

May 18 Wednesday: John Bond in for Assault was Discharged by order of the Sheriff.   38

May 20 Friday: Charles Huon Debtor was discharged by order of the Insolvent Court having found Bail.   38

May 22 Sunday: the Rev's Mr. Farrell and Mr. Benson Attended the Gaol Yesterday divine Service at 3½ P.M. –
Sent for Mr. Nash to See one of the Natives.   37

May 24 Tuesday: The Queens B Day etc   38

May 26 Thursday - 2 Debtors brought in Name Anderson & Bird The Sheriff Visited the Gaol this Afternoon. 40

May 27 Friday: Mr. Moorhouse Call at the Gaol and Saw the Native the Sick Native had Some Meat and his Chain taken off from the others So that he may walk about a little. 41

May 28 Saturday: a Prisoner Named Thomas Adams was Committed for trial about detaining Some Hurdles (the property of Philip Hollows) by C.P. Brewer Esq'r. J.P. of Willunga was this day discharged by order of the Advocate-General - the Prisoner was brot to Gaol last Night by Corp'l Pollard. 40

May 29 Sunday: Mr. Fleming & Mr Benson Attended the Gaol Yesterday divine Service at 3½ P.M. 39

June 1 Wednesday: The Sheriff Visited the Gaol this Afternoon. William Anderson a Debtor was discharged by Order of the Insolvent Court having found Bail. 43

June 2 Thursday: I went Over to the Stores about Oil Run Out. There was None that I Could have. 42

June 3 Friday: Saw the Sheriff about the Oil and Rice has [as] we had No Oil I Could Not Light the lamps. And That I Should give they Prisoners ½ lb of Extra Bread a day not having any Rice. 41

[In margin in red]
Overseer and 4 Men Commenced Cutting
Wood for the Gaol.

June 5 Sunday: Mr Benson Attended the Gaol Only this day. Mr Fleming was Out of Town and Mr. Howard Could Not Attend. 40

June 8 Wednesday: At the Supreme Court about Mr. Arthurs Case. 40

June 10 Friday - No Oil, having Overdrawn 4½ Gallons - only one Lamp Lighted. 40

June 11 Saturday: 2 Gallons of black Oil from the Stores Making 6½ Galls's Overdrawn this Quarter Gave Mr. Williams a Receipt for the Same. 41

June 12 Sunday: the Rev'd. Mr. Farrell and Mr. Benson Attended the Gaol divine Service at 3½ – Mess'rs W.H. Newenham & Lateswood Came to divine Service.   41

June 14 Tuesday: 2 Debtors Named Rich'd Novis & John Denton was brot to Gaol for Debt. R.L. Milner (Debtor) having been in Gaol 14 Months was this day discharged at 9 OC'k A.M.   44

June 15 Wednesday: At the Stores About the Oil Ordered 6 Gallons Making 12½ Gallons More than was drawn for the Quarter.   43

June 18 Saturday: the Sheriff Visited the Gaol this Morning.
Received this day from Serg't. Gardiner (Iron Stores) the following Articles as per Sheriffs Requisition for Poor Prisoners.
3 Pair of Old Grey Trousers
57 Pair of Dark Trousers
33 Flannel Jackets
Also for the Use of the Gaol
4 Wood Mauls
12 large Iron Wedges
Richard Novis (Debtor) was discharged this day by Order of the Insolvent Court having found Bail.   25

June 19 Sunday: Mr. Fleming & Mr. Benson Attended the Gaol Yesterday Afternoon divine Service etc 3½   39

June 20 Monday: John Dunford was Discharged by order of the Insolvent Court – and Matthew another Debtor by order of the Sheriff.   41

June 22 Wednesday: Received a Letter this day at the Post Office dated ... that Capt. Lipson had Sent Me for to put a Sailor on Board Ship. Saw the Sheriff about the Same and whether the Letters for the Gaol Should Not be Sent from the Post Office.   39

June 23 Thursday: Received an order his [this] day to discharge John Perryman Sailor belonging to the Ship William Fulcher and to Charge and Receive from the Capt'n 1s-/1d per day for his Keep. Sent a letter to Capt'n Lipson to Receive from the Capt'n 15s/2d for 14 days Keep.   40

June 24 Friday: the above Sailor was this day discharged.   40

June 25 Saturday: Received 3 Pair of Handcuffs Making in all 8 pair of Handcuffs Made and Supplied by Mr. Pybis as per order I Received from the Colonial Secretary and the Sheriff to get 8 prs Made in lieu of 8 pr. Sent for the Use of the Police Viz 6 pr for Port Lincoln and 2 pr for Mr Eyres Station. 39

June 26 Sunday: the Rev'd Mr. Howard and Mr. Benson Attended the Gaol this day divine Service at 3½ OC'k P.M. Mrs Green a Prisoner Committed for Trial was Taken Ill at 6 P.M. this day Sent for Dr. Nash And the Nurse. - At 9 She was a little better Dr. Nash went home the Nurse Stoped All Night. 39

June 27 Monday: at 6½ OC'k this Morning Sarah Green as above Was Delivered of a Still Born female Child Dr. Nash Attended. 42

[In margin in red]
This Child was Buried Near Stagg - at the west-end of the grave Just at the parapet of the wall.

As far as I know, this is the sole record of this burial. The nurse stayed on to look after Sarah Green for a week then, only ten days after the delivery of her stillborn child, Sarah faced the Supreme Court, charged with robbery and assault.

Sarah had been questioned in April 1842, accused of stealing from a man named Looney who had become intoxicated at a public house. He had met with her earlier at Catchlove's, a 'house of ill-fame' in Hawdon Street (though at her trial she said 'I do not remember treating you at Catchlove's'). She walked by the hotel just as a policeman had stopped him outside in the street and she offered to escort the drunk man home, saying she lived close to where he was going. Instead she sent the child with her on ahead and took him to the house at Hawdon Street. There, with the help of others, including the child, Mary Ann Davey, who held on to his leg, she emptied his pockets and pushed him out the door. He stumbled across the same policemen and all were charged with assault and robbery. Because the offence was 'committed previously to the time when the law for ameliorating punishments came in force here', Sarah Green, aged 22, along with George, Elizabeth and the 14-year-old Mary Ann Davey, known as 'Poll' and described as 'a little girl', along with Joseph Thompson, were sentenced to death.[282]

The sentences of the two men were later reduced to transportation for ten years and the women ordered to remain in gaol for the time being.[283] Sarah was transported almost a year later, in the following May.[284] The mother and child, Elizabeth and Mary Ann Davey, stayed on in gaol until they were pardoned and all were eventually pardoned.[285]

Numerous debtors continued to be escorted in and let out of gaol, also more women were 'sentenced for 14 days' (prostitutes, though Ashton never names them as such). The number of Aboriginal people imprisoned, including for solitary confinement and whipping, also increased.

The effect of solitary confinement on Indigenous people in early Adelaide can perhaps be gauged by a speech in 1864, in which Cawthorne spoke of the beliefs of the 'Adelaide Tribe':

> Every death is the result of sorcery in one shape or another. . . . As the shades of night gather round the Worley, the disease makers, the sorcerers, the wizards and evil spirits, are busy plotting the death of some one, thus they live in a continual state of fear, and more horrible because the agents are invisible – the dread dispensers of spells and charms.
>
> No white child is more frightened of the dark than the biggest warrior that ever transfixed a man. They never stir from the camp after sunset and even if they go 50 yards they . . . carry a lighted stick . . . on no account will they allow the various camp fires to become extinct.[286]

There were lamps lit in the gaol and fires in the yards. However, little light would have reached into the solitary cells.

The number of Aboriginal people in the city increased in the early part of 1842. Klose (pronounced *Klozey*), the missionary who had arrived after Teichelmann and Shurmann and now taught at the Piltawodli school, recorded many of the comings and goings of the 'Adelaide Tribe' and also kept an eye on the other groups. He wrote in his diary on 4 December 1841 that the 'Adelaide Tribe' had left for the bush:

> Sad at heart I watched them go but believed they would not stay away long, but would soon return to Adelaide. In Willunga and in the region of Ngangkiparri... they stayed until 1st March... (no-one in schoolroom all that time).[287]

While the local Aboriginal people were away 'a crowd of other tribes moved in from the North, from the Murray [and] from the east'. When the 'Adelaiders' came back, a large number then arrived from Encounter Bay and Lake Alexandrina 'so that there were more than 500 natives altogether'.[288] In the same letter, Klose wrote that when the groups visit 'they never leave again without spear or fights'. In April 1842 the Adelaide Aboriginal people went to Holdfast Bay (Glenelg) to watch a spear fight between the 'Murrays' and the 'Encounter Bays'.

> An old enmity exists between the Murray and Encounter Bay natives, whose origin they cannot explain, but only practice revenge for the last wounds received.[289]

These ritualised 'battles' that the settlers were now beginning to see were fierce and skillful. However, unlike British battles, a single fatality signified the loser. This particular battle ended with a fatality in the 'Encounter Bay Tribe'. They returned to Encounter Bay (Victor Harbour) and the victors, the 'Murray Tribe', came into Adelaide to camp. The 'Adelaide Tribe', traditional enemies of the 'Murray Tribe', took to the hills and 'only on 5 April did I again see a few children in the Lokation [sic]'.[290]

At the end of the year of 1842, on December 23, it was the 'Murray Tribe' who lost a 'battle' with seven wounded and one killed.[291] They came into the city to bury the slain man in the bed of the Torrens River. After the fight Klose wrote:

> [O]ur natives went off with the Enc Bay natives to the Ngankiparri river... So now I am again without any school children.[292]

The next day Cawthorne wrote of the burial in the bed of the Torrens where the Aboriginal people said 'Whitefella (meaning all people assembled there) you go away'.[293]

Indigenous people seemed to be in large part unimpressed with white society, and some tried to ignore the settlers and continue a traditional life. However the influx of the Europeans, the loss of wildlife, the introduction of liquor, and the pollution of the river made the impact on them hard to ignore. For the 'Adelaide Tribe' the impact was particularly severe as the settlers had landed right in their country. Now other tribes were here as well. They were to keep coming, partly for benefits of rations they saw the 'Adelaide Tribe' receiving, partly to keep tabs on the newcomers and partly probably out of curiosity.[294] Some of this was traditional visiting however a lot was new. Some, such as visiting Adelaide on the Queen's Birthday, became a 'new tradition'.

Ashton made no comment on what was happening with the Aboriginal people. Nonetheless, it was within the Adelaide gaol that those from all the various Aboriginal groups who sought to retaliate when the frontier reached them, or who in any other way transgressed British law, were collected. In just one sitting of the Supreme Court (in July 1842) five Aboriginal prisoners were brought before the judge: Moorpar, Nantes and Nweba, all from Port Lincoln, on charges of assault, spearing and driving away sheep, stealing a blanket and stealing a bag of flour, assault and inducing fear by aiming a spear; Monicha, charged with stealing a silver watch; and Boccomola alias Karri alias Turle Kurree charged with stealing from a station hut at St Peters and attempted murder.[295] By September 1842 Klose would record a total of '12 Aboriginal prisoners in the new Gaol – 4 locals, 4 Murray, 2 Encounter Bay, 2 Port Lincoln'.[296]

June 28 Tuesday: This Morning the Sheriff Visited the Gaol. - Thomas Hodges brot in for Debt by Jones.   43

July 2 Saturday: Received the Printed lists of Prisoners for Trial Next week.   44

July 3 Sunday: the Nurse left Sarah Green this day having been with her a Week – Mr Fleming & Mr Benson Attended the Gaol this Afternoon divine Service at 3½. 44

July 4 Monday: Sarah Green was taken Ill this Afternoon Sent for Dr. Nash And – took the Printed Lists Round. 43

July 5 Tuesday: the Sessions Commenced this day No Prisoners Tried. 43

July 6 Wednesday: at the Sessions All Day. 43

July 7 Thursday: at the Sessions. 45

July 8 Friday – at the Sessions. 44

July 9 Saturday: At the Sessions 2 Natives tried this day for Attempt to Murder Death was Recorded against them. – A Native in Solitary Confinement for one Week from this day. 45

July 10 Sunday: the Rev'd Mr. Farrell and Mr. Benson attended the Gaol divine Service at 3½ OC'k. 45

July 11 Monday: at the Sessions all day Alex'r Johnson for Uttering forged Notes was Aquitted Stevenson for an Attempt to Murder was Ordered by the Court to be detained until next Sessions. 46

July 12 Tuesday: at the Sessions all day Fred'k M. Scott for forgery was Aquitted – the Court was Adjourned to 11 OC'k to Morrow Morning to the Judges Chambers. 43

July 13 Wednesday: Hughes for forgery in his Own Bail to Appear within Six Months if Call'd on this under the Sessions. 41

July 15 Friday: The Native was taken out of Solitary Confinement this Evening having been in a Week – Williamson alias Green in Gaol for hard Labour was put into Solitary Confinement for Abusive Language to the TurnKey at 11 OC'k this Morning he was taken out of the Solitary Cell at 6 P.M. on his promising not to Offend again 2 Women was Sentenced this day by the R Magistrate to 14 days Solitary Confinement. 42

July 16 Saturday: the Sheriff Visited the Gaol this Afternoon and the Prisoners in Solitary Confinement and the others. 41

July 17 Sunday: Mr. Fleming and Mr. Benson Attended the Gaol divine Service at 3½ – in the afternoon. 41

July 19 Tuesday: His Excellency was this day pleased through the Sheriff to Pardon John Cullens Convicted of Stealing a Calf and was Sentenced to Transportation for life - His Excellency was also pleased to Commute the Sentence of Edw'd Saddler to 10 Years Transportation James Smith - George Morris Joseph Thomson & George Davey Each to 10 Years Transportation they having had Death Recorded Against them with the exception of Saddler who was Sentenced to Transportation for Life. 41

July 20 Wednesday: Received orders to put the Prisoners on Board the Challenger when Ready for Sea to be transported to V.D. Land. 39

July 22 Friday: I left the Gaol this Morning at 10¼ with the following Prisoners under Sentence of Transportation to V.D. Land.
    1. Joseph Thompson
    2. George Davey
    3. David Wilmot
    4. James Smith
    5. George Morris
    6. Edward Saddler

I arrived at the Port at 11½ A.M. and after inspecting the Accommodation and Provisions put the Prisoners on board the Schooner Challenger Capt'n Tapley for Hobart Town then Shortly after hove out into the Stream - and I Returned to Town at 4½ P.M. 4 Mounted Police went to the Port with Me as Guard - W.B. Ashton - Governor of Gaol 33

July 24 Sunday: The Rev'd Mr. Howard and Mr. Benson Attended the Gaol divine Service at 3½ P.M. 32

July 26 Tuesday: Eliza Brand was Sentenced to One Weeks Solitary Confinement for Absconding from the Service of Capt'n O'Halloran or pay a fine of £2-8-6. 33

July 27 Wednesday: the Sheriff Visited the Gaol this afternoon. - Dr. Nash. 33

July 28 Thursday: Mary Aldridge & May Smith was discharged this day at 1 OC'k P.M. having been in Solitary Confinement 14 days. 33

July 30 Saturday: at 8 OC'k this Morning Monicha the Native was put in Solitary Confinement – being his last week. 30

July 31 Sunday: Mr. Fleming & Mr. Benson Attended the Gaol Yesterday afternoon divine Service at 3½ P.M. 30

August 2 Tuesday: a Man was Committed to take his Trial on Rape on Hannah Hoare at Mount Barker. 30

August 3 Wednesday: John Smith was discharged this day having been in Gaol 12 Months. 30

August 5 Friday: the Native Named Monicha was Whipped this day at 12 OC'k Noon as Sentenced at the last Gaol delivery – he Received 75 Lashes in front of the Gaol in presence of the Sheriff Mr. Moorhouse and a great No of People – T.L. Scown (Debtor) was taken to the Insolvent Court & was discharged 2nd hearing. 30

The next day the *South Australian Register* reported:

> Yesterday ... Monitya the native man who was sentenced ... to one months imprisonment and a public whipping for stealing a watch ... underwent the latter part of his punishment in a triangle erected in front of the Jail. Several hundreds of persons were present, among whom we regretted to observe, a considerable proportion of women. ... secured to the triangle [he] received fifty lashes of a cat-o'nine tails, which he bore with considerable fortitude ... A considerable number of the aborigines of both sexes were present.[297]

Existing scarring on Monitya's back, the result of traditional tattooing, was reported to have protected him like a coat of leather from the worst of the flogging. Perhaps it was for this reason that the sheriff ordered 25 more lashes, making 75 in total.

August 7 Sunday: The Rev'd Mr. Howard & Mr. Benson Attended the Gaol divine Service at 3½ P.M. 23

August 13 Saturday: 2 Sailors Named Sutherland and Williams was Sent to the Port this day with 2 of the Mounted Police by order of Capt'n Lipson to Join their Ships. 27

August 14 Sunday - Mr. Fleming & Mr. Benson Attended the Gaol this day divine Service at 3½ P.M. 25

August 15 Monday: William Evans was brot to Gaol for Debt by Jones Sheriffs Officer he was Very Ill and was Allowed to Stay in the Turnkeys Lodge Dr. Nash was Sent for who Came and Saw him. 27

August 16 Tuesday: Evans Still Very Ill the Rev'd Mr. Farrell Came and Saw him and Also Saw Sarah Green Dr. Nash Visited Evans. 29

August 17 Wednesday: Dr. Nash Visited Evans John Wilson discharged this day having been in Gaol 3 Months for Assault. 29

August 18 Thursday: William Evans Still Very Ill Dr. Nash Visited him - and he was discharged by order of the Insolvent Court he having found Bail. This afternoon - he had been Supplied with one Bottle of Port wine during the time he was in Gaol. 28

August 20 Saturday: I left Town Yesterday at 10 OC'k P.M. and Returned this Afternoon and found things Correct in the Gaol. 27

August 21 Sunday - Mr. Fleming & Mr. Benson Attended the Gaol this day divine Service at 3½ in the Afternoon. 27

August 25 Thursday: William Couzens was brot to Gaol for Debt this Morning by Jones Sheriffs Officer. 27

August 26 Friday: Received from the Superintendant of Emigrants 5 Loads of Fire Wood weighing in all 13400 lbs Yesterday. 27

August 27 Saturday: Received a Letter from the Colonial Storekeeper Stating that we was to Continue to Receive the fresh Meat from Mr Pepperill untill the end of the Present Month. 27

August 28 Sunday: Mr. Fleming & Mr. Benson Attended the Gaol divine Service at 3½ P.M. 27

August 29 Monday: 2 Prisoners brot to Gaol on Warrants for Assault at 6½ P.M. by P.C. Norris. 29

August 31 Wednesday: The Sheriff Visited the Gaol this Afternoon. 29

September 1 Thursday – Certified this day Couzens's (the Debtor) Petition to the Insolvent Court. 30

September 4 Sunday: Mr. Benson (only) Attended the Gaol Service at 3½ P.M. The Rev'd Mr. Howard Sent word that he was too unwell to Attend. 30

September 5 Monday: a Private Named Thomas Wilson of the 96 Reg' for deserting Sentenced to 2 Months Hard Labour except the 1st & last 14 days which is to be in Solitary Confinement. 31

September 7 Wednesday: Dr. Nash did not Visit the Soldier (Thomas Wilson) in Solitary Confinement this day. 30

September 8 Thursday: George Stevenson of North Adelaide was brot to the Gaol for Debt – on 2 Cases at 8¾ A.M. by Borr Sheriffs Officer. 31

September 10 Saturday: Mr. George Stevenson (in Gaol for Debt) was dis'd this day by order of the Sheriff. 31

September 11 Sunday: Mr. Fleming & Mr. Benson Attended the Gaol this day divine Service at 3½ P.M. 2 Soldiers belong'g to the 96th Regiment was brought to the Gaol this Evening by the Mounted Police they having been Sentenced one to 7 days for Drunkenness the other to 3 Months for an Assault. Committed by Mr. Eyre Resident Magistrate at Moorunde – it Appears that those Men was detained at the Police Barracks all last Night. 32

September 12 Monday: Call'd at the Barracks this day about the Soldiers Relative to the discharge. 31

September 13 The Sheriff Visited the Gaol this day His Excellency was pleased to Remit the fine on John Williams this day and he was discharged the Prisoner was in Gaol for absconding from the Hawk Capt'n Brown. 31

September 15 Thursday: Mr. Moorhouse Call'd at the Gaol and Saw the Natives. 29

September 18 Sunday: The Soldier Named Thomas Wilson was this Morning taken out of Solitary Confinement and put in the felons Yard. Lieut. Huganan Saw the Soldier Named Dilby The Reverend. Mr. Farrell & Mr. Benson Attended the Gaol this day divine Service at 3½. 29

September 19 Monday: The Sheriff Visited the Gaol this Afternoon. 29

September 21 Wednesday: Several Loads of fire wood was Sent us for the use of the Gaol by the Sup't of Emigrants. 29

September 23 Friday: Several Loads of Wood was Sent by the Sup't of the Emigrants. 29

September 24 Saturday: James Austin - Debtor Sentenced by the Insolvent Court to 6 Month Imprisonment the time to Commence from the 24th March last was Discharged this Morning having Completed his Sentence. - In Consequence of Several of the Prisoners in the felons Yard informing Me that the Prisoner Named Douglas (Charged with Attempt to Murder) had Asked them to get their friends to bring him in Some Poison, I thought it Proper to put him in One of the Cells Out of the Yard, at the Same Time Allowing him to Walk at times between the walls. - James Leon & Long both brought to Gaol for Debt by John Borr Sheriffs Officer. 31

September 25 Sunday: Mr. Fleming & Mr. Benson Attended the Gaol this day divine Service at 3½ P.M. 30

September 28 Wednesday: Andrew Murray was brot to Gaol for Debt by Borr Sheriffs Officer and Katamio a Native Committed for Trial by G.C. Hawker Esq. J.P. for Killing a Calf the Property of Charles Campbell of Adelaide. 32

October 1 Saturday: John William Spicer (Attorney) was brot to Gaol this Morning at 6¼ A.M. Committed for Trial for the Wilful Murder of George Jefferay Spicer was Committed last Night by the Coroner and brot to the Gaol this Morning. 32

October 2 Sunday: the Rev'd Mr. Howard & Mr. Benson Attended at the Gaol this day divine Service at 3½ P.M. 31

October 4 Tuesday: Mary Ann Smith was this day Sentenced to 3 days Solitary Confinement for being Drunk. 32

October 5 Wednesday: The Native Named Nante from Port Lincoln was Whipped this day in front of the Gaol and discharged according to his Sentence at the last Sessions he was taken way by Mr. Moorhouse [and] the Sheriff. Mr. Moorhouse and Myself Present. - 2 of the Mounted & 6 of the foot Police in attendance Whipped by a Man Named William Hopkins The Native Received 75 lashes. 32

> At 12 o'clock, *Nante* was brought out of the gaol, and tied up to a triangle erected at about one hundred yards from the front of the gate, where he received 75 lashes.[298]

Moorhouse commented on this incident in his next quarterly report:

> Corporal punishment does not appear to be dreaded So much as transportation, they are accustomed to Severe bodily afflictions amongst themselves at tattooing.[299]

October 6 Thursday: Andrew Murray was discharged by order of the Insolvent Court - he having found Bail. 30

October 7 Friday: last Night in Consequence of So Many of the Panes of Glass being broken in the Kitchen Windows in the felons Yard and not being able to find out who broke them I had the frames taken out and put into the Store Room for Safety. - Couzens a debtor was this day taken to the Insolvent Court and was Remanded to Friday next the 14th. 28

October 9 Sunday: Wainwright alias Yorke was discharged at 9 OC'k this Morning Mr. Fleming & Mr. Benson Attended the Gaol this Day divine Service at 3½ P.M. 28

October 10 Monday: At the Stores this day for the Quarters Rations and etc Received all except the Vinegar & Lamp Cotton. 27

October 12 Wednesday: the Sheriff Visited the Gaol this Afternoon and wished Me to give Yorke a Pair of Trousers and a Shirt was given him last Sunday he having None to Wear. 28

October 13 Thursday: About 4½ P.M. a Quantity of the Bricks was blown from the Wall on to the Roof of the Females Room No other damage done except a great Many of the Bricks Very broken. 28

October 14 Friday: A Man named John S...y was brot to Gaol Charged with felony from Port Lincoln - Received this day from Thomas Wallace 12 Bushels of Limes as ordered by the Sheriff Yesterday. 30

October 16 Sunday: The Rev'd Mr. Howard and Mr. Benson Attended the Gaol Yesterday Afternoon divine Service at 3½ Mr. Howard was taken Unwell in the Middle of the Service and was Obliged to leave. 31

October 19 Wednesday: a Man was Sent from the Colonial Engineers to Repair the Pump, & the Water Closet in My house. 30

October 20 Thursday: the Sheriff Visited the Gaol this afternoon. 30

October 23 Sunday: Mr Benson only attended the Gaol this day Service at 3 P.M. Thomas Wilson the Soldier was put into Solitary Confinement to under go the last 14 days Punishment. 29

October 24 Monday: Wilson was taken Rather unwell he was Allowed to walk in the a.m for a Short Time. 29

October 25 Tuesday: Dr. Nash Visited Wilson And Stated that he thought he would not be able to undergo the 14 Days Solitary Confinement. 29

October 28 Friday: The Sheriff Visited the Gaol this afternoon. 30

October 30 Sunday: The Rev'd Mr Howard and Mr Benson Attended divine Service at 3½ P.M. During divine Service 3 Bed & 3 Rugs was burned in the Females Yard Caused by the Wind blowing the fire about the Yard the beds was left out to air. 29

October 31 Monday - Charles Gruland (Committed for Trial) was Violently Assaulted by Thomas Stewart (also Committed for

Trial) with a Belt with a Buckle. - I had Stewart put in one of the Solitary Cells where he Shortly Afterward hung himself he was discovered and taken down by Perry the TurnKey, Nearly Dead, I sent for Dr S... who Came and Bled and Shortly after Dr Nash Arrived - Douglas and Wilson have Charge of him. 29

November 1 Tuesday: Stewart Much better this day, Douglas & Wilson Still with him. 28

November 2 Wednesday: Took James Arthur to the Supreme Court on a Habius on a trial against him by Mr. Pearce for a Libel - a Verdict against Arthur Damages £250 - brot him back to Gaol at 6½ P.M. 28

November 4 Friday: James Arthur in Gaol under the Insolvent Act for Defrauding his Creditors and Sentenced to 18 Months Imprisonment his time Expired this Morning but he Knowing the Sheriffs Officer was Outside to Arrest him again Refused to leave the Debtors Yard The Officer therefore Arrested him in the Yard at the Suit of William Pearce for the Sum of £250. 28

November 5 Saturday: His Honor the Judge and the Sheriff Visited the Gaol this day went all over the Yards. 28

November 6 Sunday: Mr. Fleming & Mr. Benson Attended the Gaol this day divine Service at 3½ P.M. 27

November 7 Monday: Round with the Calendars this day. 27

November 8 Tuesday: the Sessions Commenced this day At the Court all day. 28

November 9 Wednesday: Sessions all day. 26

November 10 Thursday: ditto 27

November 11 Friday: ditto 29

November 12 Saturday: ditto 29

November 13 Sunday: The Rev'd Mr. Howard Mr. Fleming & Mr. Benson Attended the Gaol divine Service at 3½ P.M. 29

November 14 Monday: At the Sessions. 29

November 15 Tuesday: ditto 30

November 16 Wednesday: ditto 29

Ashton seems to have had a lot to do with ensuring the calendar, or list of prisoners to be tried or sentenced, was delivered to the court. No details of these particular sessions are included in the journal, except that we know Katamio was to be tried for killing a calf. The *Southern Australian*'s court reporter told of the outcome:

> Tuesday, November 15, 1842. The native *Katamio* was placed this day again at the bar to receive his sentence, which was, that he be 'transported beyond the seas for the term of ten years'.[300]

Katamio had been committed for trial, as per the journal entry, on 28 September 1842. Over a year later, on 12 December 1843, we are to find it recorded in the journal that this same prisoner was granted a free pardon and taken by Moorhouse to the Location. Aboriginal people were often known by a number of aliases and Ashton this next time recorded him as Kurti Mukarta. The offence and the timing are however the same. Moorhouse also recorded the pardon under the different name.[301] The existence of a sentence of transportation for an Aboriginal person was a harsh fact of the time and being an Aboriginal person in prison for a year, expecting transportation to be your fate, would have been punishment in the extreme.

There were to be yet more Aboriginal people sentenced to transportation. These sentences also were not carried through.

November 17 Thursday: John William Spiers Trial Commenced this Morning at ½ past 8 OC'k A.M. The Court Adjourned at 8½ P.M. till 9 OC'k ToMorrow Morning. 29

[In margin]
For the Wilful Murder of George Jeffery his Servant in Adelaide.

November 18 Friday - Spiers Trial on at 9 OC'k A.M. - Court Adjourned 8 P.M. to 9 OC'k to Morrow Morning. 30

November 19 Saturday: Spiers Trial on at 9 A.M. and lasted till 7 OC'k P.M. when he was Acquitted Sessions ended this day. 30

November 20 Sunday: Mr. Fleming and Mr. Benson Attended this Day divine Service at at 3½ P.M. 29

November 21 Monday: Received a Letter this Evening from the Sheriff Stating that His Excellency had been Pleased through the Judge to Pardon James Stevenson alias Douglas found Guilty last Week of Shooting with Intent etc Death had been Recorded against him - the Sheriff Visited the Gaol this Afternoon. 29

November 22 Tuesday: James Stevenson was Discharged this Morning at 9 OC'k. 30

November 24 Thursday: Jane Miles Discharged this Morning having been in Gaol 14 days. 30

November 25 Friday: William Couzens was discharged at 9 OC'k this Morning having been in Gaol 3 Months as per Sentence of the Insolvent Court for Defrauding his Creditors. 29

November 27 Sunday: the Rev'd Mr Howard attended the Gaol also Mr Benson divine Service at 3½ P.M. 28

November 28 Monday: the Sheriff Call'd at the Gaol this Morning. I left the Gaol at 10½ OC'k this Morning for the Port with they following Prisoners under Sentence of Transportation
Viz - William Kay alias Yorke
John Hackett
Thomas Stewart
Charles Hall
Arrived with them at the Port at 12 OC'k Noon and put them on Board the Dorset at 4 P.M. Capt'n Walsh - to be taken to Hobart Town V.D. Land - Philip Hyde also under Sentence of Transp'n Remains here for the Present. Arrived at the Gaol at 7 P.M. Escorted to the Port by Mr. Insp'r Gordon and 4 of the Mounted Police. 30

November 30 Wednesday: The Womans was Creating a Disturbance in the Yard, I had Sarah Green and Mary Ann Davy put in the Cells for the Night and etc 24

December 1 Thursday: This Morning at 9 OC'k Sarah Green and Mary Ann Davy having Stated that they was Sorry for Creating the Disturbance last Night and Promising Not to do the Same again they was taken out the Cells and put into the Females Yard. 26

December 4 Sunday: Mr Fleming & Mr Benson Attended the Gaol this day. Divine Service at 3 P.M. Thomas Jones (a Debtor) was taken Very Ill this Morning at 7½ Oc'k he was in Strong fits for Several hours Dr Nash was Sent for but he being Unwell Dr Wyatt Attended. - Jones was better in the Evening 3 of the Prisoners in for hard labour was left in his Room all Night in case of the fits Returning. 24

December 5 Monday - Jones was much better this Morning - Received Notice this afternoon that the Military Guard will leave the Gaol to Morrow Morning at 6 OC'k & be Supplied by 3 of the foot Police. 26

December 6 Tuesday: 3 of the Police Came on Duty at 6 OC'k this Morning and the Military Guard left. 26

December 8 Thursday: John K... was discharged this Morning having been in Solitary Confinement for one Month - The Sheriff and Mr. H.W. Newenham Visited the Gaol this Afternoon Saw they Prisoners and went Round the Gaol. 26

December 10 Saturday: Joseph Glass under Sentence of One Months hard Labour Refused to help in Cutting Wood Saying he was Ill Dr. Nash Saw him and Ordered him to have a Blister on each Shoulder but which he Refused to have on Stating that he would not be Able to Work when he left the Gaol. 25

December 11 Sunday: The Rev'd Mr Howard and Mr. Benson Attended at the Gaol Yesterday divine Service at 3½ P.M. 25

December 12 Monday: about 1 OC'k this Morning the Chimney in the TurnKeys Lodge Caught fire and burnt for Near an hour it was put out by going on the top of the house and throwing water down. Reported to the Sheriff this Morning that they female Prisoners Could not Attend divine Service for the want of Clothing. 25

December 15 Thursday: Patrick McMann Sentenced in Nov'r Sessions 1842 to 2 Months Imprisonment for an Assault on Borr Sheriffs Officer was this day Pardoned by His Excellency and Discharged. 25

December 16 Friday: None. The Soldiers Returned to the Gaol duty at 11 OC'k A.M. and they Police left the Gaol. 24

December 18 Sunday: Mr. Fleming & Mr. Benson attended the Gaol, divine Service at 3½ P.M. 24

December 19 Monday: went to the Port this Afternoon left Mrs Stewart on Board the Emma for Hobart Town Arrived at home at 6 P.M. Jacob Hart was brought in for Debt by Borr Sheriffs Officer. 25

December 20 Tuesday: Hart as above Petitioned the Insolvent Court this day. 25

December 21 Wednesday: Mary Lowe was brought to Gaol Sentenced to 3 day Solitary Confinement – and Jane Slackford Remanded to the 27th. The Sheriff Visited the Gaol this Afternoon went over the Yards. 27

December 25 Sunday: c/- Christmas day the Prisoners had a 1 lb of Beef each and a pint of Porter. 27

Once again, Ashton provided a proper Christmas dinner to the prisoners. It was almost the end of another year, and then – another successful escape from the new gaol. This time it was spur of the moment, a very fast runner through two open gates.

December 28 Wednesday – George Dyer a Prisoner Committed for Trial for felony Made his Escape under the following circumstances Perry was outside the Gaol getting wood with Some Prisoners – Molineux opened the Gate of the felons Yard to let Dyer Get a Bucket of Water when the Prisoner Runs Out & Round the Gaol he past Close to the Tower where they Military Guard Saw him but they had no Pieces loaded the Prisoner was pursued by Molineux to the River where he presented his Gun at him but it would not go off Perry & 3 Soldiers followed Dyer to Bowden when they lost Sight of him, either in the bend of the River or Among the houses he is Supposed to have Made for the Port or the Reed Beds The foot, Mounted, and the Port Police are informed of Dyers Escape and he being well Known I have no Doubt but he will be Soon

> Retaken it was against my Orders that Dyer was let out of the Yard at all but the Water being Close to the Gate Molineux let him out without thinking of it. 26
>
> **December 29** Thursday: Saw Mr. Tolmer about Dyer and Arranged with to go the Bay at day light toMorrow Morning. 27
>
> **December 30** Friday: left the Gaol this morning at 5 OC'k in Company of Mr Tolmer taking Gruland (a Prisoner) with Me to point out a Boat at the Bay that Dyer was Supposed to Attempt to get away in we found a Boat a long way up the Beach that any person Could easily get off in but heard nothing of Dyer Returned to the Gaol at 9½ AM with Gruland. 27

Again there was no immediate newspaper reporting of the escape. There are two official letters in the government files, one from the sheriff suggesting dismissal of Molineux for not following orders, and suggesting a reprimand for Ashton for not being present when the outside gate was open; and a reply on behalf of the governor of the colony taking a milder course of issuing a warning to all the guards to be more careful in future.[302] The first newspaper report I can find is when Dyer was recaptured. It seems to be the only one:

> About nine or ten months ago an American black named Dyer, who had come to this colony as a cook on a vessel, was taken into custody with no less than four robberies, having three times broken in to Mr Whistler's house at Unley ... Shortly after he was lodged in Gaol, the gates opened to admit firewood, and Dyer who was employed getting water in the inner court, watched his opportunity, slipped out, and being a remarkably swift runner he was soon out of sight. He then seized a boat ... at the Onkaparinga and went over to Kangaroo Island. ... returned to the mainland ... police have been in constant pursuit.[303]

The article goes on to explain that the police eventually received information that led them to Chain of Ponds, where a dog sniffed Dyer out. Dyer jumped into the river to make his escape and shed his clothing in a desperate attempt to slip free, but one of the police officers wounded Dyer with his sword, and he was taken in.

One 1919 article and two centenary-year articles look back on the escape with additional and different details, maybe based on fact, maybe embellished.[304]

There are a number of further entries in the journal concerning Dyer, such as when information was received about him (journal entries 29 January 1843 and 16 May 1843), when he was re-taken and his wounds attended (journal entries 12 and 17 September 1843) and when he was finally taken to the Port to be transported to Van Diemen's Land (journal entry 1 April 1844).

December 31 Saturday: at 11 OC'k this Night the Prisoners for hard Labour in No 5 Cell was Singing and Making a Great Noise they was told by Kennedy to be Quite 3 times but paid No Attention to him I went to them Myself When they left off making a Noise I Stoped their Meat for 3 days. They Prisoners Making the Noise were Ilbery - Iron - Rogers - Hutchinson - Glass - and Noulan the Soldier. 27

The governor's journal 1843

Some of the most compelling writings on early Adelaide are those of the young William Cawthorne.[305] Having arrived in Adelaide in May 1842 as a well-travelled 17-year-old, he lived with his mother in Morphett Street behind Trinity Church; his father was a ship's captain and so was away at sea. Cawthorne had no emotional attachment to England, nor love of the British, nor any time or sympathy for the German missionaries. He was reportedly lonely in Adelaide and fascinated by the lives and weapons of the Aboriginal people. He was a talented artist and observer. In October 1842 he began a sketchbook and diary that now provides a view of the Aboriginal people on the banks of the Torrens less than a mile from his house. He could see the gaol from his upstairs window and watched people flocking to the 'sad spectacle' of the hanging of the Aboriginal man Ngarbi in August 1843.

By the start of 1843 Cawthorne had already written of encampments, corroborees, fights, a burial, and initiation ceremonies, all occurring on the banks of the Torrens. For example, in December 1842 he wrote:

> 17 December. This evening a fray [took] place amongst the blacks who were encamped 4 or 500 yards from us on the banks of the River. I quickly put on my clothes and roved amongst them.[306]
>
> 21 December. This morning there was a stir among the blacks ... They are encamped from my place about a furlong, just on the other

side of the River ... When I came to the spot, what a scene. What an indescribable scene ... I saw about a hundred blacks, naked and armed, with the long and short spears, with their fierce looking shields, cutting the most extravagant capers, running to and fro, talking, laughing, pretending to fight, yelling etc, which all combined together produced a terrible and curious scene.[307]

On 22 December he described an initiation taking place in the river bed, noting the different but equally painful practices of the Mount Barker and Adelaide groups. He concluded this entry by saying 'Well keep me from being a blackfellow!'.[308]

On 27 January 1843 he wrote:

Nearly all the Mount Barker tribe are down at Adelaide now and have been for some time ... The other night they being encamped above the bridge, a policeman came with orders to burn all their wurlies, or huts, which was done, and the whole tribe had to decamp and it was a rather curious sight to [see] them all go, some angry, some laughing, some sullen, some jeering at the police ... The reason for them burning them out was because they swam and made the water so dirty above the hole where the whole town was supplied from. Still I thought it was hard, that the real possessors of the land could not make a fire where they liked.[309]

None of this is mentioned in Ashton's journal, however the reaction of settlers and officials to the Aboriginal people in the colony, and vice versa, provides a necessary context for some of what happens in the gaol in 1843.

The journal for 1843 begins.

January 1 Sunday & New Years day: They Prisoners in the felons Yard refused to attend divine Service Mr Fleming attended No Service Mr Benson attended had Service at 3P.M.   27

January 2 Monday: the above Prisoners except Iron refused to fetch the Wood in Consequence of their Meat being Stoped.   27

January 3 Tuesday: the Prisoners as above Saw the Sheriff about them he Said he would Come to the Gaol and See them to Morrow Morning. 28

January 4 Wednesday: the Sheriff Visited the Gaol Saw they Prisoners who all Consented Work except Rogers who told us he would not work. 30

January 5 Thursday - a dreadful dusty day Several times it was quite Dark with the dust - at 7 P.M was obliged to lock the Prisoners up in Consequence of the wind and dust Jones the debtor in fits had him in the TurnKeys lodge all Night. 30

Adelaide during this period was a dustbowl or, if it rained, a quagmire. Streets – always considered by the early settlers to be excessively wide – had been cleared, and the parklands were also on their way to being almost totally stripped of trees. Cawthorne describes a similar day just weeks later:

> Horrible dusty day. I only wish I could describe an Adelaide dusty day as it actually is. If I say dust comes in the houses so as to nearly choke you. If I say that dust, after a squall, lays thick on everything and in every part of the houses. If I say that dust makes you black, makes housekeepers savage, others sullen, others obstinate, others in a frenzy, others in despair, others mad, others desperate.[310]

January 8 Sunday: No divine Service this day in Consequence of Minister [not] Attending the Gaol etc. 26

January 10 Tuesday: the first General Quarter Sessions was held this day at the Supreme Court House His Honor C. Cooper Esq'r Chairman when they following Prisoners were disposed of - Jane Slackford - Acquitted - Robert Conner - 7 Years Transportation - Patrick Fitzgerald - Acquitted - and James MacKie - put off untill the General Gaol Delivery in March next Commenced this Morning at 10 OC'k and Closed at 4 OC'k P.M. 27

January 11 Wednesday: James MacKie was this day Bailed to Appear at the Gaol delivery (to be held on the 14th March next) by His Honour the Judge. 26

January 15 Sunday: Mr. Fleming & Mr Benson Attended the Gaol divine Service at 3½ P.M. 26

January 16 Monday: left the Gaol this Afternoon at 4¼ OC'k with Robert Conner under Sentence of Transportation for 7 Years – put him on board the Challenger Capt'n Long at the Port and left the Prisoner in Charge of Mr. Partridge Constable of Hobart-Town to be taken to Hobart-Town by him. Returned to the Gaol at 9½ P.M. 27

January 20 Friday: Jones the Debtor was this day taken to the Insolvent Court and was discharged his first hearing. 27

January 21 Saturday: a Native of Adelaide was this day Committed for Trial felony. 28

January 22 Sunday: The Rev'd Mr. Howard and Mr. Benson attended at the Gaol this Afternoon divine Service at 3½. 27

January 24 Tuesday: Mr. Wigley the Visiting Justice Visited the Gaol this day for the first time with the Sheriff & Mr. Phipson Went all over the Gaol.
Mr. Moorhouse Visited Tommy a Native. Ill. 28

January 25 Wednesday: Mr. Moorhouse Visited the Native – he was Very Ill I had his Irons taken off That he Might walk about a little. 28

January 26 Thursday: George Gandy brought this day a Load of fire wood – and one he brought on the 24th Last which he had weighed about a Ton each Load we had no way of weighing the Wood. 30

January 27 Friday: Received a letter this day from the Sheriff about the quantity of Water used in the Gaol there are altogether in the Gaol Using water 55 for using etc We have 2 Loads a day Making the expense for All the Gaol 1s/10d daily. 29

January 28 Saturday: the Sheriff showed me a letter from the Colonial Secretary that Perrys Money was to be £1-9-1 per week and not £1-11 – as he have been Receiving Since the 1st of January 1843. 29

January 29 Sunday: Mr. Benson only attended at the Gaol this day he had Service at 3 P.M. Received Information about Dyer (who made his escape a Short time ago) Perry the TurnKey was out all day which led us to Suppose he Can be taken at day light to Morrow Morning – and have Made Arrangements for Perry to go with the Mounted Police after him. 29

January 30 Monday: Received a letter this day from the Sheriff informing Me that Perrys Money would be £1-9-1 in place of £1-11. 30

January 31 Tuesday: Mr. Wigley Visited the Gaol this day No Complaint for him to hear. 30

February 3 Friday: the Dresses & Callico Shoes etc was given out to Elizabeth Davy, Mary Ann Davy & Sarah Green – allowed by the Government and Sent to the Gaol by Mr. Nation. 30

February 5 Sunday: Mr. Fleming & Mr. Benson Attended at the Gaol this day divine Service at 3½ P.M. 30

February 7 Tuesday: Mr. Wigley Visited the Gaol No Complaint for him to hear – a Native Call'd Williamy was this day Sentenced to 7 days Solitary Confinement for Assault. 33

February 9 Thursday: James Arthur in Gaol for Debt was this day discharged by order of the Sheriff having been in Gaol altogether above 21 Months. 33

February 10 Friday: Eliz'th Davy in place of Making herself a Chift of the Callico Given to her She Cut it up for a Petticoat When Mrs. Ashton Spoke to her about the Same She Swore and made use of Very Abusive Language On my Return home She was Abusive to me. I had her put into a Solitary Cell – after She had been in the Cell about one hour She beg pardon was expressed her Sorrow for what She had done and having a Young Child I allowed her to go into the Female Ward again. 32

Charlotte Ashton was very much involved in the care of the women and it could be a thankless task. The scene described above is easy to imagine: the act of defiance by a woman more attuned to dressing in frills than in gaol garb. She was to be pitied for her situation though; she had brought an infant with her into the gaol, her eldest daughter was a fellow prisoner and her husband George had been transported. William Ashton did punish her briefly for her abusive language then quickly allowed her to return to her children in the women's ward showing regard for her plight. As her infant grew he requested rations be supplied (as we see from his journal entry on 15 March 1843).

February 11 Saturday: Mr. Moorhouse and a Gentleman Visited they Natives in Gaol this day. 31

February 12 Sunday: Mr. Fleming Attended the Gaol this day divine Service at 3½ P.M. Mr. Benson did not attend. 31

February 13 Monday: Gottlieb Weisman was this day Committed for Trial for an Aggravated Assault on a child named Sarah Ann Elliott aged 5 Years. Dr Nash Visited the Gaol and Saw Several of they Prisoners. 31

February 14 Tuesday: Mr. Wigley and the Sheriff Visited the Gaol this day found All Right - a Man from the Colonial Engineers Department was down doing the Pump & Doors & also the Steps leading to the Chapel. 29

February 15 Wednesday: the Lock was put on the front door this day. 29

February 17 Friday: Sent Eliz'th Davy - Mary Ann Davy - and Sarah Greens Petition this Morning to the Sheriff by Kennedy - Mr Moorhouse Attended at the Gaol this morning and took the Names of the Natives. 30

After visiting the gaol Moorhouse wrote to the lawyer Mr Fisher asking that he defend the five Aboriginal prisoners due for trial: three, King John alias Merrainmalla, Jimmy alias Yuki Warritya and Tommy alias Kepuin, for stealing sheep and silver spoons; and two, Nultia and Moullia from Port Lincoln, for the murder of Rolles Biddle and others.[311] The *Southern Australian*'s report of the trial lists the name '*Rongist Meraimnalld* [sic] alias Murray King John', so not to be confused with the 'Adelaide Tribe's' main *burka*, 'King John', well-known as Mullawirraburka.[312]

The silver spoons can be explained:

> Mary Carson was brought up on a charge of receiving silver spoons from the natives ... a native from Moorundie ... admitted taking spoons from time to time from Captain Duff's house and sold them to a woman in Grenfell-street ... Many complaints have been lately made of Europeans receiving stolen property from the natives, and it is well if they take warning from the case which is now before the public.[313]

February 19 Sunday: the Rev'd Mr. Howard Mr. Fleming and Mr. Benson attended the Gaol Yesterday Afternoon divine Service at 3½ OC'k   30

February 22 Wednesday: Received this day from the Colonial Engineers Department
24 Tea Tree Brooms 1 Hair Broom 2 Mops and one Scrubbing Brush.   29

February 23 Thursday: one of the Military Struck another this Morning whilst getting a Bucket of water by the Iron Gates.   29

February 25 Saturday: the Sheriff Visited the Gaol this Afternoon - also Dr Nash to See Morris (a Prisoner) Ill Since Thursday last.   28

February 26 Sunday: Mr. Fleming and Mr. Benson attended at the Gaol Yesterday afternoon divine Service at 3½ OC'k.   27

February 28 Tuesday: Mr. Wigley Visited the Gaol no Complaint - etc - His Honor the Judge & Mrs Cooper visited the Gaol this Afternoon.   27

March 3 Friday: McDonald having been fined £5-15- for An Assault or 2 Mo. H. Labour and fined for another offence £1-15 or one Month

H. Labour having Served his 2 Months and Paid the £1-15- he was discharged The Sheriff Call'd at the Gaol this afternoon. 28

March 5 Sunday: Mr. Fleming & Mr. Benson Attended at the Gaol this day divine Service at 3½. 28

March 6 Monday: out with the lists of Prisoners for Trial to Morrow. 28

March 7 Tuesday: the Sessions Commenced this day There all day. 28

March 8 Wednesday: Sessions all day William Cooke brot to Gaol by Borr Sheriffs Officer for Debt. 29

March 9 Thursday: at the Sessions John Morris was this day Sentenced to 10 Years Transportation for Robbing Thomas Jones of Several one pound notes After the Sentence was passed on him he used the Most Violent Language to his Honor the Judge – and Struck they Police Several Times and Threatened to Kill Some one in the Gaol before he left this Colony in Consequence of Which I had him well Ironed and to be Kept by himself in one of the Solitary Cells – The Court was this day Adjourned to Monday Next the 13th. Just at 10 OC'k His Honor ordered the Native named Jemmy to be discharged No Bill presented against for Sheep Stealing. The Native Call Boccomola was taken Very Ill Sent for Mr. Moorhouse who Came about 2½ P.M. he wished me to Keep Jemmy (ordered as above to be discharged) untill 9 OC'k to Morrow Morning when he would Come to the Gaol for him. Allen Wilson was brot to the Gaol for Debt by Borr Sheriffs Officer. 29

Boccomola had been in gaol since 5 May 1842:

> His sentence was 'death recorded' [assault with intent to kill] . . . His behaviour in prison has been uniformly good since he was first lodged there. . . . Buccomola is about 42 years old, & an influential person amongst his tribe; he is a sorcerer & ever since his lodgement in Jail, the Northern Natives who visit Adelaide have been in perpetual fear of some great evil befalling them, on account of an individual of his rank being kept in custody.[314]

He was to be pardoned on the Queen's Birthday in 1844.[315]

A comment in the *Southern Australian* on 10 March 1843 is worth including here:

> It is a curious fact, that there are four natives at present in gaol for trial at the Sessions, who speak four languages as distinct as the English and German. Even the Encounter Bay language is so different from that of Adelaide, that there are not twenty words the same in both. The grammatical construction in all, however, is exactly the same. At the ensuing trials, Mr Moorhouse will interpret for the Adelaide black; Mr Schurmann for those from Port Lincoln; Mr Meyer for the native from Encounter Bay; and if Mr Eyre does not arrive in time, there will be no interpreter for the Rufus native, who must consequently be discharged.[316]

The injustice of too many Aboriginal people in gaol, and being judged by laws that were not their own, sits side-by-side with the very Britishness of the insistence on an individual's right to a fair trial – that if a person cannot be represented they can have no justice so must go free.

March 10 Friday: William Garlick was brot the Gaol for Debt - by Borr Sheriffs Officer Mr. Moorhouse Came to the Gaol at 9 OC'k this Morning and took Jemmy the Native away. 28

March 11 Saturday: the Sheriff & Mr. Wigley Visited the Gaol this day Saw Morris. No Complaint. 27

March 12 Sunday: Mr. Fleming and Mr. Benson Attended the Gaol divine Service at 3½ Dr. Nash Visited the Gaol and Saw the Prisoners in Solitary. 26

March 13 Monday: at the Sessions untill 5 P.M. the Court then Adjourned to Monday Next the 20th Inst - the Prisoner Boor was this day Sentenced to 12 Months Hard Labour except the 1st and last 14 days which is to be in Solitary Confinement. 26

The case of Boor speaks of the lingering nature of the financial depression:

REVERSE OF FORTUNE *James Richard Boor*, the son of a highly respectable barrister in England, was charged with stealing ... The prisoner did not deny the fact, but pleaded poverty in extenuation, he being unable to find employment, or an honest liveihood. The worthy magistrate, on committing the prisoner for trial, expressed his deep regret to see one so respectably connected, placed in such an unhappy and criminal situation.[317]

March 14 Tuesday: the Rice having been all Used in Consequence of the No of Natives that have been Confined in Gaol - I was obliged this day to allow the Prisoners ½ lb of Bread extra not having Rice. 25

March 15 Wednesday: Reported to the Sheriff this morning that we was out of Rice and who ordered that ½ lb of Bread Should be given to each Prisoner in Lieu of Rice to the end of the Quarter - also that Mrs. Davy's Child Should Receive ½ lb of Bread. 24

The Sheriff disagreed with rations for the child. He wrote to Grey:

> The Prisoner Elizabeth Davy under Sentence of 'Death Recorded' had at the time of her committal to Gaol an Infant whom she was then nursing. This Child has Since weaned and now requires to be fed. As the child is not a Prisoner I do not feel myself Authorised to allow bread to be served out to her and I would respectfully Suggest that this Child be taken from the Gaol and placed with Mrs Davys two other Children who are now at Emigration Square under Charge of a Nurse.[318]

Governor Grey showed perhaps surprising flexibility in his reply, conveyed by the Colonial Secretary:

> In reply to your letter of yesterday's date, recommending that a child of the prisoner Elizabeth Davy be placed with her two other children at Emigration Square ... His Excellency the Governor has no objection ... if the mother wishes to part with her child; but ... no objection to sanction some increase to her rations on account of the child.[319]

It may be that he was already considering granting her the pardon that was soon to come.

March 19 Sunday: the Rev'd Mr. Howard and Mr. Fleming and Mr. Benson attended the Gaol this day divine Service at 3½ OC'k. 24

March 20 Monday: At the Court this Morning when His Honor Adjourned the to [to the] Thursday Next at 10 A.M. His Excellency was this day Pleased to Remit the Remaining portion of Charles Grulands time and order his discharge - Gruland was Convicted in the last November Sessions and Sentenced to Six Months hard Labour for Felony. 23

March 21 Tuesday: The Sheriff Visited the Gaol this Afternoon. 22

March 23 Thursday: At the Sessions all day - the 2 Natives Named Nultia & Moullia - from Port Lincoln was this day tried for the Murder of Rolles Biddle at Port Lincoln in March last and Sentenced to be taken to Port Lincoln and hanged there on the 4th April 1843 - the Sessions ended this day. 24

March 24 Friday: with the Sheriff about the 2 Natives. 23

March 25 Saturday: Mr. Shurmann Visited the 2 Natives Under Sentence of Death. 23

March 26 Sunday: Mr. Moorhouse and Mr. Schurmann Visited the 2 Natives this Morning in the Gaol. Mr. Fleming attended the Gaol Yesterday also Mr. Benson divine Service at 3½ P.M. 23

March 28 Tuesday: Ordered to be Ready to leave Adelaide to Morrow for Port Lincoln. 24

March 29 Wednesday: Gov'r of the Gaol as Deputy Sheriff left the Gaol this day at 12 OC'k Noon with the Prisoners Nultia and Moullia and 2 of the Mounted Police - Nultia to be Executed at Port Lincoln on the 7th April 1843 Moullia to be taken also to Port Lincoln and to be left there and ... The Sheriff was at the Gaol at the time the Gov'r left. 24

The handwriting changes again here, until 15 April 1843, as Ashton left the gaol to travel to Port Lincoln, taking with him the two Aboriginal prisoners. Nultia was to be hanged in his own country as a warning to others and Moullia, having received a reprieve, was to be taken to the gaol in Port Lincoln.

March 30 Thursday: Prisoners unlocked & locked up all Safe. 21

March 31 Friday: the Visiting Magistrate Visited. - all the Prisoners Safe. 21

April 1 Saturday: the Sheriff Visited the Gaol and Read the Answers to the Petitions of the following Prisoners from His Excellency that their Sentences Could Not be Altered. Viz Ross - Morris - Robinson and Benson - but Hyde was to be detained untill Next Sessions. 21

April 2 Sunday: The Rev'd Mr. Howard Attended the Gaol divine Service at 3½ P/M. The Prisoners locked up all Safe. 21

April 3 Monday: Mr. Moorhouse & Mr. Eyres Call'd at the Gaol to See the Natives Prisoners locked up all Safe. 21

April 4 Tuesday: Charles Gruland was Committed for Trial this day Dr. Nash Visited the Gaol They Prisoners locked up Safe. 21

April 5 Wednesday: Patrick Nowlan was this day discharged having been in Gaol 3 Months James Ilbury was brot in for Debt. - Prisoners locked up all Safe. 21

April 6 Thursday: all Safe.

April 7 Friday: Dr. Nash Visited the Gaol found all Right. 21

April 8 Saturday: All Safe. 21

April 9 Sunday: Mr Fleming attended the Gaol divine Service at 10 A.M. Prisoners all Safe. 21

April 10 Monday: Dr Nash Visited all Right. 22

April 11 Tuesday: all Safe. 22

April 12 Wednesday: the Sheriff Visited the Gaol Thomas Freeman was brot to Gaol for Debt. All Safe. 23

April 13 Thursday: the Bread was So bad that it was Sent back and other Received Prisoners all Safe. 23

April 14 Friday: Dr. Nash Visited found All Right and Safe.   23

Ashton again:

April 15 Saturday: I returned to the Gaol at 9 A.M. from Port Lincoln where I had been as Deputy Sheriff to See The Sentence of the Law Carried into effect on the Native Called Nultia for the Murder of Rolles Biddle. The execution took place on the 7th April 1843 at 8 OC'k in the Morning at the Spot where the Murder was Committed about 20 Miles from the Town of Port Lincoln - Moullia the other Native was brot back to the Gaol at Port Lincoln and left there in Irons he having been Pardoned by His Excellency - the body of Nultia was brought to the Gaol and buried in the Yard I left Port Lincoln on the 10th Instant and arrived in Adelaide this day.

W.B Ashton Gov'r of the Gaol.   23

The newspapers reported the trial of the two men including gruesome details of the killings. A party of Aboriginal men had assembled at the shepherd's hut with spears that they had systematically thrown while stealing potatoes. They fled when threatened with guns; then later 80 men had returned, including Nultia and Moullia, both known to the several people holed up in the hut. There followed a brutal raid, killing several white men with spears and hacking at the shepherd's wife with sheep shears, after which the hut was ransacked. It was an operation not down to individuals, rather it was on a 'tribal' scale. When asked why they should not have been found guilty they answered through their interpreter Schurmann that it had not been them, 'singling out the murderers from their tribe by name'.[320]

In the same sessions a white shepherd at Mount Hughes Station was found not guilty of manslaughter of an Aboriginal woman. She was shot as she lagged behind when her people were evicted from the station in retaliation when sheep had been dispersed. There had been insufficient evidence to convict. The judge commented on this apparent disparity in justice and gave a general warning for settlers to be more careful in their treatment of Aboriginal people. He then stated that nonetheless an example needed to be made in the case of Nultia and Moullia. In the same newspaper article another sad case was described. A ten-year-old boy from Mount Barker sent to tend cattle was murdered by the 'lunatic' Hedditch who believed the boy was an evil spirit.[321]

At the gallows:

> Nultia was much affected; the tears ran down his face, and, pointing to the bush, he cried, 'Why kill me for this, who am a boy, when there are plenty big men over there who were at the murder'?[322]

Only Ashton, missionary Schurmann, the hangman, a few officials and a handful of Aboriginal people from the town witnessed the end of Nultia's life. It was a heavy duty, each playing a part in an awful colonial saga.

On 12 April Moorhouse presented his quarterly report. He agreed with Klose that the school at the Location had been poorly attended because 'the Adelaide Tribe were driven from town on the 23rd December last, by the Murray Tribe and did not return until the 7th March'. He believed that unless the 'Murray Tribe' could be kept away, the school had no future. When he and Klose had tried to include Murray children in the school, the Adelaide children would not attend, and when they instead put them in a separate room 'they are abused by the Adelaide adults and accused of obtaining food in a territory to which they have no hereditary right'. Moorhouse estimated that 150 of the 'Adelaide Tribe' and 200 of the 'Murray Tribe' were now living in Adelaide and suggested to Governor Grey that he encourage the 'Murray Tribe' to keep to their own country. He also reported that Aboriginal people coming into town for the first time were wandering the streets naked. He wrote that these people were 'placed 24 hours in the Lock-up, with a good effect probably, as I have not seen one taken twice for the offence'.[323] Moorhouse wrote to Eyre asking him to warn Aboriginal people in the interior that if they left their districts for Adelaide they would be escorted back by the police.[324]

Klose's 1843 letters regret the missionaries' lack of impact. Not one Aboriginal person had been converted. 'Unbelief has the upper hand here', Klose wrote.[325] For some time Klose had been contemplating separating children from their parents and turning the Aboriginal Location into a live-in school. The adults had long mocked the teachings of the missionaries, encouraged by the 'ungodly influence' of some of the settlers who would turn up with their pamphlets to disagree with the missionaries or wander in an out of the huts at the Location.[326]

Klose and Moorhouse both were worried about increasing immorality – venereal disease was rife, even among the schoolchildren. They moved ahead with the idea of converting the Location school to a live-in school, ostensibly to prevent disease, and employed a woman to look after the girls.[327] Klose believed that if they could keep the children away from the influence of their parents, they would have some hope with the children. The protector believed the same, having already had two of the girls from the school as servants living in his house in the hope they would turn away from their traditional ways. This was in 1842 and despite his wife and himself treating the girls well and taking them to church with the other servants, the experiment had not succeeded. Klose had written about it in his diary:

> [The children] often said that never again did they want to live in the bush with the other natives, but wanted to stay with an employer always. But what happened when, in the middle of November, the natives came back out of the bush? The girls visited their parents and friends and as a result of this visit were incited by the adults to leave the European's house. They left the house, took off their dresses and took with them only one garment which they wrapped around their bodies under the arms as the other women do, and followed the men to whom they had been promised previously. How painful that is for the teacher ... when he sees a shoot from a seed he has sown break through the earth, only to see it destroyed by a swarm of insects on the following morning.[328]

Klose believed the live-in school worked and noted his belief that 'even the parents are satisfied because they see that the children are completely cared for'.[329]

The protector and the missionary were arguably well-intentioned. Nonetheless the mindset that brought about the live-in school and the protector's employment of the girls continued, and in retrospect can be recognised as the first steps in South Australia toward the more recent Australia-wide tragedy of the Stolen Generations. Cawthorne disagreed with everything the missionaries did at the Location but he also was concerned for the morality of the Aboriginal people. He wrote:

> I am afraid the natives are getting fond of that curse to Englishmen, viz. Beer & wine, for I saw coming along 7 or 8 of them lolling about a public house, some even seemed to be quite stupid. It is a bad omen for they never stop later than sunset in town. Oh if they begin to get fond of strong drink it will lead them to Robbery and to murder.[330]

April 16 Sunday: the Rev'd Mr Howard Attended the Gaol divine Service at 3½ P.M.   23

April 18 Tuesday: Mr. Wigley the Visiting Magistrate Visited the Gaol (and Saw the Prisoner Hedditch Charged with Murder) all was quiet - Thomas Freeman (Debtor) was discharged by order of His Honor the Judge - Morris & Hedditch - was put in the felons Yard.   23

April 19 Wednesday: Saw the Sheriff about Morris & Hedditch See Yesterday.   22

April 21 Friday: William Garlick was taken to the Insolvent Court and was Sentenced to 3 Months Imprisonment from the day of his arrest.   22

April 23 Sunday: Mr. Fleming Attended the Gaol divine Service at 3½.   22

April 24 Monday: James Macloud was brot to Gaol for Debt the Sheriff Sent word for him to Stop in the Office. 23

April 25 Tuesday: James Macloud & W.A. Polden both Debtors was this day discharged by Order of the Sheriff. 23

April 28 Friday: William Cook (Debtor) was taken to the Insolvent Court this day and was discharged his first hearing.
Received an order from Mr. Gilbert Colonial Storeperson on Mr Harriott for 44 Gallons of Oil for the use of the Gaol. 22

April 30 Sunday: Mr. Fleming attended at the Gaol divine Service at 1 OC'k P.M. 21

May 1 Monday: W'm McDonald alias William Brown with his hand nearly blown off he is Charged with having with others broken out of the Melbourne Gaol – we Identify him as William Brown and that he was Convicted at Adelaide for Highway Robbery on the 9th March 1840 and left here for Sydney on the Mary Ridgeway on the 6th April 1840 under the Sentence of Transportation for life and that he has been at large Nearly ever Since. Dr. Nash Called to See Him. 22

May 2 Tuesday: Iron & Brown Slept in one of the Solitary Cells Brown wanting his hand dressed during the Night. 22

May 3 Wednesday: Gave 5 Prisoners under Sentence a pr of Trousers each as per wish of the Sheriff. 22

May 5 Friday: Browns hand a little better Dr. Nash Saw him. 22

May 7 Sunday: Mr. Fleming Attended at the Gaol divine Service at 3½ P.M. 22

May 9 Tuesday: The General Quarter of the Peace was held this day Charles Cooper Esq'r Chairman The following Prisoners where disposed of Charles Gruland – Thomas Thornton – 7 Years Transportation. W'm Williamson 3 Months Hard Labour – and William McDonald Identified as William Brown a Returned Convict – detained for His Excellencys Pleasure. Sessions ended. I Came home very Ill having fell down a hole in the place where they Prisoners are Kept at the Court and which had not been Covered Over by the Man that Cleaned the Cellar out the day before. 22

May 10 Wednesday: at home all day Sick. 22

May 11 Thursday: ditto 23

May 12 Friday: ditto 23

May 13 Saturday: ditto 23

May 14 Sunday: ditto
The Rev'd W. Howard attended the Gaol divine Service at 4 P.M. 23

May 15 Monday: went to the Sheriffs this day. 23

May 16 Tuesday: John Armstrong was brot to Gaol on a Warrant on a fine under the Waste Land Act - he Said he could point out the Spot where George Dyer (an escaped Prisoner) Could be taken I Sent Perry & Kennedy and 4 of they Mounted Police went with them to Mr. H. Watt's Station Near the Sturt - they found the Hut where Dyer had been and brought his Gun away but did not See Dyer. 24

May 18 Thursday: The Sheriff Visited the Gaol and Saw the Several places where the wet comes in about the Gaol. - A Native was brot to Gaol Committed for Trial from Mount Barker Named P... alias Williamy. 26

May 19 Friday: Ilbery (Debtor) was taken to the Insolvent Court and Remanded to Tuesday Next. John Armstrong was discharged this day by order of the Resident Magistrate. 26

May 21 Sunday - Mr. Fleming Attended at the Gaol this day at 3½ P.M. but being taken Very unwell we had no divine Service. 25

May 22 Monday: Mr. Wigley the Visiting Magistrate Came to the Gaol where the following Prisoners Applied to him for Shirts & Shoes - Morris - Brown - & Ross. 25

May 23 Tuesday: found this Morning that the above Prisoners had Shoes each Morris had 1 Shirt & Brown & Ross had 3 Shirts between them - Call'd at Mr. Wigleys office found he was not in town. - James Ilbery (Debtor) was taken to the Insolvent Court this day and was discharged Out of Custody his 3rd hearing - at 4 P.M. Morris & Gruland was fighting in the felons Yard they was brought out of the Yard and put into Solitary Cells - this is the 2nd time that they have been fighting within a few days They was not punished on the first occasion they promising it Should not take place again. 25

May 26 Friday - Call'd at the Colonial Secretary's Office with a Report of Prisoners in Gaol under Sentence of Transportation. 24

May 27 Saturday - Saw the Sheriff about they Prisoners going away he gave me the Names of Sarah Green - Charles Robinson - James Ross - William Brown - John Morris - Charles Gruland - Thomas Thornton that was to go. 24

May 28 Sunday: The Rev'd Mr. Howard Sent Word he was Ill & Could Not Attend. Mr. Benson Attended at 2½ P.M. 24

May 29 Monday: took the description of the following Prisoners to the Colonial Secretary - Sarah Green - Charles Robinson - James Ross - William Brown - John Morris - Charles Gruland - and Thomas Thornton Under Sentence of Transportation. - The Sheriff went to the Port and on Board of the Emma to See Things All Ready for the Prisoners. 24

May 31 Wednesday: I left the Gaol this Morning at 9 OC'k with They following Prisoners under Sentence of Transportation to Hobart Town - Sarah Green - John Morris - Charles Robinson - William Brown - James Ross - Charles Gruland & Thos. Thornton with 5 of the Mounted Police with Me Arrived at the Port about 11 A.M. the Brig Emma was Not Ready to Receive they Prisoners After waiting about half an hour the Hold was a little Ready And they Prisoners put on board Sarah Green in the Storage About an hour after the Prisoners was on board the Capt'n (Sproud) Arrived at the Port and in My Absence and Capt'n Lipsons he ordered the female to be put into the hold with they 6 Male Prisoners. I went and Saw Capt'n Lipson about it who went with [me] on board again and After a great deal of Abusive language from Capt'n Sproud to Capt'n Lipson & Myself Sarah Green was again put into the Storage and I left the Ship leaving the Port Police on board

> I had before this time asked Capt'n Sproud if he would like one or two of they Mounted Police to Stay on board untill he left the wharf which he Refused. 25

Sarah Green was now transported for 14 years, leaving behind her co-conspirators, Elizabeth and Mary Ann Davey as well as the buried remains of her stillborn child. Ashton insisted that she not be treated poorly on board ship, the only female on board, and that she not be put in the same place with all the men. Given the disposition of the captain however it is doubtful this was carried through.

> **June 1** Thursday: Reported to the Sheriff they Prisoners having him put on board of the Brig Emma for Hobart Town etc Yesterday at Port Adelaide. 18
>
> **June 2** Friday: the Sheriff Visited the Gaol and went all over. 18
>
> **June 3** Saturday: Dr. Nash Visited. 18
>
> **June 4** Sunday: Mr. Fleming attended at the Gaol this Afternoon divine Service at 3½. 18
>
> **June 6** Tuesday: Dr. Nash Visited the Gaol. - Went to Mr. Gilberts about Some Wine for Brown. 18
>
> **June 7** Wednesday: Henry Watson was brot to Gaol for Horse Stealing this is the Man that made his escape from the Police Some time ago Also a Man & a Boy brot to Gaol for Shooting a Bullock. 21
>
> **June 8** Thursday: Stephen Hack a Debtor was discharged this day by Order of the Insolvent Court he having found Bail. 21

Stephen Hack was brother to John Barton Hack, both well-known early settlers and both declared insolvent in 1843 after many joint ventures and changing fortunes. Stephen was the only brother to be imprisoned and became estranged from his brother for many years. Their story is told in *Chequered Lives: John Barton Hack and Stephen Hack and the early days of South Australia*, by Iola Hack Mathews with Chris Durrant.[331]

June 9 Friday: Dr Nash Visited the Gaol Saw William Brown alias McDonald and Said the wine & Extra Bread & Meat be Stoped after this date – Also Saw Williamson and Stated that – he Should Constantly Wear a Truss. 19

June 11 Sunday: Mr. Fleming Attended the Gaol this day divine Service at 11 A.M. 21

June 12 Monday: A Sailor brot to the Gaol from the Port – for 14 days Hard Labour and to Pay a fine of £1. 19

June 14 Wednesday – Sent the Pay Sheets to the Sheriff by Kennedy. 20

June 15 Thursday – took a letter to the Judge from Jolley etc About Bail. 20

June 16 Friday: His Honor the Judge Sent Jolleys letter back this day No Answer with it. 19

June 18 Sunday: Mr. Fleming Attended the Gaol this day divine Service at 11 A.M. 19

On this same day Mrs Ashton gave birth to their second daughter.[332] They called her Charlotte Maria.

June 19 Monday: the Sheriff Visited the Gaol Williamson Spoke to him About Shirts – etc – Dr. Nash also Visited the Gaol. The Prisoner Watson was this day Committed for Trial for Horse Stealing. 19

June 23 Friday: The Port Lincoln Native was taken to the Resident Magistrates Court And Again Remanded to Monday the 26th 1843. 20

June 25 Sunday: No divine Service in the Gaol Mr. Fleming not Attending. – Fred'k Medcalfe (Sailor) was discharged having Served his 14 days and a Pound having been Sent to me from the Port to Pay his fine of One Pound. 20

June 26 Monday: His Excellency Sent a Mounted Police for a Native under Remand the Policeman did not Know the Name Nor the

Crime he was in Gaol for there being 2 Natives in Gaol under Remand for this day The TurnKey (Perry) Sent the Port Lincoln Black up - who was brot back and the Policeman Said it was Williamy Native that was wanted etc - was taken before His Excellency Mr. Moorhouse & the Advocate General the Policeman brot him back and Said that I was to discharge him which I did after Sending for Mr. Moorhouse and got from him a written discharge. 19

June 27 Tuesday: The Sheriff Call'd at the Gaol on his Return from the Port and Said Brown a Prisoner was to leave on Thursday in the Terror for Sydney. 19

June 28 Wednesday: Saw the Sheriff & the Colonial Secretary about Sending William Brown to Sydney in the Terror - Received Orders to put him on Board to Morrow Morning. 19

It appears that the earlier intention to send William Brown on the *Emma* to Hobart did not eventuate. The fact that he was seen by the doctor a week later suggests he was not fit to go. He is now finally being transported, and for the second time.

June 29 Thurday left the Gaol this Morning at 9 OC'k with the Prisoners William Brown a Returned Convict from Sydney (and who was Transported from this Colony for life with Jeremiah Collins for Robbing David Campbell - left him in the Mary Ridgeway for Sydney on the 6th April 1840 -) Arrived at the Port at 10 A.M. and put the Prisoner on board the Basque Terror The Colonial Secretary Sent down the Papers by a Mounted Policeman at 2 P.M. and which I took on board and gave to the Capt'n a Policeman was left on board until the Terror left. I returned to the Gaol at 5 P.M. 19

June 30 Friday: Reported to the Sheriff having put the above Prisoners on board the Terror Yesterday. 18

July 1 Saturday: George Stevenson was brot to Gaol for Debt by Borr Sheriffs Officer. 21

July 2 Sunday: Mr. Fleming Attended the Gaol divine Service at 11 A.M. 21

Ashton's Hotel

July 3 Monday: at 12 Oc'k Night No 2 Sentry at the Wooden Fence was found to have left his post leaving his Gun etc in the Sentry Box and when it was Reported to the ... Comm'n Officer in the Guard Room it was found that a Deserter named Gilks had also left the Guard Room and Escaped with the Sentry over the Wooden fence The Sentry Answered the TurnKeys Call at 11½ and Not Answering at 12 led to the TurnKey finding out that he had left. - As Soon as it was Mentioned to Me I Sent for the Guard (Molineux) off duty and Kept all hands Under Arms the Rest of the Night - in Case any Attempt Should be Made by our own Prisoners to Escape. - No Attempt however was made. 21

July 4 Tuesday: Reported the Above to the Sheriff - all Quite in the Gaol. 21

The *Southern Australian* reported:

> On Monday night last, an alarm was given in the gaol, that one of the sentries on duty had left his post and deserted. Mr Ashton was promptly on the spot, and on examination found that a soldier under the charge of the party on guard and the sentry had both escaladed the wooden fence on the west end of the gaol.[333]

Two other soldiers working at the police barracks deserted on the same evening so it became obvious it was part of a plan. Nonetheless it is an extraordinary tale, the sentry (a soldier co-opted to work at the gaol) assisting a deserter to escape and escaping himself while still on duty, both over the wooden fence from the sentry box, he doing the right thing by leaving his gun behind.

July 6 Thursday: The Visiting Mag'te Attended the Gaol and Saw Watson a Prisoner Comm'd for Horse Stealing And is to See him again on Tuesday next. 21

July 7 Friday: Received Notice from the Sheriff to get One or 2 Men for the Gaol duty as one of the Sentries was to taken off the Gaol duty Saw a Man Named Alfred Nicholson Took him to Mr. Wigley to have him Sworn in as a Constable for the Gaol. Mr. Wigley Said he Could not do so without an Order from the Colonial Secretary Nicholson Came to the Gaol Saw Me lock up and Saw what duty he would have to do.   21

July 8 Saturday: Nicholson Came to the Gaol this Morning and Ev'g again Stating that he thought the Night duty would be too hard for him and injure his health. - At 11 Oc'k when the Soldiers Came I found in Room of [instead of] one More Comm'd Officer and 6 Men Only one Officer and 3 Men Came to do duty So that I Should have but one Sentry and he to be Stationed at the Guard room there being 2 of their own Prisoners Kept in the Guard Room - I went to the Sheriffs who not being in and as Nicholson had Resigned I Sent Marra (an old Guard) to the Gaol to do duty. - he took the Sentrys Post at the Wooden fence. Saw the Sheriff Shortly Afterwards and who told me it was quite Right in placing Marra on duty as only one Sentry had been Sent to the Gaol. Geo Stevenson Debtor was discharged by order of the Insolvent Court he having found Bail.   21

July 9 Sunday: No divine Service in the Gaol this day Mr. Fleming Not Attending. Marra went off Duty at 7 OC'k last Night So that I had no Guard at the Wooden fence All Night.   21

July 11 Tuesday: Rec'd a letter this Evening from the Sheriff Stating That Lean was to be taken on duty at the Gaol.   21

July 12 Wednesday: Lean As Above Came on Duty as Gaol Guard in the Evening.   21

July 13 Thursday: 2 Men (Convicts) was Sent to the Gaol for Safe Custody by Capt'n Lipson untill the Waterwitch was Ready to Sail for Hobart Town (Names John Davis and Francis Fides) their Keep to be paid by the Capt'n Of the Ship. N.C Kingdom was brot to Gaol for Debt this day.   24

July 15 Saturday: Received this day they printed Calendars of Prisoners for Trial.   25

July 16 Sunday: No divine Service at the Gaol this day Mr. Fleming not Attending.   25

July 17 Monday: Round delivering they Calendars etc   25

July 18 Tuesday: The Sessions (Gaol delivery) Commenced this Morning at 10 OC'k before His Honor Charles Cooper Esq'r Judge - a Girl Named Mary Brown was Sentenced to 3 Months Hard Labour for felony His Honor Mentioned for her to be Kept apart from they other Prisoners and the Sheriff approved My Sending her into My house to do any thing for Mrs Ashton which was done. - Harriet Sturgess was Discharged No Bill being found her. 25

July 19 Wednesday: at the Sessions All Day and Charles Hedditch was found Guilty of the Murder of John Murdock and the Jury found that he was Insane at the time he Committed the Murder - ordered by the Court to be Confined in Gaol untill H.M.Pleasure be known. 23

July 20 Thursday: At the Sessions When Ngarbi the Port Lincoln Native was found Guilty of the Murder of Eliz'th Stubbs at Port Lincoln and Sentenced to be Executed on the 1st of August 1843 His Excellency was pleased this day to Pardon Eliz'th Davy and Mary Ann Davy (in Gaol Since July 1842 under Sentence of Death Recorded against them for Highway Robbery -) and they was this day discharged from the Gaol. 22

Elizabeth and Mary Ann Davey were pardoned.[334] Besides being incarcerated for 12 months, they had been separated from two of the children in the family, and had lost the father of the family and the two others involved (all to transportation), for the crime of relieving a punter of his cash. At the same time Ngarbi, found guilty of participating in brutal murder, faced execution.

Cawthorne again:

> News. There is another poor native to be hung ... Many are against the sentence. They are going to petition the Governor. May they succeed in their humane endeavours.[335]

When the sentence was passed Schurmann petitioned the governor, also Moorhouse who put forward seven reasons to show mercy. Among them:

1st. He fully confessed his guilt, which is not usual amongst the Natives of the Province; ...

4th. His remaining in custody will convince the Natives that the Europeans have him still in their power ...

5th. ... his older associates took advantage of his acquaintance with Europeans and entreated him to be prominent in the attack.

6th. Whatever the majority of the older Natives decided upon, must be carried out if practicable by the younger men, the whole of the tribe agreed to attack Mr Biddle's Station; it was with them a tribal (national) decision & and he could not have prevented the melancholic attack, had he been ever so disposed.

7th. From his years he could have little influence in tribal decisions – only being about 20 years old.[336]

The petition was to have no effect: there was no pardon and Ngarbi was to be hanged. Another Aboriginal man, Henry, found guilty of stealing sheep, was the next to have his fate decided.

July 21 Friday: Henry a Native was Convicted of Sheep Stealing and Sentenced to 12 Months Hard Labour except the first and last Week which is to be in Solitary Confinement - the first Week to Commence on Monday Next - James Jolley and Theodore Heinrick was both Acquitted The Sessions ended this day about 2½ OC'k   20

July 22 Saturday: I was at the late Rev'd Mr. Howards Funeral. Kennedy & Lennon was also at the Funeral Molineux takin extra duty.   19

Reverend Howard, who had arrived on the *Buffalo* as colonial chaplain less than seven years previously, was only 36 years old when he died and apparently well loved and respected. Cawthorne told of the sadness of an Aboriginal man at Howard's passing and his eulogy, reported in the *Adelaide Observer*, told of the love of the colonists for him.[337]

July 23 Sunday: no Divine Service at the Gaol this [incomplete entry]. 19

July 24 Monday: Saw the Sheriff who Said he had not heard any more about the Execution of the Native. 20

July 28 Friday: Andrew Birrell was brot to the Gaol for Debt by Borr Sheriffs Officer. 26

July 29 Saturday: The Sheriff Visited the Gaol and told me that the Native was to be executed on Tuesday Morning Next at 9 A.M. His Honor the Judge also Call'd to See me about Woods Case. - Dr. Nash also Visited the Gaol Saw Hedditch and wished him to be Set to Some Sort of light work. 26

July 30 Sunday: Mr. Fleming attended at the Gaol - Divine Service at 12 OC'k Noon. 26

July 31 Monday: Saw the Sheriff about the Native for Execution - also Saw His Honor about they Prisoner Woods Case and Witnesses. - the Sheriff Came to the Gaol with Me about the Drop. - Robert Gibbions Sentenced to a Months Imprisonment and to pay a fine of £2 - his Time was up Yesterday but Could not pay the fine it was paid this day & he was discharged. 27

August 1 Tuesday: The last Sentence of the Law was Carried into effect on the Native Call'd Ngarbi alias little Jemmy in front of the Gaol for the wilful Murder of Eliz'th Stubbs at Port Lincoln on the 29th day of March 1842 - at 9th OC'k A.M. the Sheriff gave the Signal and the Unfortunate Man was Launched into Eternity After hanging the usual time (one hour) the body was Cut Down and Buried between the walls of the Gaol Close to where Joseph Stagg was Buried. - The Drop was put up and taken down by Mr. Porter & Men from the Colonial Engineers Department. 27

That night Cawthorne wrote in his diary:

> This morning justice demanded the fulfillment of a decree passed a few days ago on the body of a Port Lincoln native for the murder of a Mrs Stubbs. He was hung. . . . I did not get to see this heart-rending spectacle and oh how I was not shocked to see men and boys running actually to see this sad spectacle, as if to an Exhibition. Not only

these, women went also – where are their finer feelings? ... Instead (as I had expected) of seeing the females melt into tears, Alas! Laughs resounded from their mouths. Instead of the men turning away with real sorrow, Alas! Swearing, nonsensical remarks and ribaldry formed their conversation.... [I] could see the jail from our upstairs window.[338]

August 3 Thursday: went to Col'l Stores and got 2 lbs of Tea for Prisoners we being out And A Birrell was this day discharged by Order of the Insolvent Court he having found Bail.   25
August 4 Friday: The 3 Natives was taken before the Resident Magistrate for the Robbery at the Port and was again Remanded.   24
August 5 Saturday: about 6½ P.M. as 2 Men and a boy attempted to Cross the River near the Gaol with 2 Bullocks and a Dray was washed away the boy was drowned the 2 Men was got out with Ropes. – also the Dray and bullocks. One Man Named Hanna (the Father of the Boy Drown) was driving I afterwards gave into Custody for being Drunk & wilfully driving and thereby Causing the death of his Son James Hanna.   24
August 6 Sunday: Mr. Fleming attended the Gaol this day divine Service at 11 A.M. We was unable to find the body of the boy drowned Last Night this day.   24
August 7 Monday: The Visiting Magistrate Attended the Gaol this day Saw Mr. Kingdom (Debtor), attended the Magistrate Court this day about the Man Hanna and the Magistrate held him to bail to appear this day week. Body of the boy not found.   24
August 8 Tuesday: Thomas Selfs was brot to Gaol this day for debt.   24
August 10 Thursday: took Jemmy the Native down the River looking for the Boy that was Drown on Saturday last Could not find the body.   24

The 15-year-old boy's body was found two months later, on 11 October 1843. A man 'had seen a hand of some person in the river', snagged in a tree below the slaughterhouse. He alerted Perry, the turnkey at the gaol, and along with Ashton they returned to the river. Together they pulled the body out and took it to the market house for the coroner's inquest. The opinion was that the drowning was the tragic result of a simple misjudgement resulting in the death of a much-loved child – and although the father had been drinking earlier in the day it was deemed not excessive and a verdict of accidental death was returned.[339] Ashton and Perry had been involved from the start – when Perry had first heard cries from the flooded river he and Ashton, and Ashton's son, probably the oldest, William James, had rushed down from the gaol and saved the rest of the party and some cattle. The boy, James Hanna, had already disappeared.[340] After all this time they now helped retrieve the body. It had been a distressing time.

August 11 Friday: His Excellency was pleased to Grant a free Pardon to William Wood (a prisoner Convicted at the last Sessions with Uttering a forged order to Mrs. Fisher) and Sentenced to Transportation for life and he was discharged from the Gaol at 11 OC'k this Morning The Colonial Secretarys letter was dated the 10th but I did not Receive the Same from the Sheriff until 11 OC'k this day. - The Sheriff Visited the Gaol this day Dr. Nash also Visited the Gaol. 24

August 12 Saturday - Received a letter from the Sheriff this Evening Requesting Me to Send to the Advocate General Capt'n Lipsons letter about the 2 Prisoners from the Waterwitch. 24

August 13 Sunday: Sent Perry to the Advocate General with a Copy of the Colonial Secretarys letter and also the letter from Capt'n Lipson Relative to the Prisoners in Gaol from the Waterwitch - Mr. Fleming Attended the Gaol this day divine Service at 11½ A.M. 24

August 14 Monday: Saw the Advocate General and the Sheriff about the 2 Prisoners from the Waterwitch. 24

The *Waterwitch* carried convicts destined for Hobart Town. The ship leaked and diverted to Adelaide where the two prisoners were temporarily held in Ashton's gaol.[341]

August 15 Tuesday: went over to the Stores this Morning with Kennedy and a Prisoner and Received 10 lb 2 oz of Tea - 55 lbs 2oz of Salt - 6 lbs of Sago - and an order on Mr. Harriett for 623 lbs of Rice and for 6 lbs of Oatmeal - the Sheriff Visited the Gaol this day. - Dr. Nash also Call'd and Saw Hedditch. 25

August 16 Wednesday: Call'd at the Sheriffs Office When did not See him left a letter from Skelton (a prisoner) for His Honor the Judge at his office Mr. H. Newenham. 26

August 17 Thursday: Thomas Williams was brot to Gaol for Debt by Borr Sheriffs Officer 2 Native Women was brot to Gaol for Stealing Potatoes from Mr. Phillipson near Walkerville. The Rev'd Mr. Farrell attended the Gaol this day divine Service at 1 OC'k P.M. 28

August 18 Friday: Selfs (Debtor) was this day Discharged by Order of the Insolvent Court he having found Bail. 28

August 19 Saturday: 2 Native Women for Stealing Potatoes taken before the Magistrate this day was not brought back. 27

August 20 Sunday: Mr. Fleming Attended the Gaol this day divine Service at 11 OC'k A.M. 25

August 21 Monday: Mr. Wigley Mr. ...ham and Mr. Rev. Bean of the Water Witch Came to the Gaol to See the 2 Prisoners which are left here for Safe Custody from the Waterwitch. 25

August 22 Tuesday: 2 Prisoners Was brot to Gaol for Cutting Timber on the Crown Land without a Licence. 28

August 23 Wednesday: Received a letter through the Sheriff from the Advocate General to Discharge Henry Poeverall a Private of the 96th Regiment and to be handed over to the Military Authorities he was discharged and by Capt'n Butlers Request was given over to the Officer on duty at the Guard Room in the Gaol - the Prisoner was Committed to Gaol for Trial for Shooting a Sheep with intent to Kill the Same. Com'c by M Moorhouse Esq'r from the Murray River district Thomas Williams in Gaol for debt was this day discharged by order of the Insolvent Court he having found Bail.
The Capt'n Of the Sans Parielle (Brodie) Call'd at the Gaol and left £2- the fine for 2 Sailors belong'g to his Ship named Robertson & White. 27

Ashton's Hotel

August 24 Thursday: the above 2 Sailors was Discharged having Served their Month and the fine having been paid. Received from Mr. James Fisher a Load of Straw for filling Prisoners Beds - Beds filled Same time. - Received from Colonial Engineers Department 3 Hair Brooms without handles - & 2 lbs of Sewing Twine for Assembling Beds. 25

August 25 Friday: Henry White and James Robinson - was discharged this Morning and paid their fine of one pound each as disorderly Sailors belong'g to the Sans Parielle. 23

[In red overlay handwriting]
Sentenced by Mistake

August 26 Saturday: paid to the Sheriff this day £2- the fines for 2 Sailors. - and also 5/- for the Discharge of Thos. Williams a Debtor - William Cock in Gaol for a fine was this day discharged by order of His Excellency. 23

August 27 Sunday: divine Service at 11 A.M. Mr. Fleming attended. 22

August 29 Tuesday: Mr. Pybus Supplied a Truss for James Iron a Prisoner in Gaol Saw the Sheriff this day about the time I went to Sydney. 22

August 30 Wednesday: They Pay Sheets was made up the 31st Aug't 1843 as the Men are to be Paid Monthly from the 1st September. 22

August 31 Thursday: the Sheriff Visited the Gaol this day Found All Right. 22

September 2 Saturday: The Sheriff told me this day that His Excellency had Ordered that Philip Hyde under Sentence of Transportation was not to leave this time with the other Prisoners. 25

September 3 Sunday: No divine Service this day Mr. Fleming not Attending. 25

September 4 Monday: Charles Stevens was brot to Gaol at 7 OC'k this Morning for debt by Pat'k Kelly one of Borr's Men. 26

September 5 Tuesday: the above debtor applied for Rations he having nothing to eat nor had nothing all day Yesterday only what

I Supplied with from my own Table - Allowed him from this
date. 24

September 6 Wednesday: Isaac Nonmus was brot to Gaol for Debt on
2 Habias's at the Suit of William Moore by Mr. Borr Sheriffs
officer. 25

September 7 Thursday: Dr. Nash Visited this day and Saw
Hedditch. 25

September 8 Friday: Mr. Wigley Visiting Magistrate Visited the Gaol
Found all Right. 25

September 9 Saturday: Isaac Nonmus debtor Petitioned this day for
Rations Saw the Sheriff about the Same told to let him have
Rations for the Present. - The Sheriff Visited the Gaol this day
And Read His Excellency's Answer to Boors Petition. 25

September 10 Sunday: Mr. Fleming Attended the Gaol this day divine
Service at 11½ A.M. 22

September 12 Tuesday: the Quarter Sessions was held this day His
Honor C. Cooper Esq'r Chairman One Prisoner only tried Named
William Williamson and Sentenced to 7 Years Transportation
George Dyer a Prisoner who made his Escape from the Gaol on
the 28th Dec'r 1842 was retaken and brought back to the Gaol this
day by the Mounted Police he was wounded in two places with a
Sword by the police in taking of him - he was put into one of the
Solitary Cells and Attended by Dr. Nash. 23

September 14 Thursday: Saw the Sheriff About the Prisoners going and
took Their Description to the Colonial Secretarys Office. - The
Sheriff Visited the Gaol. 24

September 15 Friday: Saw Mr. Tolmer and the Resident Magistrate
about Dyer and the Persons that had Keep him at their house well
Knowing that he had Made his Escape from the Gaol. 24

September 16 Saturday: Saw the Commiss'r of Police this Morning and
handed to him Two Pounds to be given to They Police for their
good Conduct - in Retaking George Dyer a Prisoner that had
Escaped from Gaol. Saw the Sheriff who Showed Me a letter that
he had Received from His Excellency that a Report was to be Sent

> to His Excellencys Office every Saturday Morning by the Gov'r of the Gaol of the No of Prisoners. 24
>
> **September 17** Sunday: George Dyer much better Dr. Nash Visited him. Mr. Fleming attended the Gaol divine Service at 11 OC'k A.M. - Dr. Nash visited him. 24

Despite all the drama, Ashton is matter-of-fact about Dyer's escape and recapture. He is also generous in his gift to the police, a clue to his relief that all was in order again. Two nights later he had reason to be worried again and to reprimand the military sentries.

> **September 19** Tuesday: At 12 OC'k last Night the Sentry at the Guard Tower did not Answer the Call I went Round with Kennedy the TurnKey and Asked the Reason of Not Calling out. - he Said that he did Not Hear the Guard Call - and that he was Very deaf I told Kennedy to tell the Corporal I wanted to Speak to after his Working Several times at the Guard Room door he went in and found the Soldiers All Asleep the Corporal Came out and and I told him he ought to be Very Cautious as whilst he was So fast Asleep his own Prisoners Might Make their Escape from the Guard Room and that Something Serious might take place between their Prisoners and My Guard and wished him to be Very Particular - I mentioned this Circumstance to Mr Houganon this day when he Visited the Military Guard of the Gaol this day. - Dr. Nash Visited Dyer this day and Said he was much better. - a Native Boy was Remanded to Gaol this day for Stealing Oil. 25
>
> **September 21** Thursday: The Sheriff Visited the Gaol this day Dyer much better. 25
>
> **September 22** Friday: Saw the Sheriff about They Prisoners leaving for V.D. Land. 27
>
> **September 23** Saturday: left the Gaol at 1 OC'k P,M, with the following Prisoners - Henry Watson - William Williamson - John Davis and Francis Fid...s (the latter 2 left here by the Waterwitch) and put them on board the Joseph Albino Capt'n Finness

at the Port to be taken to Hobart Town under Sentence of Transportation – Watson for 10 Years they others at 7 Years each Returned to the Gaol at 6 P.M. Robert Craiggie was brot to Gaol this day for Debt. 27

September 24 Sunday: George Dyer had Irons put on him and he was Allowed to Go into the felons Yard. Mr. Fleming Attended divine Service at 11 A.M. 23

September 25 Monday: Saw the Sheriff this Morning and Sent the Gaol Books to him Viz – Bread Book – Meat Book – Water Book – Wood Book – Pay Book and Requisition Book. 23

September 27 Wednesday: took the Pay Sheets to the Sheriff this day for the Monthly Pay. 25

September 28 Thursday: Mr. Wigley the Visiting Magistrate Visited the Gaol this day. 26

September 29 Friday: Robert Craiggie (Debtor) was Discharged this day by order of the Insolvent Court – he having found Bail. 25

September 30 Saturday: Raised the pay this day for the Month. 25

October 1 Sunday: No divine Service in the Gaol this day Mr. Fleming not Attending. 25

October 2 Monday: The Sheriff & the Commiss'r of Police Visited the Gaol and went all over the place. 25

October 3 Tuesday: John Shand was brot to Gaol for debt – by Borr Sheriffs Officer Mr. Gilbert Call'd at the Gaol and Said Mr. Martin had the Contract for this Quarter for the Meat for Prisoners. 26

October 4 Wednesday: a Man Named Beck was Stoped by Perry with a Bottle of Brandy which he was takin into Kingdom in the debtors Yard he being a Poor Man and Saying he Could Not Read the Board on the Outside of the Gaol Door he was not detained but the Spirits was taken from him and thrown away in his presence. – Shortly after a person named Mitchell brot a Bottle of Wine which he was takin into the debtors Yard which was also taken from him and thrown away in his presence – Received a letter this day from the Sheriff Relative to our Guard and the Military Prisoners in the Guard Room. 26

October 6 Friday: Mr. Thomas Williams was Sent back to Gaol by the Insolvent Court his former Petition having been dismissed but with leave to Petition Again within 21 days - I Certified another Petition for him this day brot to Gaol by Payne Judges Mess'r. 27

October 8 Sunday: Mr. Fleming Attended divine Service at 11 A.M. 27

October 10 Tuesday: Saw the Sheriff this day told me he wished to See Me to Morrow Morning at 11 OC'k. 28

October 11 Wednesday: found the body of the boy that was drown on the 5th of Aug't last - took the body to the Market house. 29

October 12 Thursday: the inquest was held on the Body of James Hanna by Mr. Nicholas Coroner at the Market House this day at 12 Noon - They Jury Returned a Verdict of Accidentally drowned. - The Rev'd Mr. Farrell Came to the Gaol but being told by Kennedy that Myself & Perry was at the Inquest he did Not Stay So that there was no divine Service.
John Shand (Debtor) was discharged by order of the Insolvent Court he having found Bail. 29

October 13 Friday - The Sheriff Visited the Gaol this day. - Mr. Thomas Williams (Debtor) was discharged by order of the Insolvent Court - he having found Bail. 30

October 15 Sunday: Mr. Fleming Attended at the Gaol divine Service at 11 A.M. 29

October 16 Monday: a Woman Left a Child this afternoon with Stevens (a debtor) in the debtors Yard after the felons was locked up I told Stevens the Child Could not Stay in the Gaol and it was taken by Kennedy to Stevens friends in the Town and left - Perry had told the Woman when She was leaving the Gaol that the Child would not be Allowed to Remain in the Gaol during the Night She Said She would Come back for it but did not. 29

October 17 Tuesday: Mr. Gilbert Call'd about the Rations for Prisoners he Not having Received the Orders before from the Colonial Secretary. 29

October 18 Wednesday: Mary Brown Sentenced to 3 Month Hard labour for felony by His Honor in July last was this day discharged – The Sheriff Visited the Gaol. Police Constable Norris brot down word that the Native Ned was to be discharged he was Remanded to Saturday but the Police did not Come for him it Appears that he was to have been discharged that day but No Order was Sent to Me to that effect and I only Know of it at 5 OC'k this Afternoon when he was discharged. 30

October 19 Thursday: Dr. Nash Visited the Gaol Saw Isabella Anderson in Solitary Confinement Also Charles Hedditch. 28

October 20 Friday: Dr. Nash Visited the Gaol Saw Isobella Anderson in Solitary Confinement & Hedditch. Isaac Nonmus (Debtor) was discharged by Order of the Sheriff. 28

October 21 Saturday: John Noonan was this Day Committed for Trial for an Assault on a little Girl 9 Years of age with intent and etc This Man was a School Master at North Adelaide. 28

October 22 Sunday: No divine Service at the Gaol this day Mr. Fleming not Attending. 28

October 23 Monday – Moullia the Native that was Taken and left at Port Lincoln at the time the Native was executed there for the Murder of Eliz'th Stubbs was brot back to the Gaol by Serg't ... of the Police – without any papers. 31

October 25 Wednesday: Capt'n Frome and Mr. Dashwood Visited the Gaol and went – and went all over. 32

October 26 Thursday: Dr. Nash Visited the Gaol & Saw they Prisoners in Solitary Confinement and Hedditch. 30

October 28 Saturday: Mr. Wigley the Visiting Magistrate Visited the Gaol this Morning. 30

October 29 Sunday: Mr. Fleming Attended the Gaol divine Service at 11 OC'k this Morning. 29

November 1 Wednesday: the Sheriff Visited the Gaol this Morning and went Over the Several yards. Received the Cheque this day for the Months Pay etc from the Treasury. 27

November 4 Saturday: Received this day for Safe Custody 6 Prisoners by the John Pirie from the Mauritius under Sentence of Transportation to V.D. Land. Mr. Hamilton to be Answerable for their Rations - also 2 Soldiers as Sentenced by Court Martial. 35

The Adelaide gaol was again used as a place of custody for convicts in transit. The *John Pirie* had travelled via the island of Mauritius (in British hands since 1810), arriving in Adelaide 7 August 1843.

November 5 Sunday: No divine Service at the Gaol this day Mr. Fleming Not Attending. 35

November 6 Monday: I took the Printed Callendars to his Excellency - the Judge. - The Sheriff & Mr. Hamilton Came to the Gaol to See the Prisoners from the Mauritius and etc 35

November 7 Tuesday: the Sessions Commenced at 10 OC'k this Morning and was Adjourned at 1½ P.M. till 10 to Morrow Morning Not being able to get a Grand Jury. 35

November 8 Wednesday - Court All Day Joseph Hardy was Convicted of Stealing a Bullock the property of Mr. Frew and Sentenced to 10 Years Transportation. 36

November 9 Thursday: Court all day - A Native called Warrimirru was Sentenced to 12 Months Hard Labour and to be Publicly Whipped during the first week of his imprisonment. 34

November 10 Friday: At the Court John Noonan Schoolmaster was this day Sentenced to 18 Months imprisonment and to pay a fine of £5 for an Indecent Assault on Jane Grant 10 Years of age The trials ended this day and the Court Adjourned at 2 P.M. to Tuesday Morning next at 10 OC'k. 30

November 12 Sunday: No divine Service at the Gaol this day Mr. Fleming do not Attend. Mr. Benson Visited they Prisoners from the Mauritius at 2 OC'k P.M. 30

November 13 Monday: the Native Call'd Warrimirru alias Jemmy was this day Whipped this day at 12 OC'k Noon in front of the

Gaol and Received 50 lashes Present - the Sheriff Dr. Nash Mr. Moorhouse the Gov'r of the Gaol Insp'rs Litchfield, Shaw and 3 of they Mounted Police. - this Prisoner was Sentenced on Thursday last by His Honor the Judge to 12 Months Hard Labour and to be publicly Whipped for Stealing Tobacco from the Premises of Mr. Waterhouse.   30

November 14 Tuesday: Mr. Benson Visited they Prisoners from the Mauritius at 8 OC'k A.M. Mr. Wigley the Visiting Magistate Visited the Gaol.   30

November 16 Thursday: Sent Dyers Petition to the Sheriff this day.   30

November 17 Friday: Mr. Moorhouse Call'd and Saw the Natives he wished me to have the Irons taken off Buccomola the Native he having burnt his feet I do So. - Sent Hayters Petition to the Sheriff - the Sheriff Sent Me the Answer to Maria ...s Petition. Thomas Williams was Sent to Gaol from the Insolvent Court for 6 Months to Commence from the 17th day of Aug't 1843.   31

November 18 Saturday: Saw the Sheriff this day with the Reports and etc.   31

November 19 Sunday: No divine Service at the Gaol this day Mr. Fleming did Not Attend.   31

November 21 Tuesday: Call'd the Sheriffs Office he was not in Town.   33

November 23 Thursday: 2 Panes of Glass broken in the felons Yard one in No 3 and one in No 4 Caused by the wind blowing the Windows Open Reported the Same to the Sheriff. The Sheriff Reported 3 Panes broken.   32

November 24 Friday: Mr. James (Attorney) Came to the Gaol and demanded the discharge of Mr. Williams I told him I Could Not discharge him he having been Sentenced by the Insolvent Court and that I had the Warrant Signed by the Judge to detain him but that I would See the Sheriff about the Same to Morrow Morning and let him Know - as it was to late (4 P.M.) to See the Sheriff this day.   36

November 25 Saturday: Saw the Sheriff this Morning about Mr. Williams discharge The Sheriff wrote me this -
Mr. Ashton

> The Insolvent Cannot be discharged without an application to the Court.
> C.B. Newenham Sheriff 15th November 1843 -

I told Mr. James the Same. 36

November 26 Sunday: Mr. Fleming Attended the Gaol Divine Service at 11 A.M. 36

November 27 Monday: the Sheriff Visited the Gaol this Morning went all over etc. Reported to him about lamps being broken - Windows they Cells doors etc. 36

November 30 Thursday: Mr. Thomas Williams In Gaol under the Insolvent Act was this day Discharged by Order of the Sheriff. 39

December 1 Friday: Charles Stevens (Debtor) was this day taken to the Insolvent Court and was Remanded back to Gaol for 4 Weeks - Mr. Hamilton Came to the Gaol to See they 6 Prisoners from the Mauritius he Said he Thought they leave here for V.D. Land on Tuesday or Wednesday Next. 38

December 2 Saturday: took they 6 Prisoners (from the Mauritius) to the Port and put them on board the Schooner Victoria Capt'n Derke to be taken to Hobart Town all under Sentence of Transportation put them on board about 6 P.M. Mr. William Moore went with them. 39

December 3 Sunday: No Divine Service at the Gaol this day. 33

December 4 Monday: Saw the Sheriff and Mr. Hamilton this day Reported to them that they Prisoners was put on board on Saturday. 33

December 6 Wednesday - Received from Mr Hamilton on Account of the 6 Prisoners from the Mauritius and placed in this Gaol for Safe Custody for the under mentioned Articles -

70 lbs of Bread	£1-0-5-10
114 lbs of Meat	?-16-7½

5 lb of Salt	-4
¼ lb of Tea	-6
3 Bottles Lime Juice	-3-6
	£1-6-9½

I paid the above Sum to the Sheriff on an Account of Government. 33

December 7 Thursday: Mr. Porter from the Colonial Engineers Department and went Over the Gaol to See what Repairs was Wanted. - Mr. Wigley the Visiting Magistrate Visited the Gaol. 34

December 9 Saturday: His Excellency was pleased this day to Grant a free Pardon to Philip Hyde under Sentence of Transportation for Robbing a Person named ... Convicted in November Sessions 1842 and Sentenced to 15 Years Transportation - discharged this day out of Custody. 31

December 10 Sunday: No divine Service at the Gaol this Day. 30

December 11 Monday: Call'd at the Sheriff's Office he was Not in Town Mr. Moorhouse Call'd at the Gaol and Said that the Sheriff had Received the discharges from the Colonial Secretarys Office for the Discharge of a Native Call'd Kurti Mukarta I Received None from the Sheriff. 31

December 12 Tuesday: Received this day from the Sheriff His Excellencys Free Pardon for the Native Called Kurti Mukarta - he was discharged and taken by Lennon over to Mr. Moorhouse's This Native was Convicted at the Nov'r Sessions 1842 and Sentenced to 10 Years Transportation for Stealing a Calf the property of Mr. Campbell. 31

December 14 Thursday: Received Yesterday from Mr. Harriotts lbs of Rice as Ordered by the Colonial StoreKeeper Extra Applied for in Consequence of having had So Many Natives in the Gaol this Quarter they Natives Receiving Extra Rice in place of Meat Tea & Sugar. 31

There is certainly an impression of a great many Indigenous people having dealings with the gaol throughout 1843. A few snippets from

Cawthorne's diary provide a snapshot of the mood and situation for Aboriginal people living in or visiting Adelaide at the end of 1843:

> 3 October 1843 – All the natives have lately gone away into the country and hardly one is to be seen about now. It would be better if all were permanently to remain in the country for the vices they learn in the town amongst the English ... are prejudicial ... to themselves ...
>
> 21 October 1843 – I have often told you that our present Governor is invariably disliked. Let me add an original anecdote ... by one of the natives. [For the Queen's Birthday the former governor was] ... very good – long time ago came here – give lanty tuckout – lanty blanket – lanty Bullocky – lanty sheepy. This man (the present Governor) no good, give piccaninny meat ... Gubnor Gay no good. Gubnor Gay bloody rogue!!
>
> 2 November 1843 – I went amongst the natives this morning for latterly a great number have arrived from different districts – at the present time I should say there are no less than 400. There are 3 different tribes, viz. – the 'Moorunde', the 'Mount Barker' and the 'Adelaide' ... a grand fight is the object that has attracted them here ... I shall try to see this barbarous spectacle but I think the authorities will not permit the fight to take place.

Again on 2 November 1843 he wrote:

> I went to the tribe which was encamped not a dozen yards distant – the Mount Barker. 'What for all black men come out down here' [the answer was to keep an eye on the white man] ... 'white fellow no give rice, bullock, sheepy, sugar, no nothing, black man come down here and kill white man, police man, shentleman, white man, all!! all!! Black man spear ... black man will come far away, will come from there (pointing to the north) from there (pointing to the S) from there (pointing to the E) all!! lanty, lanty, black fellow come. Come out, down here. Come kill all white man. White man no more good, bloody rogues' ... This will give some faint idea how the natives

hate the whites, but as to their killing us, it is only bravado – at least I should think so.

And on 13 December 1843:

[T]he Zangary (gum) is now no more and the native wails in vain . . . Hang the rapacious Englishman. They are stripping every wattle tree that can be found . . . Britons you would sell the earth if you could find a purchaser.

Aboriginal people were employed to strip the wattle bark for export of the gum, and in doing so depleted a main source of food, relied on by the Kaurna mothers to feed and comfort their babies.

16 December 1843 – The 'Korrobbery' of the blacks – how affecting their plaintive wail. . . . The moon is shining, silence prevails, and the wild song of the blacks comes melancholy through the tall gum trees. This is the last remaining custom they enjoy. They are becoming gradually absorbed in the habits of the English. Their manner and customs are being forgot. The Korobbery will soon follow their language [and] will become extinct and lastly not a black will be able to sing the song of former days. Alas! Such will be the case. May I not see it. . . . wail on natives.[342]

December 15 Friday: Reported to the Sheriff 2 Keys of the Iron Gates - the R. . . Block broken & the privy in the felons Yard wants emptying etc   31

December 16 Saturday: got they Prisoners last Night & this Morning Opened the door and had the privy in the felons Yard cleaned out had a dreadful Mess with the Same gave they Prisoners a bottle of Brandy for doing the Same. - The Sheriff Visited the Gaol this day Saw they Prisoners.
They 3 Prisoners (Soldiers) that have been Confined in the Guard Room Some days was taken away at ¼ to 5 OC'k this Morning.   31

December 17 Sunday: Mr. Fleming Attended divine Service at 11 A.M. Dr. Nash Visited the Gaol.   31

December 18 Monday: Call'd at the Sherriffs Office this day he did Not Come to Town. 31

December 19 Tuesday: Saw the Sheriff this Morning Mentioned to him about Gilks. – I also took him the list for Articles & Rations for Next Quarter. 31

December 22 Friday: William Pearce was brot to Gaol for Debt – brot to Gaol by Borr. 33

December 23 Saturday: William Pearce was discharged for Debt by Order of the Sheriff – the Locks & Keys of the Gates (Debtors & the one by the Coppers) was Repaired by a Man from the Colonial Engineers Department this day. 32

December 24 Sunday: No divine Service at the Gaol this day Mr. Fleming did Not Attend. 31

December 27 Wednesday: John Haytor (in Gaol for a fine etc) was discharged he having Served his 3 Months. 30

December 30 Saturday: Received a letter from Capt'n Lipson this Afternoon Ordering the 2 Sailors (McKenzie & Glanville) belonging to the Madras to be taken to the Port this day I took Them down and left them Capt'n Lipson Saying he had Received their fines. 28

December 31 Sunday: No divine Service A prisoner Named Baker was brot to the Gaol on a Warrant for an Assault – at 11 OC'k Night. 27

The governor's journal 1844

January 2 Tuesday: Saw the Sheriff at his Offices. 28

January 4 Thursday: The Sheriff Visited the Gaol Saw the Prisoners and went over the Gaol etc The Rev'd Mr Farrell Call'd at the Gaol but did not Stay for divine Service. 30

January 7 Sunday: divine Service in the Gaol at 11 OC'k A.M. Mr. Fleming Attended. 31

January 8 Monday: Saw the Sheriff at his Office this Morning also took a Letter for His Excellency from Hardy a Prisoner gave it to Mr. F... at the office. 32

January 10 Wednesday: Saw Mr. Gilbert about the Rations for the Prisoners - to See him tomorrow Morning about the Orders. 32

January 11 Thursday: Went to the Stores for the Orders for the Rations for Prisoners Call'd at the Sheriffs - The Sheriff Visited the Gaol told the 2 Prisoners under Sentence of Transportation was likely to go away in a day or two and that 2 Guards Mara & Lean was to leave the Gaol duty on Next Saturday Week - the Rev'd Mr. Farrell Attended the Gaol at 1 OC'k P.M. divine Service. 30

January 12 Friday: Turner the Military Prisoner was put into Solitary Confinement this Morning According to his Sentence. 29

January 13 Saturday: Saw the Advocate General this day About the Prisoners for Trial on Tuesday Next at the General Sessions of the Peace. 29

January 14 Sunday: No divine Service at the Gaol this day Mr. Fleming did not Attend and etc 29

January 15 Monday: Mr. Pearce brot to Gaol for Debt. 30

January 16 Tuesday: the General Sessions of the Peace (Charles Cooper Esq'r Chairman) Commenced at the Court all day - Lieutenant Hugonin left word with Perry that the 2 Military Prisoners now in Gaol (Gilks & Turner) was to be treated every way the Same as the Other Prisoners in the Gaol either in the Solitary Confinement or otherwise and that if the Other Prisoners had only bread & water they to have the Same. 31

January 17 Wednesday: at the Sessions all day - James Wilde - John Howard - and Harry Metcalfe Cases was put off until the Gaol delivery in March Next - Harriet Spencer was this day Sentenced by the Court - to One Months Middling Hard labour and not to let her Mix if Possible with they other Prisoners - She was taken into the TurnKeys House (Perrys) for the Present by the Sheriffs wish. - I Mentioned to the Sheriff what Lieutenant Hugonin told Perry he wished me to let it Stand as it then did untill after the Sessions and he would Come down to the Gaol & Arrange with Me about the Soldiers & the Girl. - the Trials of the Prisoners was finished at 5 OC'k this day and the Court was Adjourned to 10 OC'k to Morrow Morning. 33

Harriet Spencer was yet another child prisoner. She had been apprenticed to a Mrs Watts but had been dismissed after just a month. Before she left she was caught stealing lace and ribbons.[343] Again Ashton did what he could to juggle arrangements in the gaol. The principle of 'classification' or physically separating different classes of prisoners (to prevent moral cross-contamination) was an ideal in prison systems of the time, however Ashton had little means to do so in his gaol. He certainly had nowhere for child prisoners. He had to rely on Perry the turnkey's house, the guards' room (that was also used for military prisoners), or else his own house.

January 18 Thursday: Saw Mr. Richman about the Prisoners Sentenced this Evening. - Lieut't Huganin Told Me the Same this Afternoon has he had told Perry on Tuesday last and Said the Sixpence per day for the 2 Soldiers would be paid and that the next night to have been back on Inside the Gaol. 32

January 19 Friday - A pane of Glass was this Afternoon broken in the debtors Yard No 2 Room Caused by the wind One of Porters Men Commenced the Work at the Gaol Yesterday the felons Kitchen fire place was the first job done. 32

January 20 Saturday: Mara & Lean 2 Guards left the Gaol duty this day by order of the Government - The Sentry was moved Round to the Wooden fence. 33

January 21 Sunday: No divine Service at the Gaol this day. Mr Fleming did Not Attend. 33

January 22 Monday: Call'd at the Sheriffs Office he was Not in. 33

January 23 Tuesday: Saw the Sheriff this day with the Return of No of Prisoners in Gaol during the Year brought it back to alter. 33

January 24 Wednesday: Sent Perry with the Return of Prisoners to the Sheriffs this Morning. At 9½ OC'k this evening Mr. Ha... - Mr. Gwynne & Mr. Smith Came to the Gaol. Mr. Ha... Said he wished to See Mr. Pearce a debtor about some property - and altho the Prisoner was locked up for the Night I allowed him to See him. - he Saw him about Some Articles they had discovered at the Bay. 33

January 25 Thursday: Gilks the Soldier was put into Solitary Confinement to Serve his Month According to his Sentence. 33

January 28 Sunday: No divine Service - in the Gaol this day Mr. Fleming did Not Attend. 33

January 29 Monday: Received an Order from the Sheriff this Morning to take Mr. William Pearce (a Debtor) before the Resident Magistrate to be Ex'd on a Charge of felony Took him to the Court Accordingly Pearce was Remanded until 11 OC'k to Morrow Morning. 33

January 30 Tuesday: a Carpenter Sent by Mr. Porter to do the work in the Gaol Took Mr. Pearce to the Court at 11 OC'k this Morning brought him back at 4 P.M. Remanded until 11 Oc'k on Thursday Morning Next The Magistrate Requested Me Not to let him have any Communication with any one while under Remand - I therefore gave Perry orders not to let any Person go into the debtors Yard but if any one wanted to See either of the Other Debtors to let the debtors Come out and See any one in the TurnKeys lodge. - The Prisoner Little from his foolish talk was likely to Make a disturbance with they Other Prisoners in the felons Yard I ordered Perry to let him Sleep in one of the Cells Out Side of the Yard. 33

[In margin]
Received this day from Sarg't Clarke of the 96 Regiment £4-7- for the Keep of 2 Soldiers 6d per day each being 87 days.

January 31 Wednesday: Mr. Polden the Attorney Came to the Gaol this Morning and Saw Mr. Pearce in the TurnKeys lodge. 33

February 1 Thursday: Mr. Pearce the Debtor was this day taken before the Resident Magistrate and was Remanded to Saturday Next at 11 OC'k. Paid the Sheriff this day £4-7-0 for the Keep of 2 Soldiers 27 days at 6d per day each. 34

February 3 Saturday: took Mr. Pearce the debtor to the Magistrates Court & he was Remanded again to the 8th Inst Thursday - Received an Order from Capt'n Lipson that the Sailor William Newman belonging to the Dorset was to be put on board this Afternoon and he was taken to the Port by P.C. Dean - I told Dean to Remind Capt'n Lipson about the fine etc - which was to be paid by the Capt'n of the Dorset. 35

February 4 Sunday: No divine Service at the Gaol this day Mr. Fleming Not Attending. 34

February 5 Monday: the Sheriff Visited the Gaol this day went all over etc he found they Military all up Stairs and their Fire Arms Standing outside the Guard Room door Call'd them down and Cautioned them. 34

February 6 Tuesday: took Pearce to the Magistrates Court at 11 A.M. he was again Remanded untill 11 OC'k on Thursday Next – whilst at the Court this day Perry the TurnKey Sent Me word that Dyer & Oakey Prisoners under Sentence of Transportation had Made up their Mind to Make their Escape from Gaol Not being able to leave the Court Capt'n Litchfield was Kind enough to Send down one of the Police till My Return We had Work Men in the Yard with Ladders etc – on My Return home I found all Right and Sent the Police Constable home. 34

February 8 Thursday: took Mr. Pearce (Debtor) to the Magistrates Court and he was Committed for Trial for Concealing Some Property with intent to defraud his Creditors he was Bailed as to the Charge of felony brot back & put in the debtors Yard. 32

February 9 Friday: A Man named Pearson was this day Committed for Trial for Stealing a Bell. 38

February 10 Saturday: the Sheriff this day Certified that Rations Should be Allowed to William Pearce a Debtor from this day. Saw the Colonial Secretary about the Whitewash Brushes for the Gaol – he told me I had better purchase 2 Brushes and put the Same in the Bill for the limes & Rivets –
Paid Mr. Pybers 3/- for 2 Dozen of Rivets for Prisoners Irons etc – 33

February 11 Sunday: No divine Service in the Gaol this day Mr. Fleming did not Attend. 32

February 13 Tuesday: Received from Capt'n Finnis 4 pr of Leg Irons which had been taken to Hobart Town Some time ago with Prisoners. 33

Dyer, who had escaped once already, caused nervousness in the gaol. The quality of iron to make leg irons in the colony was extremely poor and iron of any type was scarce, hence the attention to replacing rivets and noting any leg irons returned. The presence of workmen, ladders and firearms left unattended would be the perfect opportunity for Dyer.

February 15 Thursday: 4 Squares of Glass was broken in the Lamps by they Prisoners Scrubbing them to get the oil off. Reported the Same to the Sheriff. 33

February 17 Saturday: the Girl Spencers Father Came and [took] her away She was discharged Yesterday but was allowed to Sleep in Perrys House untill this day when She was taken away. 31

[In margin]
Stevens Debtor was discharged by order of the Sheriff having Settled with his Creditors.

February 18 Sunday: No divine Service in the Gaol this day Mr. Fleming did not attend. About 10 P.M. Isabella Anderson was Creating a disturbance in the Females Yard I had her put into one of the Solitary Cells for Safety. 30

February 19 Monday: They Prisoners in the felons & debtors Yards Refused to take their bread this Morning I Saw the Refused without a Cause Showed Some of the bread to the Colonial Storekeeper & to the Sheriff who all So Said it was good and gave me a written order to give them no other Sort. - Perry in my Absence gave they Prisoners in the felons yard 5 loaves of the Same Sort of bread but further baked - that was all they had during the day. - They Prisoners was all Very - quite [crossed out] quiet about the Same. - the Visiting Magistrate Visited the Gaol this day & found all Right Isabella Anderson Still in the Cell Made a Great Noise all Night. 31

February 20 Tuesday: the Sheriff Visited the Gaol & found All Right. - a Square of Glass in a lamp was broken this day whilst being Painted. All they large Lamps was painted this day by a Man Sent by Mr. Porter. - Isabella Anderson Still in the Cell She was Quite Mad this evening. 32

February 21 Wednesday: Isabella Anderson Making a Noise All Night was in a dreadful Mess this Morning and So was the Cell by her doing her Occasions about the Place Saw Lieut't Huganin this day & Yesterday about the Soldier Turner I Having Received a letter from Serg't Clarke Stating that the Sentence was 9 Lunar Months but Lunar Months not having been Mentioned in the Committal he have been presumed by the Calendar Month So that when his 7 Month in Solitary was up his time by the Lunar Month was to go in again Mr. Hugonin wished Me to let the Prisoner Remain out in the Yard for the present untill he has Spoken to Capt'n Butler about the Same. 32

February 22 Thursday: Saw Liet't. Hugonin again Told he had Spoken to Capt'n Butler and the Prisoner Turner was to Remain as he was for the present W.C. Kingdom (Debtor) was Discharged this Morning by Order of the Sheriff the discharge was dated the 21st but I did Not Received untill 9 O'Ck this Morn'g when he was discharged - Isabella Anderson Still in the Cell Very bad. Saw the Sheriff this day. 31

February 23 Friday: Received this day by Kennedy from the Colonial Engineers Storekeeper 4 Buckets (Old) & One New Shovel as per the Quarter Requisition Isabella Anderson Still in the Cell Appears a little better this day. 31

Isabella Anderson takes up much of Ashton's time and attention during 1844 and continued to do so for some years. The journal for 1844 provides a sobering insight into the place of gaols in the history of care for the mentally ill. 'Bella' was known as the town drunk and notorious for her outrageous talk, however her situation had gone beyond public entertainment with her quick and foul mouth; her mind had now seriously deteriorated. Ashton starts his journal entries regarding Bella in a relatively objective way, however his vigilance concerning her, noting her ups and downs, and his sometimes lengthy descriptions of her behavior, show his true concern. He did not seem to judge, and without saying as much, seemed particularly touched by her plight. There is the clear impression that he was much relieved and hopeful at brief moments when she 'appears a little better'.

Bella was not the only one who was in gaol enduring a mental illness – 1844 seemed to be a year for it. Mary Rhodes was one who had been in and out since the old temporary gaol and was now considered 'insane', suffering from delirium tremens. At one point she lashes out seriously at Mrs Best, another of the women prisoners. Both Mary Rhodes and Bella were permitted in the women's section when possible, however the situation could deteriorate quickly and one or other would need to be removed to a solitary cell to protect the other women. As with the category of 'children' there was no separate space for the category 'lunatics'. Ashton tried to solve this dilemma by asking for a female assistant to be employed to help, particularly with Bella, as she was messing herself and ripping off her clothes.

Hedditch, who had murdered the young boy near Mount Barker and been deemed 'insane', was still in the gaol, looked after by two of the debtors. McPherson, who was suspected of lighting the 1841 fire at Government House, was also thought to be a 'lunatic' (though there had been some official dispute – in a Supreme Court writ *de lunatico inquirendo*, doctors' opinions were divided and six jurors thought him 'lunatic' and six not).[344] Three more sufferers, all men, were to be gaoled on the charge of being 'dangerous lunatics' before the year was out. The first of these, Ernest Hagen, was looked after with some success by the debtors. However, when towards the end of the year two extremely violent and unpredictable men, Berkely and Wilkins, were brought in, the situation became impossible. Though Dr Nash, Ashton, the guards, and the other prisoners were all doing their best, their time (and the journal entries) seemed to be consumed with the 'lunatics'. The sheriff decided to employ an extra turnkey, later described as extra turnkey and 'Keeper of Lunatics'.[345] In no time it was clear that the new employee could not cope. The colony had pitifully little provision for such illness. Dr Nash had done his best in the gaol, however a dedicated 'lunatic asylum', first mooted in Gawler's time had not yet been decided.

February 25 Sunday: No divine Service at this day the Rev'd Mr. Farrell did not Attend.   31

February 26 Monday: A Person Named Robert Davis was this day brot to Gaol from the Port Sentenced by Capt'n Lipson & Mr. T... to 2 Months Solitary Confinement on 2 Separate Charges of an Assault in default of paying the fine.   33

February 27 Tuesday: Saw Mr. Wigley the Visiting Justice about the above named Prisoner Davis he gave me a Written Order to take the Said Davis out of Solitary Confinement and put him into the Yard with the Other Prisoners untill further Orders which was done Isobella Anderson a little better but Still in the Cell.   35

February 28 Wednesday: Mr. Wigley Visited Saw Mr. Pearce & Isabella Anderson. - Dr. Nash Also Saw Anderson Said She was better and as her time of Imprisonment would be out to Morrow he thought She would be better when Set at Liberty.   35

February 29 Thursday: Isabella Anderson was discharged this day and etc -   35

Two days later Bella was back, a common occurence for her – newspapers often mentioned it. One newspaper report, six years later, conveyed the resignation of everyone including herself to her fate:

> Isabella Anderson, alias Scotch Bella, was charged with making use of obscene language. Constable Dyke said that the woman came out of gaol on Thursday week, and had been behaving most outrageously ever since. On Saturday night she behaved so offensively that he felt compelled to apprehend her.
>
> The prisoner said that she had been 14 years in the colony, and that the greater part of the time she had been in prison. The Commissioner said ... She was much better in prison than in the streets, and he would therefore commit her for one month.[346]

In another version of the same decision His Worship noted that she 'had only just returned from a three month's visit to Ashton Castle' and declared he would now 'return her to her old friend Mr Ashton'.[347]

March 1 Friday: Received the Months pay this day from the Colonial Treasurer and paid they Men.   34

March 2 Saturday: Isabella Anderson was brot to Gaol again this day for a Month. The Sheriff Visited the Gaol this After Noon and 2 Men Committed under the Masters and Servants Act for One Month each.   36

March 3 Sunday: No divine Service at the Gaol this day. 36

March 4 Monday: they Calendars was delivered this day. 36

March 5 Tuesday: the Gaol delivery Commenced this day No Prisoners tried at the Supreme Court all Day. Isabella Anderson Still Very Bad Dr. Nash Ordered her head to be Shaved and Kept Wet with Spirits and Water etc which was done. 35

Applying the spirit ether to a shaved scalp and letting it evaporate was one of the standard treatments for agitation, meant to cool the system and deflect the patient's attention through shock, thus inducing sleep. There is no evidence that it improved Bella at all – she remained extremely disturbed throughout the following days. It may have provided her with some relief (she was possibly tearing at her hair) or else she may have felt completely devastated to be stripped of her hair.

There is a rare physical description of Bella that happens to mention her hair. It is in a verse written by a police officer in 1841. He was patrolling the Torrens River at night, admiring the beauty of the scene, when:

> A spectre arose on my vision! The son of my mother was frightened! The figure was that of a female! Flowed her locks, like a dark stormy midnight! Rolled her eyes like a couple of coach-wheels! 'Son of Murder' said she 'Where art walking?' I fled like night's shadow at morning. I beheld in my vision Scotch Bella. W.X.[348]

She was often called Scotch Bella, a term she hated. Scottish people generally would have found the adjective demeaning when applied to people and only acceptable when describing things, such as whisky. Perhaps it was a pun because she was an alcoholic. Years later she complained that boys in the street 'old enough to be at their trades' were taunting her, calling her 'Scotch Bella' and 'Vandemonian lag'.[349]

March 6 Wednesday: at the Court all day Henry Wilson & Eliz'th Mason was Convicted of Stealing Timber & Sentenced to 6 Months Hard Labour. 36

March 7 Thursday: at the Court all day Isabella Anderson is Still Very Bad Obliged to Keep her in a Cell by her Self. 36

March 8 Friday: at the Court untill 8 P.M. The Trial of William Pearce Comm'd this Morning Adj'd till to Morrow Morning at 9 OC'k. 32

March 9 Saturday: Pearce Trial on till 11 P.M. Adj'd untill 9½ Monday Morning they Jury Kept till that time. 31

March 10 Sunday: No divine Service at the Gaol this day. 31

March 11 Monday: At the Court all day The Jury found Pearce Guilty this day Sentence Not past on him to be taken to Court on the 13th (Wednesday) at 10 A.M. 31

March 12 Tuesday: James Wild - & John Howard for Stealing Oil was this day Acquitted This was the last Case in the Calendar for Trial - Isabella Anderson Still Very bad in the Cell Still. 31

March 13 Wednesday: William Pearce was taken the Court at 10 OC'k this Morning for Sentence - to be brot up again for Sentence to Morrow Morn'g at 10 A.M. Isobella Anderson Still Very Ill - Still in the Cell. 33

March 14 Thursday: Pearce was taken to the Court at 10 this Morning and in Consequence of the Indictment on which he had been found Guilty on being Defective His Honor discharged him as to the felony and Ordered Me to take him back in the Same Custody as he was in before tried brot back to Gaol and put into the Debtors Yard This ended My duty at the Court - The Rev'd Mr. Farrell Attended - divine Service at the Gaol at 1 P.M. Joseph Hardy under Sentence of Transportation was Baptised in the Chapel. 32

March 15 Friday: Saw the Sheriff about They Prisoners going to V.D. Land told Me they was not likely to go before the end of the Next Week. 30

March 16 Saturday: The Sheriff Visited the Gaol this day found All Right. 30

March 17 Sunday: No divine Service in the Gaol this day Isabella Anderson Still Insane & in the Cell. 28

March 18 Monday: took the Reports to the Sheriff for the Next Quarters Supplies - Saw Mr. Gilbert about the extra Rice he Sent us 58 lbs.

Isobella Anderson went to the Tower and into Kennedys bed Room.

March 19 Tuesday: John Turner (a Soldier) was discharged and taken from the Gaol by the Military he having Served his 9 Lunar Months - he was Committed for 9 Months but Nothing was Mentioned about Lunar Months. I took his Sentence as Calendar Mo. His 7 & 9 Months was to be in Solitary Confinement - The Consequence was having only heard a Short Time Ago from Serg't Clarke that it was to be Lunar Months he was only in Solitary Conf't 6 days of his last Month before he was discharged.

March 20 Wednesday: Reported to the Sheriff this day that Eliz'th Mason (a Prisoner under Sentence of 6 Months hard Labour) Could not eat the Prison Rations being in deteriorate health and that her Husband wished to Supply her himself with food during the time She was in Gaol - The Sheriff told Me to Allow him to do So for the present and Allow her Nothing from the Gaol Rations - which was Accordingly done Isabella Anderson Still Very Bad.

March 21 Thursday: a Man Named Charles Thompson was brot to Gaol as a Runaway Convict from New South Wales. Remanded till to Morrow.

March 22 Friday: Isabella Anderson Very bad Made a Great Noise all Night tore All her Clothes off her back and Mest herself all over - and the Cell and walls - Dr. Nash Saw her and Ordered her head to be again Shaved and a blister to be put on which was done - Sent to the Hospital and got a Straight waistcoat and put on her She was So bad that we Obliged to fasten her to the Wall All Night. Thompson as Mentioned Yesterday was again Remanded for a Week. - 8 Sailors was Committed this day for 3 Months each for Refusing to Work on board their Ship the Augustus now at Port Adelaide Committed by Mr. Finnis & Mr. Bonney.

March 23 Saturday: Isabella Anderson Still Very bad.

A number of treatments for Bella are mentioned in this part of the journal. The blister is the least known now. It was a plaster containing an irritant, placed on the extremities to induce blisters and heat. The 'blister' was left on the skin until it was almost unbearable. It was both a deflection technique to distract the agitated patient and also meant to draw the blood to the blister, away from the affliction. In this way it was similar to blood letting or being 'bled' with leeches, which was meant to mobilise 'stagnant blood' into flowing again.

Years later, Perry and Ashton publicly mentioned their practice of tying Bella down. They were at the court presenting the case that she was 'lunatic' and not fit to be released:

> Thomas Perry, turnkey of the gaol, deposed that the woman had been in custody for the last three months, during which time she had been very violent, tearing off her clothes, and striking witness and the other turnkeys. On one occasion she threw her dinner at witness. The straight-waistcoat had often to be used, and at times she was obliged to be strapped down. Her language was most abusive ...
>
> By Mr Ashton, – Had even tied her down to prevent her destroying herself, which she several times attempted to do by beating her head against the wall and the pavement ... William Baker Ashton ... gave evidence ... She had thrown her food about and broken the pannicans. Had remonstrated with her, when she took off her shoe and struck him with it. ...
>
> Here the woman attempted to make a rush at the witness, but was restrained by the police. Witness continued. – Considered her so dangerous that he could not place her with any other person ... Last night she might have been heard for a mile. She was not a fit character to be at large.[350]

March 24 Sunday: No divine Service in the Gaol this day Mr. Fleming did Not Attend. 37

March 25 Monday: 4 of they Sailors brot to Gaol on Friday last was Discharged by Order of Mr. Finnis and Mr. Bonney and taken from the Gaol by the Police to be put on board their Ship at Holdfast Bay at 1 P.M. 39

March 26 Tuesday: Isabella Anderson Still Insane – and Very bad. 36

March 28 Thursday: Charles Belfour Elphinstone and George Davis was Committed for Trial for an extensive Robbery At Mr. James Saunders Baker of Hindley Street Adelaide – Isabella Anderson is Still Insane. – Call'd at the Sheriffs Office this day about the Quantity of Bread we had overdrawn he was not in Town. 36

March 29 Friday: The Sheriff & Dr. Nash Visited the Gaol this day and Saw the Prisoners. Charles Thompson under Remand Charged as a Runaway Convict from New South Wales was this day taken before the Resident Magistrate & B.F. Finnis Esq'r J.P. and was discharged on His Own Recognizance in a £100-0 to Appear at the Next Gaol delivery to Answer to being Bill of indictment that may be prepared Against him by the Advocate General Isabella Anderson Still insane. 36

March 30 Saturday: Saw Capt'n Finniss and the Sheriff about they 3 Prisoners going to V.D. Land Capt'n Finniss Said he would let me Know on Monday Morning The Sheriff wrote to the Colonial Secretary this day about Isobella Anderson to Know What is to be done with her as her time will be to discharge her on Tuesday Next 2nd April 1844 She not being in a fit State to be Set at large in Consequence of being Insane. Saw Mr. Gilbert the Colonial StoreKeeper who told Me that the New Contractors for the Bread & Meat where for Bread Mr. Layton & for Meat Mr. Marton both of Grenfell Street and Would Commence Supplying the Gaol on Monday the 1st April 1844. 39

The letter written by the sheriff, regarding Bella, read as follows:

[A] female prisoner now in HM Gaol of the name of Isabella Anderson, a woman hitherto of very abandoned character and a most confirmed drunkard ... has now become decidedly insane, and since her last committal has been getting worse every day ... due for release ... not a fit subject to be allowed to go at large ... request instructions as to what is to be done with this woman.[351]

The colonial secretary replied:

I am directed by His Excellency the Governor to request that you will retain this unfortunate woman in Gaol, and cause such care and attention to be paid as you have it in your power to afford.[352]

March 31 Sunday: No divine Service at the Gaol this day.

April 1 Monday: Capt'n Finniss Call'd at the Gaol this Morning and Said they Prisoners Must be on board this afternoon at 4 OC'k - Saw the Sheriff and Received Instructions from him to take and put on board the Joseph Albino (Capt'n Finniss) at Port Adelaide the following three Prisoners under Sentence of Transportation to V.D. Land and to be taken to Hobart Town in the above Vessel
Joseph Hardy
George Dyer - and
James Oakey -
I left the Gaol with them at 1½ P.M. in the Police Cart Escorted by 2 of they Mounted Police and arrived at the Port about 3½ P.M. The Ship Shortly after left the Wharf and went down the River Capt'n Lipson Placed a Police Constable on board in Charge of they Prisoners and to Remain on board untill the Pilot left the Ship. I Returned to the Gaol at 6½ P.M.

April 2 Tuesday: Saw the Sheriff this day and Reported to him my having taken and Put they Prisoners on board the Jos'ph Albino Yesterday. - he told me that he had not heard from the Government Relative to Isabella Anderson but that we Should Keep her in Gaol untill he did hear for her own Safety.

April 3 Wednesday: the Sheriff told Me this day that he had Seen the Governor about the Woman Isabella Anderson and That She was for the present to be Kept in the Gaol untill they Considered what Could be done with her. - She is Still very bad.

April 4 Thursday: Received from Serg't Clark the Sum of two pounds fourteen Shillings for the Keep of 2 Soldiers under Sentence by the Court Martial - Viz
John Turner 48 days at 6d per day from the 1st Feb'y to the 19th March 1844   £1-4-
George Gilks 60 days at 6d per day from the 1st Feb'y to the 31st March 1844   £1-10-
Total Sum of   £2-14-0
Isobella Anderson Very Noisey This Morning.

April 5 Friday: being good Friday it is a Holy day at the Government Offices. Isobella Anderson is better this day Allowed her to go into the females Yard and walk about.

April 6 Saturday: went to the Sheriffs Office to pay the £2-14 for the above 2 Soldiers the Sheriff was not in Town. 30

April 7 Sunday: Eliz'th Forbes was brot to Gaol this Morning on a Warrant for not having paid a fine of 10s/- Sentenced to 14 days the first & last 3 days in Solitary Confinement The Police it Appears took her late last Night Isobella Anderson was Very Violent to the female prisoners in the Yard Obliged to Confine her hands etc Dr. Nash was Sent for to See her. No divine Service at the Gaol this day. 31

April 8 Monday: Easter Monday a Holiday at the Public Offices. - Isobella Anderson was Very bad this day Struck the female Prisoner and made a Mess all over the place was obliged to put her into the Cell. 31

April 9 Tuesday: Saw the Sheriff this day Sent the Meat over for Mr. Gilbert to see Mr. G. was not at home The Contractor Sending us Scarcely Any Thing but Necks of Mutton and the best part of the Meat Cut off. 31

April 10 Wednesday: Sent the Meat again to Mr. Gilberts who Said he would See the Butcher about it - and they Prisoners Must have better Meat. - Reported to the Sheriff that if Isobella Anderson Remained in Gaol She Must have 2 Changes of Dress and a Woman to look after her as She was getting worse and there being no female Attendant on the Gaol Establishment to do any thing for her. 31

Ashton's demands were answered, His Excellency authorising both the new clothes and a woman already being supported by the government, to be a nurse.[353]

April 11 Thursday: Saw the Sheriff this day and gave him the Petition of Elizabeth Mason to be forwarded to His Excellency the Governor praying for a Commutation of the Sentence. Dr. Nash Visited. 31

April 12 Friday: went over to the Stores and Saw Mr. Gilbert gave the Receipt for the Quarters Rations and Mentioned to him about the Meat I told him What we Received generally Meat he told me he would See the Butcher this day and that if he did not Send us better Meat the Contract Should be taken away from him The Sheriff Visited the Gaol this Afternoon Saw all they Prisoners and went over the Gaol Mr. Tolmer Sent down and asked me to let him have the description of Charles Thompson alias Richard Lewis a Supposed Runaway Convict from Sydney - Sent Accordingly. 31

April 13 Saturday: Received an Order from Mr. Gilbert on Flett & Linklater for 3 lbs of Tea & 12 lbs Sugar on Account of Quarters Supply - Received. 31

April 14 Sunday: Much Rain during the Night the wet Came in a great Many places about the Gaol and house - Felons Yard Debtors Yard. - Bella was Very bad again this day - No divine Service in the Gaol or have we had a divine Service in the Gaol on Sunday Since the 1st January 1844 except once Viz on the 7th January 1844 - when Mr. Fleming attended. 31

Mr Fleming was not to return until November so was away almost the entire year. With Reverend Howard deceased and Mr Farrell attending rarely, the chapel was little used.

April 15 Monday: Saw the Sheriff he told Me that he had not heard about the Quantity of fire Wood for the quarter as Altered by the Government. Bella Very bad still Dr. Nash Saw her. Several Slates was blown off the house during the Night by the high Winds. 31

April 16 Tuesday: Mr. Gilbert Call'd at the Gaol about the Rations and afterwards Sent me the Orders for all the Articles except for Oil & Soap which there had been no Tenders for. - Sent the Orders Round by Kennedy Mr. Porter Sent a Man who put the Lead to the Windows to prevent the Wet Coming into the house. 31

April 17 Wednesday: Call'd and Saw the Sheriff he gave Me the letter he had Received from the Colonial Secretary about the fire Wood which Stated that we must not exceed 9590 lbs per Week in Winter and not More than 8540 lbs in Summer - Winter from 1st April 1844 to the 30th September 1844 Summer from the 1st October 1844 to the 31st March 1845. 31

April 18 Thursday: Isabella Anderson about the Same. Eliz'th Forbes went into Solitary this day for the Remainder of her Sentence. 31

April 19 Friday: Went to the Sheriffs Office to see him about the Clothes for Bella Anderson he was not in Town. 30

April 20 Saturday: Saw the Sheriff he gave me £2 for Mrs Ashton to Get they Articles to Make the Dresses for Bella Anderson 2 Prisoners was discharged this day Capt'n Lipson & the Capt'n Of the Vixon Call'd at the Gaol & Saw the Crew of the Augustus they where trying if the Government would Pardon the Sailor as they wanted Some of them to Join the Vixon to go to Hobart Town The Capt'n told Me that the Colonial Secretary would let them Know on Monday Morning. Dr Nash Visited the Gaol & Saw Isobella Anderson. 30

April 21 Sunday: No Divine Service in the Gaol this day Bella Anderson Appeared Much better this day. 28

April 22 Monday: Mrs Ashton bought the Articles for Bella Clothes this day 2 Sailors Runaways from the Vixen brot to Gaol for One Months Hard Labour Sentenced by Capt'n Lipson. 32

April 23 Tuesday: Saw the Sheriff heard that they 8 Sailors was likely to be discharged told the Sheriff I would Call at his Office at 4 OC'k to See if there was a letter from the Colonial Secretarys There was None James Craig brot to Gaol for Debt - Bella Very bad again and tore her New Gown & Shift this day. 31

April 24 Wednesday: Went to the Sheriffs office this Morning Received the Colonial Secretary's Letter in Answer to the Petition of the 8 Sailors to be discharged from Gaol the Answer was that their petition had been Considered and that under all the Circumstances attending their Conviction did not feel justified in disturbing the Sentences which had been passed upon them. - I Read the Answer to they Men. - the Sheriff was Not in Town. - Mr. Porter Sent a Man to put they Slates on the Roofes about the Gaol. 31

April 25 Thursday: Bella Still Very bad. 31

April 26 Friday: William Pearce a Debtor was discharged by Order of the Insolvent Court he having found Bail. He paid the 5s/1 on his discharge. Elizabeth Forbes was brought to Gaol for 14 days She had been discharged from Gaol a day or 2 ago. 32

April 27 Saturday: the Sheriff Visited and went over the Gaol Saw they Prisoners etc – we having no debtor in Gaol Receiving Rations. The Sheriff ordered that in future when debtors Applied for Rations they Should only be Supplied with the Same as the Other Prisoners was Receiving Viz 1 lbs Bread ½ lbs Meat ¼ lbs of Rice daily and 2oz of Tea & 4 oz Sugar & 4oz Salt per week. 31

The news of Bella's illness spread and a false report of her death was published in the paper:

> The person so well known to the police and to the Colonists as *Bella*, expired yesterday in gaol, of *delirium tremens*.[354]

> Scotch Bella, to whom we referred as dead in our last, is, we hear, only mad. The report of her death was very current in town on Friday last, but it turns out not to be true.[355]

Inside the gaol life was extremely busy and heavily focused on Bella; outside the gaol other things were happening. Before April 1844 ended there was another annual fight between the Aboriginal groups. Cawthorne noted:

> The natives are in high glee ... making warlike preparations for a terrible contest ... They fight annually, sometimes out of fun, to try the respective strength of the young men, sometimes because one of their women were stolen ... and sometimes out of revenge for the death of one of their tribe ... It is but an everlasting retaliation, annually performed. All are in high expectancy, parading up and down the streets in small parties with their spears and cuttas, wirris and shields.[356]

Moorhouse reported the event:

> On the 22nd April there was an attempt to repeat the annual contest between the Encounter Bay Tribe and Murray Tribes. From three to four hundred natives were assembled near the Emigration Square

armed with weapons for attack, but the prompt interference of the Police Force effectually prevented it.[357]

Cawthorne wrote:

> ... unluckily, the horse police got scent of the fight and three armed up to the teeth soon galloped past us to stop proceedings, which they accordingly did ... by having every spear and shield laid on the ground – and afterwards broke up. ... Oh it was cruel of the police.[358]

If they were watching, William and Charlotte Ashton and their children would have seen the gathering battle and sudden carnage of the weapons clearly from their upstairs window.

Cawthorne made a note of his painting of the smashed spears and shields. This painting is particularly affecting with a Guernica feel to it. It is not well known, and is kept in the State Library of New South Wales, but it's a treasure of Adelaide history.

W.A. Cawthorne, *Shields and spears of the Natives on the battlefield*, watercolour on paper, in *William Anderson Cawthorne papers 1842–1844*, p. 53 [Mitchell Library, State Library of New South Wales, Sydney ML A105, item 17][359]

Cawthorne could not dismiss the injustice and wrote next day to the paper:

[T]hree horse police very unceremoniously stopped them, and had every spear and shield laid on the ground, and broken up. The astonishment that this act produced, was truly remarkable – some looked quite aghast, others were confounded . . . 'What for policeman do this? When white man fight in Adelaide, black fellow say nothing. When blackfellow fight, policeman come break spears, break shields . . . What for you no stop in England? . . . 'But what for you fight', I asked . . . replied King John, 'but no good tell you. You write in paper and tell white man what for we fight. Before white man come, Murray black fellow never come here. Now white man come, Murray black fellow come too. Encounter Bay and Adelaide black fellow no like him. Me want them to go away. Let him sit down at the Murray, not here. This is not his country. . . . Let him stop in his own country.[360]

Uncle Lewis O'Brien has studied King John's speech. He says Kaurna people still have this style of talk, a style he calls speaking in 'doubles', 'saying one thing but meaning two things'.[361]

At the end of April 1844 the Location school across the river from the gaol was reportedly going well, with between 30 and 40 children attending each week. The problem with including the Murray children had been solved – a separate school at Walkerville was about to open.[362] A government teacher, Mr Ross teaching in English, was employed at Walkerville. It was a major change – the beginning of the end for the control of education of the Aboriginal children by the German missionaries, who had taught the children in their own Kaurna language. In a little over a year, Piltawodli would be closed, and the schools combined into an English-speaking 'Native School Establishment', at a new site adjacent to the track that became Kintore Avenue in the city. It was to be run by Mr Ross from the Walkerville school, and his wife, with no involvement at all from the missionaries.

April 28 Sunday: No Divine Service in the Gaol this day Bella Very bad this day.   31

April 30 Tuesday: Eliz'th Mason & Eliz'th Forbes and Bella Prisoners All Very Ill this day Sent for Dr Nash who Came down in the Evening & Saw them Mrs Ashton Saw them Made & Sent them in Some Sago. Mr. Porter Sent a Plumber to Repair the Gutters The Man put they Slates on the Top of the House. 31

May 1 Wednesday: They Above females All Ill Still. 31

May 2 Thursday: Dr. Nash Visited the Gaol & Saw They Prisoners. 31

May 3 Friday: The Man finished the Roofs and the Other Man the Gutters About the Gaol. Dr Nash Call at the Gaol and Saw the Prisoners I have been out with Some of they Prisoners the last 2 days Cutting down 2 trees to Repair the ditch and load in front of the Gaol. Ann Bent was brot to Gaol on a Charge of felony Remanded untill Monday Next - and Jane McKinsted alias Jane Ewing Sentenced to 7 days Imprisonment for leaving the Service of B.A. Kent without leave. 33

May 5 Sunday: No divine Service at the Gaol this day Bella Still Very bad. 33

May 6 Monday: Ann Bent was Committed for Trial, Dr. Nash Call'd and Saw they Prisoners. 33

May 7 Tuesday: Howey & Smith was discharged this day having Served their 6 Months each James Craig (Debtor) was discharged by Order of the Insolvent Court he having found Bail. A Woman Named M...y was brot to Gaol Sentenced a Month for ... also 2 Natives Black Men was brot to Gaol Remanded etc on charges of felony. 36

May 8 Wednesday: Serg't Hollinsworth of the 96th Regiment Paid me fifteen Shillings for the Keep of George Gilks for 30 days at Sixpence per day from the 1st April to the 30 April 1844 - Received a Note from the Sheriff wishing Me To go to the Port and take Henry Lee as per Warrant for Contempt of Court. Went to the port with Mr. Mathew Smith and took Henry Lee and brot him to Gaol at 10½ P.M. 35

May 9 Thursday: Borr Sheriffs Office Brot to Gaol for Debt John Smith Johnston at the Suit of Edw'd Stephens and others. 37

May 10 Friday: Call'd at the Sheriffs office Saw him and he after wards Call'd at the Gaol went All Over and Saw all the Prisoners. 35

May 11 Saturday: did not go to Town Sent they Reports by Kennedy to the Colonial Secretarys & to the Sheriffs Office. 37

May 12 Sunday: No Divine Service in the Gaol this day. 37

May 13 Monday: Call'd at the Sheriffs and paid him the 15s/- for the Keep of George Gilks 30 days at 6d per day from 1st to 30th April 1844 - Mary Ann Smith brot to Gaol for 14 days Imprisonment the first 7 days in Solitary Confinement or to pay fine of £1-5- - In Consequence of the Wet and Cold and Isobella Anderson not being well I have her Sent to Sleep in the females Ward as being much warmer They Said they was afraid of her & Should Not Sleep Dr. Nash Said there was no fear I let them have a Candle and told them we would try for One Night She laid down Very quiet - about 11½ they Created a Great Noise and on the TurnKeys and Myself going in Mrs Mason Said that Bella had put the Broom which They Women had left inside into the Pot Containing Some hot Coals and was Carrying it about there was a Small hole burnt in Bellas Bed Rug but from All appearances they TurnKey & myself think that it was not done by Bella but by the Women as they was Very Anxious for Bella not to Sleep in the place with them I had Bella taken out and put into a Cell by herself where She was very Quiet all Night - Capt'n Brown came to the Gaol at 2 P.M. and Stated that Mr. Montefiore and himself had Seen the Colonial Secretary & the Advocate General About the 8 Sailors late belonging to the Augustus and that the Colonial Secretary wished him to get a written down merit from the Sailors that they would Stop with him Also to get a Certificate from the Gov'r of their Conduct during the time of their Imprisonment which was given to him as he Said he was going back to the Colonial Secretarys Office. 38

May 14 Tuesday: Bella a little better this Morning. 38

May 16 Thursday: George Gilks Military Prisoners was put into Solitary Confinement Dr. Nash Visited and Ordered Gilks to be allowed extra ½ lbs Bread per day during his Solitary Imprisonment he also Saw they other Prisoners. 40

May 17 Friday: Received an Order this day at 12 Noon (dated the 16th Yesterday) to Send to the Port the 2 Sailors belonging to the Vixon to be Put on board that Vessell Sent them to the Port in Charge of a Mounted Policeman who Mr. Tolmer had Sent by My Request for that purpose. 40

May 18 Saturday: Saw the Sheriff at his Office he also Visited the Gaol and told Mrs Mason that he had Received an Answer to her Petition and that His Excellency Regretted that he Could not interfere with the Sentence Past on her by His Honor the Judge in March last. The Sheriff Mentioned about the Quantity of Water Standing about the Gaol. 40

May 19 Sunday: No divine Service at the Gaol this day Mary Ann Smith was taken out of Solitary and put into the females Yard. 41

May 20 Monday: Capt'n Frome Call'd at the Gaol to look at the Tower & the Ditch. I went with him and Showed him the quantity of water Standing in Several Places inside the Gaol and in Front and the dreadful State the Ditch was in. Thomas Tomkins brot to Gaol for Debt at 9 P.M. 42

May 21 Tuesday: the Sessions was held this day No Prisoners tried They Witnesses in Several Cases was bound over to Appear at the Gaol Delivery in July Next - A Pane of Glass broke in the Cell where the Natives Sleep by Boccomola by Accident Also a one broke in the lamp under the Arch in Changing. They female Prisoners was quarreling this day when I went in the other women told me that Mrs. Mason was Continually Abusing them I told her if heard any More of her quarrelling or abusing they other Prisoners that She Should be put into one of the Cells by herself After which they where quiet. -

Received a written Order this day to Allow Mr. Polden to see and Copy the warrant on which Henry Lee (in the Debtors Yard) was Arrested. a Copy of which was given. 44

This is the second indication that the Aboriginal male prisoners had their own cell in either the felons' or the debtors' yard. In a journal entry from 20 May the following year we find that Governor Grey was to object to the conditions in this cell. Aboriginal woman prisoners were placed in the female yard.

May 23 Thursday: The Sheriff Call'd at the Gaol this Afternoon. 46

May 24 Friday: This being the Queens Birthday His Excellency was Pleased to Pardon they following Prisoners Viz - Boccomola a Native - Henry Wilson - and Catherine ...rry Boccomola was Sent up to Government house - And the Sheriff Came down to the Gaol about 3 OC'k and discharged the Other 2. 46

May 25 Saturday: Sent they Reports this day to the Colonial Secretary & the Sheriff by Kennedy the TurnKey. 43

May 26 Sunday: No divine Service in the Gaol this day Mary Ann Smith having Served her 14 days was discharged at 6 P.M. 43

May 27 Monday: Saw the Sheriff and Reported to him that we Should want Some Rice in Consequence of the No of Prisoners brot to Gaol. 43

May 28 Tuesday: 2 Prisoners brot to Gaol this Morning They was Committed for Trial on the 23rd May 1844 by G.C. Hawker Esq'r J.P. for felony at his Station in the North. 45

May 29 Wednesday: Received an Order this Morning from the Sheriff to Send up to the Supreme Court J.S. Johnston (Debtor) to Give Evidence. Sent him up by Kennedy who brot him back again at 2 P.M. Thomas Tomkins in Gaol for Debt was discharged by order of the Insolvent Court he having found Bail to Appear before the Court from time to time. - Isabella Anderson has been Very bad this day in fact we Could do Nothing with her.

Received this day from the Sheriff the Colonial Secretarys letter Relative to the Prisoners Pardoned on the Queens Birthday. - the following is a Copy. -

No. 752. Colonial Secretarys Office
Adelaide 24th May 1844
Sir,

In Reply to Your Memorandum of the 23rd Instant Recommending Certain Prisoners Confined in Her Majesty's Gaol to the Merciful Consideration of His Excellency the Governor, I am directed to inform you that His Excellency has been pleased to exercise his prerogative of Mercy towards the

prisoners Specified in the Margin All of whom you are hereby Authorised to Discharge from Custody Accordingly
I have the honour to be Sir

       Yr. Most Obedient Servant
       A.M. Munday
       Colonial Secretary

The Sheriff
Names of Prisoners Discharged on the 24th May 1844 –
Cath'e Mu...y Committed 7th May 1844
Henry Wilson ditto 7th May 1844
Bocomola Sentenced 9th July 1842

Bella was much worse this Ev'ing and Created a Great Disturbance in the Gaol. 44

May 30 Thursday: Bella Making a Dreadful Noise All Night She tore her Clothes off and her person all exposed whilst they Turnkeys was putting on The Straight Waistcoat etc – in fact She is quite enough for they Guards to look after with watching they other Prisoners She is So Outrageous that the female Prisoners Cannot do any thing with her A Great Quantity of Water in the Yards and in fact All about the Gaol in Consequence of the heavy Rains. 43

May 31 Friday: Bella have been more quiet during the Night. 44

June 1 Saturday: Henry Lee (Debtor) was discharged by Order of the Sheriff Bella a little better. 44

June 2 Sunday: No divine Service in the Gaol this day. 48

June 4 Tuesday: Bella Much worse this last Night making a Great Noise. 43

June 6 Thursday: His Honor the Judge Visited the Gaol this day etc And went over the Gaol in they females Yard and outside round the ditch. 43

June 7 Friday: Bella Still Very Noisey. 43

June 8 Saturday: Saw the Sheriff at his Office this day His Honor the Judge Call'd at the Gaol & Saw Ann Bent a Prisoner. Bella was much worse this evening both in Mind and Body Sent Perry up to Dr. Nash who Ordered her to have Some Castor Oil Laudanum with Gin which was given to her after a great to do to get her to take it She was afterward tied down on her bed and about an hour after She was a little better. 43

The combination of castor oil, laudanum and gin was a common remedy for almost any ailment, usually working by inducing sleep.

June 9 Sunday: Bella better this Morning Dr. Nash Visited her. No divine Service in the Gaol this day. 43

June 10 Monday: Bella Still Very bad The Sheriff Visited the Gaol. 44

June 11 Tuesday: Nultia a Native Prisoner Very Unwell Sent to Mr Moorhouse who Came and Saw him and Said he was Suffering from Debility and that it was Necessary that he Should [have] 1 lbs Meat 3 Oz of Sugar Tea etc daily and that it was Necessary for the Prisoner that his Irons Should be taken off which was Accordingly done. 44

June 13 Thursday: I Saw the Sheriff at his Office this day. Bella a little better this Day. 42

June 14 Friday: Bella was Very Noisey this day. 41

June 15 Saturday: Saw the Sheriff Mentioned to him that Mathew Dean Sentenced to 60 days Imprisonment was a Shoe Maker & that Mr. Chanter of Hindley St wished him to make Some Shoes for him whilst in Gaol and to pay for his Keep. The Sheriff told me to let him work for the present and to Give him Working Rations and to Receive the Money for the Same to be handed over to the Government. 42

June 16 Sunday: Bella Making a Dreadful Noise All day. No divine Service in the Gaol this day. 42

June 17 Monday: 2 Natives brot to Gaol for 7 days for damaging Trees on the Park land. William Pearce was Remanded back to Gaol by the Insolvent Court at the Suit of E.C Gwynne his Petition having been dismissed Brot to Gaol by Borr Messenger to the Insolvent Court. 45

June 19 Wednesday: the Sheriff Visited the Gaol Also Dr Nash 2 Girls Named Julia & Merlina Hyrdess was brot to Gaol Remanded on a Charge of Murder.   46

June 21 Friday: The Rev'd Mr. Farrell Attended Divine Service at 10½ A.M.   46

June 22 Saturday: Saw the Sheriff at his Office who Told me to let Pearce the debtor have the Rations for the present.   44

June 23 Sunday: No divine Service at the Gaol. The 2 Natives for Damaging Trees on the Park land was discharged Bella was Dreadfully Noisey all this day Obliged to put her into the Cell. She tore all her Clothes off Several times.   40

June 24 Monday: Rosa Ann Dew Hyrdess aged 19 - was brot to Gaol for the Murder of her Bastard Infant female Child on the Coroners Warrant She was Committed on the [18 June] 1844 but was too unwell and was taken to the Hospital - her 2 Sisters Named Julia & Merlina Hyrdess aged 15 & 14 was also Committed this day for the Wilful Murder of the Same Child. Call'd at the Sheriffs Office he was not in Town I wanted to See him about the Rice being Out. - left the pay Sheets And Report with Borr his Officer - Pearce Debtor Discharg'd by Order of The Sheriff.   39

The Hyrdess sisters were to remain in gaol for some time. Ashton says little about them however their story was in the papers:

> On Thursday last, two young girls (sisters) named Julia and Merlina Hyrdess aged 15 and 14 years, were brought before the Commissioner of Police ... charged with the willful murder of a female infant, on the 11th instant, at Syleham, on the Torrens, of which another sister named Rosa Hyrdess had just been delivered. ... The dead body was scented on Mr Mann's Section, by a couple of dogs, who accompanied two of Mr Mann's servants in an afternoon's stroll on Sunday last. The child's head was nearly severed from the body, by some sharp instrument, probably a razor; but the wretched mother, who confessed to the murder, declined to say in what way she had destroyed her illegitimate offspring.[363]

There were many questions – the death was not notified until after the body was found, yet the birth had occurred in a house with no partitions when her sisters and father were present. A young man was questioned and released. The judge clearly suspected involvement of Rosa's father, however in the absence of proof, warned settlers of the circumstances where immorality could take hold.[364]

June 25 Tuesday: Saw the Sheriff this day he Told me he would See about Something to be done Relative to Prisoners at the Court it being Dreadfully Cold when they are being Tried Mr. Hance told me that John S. Johnstone was to be brot to the Insolvent Court on Thursday Next (27th) at 12 OC'k Received an Order this Morning from Mr. Gilbert for a 100-12 lbs of Rice for Prisoners Sent the order to Mr. L... 38

June 26 Wednesday: Received the Above Rice this day Dr. Nash Visited this day - Mr. Farrel Call'd to see Rosa A.D. Hyrdess Charged with Murder he saw her in the office The Rev'd Mr. Mahoney Catholic Priest Came and Saw the Catholics in Gaol. 38

June 27 Thursday: the Rev'd Mr Farrel Came to the Gaol & Saw Rosa Hyrdess for Some time in the Office - John Spick Johnston Debtor was taken to the Insolvent Court and was Discharged on his Petition his first hearing. - Bella Dreadfully Noisey again this day. 38

June 28 Friday: the Sheriff Visited the Gaol also Dr. Nash. Anthony Best brot to Gaol for Debt. 38

June 29 Saturday: Saw the Sheriff at his Office this day Ulricke Hubbe was brot to Gaol for Debt at the Suit of Edward Stephens. 40

June 30 Sunday: Mr. Fleming Came to the Gaol and Saw the Girls Hyrdess's Some time talking to them in the Office. No divine Service in the Gaol. 40

July 1 Monday: took they Calendars to His Excellency - the Judge. 37

July 2 Tuesday: the Court of Oyer & Terminus and General Gaol Delivery Commenced this Morning at 10 OC'k His Honor Charles Cooper Esq'r Judge the Court Adjourned at 4½ P.M. 37

July 3 Wednesday: The Court Opened at 10 A.M. Elphinstones & Davis's Trial Commenced at 10 & was on till 9½ when the Court Adjourned to 10 OC'k to Morrow Morning. 37

July 4 Thursday: Elphinstones & Davis's Trial Commenced at 10 OC'k and about twelve the Jury brought in the Verdict of Guilty Against both Prisoners for felony. Davis was Sentenced to 7 Years Transportation and Elphinstone was Sentenced to 6 Months Hard Labour. The Court Adjourned to 10 to Morrow Morning. 36

July 5 Friday: at the Court all day. 33

July 6 Saturday: All they prisoners disposed of And the Court broke up at 4½ P.M. they 3 Girls (Hyrdess's) Trials postponed to the Next Gaol delivery. 31

July 7 Sunday: No divine Service at the Gaol this day. 31

July 8 Monday: Thomas Wilson a Private of the 96th Reg't brot to Gaol this day as Sentenced by a Court-Martial at Adelaide to 6 Months (Lunar) Imprisonment the first & last 28 days in Solitary the Remainder with Hard Labour The Sentence to Commence from the 17th May 1844 and therefore he having been brot to Gaol on this date the first 28 days Solitary had gone by. 31

July 10 Wednesday: One of the Mounted Police brot a Warrant against Hubbe a Debtor to be Imprisoned for 3 Months for Not having paid his Workmen. The Warrant was Signed by John Elles 8am dated the 3rd July 1844. 30

July 11 Thursday: Bella Very bad this Morning – Made a Dreadful Mess all over the place. 30

July 13 Saturday: The Sheriff Visited the Gaol this day and Saw all they prisoners Dr Nash also Visited the Gaol. Bella a little better this day. 30

July 14 Sunday: No divine Service in the Gaol this day. 30

July 15 Monday: Saw the Sheriff at his Office this day he told me there was a Mistake in the Receipt for the Quarters fire wood. 31

July 17 Wednesday: Mr. Moorhouse Visited a Native in Solitary Confinement and also Saw they Other Natives in Gaol. 31

July 18 Thursday: the Native Harry was discharged having Served his 12 Months Imprisonment he was Sent over to Mr. Moorhouse. Bella was Very bad again this day - I had no paper to make the Sheriffs Report out Yesterday. 31

July 20 Saturday: Very unwell Sent the Reports by Kennedy. 31

July 21 Sunday: no divine Service in the Gaol this day. Bella Very bad. 29

July 22 Monday: Mr. Bartley was at the Gaol for Some time waiting for His Honor the Judge but he did not Come. 29

July 23 Tuesday: His Honor the Judge Came to the Gaol to witness Mrs Bent (a Prisoner) Signing a Deed. - the Sheriff also Visited the Gaol Saw they Prisoners. 29

July 24 Wednesday: Borr the Sheriffs Officer brot to Gaol a Debtor named Charles Bower he had no money for food and Borr told me he Knows he had nothing Consequently I ordered him the Gaol Rations untill I see the Sheriff. 30

July 25 Thursday: Mary Smith was discharged She having Served her time with Solitary. - Received our Rice & Tea this day from Messrs. Hamiltons. 30

July 26 Friday: the Rev'd Mr Farrel Attended the Gaol this Morning divine Service. 29

July 27 Saturday: Bella Not So Noisey this day. 29

July 28 Sunday: No divine Service at the Gaol this day. 29

July 29 Monday: 3 Natives brot to Gaol this day. 32

On this same day Cawthorne reflected in his diary on the poor state of health of Aboriginal people in Adelaide:

> The natives are dreadfully affected at present with the itch. They are shocking spectacles from head to foot, they are one scab. Poor wretches.[365]

Venereal diseases had been mentioned by Klose and Moorhouse in 1843 and the situation had not let up. Klose wrote home that the oldest schoolgirls were lured into four of the huts by the colonists when the adults were away and that when the governor heard of this he ordered the huts, built for those in the 'Adelaide Tribe', be torn down.[366] At the end of 1844 the *Register* reported that Aboriginal people camped near the Torrens River were still in 'a beastly state of disease'.[367] Further back, in 1838, the situation had been different – James had written at that time that the settlers were

> remarkably healthy and nothing has been seen in the shape of epidemic of any kind. The Natives, who are small in numbers and perfectly friendly, are almost invariably free from disease'.[368]

Folland later recalled that in 1839 when he had arrived, the hundreds of Aboriginal people camped on the Torrens between Walkerville and North Adelaide

> appeared to be enjoying life immensely. That they had plenty of food was evident from their fat and sleek appearance.[369]

This picture of health was despite the small pox epidemic that had drastically reduced their population prior to the 1836 landing.

July 30 Tuesday: the Rev'd Mr Mahony the Catholic Minister attended and Saw the Catholic Prisoners. 32

July 31 Wednesday: A Soldier was this day Remanded on a Charge of felony and 4 Prisoners was brot from the Port Committed for Trial one for indecent Assault & 3 for felony from on Board of the Augustus - I Call'd at the Sheriffs Office this day did not See the Sheriff. - Received this day from the Serg't of the 96 Reg't 11s/6d 23 days Keep of Thomas Wilson a Military Prisoner from the 7th to the 31st July 1844. 37

For some reason there is a change of focus in the journal for the next two months. Many of the entries are suddenly quite boring, concerned with money and the recording of payments and receipts. Among these monotonous entries are occasional glimpses of what else is happening at the gaol, for example the three Hyrdess sisters are visited by their father and go to their trials, little Jemmy is forced to stay at the Location because the river is too high to return to the gaol after school and Mary Lowe deliberately contrives to be put in gaol so she can get well. For the sake of completeness all entries have been included here, but the pace picks up again toward the end of September.

August 1 Thursday: Call'd at the Sheriffs Office did not See him Received the Months money and Paid they Men. 37

August 3 Saturday: Saw the Sheriff at his Office gave him the 11s/6d for the Keep of Thos. Wilson a Military Prisoner 23 days from the 9th to 31st July 1844 which I Received from the Serg't of the 96th Reg't. 38

August 4 Sunday: Bella Very Noisey this Morning No divine Service at the Gaol this day. 38

August 5 Monday: Thomas Neilson Mitchell was brot to the Gaol this day to pay a fine of £2 - Costs £1 - and warrant 5s/- or to be Imprisoned for one Calendar Month for an Assault brot to Gaol about 1 P.M. was in the Yard about ¼ of an hour he then paid the fine and Costs and was Discharged - Received Yesterday and handed over this day to the Sheriff the Sum of 15s/6d for the keep of John Stratton a Sailor belonging to the Barque Taglioni 31 days at 6d per day the above Sum was paid by Capt'n Black and Came to Me through the hands of Mr. Litchfield Inspector of Police. 39

August 7 Wednesday: Call'd at the Sheriffs Office and paid him the Money that I Received on the 5th Instant £3-5- the fine and Costs in the Above Case T.N. Mitchell. - the Sheriff Visited the Gaol this day Saw the Prisoners. 38

August 8 Thursday: Matthew Dean the Shoemaker that have been Allowed to Work in the Gaol was discharged he having Served his today.
Bella Much better this day. 40

August 9 Friday: Dr. Nash Visited Saw Bella and Said She was much better. 39

August 11 Sunday: No divine Service in the Gaol this day The Father of They 3 Girls Hyrdess's Call'd at the Gaol and I Allowed him to See them. 38

August 12 Monday: Saw the Sheriff this day At his Office. Bella Much better. 36

August 14 Wednesday: Call'd at the Sheriffs Office this Morning and left the Report did Not See him. 36

August 15 Thursday: A Native Named Jacky was this Morning discharged Mr. Moorhouse Came & Saw him when he was discharged. 37

August 16 Friday: Bella Much better this day. 36

August 17 Saturday: handed over this day to the Sheriff on Account of Government the Sum of £2-5- for the Keep of Mathew Dean for 45 days whilst he was working Making Shoes. And £2-15- Viz the fine and Costs in the Case of George King for Assault. - paid to me on the 16 Aug't 1844. 35

August 18 Sunday: No divine Service in the Gaol this day Bella Much better. 35

August 20 Tuesday: Saw Mr. Mann, Master of the Supreme Court, about Hubbe the Debtor Mr. M told me that he would Come to the Gaol tomorrow & see him. 35

August 21 Wednesday: Bella Much better. 35

August 23 Friday: the Sheriff Visited the Gaol and Saw the Blankets that was Sent by Miller & Brydon for us to look at he Said I had better Order the Others at Once. Dr Nash also Visited. 34

August 24 Saturday: Miller and Brydon Sent the Remainder of they Blanket 10 pr. Saw the Sheriff this day at his Office. Little Jemmy the Native has Stoped over at the School the last 2 Night in Consequence of the River being too high for him to Cross he came to the Gaol this After Noon - Mr Moorhouse Visited the Natives in Gaol this Morning. 35

August 25 Sunday: No divine Service in the Gaol this day - Bella Much better. 35

August 26 Monday: Saw the Sheriff he told Me to Allow Boll to See Rosa Hyrdess in My presence for a few Minutes. Bella Much better Dr Nash Visited the Gaol Mary Lowe was brot to the Gaol for a Month She Said had Created a disturbance at the Police Station for the purpose of being Sent to Gaol to get her Self well. 36

August 28 Wednesday: Saw the Sheriff this day he gave me a Cheque to pay for the Blankets bought off Miller & Brydon on account of the Government. 34

August 29 Thursday: Paid Miller & Brydon this day for the 24 Blankets £5-5- 33

August 30 Friday: the Rev'd Mr Farrel Attended at the Gaol divine Service at 10½ A.M. Bella Much better and went To Church also the Native one Arm Charley. 33

August 31 Saturday: a Prisoner named Robert Deplege was brought to Gaol Sentence to pay a fine of £2- and warrant 5s/- or one Months imprisonment for being Drunk. His wife Came to the Gaol and paid the fine and the Prisoner was discharged. 34

September 1 Sunday: No divine Service in the Gaol this day Bella much better. 33

September 2 Monday: The Native Williamy was discharged this day and One Arm Charley was put into Solitary Confinement - for his last Month. 33

September 3 Tuesday: His Excellency was pleased this day to pardon the Native Call'd One arm Charley Mr. Moorhouse brot his discharge from the Sheriff - he was discharged and Mr Moorhouse took him away with him. 34

September 4 Wednesday: Call'd at the Sheriffs Office this Day he was not in Town Chas Bower Debtor was discharged by order of the Insolvent Court. 32

September 5 Thursday: Eliz'th Mason was discharged She having Served her 6 Months for Stealing Timber. Saw the Sheriff this day and paid him on account of Government the following Sums of Money, £2-5 - being the fine & Costs paid by Robert Deplege Sentenced by Mr. Finniss for being Drunk on the 31st Aug't 1844, 15s/6d for 31 days Keep of Thos Wilson a Military Prisoner at 6d per day from 1st To 31st Aug't 1844 paid to me by Serg't Clark of the 96th Reg't, and 5s/- for the discharge of Charles Bower a debtor discharged on the 4th Inst't, Making Altogether the Sum of £3-5-6 which I Received a Receipt for. 30

September 6 Friday: Dr. Nash Visited Said that Bella was Very Much better. 29

September 7 Saturday: Saw the Sheriff at his Office this Morning wished Me to tell Davis that His Excellency would not grant his Request Viz that Davis would not be Allowed to remain here untill he Could Receive Letters from V. D. Land as to his character. I mentioned this to Davis. Charles Turner a lad in Gaol for 7 days for being Drunk at the Port was Annoying the Prisoner Noonan he was put into a Solitary Cell untill the Evening and then on his begging Pardon and promising to behave better - he was put into the Yard again - His Honor the Judge Came to the Gaol this Afternoon to See Hubbe the debtor and took an Affidavit as to his having No money to pay for his going through the Insolvent Court. 29

September 8 Sunday: No divine Service in the Gaol this day Bella Still Much Better. 29

September 9 Monday: Saw the Sheriff this day he told Me that the 2 Prisoners Under Sentence of Transportation would have to be Put on Board Ship to Morrow for V. D. Land. 30

September 10 Tuesday: left the Gaol at 2 OC'k this day with Patrick Howie and George Davis Under Sentence of 7 Years Transportation arrived at the Port at 3½ OC'k and Put the Prisoners on board the Schooner Eliza bound for Hobart Town and which Shortly after left the Port - Returned to the Gaol about 6½ P.M. 31

September 11 Wednesday: None. W B Davis a Debtor was discharged by order of the Sheriff Paid 5/- 29

September 12 Thursday: Mr. Farrel Sent word that he Could not attend the Gaol this day but would be at the Gaol to Morrow morning at 9½. 29

September 13 Friday: Mr. Farrel Attended divine Service at 10½ A.M. Capt'n Lipson Call'd at the Gaol and Told me that John Dark the Sailor belonging to the Schooner Scotia was to be put on board his Ship. Sent him Down to his Ship by Police Constable Pollard who brot Me back 5s/-6d for his Keep 11 days 6d per day from the 3rd to the 13th Sept 1844 - The Sheriff Visited the Gaol this day Saw all they Prisoners. 29

September 14 Saturday: Saw the Sheriff this day And paid him 5s/6d for the Keep of the above Sailor and 6s/- for the discharge of William B Dawes the above Debtor. 8 Prisoners was this day brot to Gaol under Remand. 36

September 15 Sunday: No divine Service at the Gaol this day - Bella Much Better. 36

September 16 Monday: took they Calendars Round this day. 36

September 17 Tuesday: the Sessions Commenced this day At the Court all day William Winch was Discharged by Order of the Court the Bill against him having been Ignored. 36

September 18 Wednesday: at the Court all day the Grand Jury was this day discharged by the Judge 5 Prisoners was this day discharged. 35

September 19 Thursday: Rosa Ann Dew Hyrdess was Tried this Day for the Murder of her Bastard Child and her Sisters Julia & Marlina was Tried as accessory after the fact they was All Acquitted Julia & Marlina was Discharged by the Court Rosa to be brot to the Court to Morrow Morning The Court Rose at 9½ P.M. 30

September 20 Friday: Rosa Hyrdess taken to the Court this Morning And She was ordered to be Detained to Next Gaol Delivery for the Advocate General to Indict her Again The trial ended this day at 12 noon. 27

September 22 Sunday: we had a Dreadful Rough Nights both last and Friday Night the wind blew 6 Squares of Glass out of they lamps between the walls and 3 panes was Broken in the windows in the felons Yard. 27

September 23 Monday: Reported to the Sheriff this day the Above lamps & windows being broken. 27

September 24 Tuesday: The Sheriff Visited the Gaol Saw they Prisoners. 26

September 25 Wednesday: a Man Named Ernest Hargen a German (Insane) Came to this Colony as a passenger in the George Washington was brot to Gaol to be taken Care of by order of this Government he was put into the Debtors Yard with D Hubbe the Debtor and Rolland out of the other yard to look after him. 26

September 26 Thursday: Saw the Sheriff this Morning at his Office Mentioned to him that Hargen had been brot to Gaol and he Showed me the Colonial Secretary's letter to that effect. Dr Nash visited the Gaol Saw Hargen and they other Prisoners. 26

September 27 Friday: The 2 Native Women brot from Kangaroo Island was taken before the Magistrate and was discharged. 26

September 30 Monday: McDonald in Gaol on Suspicion of being a Runaway Convict was again Remanded for a Week. 24

October 1 Tuesday: Received the Months Pay this day from the Treasurer Quite out of fire wood. 24

October 2 Wednesday: Mr. Gilbert Call'd and gave me the Orders for the different Articles applied for the use of this Quarter. 24

October 3 Thursday: Received this day from Hamilton & Company Rice, Sugar, Tea. 24

October 4 Friday: Ernest Hargen and Isabella Anderson in Gaol - Insane - both better. 24

October 5 Saturday: Thos. N Mitchell brot to Gaol Under a Fine for Impounding horses and a Woman Named Mary Rhodes for a fine for being Drunk & Disorderly was found to be Insane - put her into one of the Cells to Sleep. 26

October 6 Sunday: Dr. Nash Came & Saw Mary Rhodes - Said She was Suffering from Delirium Tremens he prescribed for her She was Very Noisey all day Obliged to put the Strait waistcoat on her. 27

October 7 Monday: Dr. Nash Saw Mary Rhodes She was about the Same as Yesterday Also Saw Wilson in Solitary Confinement Ordered him ½ lb Bread per day extra. 27

October 8 Tuesday: The Sheriff Visited the Gaol Saw all they prisoners Insane Persons. Received this day from Serg't Clark of the 96th

Reg't the Sum of 15s/- for the Keep of Thos. Wilson a Military Prisoner 30 days from the 1st to the 30th Sept'r 1844. 28

October 9 Wednesday: Mary Rhodes (Insane) Very Much beat Mrs Bent about the face She had just had the Strait waist Coat taken off to Wash herself in the Womens Yard She was Very Violent the Waistcoat was put on her and She was put into one of the Cells and Kept there Sent for Dr. Nash who Came & Saw her & also Mrs Bent. 28

October 10 Thursday: Ulrich Hubbe (Debtor) was taken to the Insolvent Court to have his first hearing he was Remanded back to Gaol untill Tuesday the 15th Inst't Saw the Sheriff and Reported to him about Mary Rhodes having Assaulted Mrs Bent - also that her (Mary Rhodes) time of Imprisonment would Expire to Morrow but that She was not in a fit State of Mind to be Set at Large - he Said that he would Report the Same to the Government. 28

October 11 Friday: the Sheriff Sent Me down The Answer that he had Received from the Colonial Secretary Concerning Mary Rhodes which Stated that She was to be detained in Gaol untill in a fit State to be Set at large. She is still Very Violent. 28

October 12 Saturday: paid the Sheriff this day the 15s/- for the Keep of Thos. Wilson. Mary Rhodes a little better Anthony Best was brot to Gaol this day on a fine for not having obed the Order of the Resident Magistrate in Supporting his Wife. 28

October 13 Sunday: Dr. Nash Visited Said Mary Rhodes was better. No divine Service at the Gaol. Hargen - Insane - Very Bad. 28

October 14 Monday: the Sheriff Call'd at the Gaol and Read a letter that he had Received from the Col'l Secretary to T.N. Mitchell Stating that his Excellency had Remitted 2 £5 fines but that he Mitchell must pay the Costs. - which he Refuses to do and was therefore detained in Gaol. Mr Breeze brot to Gaol for Debt. 29

October 15 Tuesday: Ulrich Hubbe was taken before the Commiss'r of the Insolvent Court and was again Remanded untill Next Thursday Week. Saw the Sheriff told him that Mr Bailey as Agent to the Vixon would Supply Some Clothing to the 2 Prisoners Who had made their Escape from that Vessel. 29

October 16 Wednesday: Dr Nash Visited the Gaol and Bled Mrs Bent Saw Mary Rhodes her Mouth was Very bad – Bella is Much Better. 29

October 17 Thursday: the Native Call'd Karri Kudnutya Sentenced as Sentenced in Sep'r last to One Months Imprisonment was discharged this Morning and handed over to Mr. Moorhouse. 29

October 18 Friday: His Honor the Judge Visited the Gaol this day Went Over the Place Saw they Prisoners. 28

October 19 Saturday: Hargen & Rhodes Insane Very Outrageous this day. 28

October 20 Sunday: Several Slates was blown from off the tope of the House and others nearly off during Yesterday and this day also a Square of Glass broken in No 2 Room in the felons Yard Caused by the Wind. 28

October 21 Monday: Reported to the Sheriff the Slates & the Pane of Glass. – The Visiting Magistrate Visited the Gaol. 29

[In margin]
Mitchell cheque from Port Lincoln 1-10-0

October 22 Tuesday: Robert Smith Breeze (Debtor) was discharged this day by order of the Insolvent Court he having found Bail. 30

October 23 Wednesday: A Square of Glass broken in No 3 felons Yard by Wind. 30

October 24 Thursday: Dr. Hubbe taken to the Insolvent Court & Remanded back to Tuesday Next Mary Rhodes Insane Very bad. 30

October 26 Saturday: Anthony Best & Thomas Neilson Mitchell 2 Prisoners in Gaol for fines etc are from this day to find themselves in Gaol by a written Order from the Sheriff dated the 24th October 1844 when told the Same they was inclined to be abusive etc but was Very Soon quiet. 30

October 28 Monday: the Sheriff Call'd at the Gaol and wanted a Return for the Governor of they No of Prisoners Tried in the Supreme Court for the Years 1840-41-42-43 – each Year ending the 30th

September. H- he Saw they Prisoners. Mr Crawford Paid the 30/- (Costs) for T.N. Mitchell & he was discharged.   29

October 29 Thursday: Dr. Hubbe was again taken to the Insolvent Court & was discharged Saw the Sheriff gave him the No of Prisoners Tried as above.   29

October 30 Wednesday: Dr. Nash Visited the Gaol and Saw all the Prisoners.   27

November 1 Friday: Isabella Anderson who have been in Gaol Some time being insane was this day given over to Mrs Grace Sloggett by Order of the Sheriff and was by her taken into the Country to Anthony Bests Station. She Grace Sloggett Promising to take Care of her.   26

Bella is for now being taken care of. After her stay with the Bests it was said 'she looks *almost* respectable' and 'we should hardly have known her'. However she was soon back to her old ways.[370] Despite a break from the care of Bella, Ashton gets no reprieve; his attention is suddenly now taken up with another attempt at escape, this time a concerted attempt by a mass of prisoners:

November 2 Saturday: A Desperate Attempt was made by 8 or 9 Prisoners to Escape from the felons Side of the Gaol during the Night - the following Report to the Sheriff will Explain -

       Her M Gaol of Adelaide
       2nd Nov'r 1844

Sir,
  I have to Report that Molineux the Guard Call'd me this Morning at ½ past 12 OC'k and told me that he thought Some of they Prisoners was getting out through the Roof in the Felons Yard On going to the Spot I found that it was the Case I Sent Round to the Corporal of the Guards to that effect and for him to Place a Sentry at each Corner which was done 2 or 3 of they Prisoners being on the Roof at this time and Seeing that we was Prepared for them they Returned back to their Cells - On Examination I found a large hole in the Ceiling in

No 1 Cell where the 2 Prisoners of the Vixon – and McDonald (in Gaol on Suspicion of being a Runaway Convict) Was Confined All of whom had Cut the Chain of their Irons In No 2 Cell where Gilks and the other Prisoners Committed for Trial a Large Hole was Made in the Ceiling and the Slates taken off the Roof I had McDonald and the 2 Vixon Men brought out and extra pair of Irons put on them and put into Separate Cells Gilks and Wood out of No 2 Cell I had put into Irons and put into Separate Cells and the Remainder 4 Prisoners I had Removed from No 2 to No 4 Cell At the time this was discovered the Wind was blowing Very Strong and I have no doubt but that it was the intention of 6 or 8 of they Prisoners to have dropt off the Roof at Kennedys Tower go Round to the Back Rushed the Sentry and escaped over the Wooden fence had they not been detected. It was Very Dark and Rough Weather at the time So that We Could Scarcely hear or See any thing Much praise his due to the Military and My Men for their Steady and Resolute Conduct on this Occasion.

    I have the honor to be Sir

                Yr Ob't H'ble Servant
                W. B. Ashton
                Gov'r of the Gaol

C. B. Newenham Esq'r
Sheriff

Mrs Ashton Saw from the Chapel Window 3 or 4 of they Prisoners on the Roof at the time we was Stationed at the ends of the Buildings. All was quiet during the Remainder of the Night. The Sheriff Visited this Afternoon Saw the hole Where the Prisoners had Attempted to Escape, he Saw All they Prisoners and approved of what I had done and the Steps I had taken to Secure the Prisoners Saw the Commiss'r of the Police and Mr. Insp'r Tolmer who Said He would Send me a Policeman for a few Nights – as the Gaol was in Such an insecure State. – I had this Afternoon they following Prisoners put in Irons they being in No 2 Cell at the time of the holes being Made in the Ceiling; having no doubt that the greater part if not All had intended to have escaped. – Wilkinson (Soldier) under Sentence of 12 Months

Hard labour for an Assault and Robbery - Smith & Brown both for trial for felony. 26

November 3 Sunday: Prisoners all as Yesterday All Quiet. A Policeman all Night. 26

November 4 Monday: The Sheriff - Visiting Magistrate Mr. Moorhouse J.P. Visited the Gaol went all over the Cells - Saw all the Prisoners in Irons and in the female Cells I told them that they Prisoners was in Irons & in Separate Cells for having attempted to Escape from the Gaol. None of they Prisoners Made Any Complaints to the Magistrate. - A Police man again all Night. 27

November 5 Tuesday the Commiss'r of Police & Mr. Insp'r Tolmer Visited the Gaol and Said the Gaol was Very insecure - The Prisoners all quiet. A Policeman all Night. Thos. Holly paid his fine £1-5. 27

November 6 Wednesday: This Morning I had the Cut Irons taken off McDonald & the 2 Vixon Men and allowed them to walk out Side of their Cells for a half an hour each at a time - told the Military to that effect - a Police Man was Sent me last Night. 34

On 6 November 1844 the *South Australian Register* described the incident:

> The whole, we believe, of the male white prisoners ... attempted to make their escape. ... the guard on duty ... hearing an unusual noise on the roof ... called Mr Ashton ... Mr Ashton immediately got up, told the guard to call the head turn-key, and keep as quite [*sic*] as possible. He then armed himself, and went down, having called out the military guard, and stationed them on the east end of the row of buildings from whence the sounds proceeded, he collected his own men, and stationed them at the west end, these being the only points at which it was possible the prisoners could escape – the whole party being well armed. By this time ... the party could hear them scrambling on the roof; and Mrs Ashton, who was looking through the chapel window that opens on the roof, says she saw them distinctly. ... the prisoners found they were discovered and that no hope remained of their escape as they were hemmed in on all sides,

hastened back through the holes they had made into their cells; one of them ... calling upon them to come back and rush the party. ... For some time it was a mystery how the prisoners had managed to get their irons off but on examining No.1 cell, a knife, which had been missed some time since, was discovered, jagged on the edge to form a saw, stowed away between the ceiling and the roof, and which it is probable was the instrument by which they had taken off their irons ... No doubt exists but that the scheme had been some time in preparation.[371]

November 7 Thursday: Mr Wigley the Visiting Magistrate and the Sheriff Attended at the Gaol and Made further enquiries Relative to the Attempt Made by they Prisoners to Escape on the 2nd Inst, A Police man done duty with us at the Gaol last Night.   34

November 8 Friday: a person Named Alexander Berkeley brot to Gaol as Committed by Mr. Finnis & Mr. McDonald as a dangerous Lunatic - this is the first Case that have been Committed to Gaol under the Act past in the Council a Short time ago He was put into the Debtors Yard and Jellet and Hedditch to take Care of him and Hargen - Perry the Turnkey was taken Very Ill Yesterday Afternoon Dr. Sherman was Sent for - and he is Very Ill this day a Police Man Came and took Duty again at the Gaol Last Night Mary Rhodes Very Outrageous this day they Prisoners all quiet.   35

[In margin]
8th Nov'r 1844 Mr. H...t put in 6 Panes of Glass in the Windows and 7 ditto [in the] Lamps.

November 9 Saturday: Paid the Sheriff this day £1-5- As Received by Me from Thomas Halley as Sentenced by the Commiss' of Police to pay for being Drunk and Disorderly. - Saw Mr. Tolmer Told me that the Commiss'r of Police would not let a Man on duty at the Gaol without the Governors Order as we had time to have Made Other Arrangements and I went and told the Sheriff the Same and that it was Necessary that I Should have a Man as Perry was Ill and Kennedy doing day duty He told me that he would take

Care that I should have a man for the Night. - No Man however was Sent me and we done the best we could. 35

November 10 Sunday: Mr. Fleming Attended the Gaol this Morning for Divine Service but in Consequence of Perry being Ill and the State of the Gaol I did not think it Safe to have Prisoners brot together. - Berkely & Rhodes Insane was Very Outrageous Nearly all this day. Perry was a little better and was able to take they Keys for a Short time this day. 33

November 11 Monday: Saw the Sheriff and told him that I had not a Policeman either on Saturday or Sunday night Prisoners all quiet. 33

November 12 Tuesday: Anthony Best was discharged he having Served his Months imprisonment This Prisoner have not been Supplied with the Gaol food Since the 25th Oct 1844 by Order of the Sheriff to me in writen. 32

November 13 Wednesday: None, 8 Sailors left. 31

November 14 Thursday: Mary Rhodes & Alex'r Berkely (Insane) Very Violent this day & Noisey. 23

November 15 Friday: Saw the Sheriff this day gave Me the Colonial Secretarys Letter Relative to putting the 2 Vixon Prisoners on board the Eliza to Morrow for Hobart Town. 23

November 16 Saturday: took Joseph Blundell & Henry Worth to the Port and put them on board the Eliza Schooner for Hobart Town Capt'n Litchfield went with me to the Port - the Schooner left the Wharf about 6 P.M. 23

November 18 Monday: Reported to the Sheriff about Putting the 2 Prisoners on board Ship on Saturday. 21

November 19 Tuesday: the following Gentlemen Attended at the Gaol as a Board of Survey on our Old Articles - when the following Articles seen by them

Old Articles -

22 pair of Shoes - 5 pair of Canvass Trousers - 2 pair Fustian Trousers - 2 Fustian Jackets - 2 Guard Coats - 12 Beds - 60 Bed Legs - 23 large Pad locks - 3 Small ditto - 13 Tin Pannicans - 1 Water Buc't - 8 lime Buckets - 1 Water Buc't - 1 large Fireb' - 2 Small ditto - 2 Spades - 2 Shovels - 4 Iron Pots - 2 Iron

Rakes - 2 Frying Pans - 18 Hair Brooms - 25 Mops - 10 Scrubbing Brushes - 5 White Wash Brushes. -
The Sheriff Saw they Prisoners.   23

[In margin]
An Extra Sentry was Sent to do Duty at the Gaol & Stationed at the Guard Room.

November 20 Wednesday: the Cells are Still in the Same State.   23

November 21 Thursday: Received from Mr. Harris Official Assayer to the Estate of Ulrick Hubbe an Imprisoned Insolvent Debtor the Sum of £5-0-10 for 121 days Keep in Gaol of the Said Ulrick Hubbe from the 1st July to the 29th Oct' 1844 at 10s/- per day Agreeable to the Insolvent Act.   23

November 22 Friday: Mary Rhodes Very bad and also Berkley & Hargen.   23

November 23 Saturday: Paid the Sheriff this day the £5-0-10 for the Keep of the above Ulrick Hubbe whilst in Gaol. I Received this Day from Mr. Edward Bayley the Sum of £3-4- for the Keep of Joseph Blundell and Henry Worth the 2 Prisoners that Made their Escape from the Vixon Some Months Ago and for which Respect Mr Bayley is the Agent - 64 days in Gaol at 6d per day each from the 14th Sept'r to the 16th Nov'r 1844 - had 50 Calendars of Prisoners for Trial Printed.   24

November 25 Monday: Took the Calendars of Prisoners for Trial to His Excellency the Judge and Government Officers.   24

November 26 Tuesday: the Gaol delivery Sat this day at Court.   23

November 27 Wednesday: At the Court all day.   21

November 28 Thursday: at the Court Rosa Hyrdess was Tried this day for the Murder of her Child Acquitted of the Murder but found Guilty of Concealing The Birth and Sentenced to 15 Calendar Months with hard labour The trial lasted from 9 A.M. to 12 Midnight.   18

November 29 Friday: at the Court all day And Finished trying Prisoners at 10 P.M. Court Adjourned. McPherson being the Last Case. Alexr. Berkley was Very Outrageous and Violent this day and broke a Square of Glass by pushing his head through it.   18

November 30 Saturday: Reported the Above Square of Glass to the Sheriff. 18

December 1 Sunday: All they Mad Prisoners Very Violent this day. 18

December 4 Wednesday: Mary Rhodes Very bad and So was Berkley. 18

December 5 Thursday: the Sheriff Visited the Gaol. - Saw all they Prisoners. 18

December 6 Friday: George White was Put Into Solitary to under go his last 28 days and then to be Discharged. 20

December 7 Saturday: William Wilkins was brought to Gaol under Remand as a Dangerous Lunatic. 22

December 8 Sunday: The Above Wilkins and Berkeley (Insane) have been Very Outrageous and Violent all Night Making So much Noise that it was impossible for us to hear any thing else. And broke 3 Stretchers to pieces during the Night Robert Wilkinson one of they Prisoners that attempted to escape a Short time ago and have been Kept in Irons Since that time I was obliged to have his Irons taken off and get him to go into the Debtors Yard to Assist in takin Care of they Mad Men Confined in Gaol. 22

December 9 Monday: a Pane of Glass was broken in the felons Yard but I could not learn by What Cause Noonan Said he thought the Dog had broken it. 22

There is a dog sitting at Ashton's feet in Glover's 1850 painting of the staff at the gaol (see front cover). It is tempting to imagine that it was this dog (or else a previous family dog) that had broken the pane of glass. There is also a boy in the painting. Ashton's son Albert Gawler is said to have told his children that, as his father's constant companion, he was the boy in this painting.[372]

December 11 Wednesday: They Mad Prisoners are All Very bad Wilkins Could not be taken before the Magistrate he was therefore Remanded without going up. 22

December 12 Thursday: Wilkins & Mary Rhodes Very Noisey & Violent All Night and day. 22

December 13 Friday: Dr. Nash & the Sheriff Visited the Gaol. Dr Nash Said he had heard from the Government and that there was to be a person Appointed to look after the Insane prisoners. The Sheriff & Dr Nash Saw All they Prisoners. The Rev'd Mr Farrel Attended divine Service at 10½ A.M. 23

December 14 Saturday: Wilkins Insane – was taken before the Police Magistrate and Committed to Gaol as a Dangerous Lunatic. 23

December 16 Monday: Wilkins Insane – broke a Pane of Glass in the lower Cell debtors Yard by Knocking his fist through. 22

December 17 Tuesday: All they Insane Prisoners a little better. 23

December 18 Wednesday: Call'd at the Sheriffs Office but did Not See him. 23

December 19 Thursday: Mary Rhodes (Insane) Violently Assaulted TurnKey Kennedy as he was Passing her between the walls The Straight waistcoat put on her and She was Confined to her Cell untill She was quiet – her language was Dreadful – Dr Nash had Visited previous to this. 22

December 20 Friday: None. Ann Bent went into Solitary Confinement. 22

December 21 Saturday: Wilkins & Mary Rhodes (Mad) Very outrageous day And Night. 22

December 22 Sunday: Same as above. Dr Nash Visited. 22

December 23 Monday: the Sheriff Visited the Gaol and Saw they Prisoners etc – he told Perry a Man Named Morris had been Appointed to look after the Insane Prisoners. 22

December 24 Tuesday: Saw the Sheriff he Showed Me Morris's Appointment etc with the Same Salary as TurnKey Kennedy Viz £67-12- per Year and the Said William Morris Commenced his duty this day. – he Ranks as Turnkey to the Gaol but his duty Is to look After the Insane prisoners and to Assist the Other TurnKeys if Call'd on. 27

December 25 Wednesday: Christmas Day They Prisoners had Plum Pudding & Roast Beef and a Pint of Colonial Ale each Her

Majesty's and the Governors health was drank And they Appeared Happy for the day. 27

December 26 Thursday: Saw Mr Tolmer about McDonald the Supposed Runaway Convict. 26

December 27 Friday: John McDonald who have been in Gaol for Some Months Charged with felony and a Supposed Runaway Convict was this day taken before the Police Magistrate and was Discharged. 25

December 28 Saturday: Wilkins (Insane) was Very bad Yesterday and this day and Also Mary Rhodes Morris had Much Trouble with them Charles Hedditch Acting as lamp-lyter having No Other prisoner that I Can Appoint. 25

The end of 1844 is summed up in the expressions 'all they Mad Prisoners Very Violent this day' and 'They Mad Prisoners are All Very bad'. It was chaotic in the gaol at this time, with physical damage caused by the recent attempt at mass break-out, plus the seriousness of the behavior of the mentally ill prisoners, affecting everyone. Ashton was thankful for any help from the prisoners, and his journal entry on Christmas day seems to recognise how much the prisoners had suffered – 'They Prisoners had Plum Pudding & Roast Beef and a Pint of Colonial Ale each Her Majesty's and the Governors health was drank And they Appeared Happy for the day.'

It was thought that Ashton supplied much of the Christmas meal himself:

> Wednesday (Christmas Day) was observed as a holiday even in the Jail. Roast beef, with abundance of vegetables, was served out to the unfortunate inmates by Mr Ashton, each person was afterwards regaled with a pint of ale. This is said to have been in consequence of voluntary subscription, but we rather suspect that the *large subscriber* was the kind-hearted Governor of the Jail.[373]

The governor's journal 1845

Throughout 1845 Adelaide continued to transport its worst prisoners to Van Diemen's Land, with four ships leaving during the year. Adelaide's ability to rid itself of convict taint was however under threat. This threat came from two directions in just one year: early in the year from the English government, which proposed sending juvenile criminals (the 'Parkhurst Boys') to South Australia and pardoning them as they arrived and, later in the year, from Van Diemen's Land where conditionally pardoned convicts now had permission to go anywhere except back to England.

Having such people be allowed to come to Adelaide was seen to be against the promise to emigrants that South Australia would be convict-free, and both proposals sparked public outrage. People objected vehemently via public meetings to accepting the boys from England; they wanted to 'stay the plague'.[374] Nor did they want the convicts ('pardon men') from Van Diemen's Land. Governor Grey was lukewarm in his response and accepted pardoned criminals and ex-convicts from both schemes into the colony. It was said in the *Observer* that he 'lacks courage to resist their landing'.[375] This was said in September 1845 when Governor Grey had less than a month to go before he left the colony.

Adelaide citizens did not want more people, particularly if they were of a dubious character. It is true that in the hard years many had left Adelaide. In 1844 the population had dipped, and with falling revenues the city council had collapsed, but over 1000 people had already moved to Adelaide from the eastern colonies since then. With continued emigration there would be a population of close to 21,800 in the colony by the end of the year.[376] The number of Indigenous people in Adelaide varied with the time of year and the number of visiting groups. The *Return of Coloured Native Population in Occupied Districts of SA for 1845* recorded 300 for Adelaide in a total of 3730 for the colony.[377] On the Queen's Birthday, 384 Indigenous people attended in Adelaide, 'mainly locals with only a few from the Murray'.[378] In an effort to discourage visitors the government was now distributing Queen's Birthday rations of blankets and food in many of the outlying districts.

There continued to be a small number of settlers living in the parklands and people were still complaining about

> the filthy state of the streets, and of nuisance of pigs, goats, &c. The police are shooting unclaimed dogs.[379]

The Aboriginal Location at Piltawodli ended midway through 1845, the government sending in soldiers to tear the roofs down so the huts could no longer be used.[380]

Inside the gaol in 1845, the final year of the journal, much was happening, so much so that Isabella Anderson no longer got a mention. Another Indigenous prisoner was hanged, five prisoners attempted a group escape, and an unusual number of prisoners were incarcerated for horrific crimes. There were several scandals and events that impinged on the gaol. The main reason for being so busy however was that there were now up to 12 'lunatics' in the gaol at any one time.

Morris's two most difficult charges, Wilkins and Berkely, the principle reason for his appointment, were released into the care of their friends as early as January, however Morris stayed on as 'keeper of the lunatics'. He continued to be assisted by prisoners, some given extra rations to help out. Without the help of these prisoners it would have been impossible. The number of debtors declined and the debtors yard became used for the mentally ill, with any debtors still left likely to be looking after them.

The first sad event and scandel of 1845 concerned 'Poor Wilkins' –

given up to the care of his friends. Ashton wrote in the journal that he visited Wilkins at a house in Thebarton and because he looked so ill arranged for a doctor to visit. However, shockingly, Wilkins died:

> [A]bout 8th of OC'k this Night Poor Wilkins Died, I fear Through the Neglect of Dr. Wright...[381]

Ashton was much distressed by these events. He alerted the coroner and later gave evidence to the Supreme Court.

Not mentioned in the journal but significant to early Adelaide was that on the first day of 1845 Mullawirraburka died:

> King John, one of the natives is dead. His bier is stuck around with spears and he is going to be carried down to his own country 'Mypunga'. One has gone to call up the other tribe. He is lamented by whites and blacks.[382]

Mullawirraburka was probably known to everyone in Adelaide.

The journal for 1845 begins:

January 4 Saturday: Saw the Sheriff. 28

January 6 Monday: The Sheriff Visited the Gaol Saw the Prisoners. 28

January 7 Tuesday: Perry took the Report to the Sheriff Relative to the No of Prisoners brot to the Gaol during the year 1844. - 27

January 8 Wednesday: Saw the Sheriff he told Me he had Received an Answer from the Governor Relative to Frederick Smiths Petition. 25

January 9 Thursday: Mr. Porter Commenced doing the 2 Cells No 1 - & 2 - in the felons Yard which was ordered to be done Some Time Ago. 24

January 10 Friday: The Rev'd Mr. Farrel Attended at the Gaol this Morning divine Service at 10½. - 2 Debtors brought to Gaol Named B... and Sheppard. 26

January 11 Saturday: William Wilkins and Alex'r Berkely both - Insane was this day dis'd And given over to their friends by order

of they Magistrates who Committed them to Gaol as Dangerous
Lunatics. 26

January 13 Monday, Call'd at the Sheriffs Office. 26

January 14 Tuesday: Mary Rhodes Very Bad. And broke a Pane of Glass in the Debtors Yd. 26

January 18 Saturday: W'm Wilkins (Insane) who left the Gaol on the 11th Inst't was brot in from the Country and placed in a little House in Thebarton in Charge of 2 Men by his wife. 28

January 20 Monday: Saw the Sheriff. 28

January 22 Wednesday: Went with Mr. Crawford and fetched Dr Wrights Son Charles at 10½ P.M. to See Poor Wilkins who Appeared Very Ill. 36

January 23 Thursday: about 8th of OC'k this Night Poor Wilkins Died, I fear Through the Neglect of Dr. Wright I went And Saw the Coroner who Told me he Should hold an Inquest on the body to Morrow Morning At Thebarton. 30

January 24 Friday: at the Inquest of Poor Wilkins Nearly All day. Cells finished [crossed out] the Workmen broke a Pane of Glass in each Cell No 1&2. 30

January 25 Saturday: at the Inquest all day. 30

January 26 Sunday: Morning 9 OC'k Poor Wilkins Was Buried the Morning. 30

The full story is told elsewhere. Wilkins had been a hard-working man, in charge of the Market Inn in Thebarton, with a wife and six young children. He had built a bridge over the river for the use of the public and in doing so had spent beyond his means. The stress of this venture was said to have caused the severe 'lunacy' he had only recently suffered.[383] After being placed in gaol, and then released into the care of two of his friends in Thebarton, his wife had taken him with her to the country. However, she found he 'was getting too strong for me; I was knocked up and exhausted' so she returned him to the house at Thebarton.[384] It was there that Ashton visited and found Wilkins ill. He sought out Dr Wright's son Charles, who was also the doctor's assistant, to fetch his father.

What happened next was a disaster for Wilkins. Dr Wright declared the patient was in a 'chronic state of lunacy', prescribed pills, and promised to return. Over the next few days, however, the doctor was intoxicated and when he did return he prescribed more pills. Dr Wright took this second prescription, as he had done with the first, to Mr Paxton the chemist who reluctantly dispensed it, after arguing with the doctor that the dose was too high and too frequent. The doctor pulled rank, saying that Mr Paxton 'had nothing to do with it ... – and that if he killed him he and not Mr Paxton would be reponsible for his death'.[385] At the inquest, held in the Wheatsheaf Hotel in Thebarton, an excess of morphine was declared the cause of death. The doctor was charged with manslaughter due to negligence in prescribing the drug and not monitoring its effects after each dose. At the trial the chemist testified that:

> On the first occasion of his going to his shop Dr Wright was *so excited with liquor* that he could not make the chemical sign for the quantity of morphine he ordered, and that when he returned for the second dose, *he was so drunk that he was obliged to assist him off the cart*.[386]

The chemist had decided to allow Wilkins's friend to take the second bottle with him using instructions on frequency given by the doctor on a previous occasion when sober. The doctor's son Charles agreed and accordingly removed the label that the chemist's assistant had just placed on the second bottle.[387]

At Dr Wright's trial, in March 1845, the part played by the chemist was submitted as a complication and the doctor was found not guilty.[388] He had spent only one night in gaol and that was to await the second of his two-day trial. The judge could not convict; he stated that he thought Dr Wright morally guilty and urged him to mend his ways. Had he been able to convict the offence would have been punishable by transportation for life.[389]

Probably unknown at the time was that Dr Wright had a history.

Before emigrating to Adelaide he had been dismissed from his practice at Bethlem hospital (the famous 'Bedlam') due to his alcoholism.[390]

It is clear in the journal that Ashton considered the doctor guilty. It can only be imagined his thoughts on the whole sad affair.

January 27 Monday: Saw the Sheriff this day.   30

January 28 Tuesday: Patrick Noonan was taken by Kennedy on a Habeas Corpus to the Military Barracks to give evidence on a Court Martial. - brot back to Gaol again at 2½ P.M.   30

January 29 Wednesday: left the Gaol at 2 OC'k this day for Port Adelaide And Placed on Board the Ship Palmyra at 3½ P.M. they following Prisoners under Sentence of Transportation to V.D. Land
Viz Thomas Marshall alias Thomas Wood - 10 Years
George Gilks - 7 ditto
Frederick Smith - 7 ditto
The Ship Shortly after left the Wharf. And I returned to the Gaol.   30

January 30 Thursday: Reported to the Sheriff My having Put they Above Prisoners on Board the Ship Yesterday to be taken to Hobart Town.   27

February 1 Saturday: Harry Hall & John Smith 2 Prisoners Detained here for having Committed a Burglary at Port Fary - was this day taken from the Gaol in Charge of the Mounted Police to be taken in the Governor Gawler to Portland Bay. They left the Gaol at 11 A.M. - Mr. Sheppard a Debtor was Discharged this day by Order of the Insolvent Court he having found Bail.   26

February 3 Monday: Robert Hamilton was brot to the Gaol at 10 P.M. for Debt.   24

February 4 Tuesday: Levi Bigwood (a Debtor) was discharged by order of the Insolvent Court he having found Bail.   24

February 5 Wednesday: The Sheriff Visited the Gaol and Saw all the Prisoners, he Saw the Rice and Said he would Call at Mess'rs Hamilton and get them to Change it.   23

February 7 Friday: Summoned to Appear before the Police Magistrate to give evidence Against Dr. Wright for Causing the Death of William Wilkins - when the Dr. was boundover to Appear and Answer any indictment that May be Preferred Against him at the Next Gaol delivery. 24

February 8 Saturday: Sent the Sheriffs and the Colonial Secretarys Reports this Day by Kennedy being too unwell to go to Town myself -
Robert Hamilton (Debtor) was Discharged this Day by Order of the Sheriff on both Suits. 24

February 10 Monday: Saw the Sheriff at his Office. 23

February 11 Tuesday: None, 1 Bag of Rice from Mess'rs Hamilton in Room of [in place of] Bad. 23

February 13 Thursday: the Sheriff Visited the Gaol this day and Read the Answer to Ann Bents Petition which was That His Excellency Could not interfere with her Sentence only that part which Related to the Solitary Confinement which His Excellency was pleased to Remit. - From a hint I Received this Afternoon and from Other Circumstances I was led to Suppose that they 5 Prisoners Committed for trial intended to Attempt their Escape this Night Douglas (for Rope) at the Head of them I had them just at locking up time Removed into No 1 Cell. - lately lined with Slabs So that they were Stoped in their Attempt for the Present About ½ past 10 P.M. I heard a Dreadful Noise in the Gaol and on going Round I found that one of they Soldiers on Guard was in a fit which took 6 Men to hold him a Nother Soldier was Sent from the Barracks to Relieve him at 12 Night. 23

February 14 Friday: they Prisoners Appeared to be Very Uneasy this Morning at having been put into a fresh Cell last Night Douglas More So than the Others. 23

Ashton had quietly foiled another attempt at mass prisoner escape, simply by having his ear to the ground and calmly moving each potential escapee to a newly reinforced cell. This was cell no. 1, damaged in the last escape attempt and rebuilt with solid slabs.

February 16 Sunday: Mary Rhodes (Insane) brok a Pane of Glass in No 3 Cell Debtors Yard with her fist.   23

February 17 Monday: About 10 O'Ck this Night Noone Committed for Trial for felony was Making a dreadful Noise in the felons Yard So Much So that the Military Came Round I went to him and Asked him What he was Making So Much Noise About – he said it was in Consequence of Mrs Rhodes (Mad) was doing So I expected that he was Making the Noise for other purposes and I had him and Douglas brought out and put into One of the Outside Cell for the Night.   23

February 18 Tuesday: All was Quiet during the Night.   23

February 19 Wednesday: Call'd at the Sheriffs and told him that Noone (the Prisoner that I had put in the outside Cell) wanted to See him he the Sheriff Referred the Case to the Visiting Magistrate who Told Me that he would Call at the Gaol on the Next Day.   24

February 20 Thursday: the Magistrate did not Call at the Gaol this day.   26

February 21 Friday: the Magistrate did not Attend Again this day.   27

February 22 Saturday: Saw the Sheriff who Told Me that he had been So much Engaged that he had not been able to Visit the Gaol, but that he would if possible on Monday Night – but that if Noone had any Complaint to Make he was to do it in writing And it Should be Attended to. Noone was told this on my Return from town who Answered that he had No Complaint to Make.   27

February 24 Monday: the Meat Sent for they Prisoners Yesterday was Sent back it being nearly all bone Mr. Martin Sent other in the place.   27

At the beginning of March 1845 another scandal arose. The 'Reverend Mr Farrell', who visited the gaol to perform divine service, was himself in court. The Reverend Howard, who had also visited the gaol but was now deceased, had been well-loved and beyond reproach, however the Reverend Mr Farrell was now accused of indecent assault against a young girl. He was now colonial chaplain, and living in the widow Mrs Howard's house. The girl was a servant in the house. After a long and dramatic trial Sarah Charlesworth was deemed to be a liar and the case dismissed. It was perhaps the most sensational trial yet in the young city of Adelaide, watched by crowds who squeezed into the courthouse. The girl herself fainted in the heat. She had been a servant in the houses of so many well-known families that the list of witnesses to her character was a 'who's who' of Adelaide at the time. The record of trial is 28 newspaper columns long and reads like a gripping drama.[391] In his journal Ashton makes no mention of the scandal though it must have been on his mind. None of his journal entries betray his thoughts on the matter. The Reverend Farrell then married the widow Mrs Howard and was later appointed Dean of Adelaide.[392]

March 1 Saturday: Saw the Advocate General About the Calendars he Told Me Dr. Wright would be Indicted for Manslaughter. 25

March 3 Monday: Saw the Sheriff. 27

March 5 Wednesday: to the list of Prisoners to be Printed – to be printed by Friday Night. 32

March 7 Friday: they Calendars brought to the Gaol. 33

March 8 Saturday: delivered the Calendars of they Prisoners for Trial His Excellency the Judge Government Offices. 33

March 10 Monday: the Gaol delivery Commenced at 10 OC'k this Morning at the Supreme Court House – at the Court All Day. 36

Cases to be dealt with at this sitting were all serious. The judge bemoaned the nature of the crimes on his list declaring that they 'throw a dark shade on the moral character of the province'. As well as the case of Dr Wright, there was murder by an Aboriginal man, rape, and illegal manufacturing of coins; also allegations of 'wilful murder of a native man ... and a native woman', deliberate setting fire to a house, numerous cases of theft, and suspicions of murder of a newborn.[393] Several of these cases were not proceeded with; some were acquitted; and, of those where the perpetrator was found guilty, two were sentenced to be hanged and 11 to be transported.

March 11 Tuesday: at the Court James Douglas was found Guilty this day of having Committed a Rape on the Person of Helen Grant and was Sentenced to be Executed on the 29th Inst't. 36

March 12 Wednesday: At the Court all day. 36

March 13 Thursday: At the Court All Day the Native Call'd Wera Maldera alias Peter was found Guilty this day of the Wilful Murder of George McGrath on the 3rd June 1842 - at Coorong and was Sentenced To Be Executed on the 29th Inst - and his body to be buried within the Gaol. 33

March 14 Friday: at the Court the Trial of Edward Wright M.D. Commenced this Morning at 9½ for the Manslaughter of William Wilkins the Court adjourned at 8 P.M. and the Dr. who has been on bail was brought to the Gaol for the Night. 34

March 15 Saturday: The Court Sat at 9½ when the Dr. was again placed at the bar and Acquitted - the Court Adjourned early this day to Monday Morning at 9½. 31

March 17 Monday: the Court Sat this Morning at 9½ when the 7 Prisoners in Custody for Making Base Coin was placed at the bar and they was all found Guilty of Making and Sentenced to 10 Years Transportation Trial lasted all day. 30

March 18 Tuesday: the Court Sat at 9½ this Morning when the last Case for trial was Call on James Clare for Shooting a Horse etc Guilty and Sentenced to 15 Years Transportation The Trial lasted all day. - The Sheriff & Dr. Duncan Came to the Gaol And Saw Douglas Under Sentence of Death. 29

March 22 Saturday: Some of They Prisoners attempted to get their Irons off. 27

March 24 Monday: Saw the Sheriff this day about the Prisoners leaving for V.D. land. 26

March 26 Wednesday: the Sheriff Visited the Gaol Saw Douglas & they Prisoners Talked a good deal about the Comm' of Police - I afterwards Saw the Sheriff and His Excellency was this day pleased to Commute Douglas's Sentence to Transportation for life as Soon as I Mentioned this to him he was Very Abusive and Noisey - up to this time Since his Conviction he had been Very Quiet And Resigned the Catholic Bishop had Seen him every day. 26

March 27 Thursday: Douglas Still outrageous. 26

March 28 Friday: as above. 26

A group of citizens had formed a society committed to abolishing the death penalty and had petitioned Governor Grey to save the lives of James Douglas and Wera Maldera. Abolishing death as a penalty was a growing cause in the 'civilised world'. Those who espoused it in Adelaide were not soft on punishment though – they only wanted a suitable alternative to death. The society in Adelaide believed that in England, transportation was a reasonable and suitably harsh alternative. However, in Adelaide transportation lacked the same effect. They suggested that perhaps close confinement for life or working in chains for life would suffice, or whatever the governor might decide.[394]

The society could not win. James Douglas, found guity of rape, did not appreciate their successful petition to save him from the rope and the governor did not agree with them in the case of Wera Maldera – he believed the Aboriginal man had betrayed the white man's trust and should hang. In his sentencing speech he explained:

> I believe that when you committed the crime for which you are to suffer, you knew that you were doing wrong – that you were doing what neither the white people nor your own people ever suffer to pass unpunished. You and your companions had lived much among white men, and had been treated with much kindness, and you were fond of

their society; but no sooner was the crime committed, than you fled away and hid yourself ... your companions are still hidden ... The kindness with which you were treated ... by Chase in particular, adds to the enormity of the crime. He treated you with ... confidence, not only lying down to sleep in your company, but suffering you to even share his blanket. It was in the midst of these tokens of confidence and security that you crept ... gently from his side [and] murdered one of the party while defenceless and asleep ... You have been hidden from justice long; but I trust your example will teach your fellows that justice, though slow is sure. ... the white men also, who will see that when crime is brought home to the native, punishment is certain, and that they are therefore without excuse if they dare to take the law into their own hands.[395]

After the court was dismissed the colonial secretary directed the sheriff to arrange for a scaffold to be built for two – for Wera Maldera and James Douglas.[396] As it turned out, it only needed to be for one. As it also turned out, Wera Maldira behaved calmly at his death whereas James Douglas, who had received a reprieve, was 'very violent, noisy and abusive'.[397] Ashton described the scene in his journal:

March 29 Saturday: The Native Call'd Wera Maldera alias Peter – for the Murder of George McGrath was Executed this Morning at 8 OC'k and After the Body hanged one hour was Cut down And Buried inside the Gaol (agreeable to the Sentence) in the usual Place and the Grave will be No. 3 –
C.B. Newenham Esq'r Sheriff present. They Mounted & foot Police was in Attendance – After the above Execution was over the Reprieved Convicted Prisoner Douglas (and which Reprieve was Read to him this Morning by the Sheriff) he became Very Outrageous and Violent threatening the TurnKeys (Perry's) life etc And in the evening I was obliged to have him hand Cuffed and Chained Down to his Stretcher and he Made a dreadful Noise all Night – Wilkins One of the Prisoners for Coining Attempted to break his Irons off this was the Second time he had done the

Same I had him placed in one of the Cell out Side and Kept him there All Night. 26

March 30 Sunday: Douglas Much Quieter this Morning beg'd My Pardon. Received Instructions this day to take the Prisoners under Sentence of Transportation to the Port to Morrow Morning and Put them on board the Schooner Scotia for Hobart Town. 25

March 31 Monday: left the Gaol this Morning at ¼ past 9 with they following Prisoners under Sentence of Transportation to V.D Land
Viz James Douglas – life
James Wilkins – 10 Years
John Walker Wilson – 10 Years
William Somers – 10 Years
Henry Booth – 10 Years
John Walker – 10 Years
Thomas Brown – 10 Years
Henry Dowing alias Cope – 10 Years
I Arrived at the Port at 10¾ A.M. the Vessel Not being Ready to Remove Them I placed Them in the Police Station untill 3 P.M. when the Schooner Scotia Capt'n Wardel being Ready I put Them on board to be Taken to Hobart Town the Capt'n gave Me a Receipt for they Prisoners also for 8 pr of Irons and 3 pr of Hand Cuffs to be Returned to the Gaol on the first Opportunity – I Returned to the Gaol at 6½ P.M. with Kennedy the Turnkey. 25

April 1 Tuesday: Saw the Sheriff Reported to him My having put they Above Prisoners on board the Scotia Yesterday for Hobart Town They Mounted Police went to the Port with Me Yesterday and Remained there untill the Prisoners was on Board Ship. 17

The *South Australian Register* filled out the details:

> EXECUTION OF THE NATIVE, AND TRANSPORTATION OF DOUGLAS AND THE COINERS: ... On Saturday morning the sentence of the law was carried into effect upon the native, Wira Maldira, for murder; but to Douglas, the warrant for commutation of punishment to transportation for life was read by the Sheriff.

The native had been crying during the whole night, which had been passed with four other blacks. He so far braced his nerves as to show the white men little emotion . . . He had begged that the blacks should carry him to his grave, and no white man be allowed to touch him after death. This request was strictly complied with. [The Aboriginal prisoners] . . . received him in their arms, placed him in the coffin, and buried him in the gaol-yard by the side of the other murderers. Douglas was afterwards very violent, noisy, and abusive . . . threatened the turnkey . . . up to four o'clock on Sunday morning, he disturbed the whole prison with oaths, singing, and execrations. At length he fatigued, became humble and penitent, and left the gaol pretty quietly for the port on Monday with the coiners. At the Half-way House, Mr Ashton kindly gave each a glass of porter, which they drunk, as his back was turned; to the sinking of the ship.[398]

At the previous execution of an Aboriginal man, Ngarbi, Cawthorne had watched the crowds from his window; this time he was right there:

Yesterday I saw for the first time an execution. Poor blackie had to be hung by the laws of a country he never recognized, he never knew and which had usurped his freedom and rendered him obedient to laws he knew not, nor understood. Poor fellow, He went like a sheep to the slaughter. He seemed to be utterly lost and bewildered by the pomp. He spoke not, looked not, no one said good bye to him. . . . His mortal enemies the natives of another tribe stood looking on gloating. The white man his murderers, stood round in hundreds, some with swords, and guns and pistols, no one sympathized with him but myself. . . . Alas 'Wira Maldira' thy tribe shall wail for thee in vain.[399]

Cawthorne remained passionate about the plight of Aboriginal people in South Australia. By the time he gave his speech to the Temperence Society in 1864, 31 prisoners had been hanged in South Australia. Twenty-one of these had been Aboriginal.[400]

The last Aboriginal prisoner to be hanged had been in 1862. Hangings ended in 1964 and no more Aboriginal people were hanged in that time. Rupert Maxwell Stewart came closest to that fate when he was sentenced in 1959, but he was spared the death penalty after a media campaign in 1960. Nonetheless, the unending history of grief and incarceration of Aboriginal people in South Australia appears to have had its seeds in that very early time in the colony.

April 3 Thursday: A Prisoner was this day brot to Gaol as Sentenced by Mess'rs Hawker & Price - to 3 Months Imprisonment for loosing Sheep. 18

April 5 Saturday: took the Committal of the Above Charles Turner to the Visiting Magistrate and who Referred it to the Advocate General and he Requested that the Prisoner Might be discharged out of Custody - and the Visiting Magistrate gave Me an Order to discharge him Accordingly which I did - on the grounds of Informality of the Committal. 17

April 6 Sunday: None, Mr. Gleeson brot to Gaol for Debt. 17

April 7 Monday: Saw the Sheriff this day. 17

April 11 Friday: the Sheriff Visited the Gaol this day Saw the Prisoners. 19

April 18 Friday: Rebecca Somerville was Brot to Gaol as a Lunatic by order of Dr. Nash. 18

April 22 Tuesday: Mr. J. Fleming brot to Gaol for Debt at the Suit of Edw'd Stephens. 22

April 25 Friday: Thomas Millard brot to Gaol for debt at the Suit of Edw'd Stephens. 23

April 26 Saturday: the Sheriff Visited the Gaol Saw they Prisoners. - and ordered Rations to be allowed to Mr. Fleming - Millard the Debtors. 23

April 29 Tuesday: E.B. Gleeson (Debtor) was Discharged by Order of the Insolvent Court he having found Bail. 25

Edward Burton Gleeson had owned a property he named 'Gleeville' in the Tiers (now a large part of the suburb of Beaumont) and by 1840 had over 7000 sheep. He was one of a number of well-known colonists who suffered financially and later recovered, going on to buy land in the Mid North. He laid out and was therefore the founder of the town of Clare, and, in 1868, became its mayor.[401]

Ashton had not mentioned Bella in the journal all year, however she was still a regular presence in the gaol. On 1 May 1845:

> *Isabella Anderson*, better known as '*Scotch Bella*', charged for the no-one-knows-how-manyeth-time with being drunk and disorderly, was committed to gaol for fourteen days.[402]

Fifteen days later:

> *Friday May 16* ISABELLA ANDERSON *alias* SCOTCH BELLA – Was charged with being drunk and disorderly...
>
> Sergeant Lorymer – ... she has been dis-orderly to-day; she was intoxicated before she came into court, and she behaved there in a riotous manner.
>
> Committed as an idle and disorderly person, for one month.
>
> Prisoner – Thank you. Mr Finniss: you were always a friend to Miss Anderson.[403]

Bella's pattern was now established. In years to come she spent time in asylums and time in gaol. In 1851 when asked how long she had been out of gaol she replied: 'Full a fortnight between my getting out and being sent back; there's seldom so much time lost'.[404]

May 4 Sunday: Mr. Insp'r Shaw took a Sailor from the Gaol Named Barrett to put him on board his Ship Falcon at the Port. 28

May 6 Tuesday: a Sailor was taken from the Gaol by a Mounted Policeman to be put on board his Ship Falcon by Order of the Police Magistrate. 27

May 8 Thursday: None 25
A Pane of Glass [smashed] in they females Yard by the Sound.

May 9 Friday: W.T. Fleming (Debtor) was discharged by order of the Insolvent Court he having found Bail. 24

May 13 Tuesday: George Souter & John Kelly Committed from the Port for Stealing Gin. 24

May 14 Wednesday: G.G. Emmett was brot to Gaol for Debt by Borr Sheriffs Officer who told Me that Emmett had No Money to Support himself in Gaol he therefore was Allowed the Gaol Rations. 25

On the evening of 14 May 1845 Ashton went for a drink with W.T. Fleming, a debtor only days since discharged from gaol. The story of what happened next has a particularly local and familiar feel to it:

> George Rogers and Elias Jaffray were charged with a violent assault on Mr W.B. Ashton, at the Market-House Inn, Thebarton, on Wednesday evening last.[405]

The Market-House Inn had belonged to 'Poor Wilkins' the 'lunatic' who had died. Inside the hotel, according to the police report, Ashton pulled apart two men in a fight and then had tried to evict another man for making improper suggestions to the proprietor, the widow Mrs Wilkins. He removed the offending man from the premises and had just got him outside when he was struck by another man with a violent blow to his body and then by another from behind to the head. He at first thought that 'the scoundrel has stabbed me' as he was 'bleeding like a pig' but nonetheless sent someone after a fleeing man, in the meantime sending for police. The policeman 'knocked up' Mr Paxton (the chemist in the Dr Wright affair) as he was closed, who then dressed Ashton's wounds. Ashton 'nearly fainted from loss of blood [so] Mr Paxton gave him some brandy'. Ashton then went immediately to the police station to sign the charge sheet. The probable weapon was a bridle bit, seen with the offender at the hotel and afterwards found in a puddle. At the trial Ashton gave a detailed account and Fleming the debtor agreed that all was as Ashton had said.[406]

May 16 Friday: His Excellency Visited the Gaol this day in Company with the Private Secretary and Colonial Secretary went all over the Gaol (Except the Female Yard -) He Mentioned about the Natives Sleeping and that they Ought to Attend divine service The Prisoners Meat ought to be Supplied daily - and Visiting Books for the Visiting Magistrate and the Colonial Chaplain ought to have been Kept etc - he Also Saw the Gaol Book and expressed his Satisfaction in the Manner in which they was Kept The Military Guard Tower to be whitewashed and the windows to be Repaired His Excellency Spoke to James Clare under Sentence of Transportation for 15 Years and told him that he Should grant him a free Pardon and that it Should be Sent down either this day or tomorrow he was also pleased to Say that the Rooms in My house Should be whitewashed. - The Sheriff afterward Visited the Gaol and went All over. 30

May 17 Saturday: Saw the Sheriff and Mentioned to him His Excellencys Remarks at the Gaol Yesterday - and His Excellency was this day pleased to Grant a free pardon to James Clare Mentioned above and the Prisoner was discharged The discharge Came from the Sheriff. James George Witt brot to Gaol for Debt by Borr. 31

May 19 Monday: Reported to the Sheriff the Soldiers Tower and Windows and lamps which wanted Mending and which had been broken Some time also about My house. 32

May 20 Tuesday: Received from the Sheriff a letter which he had Received from the Colonial Secretary directing that in future the Natives when Sentenced to Transportation Should be Supplied with a Suit of Clothing Complete Native Prisoners in Gaol for a Short time to be Supplied with Blankets. Mr. Moorhouse to Supply them with Clothing on their being discharged from Gaol. - And that the Native Prisoners in future be Supplied with beds and bedding in all Respects the Same as those Supplied to European Prisoners the Officers of the Gaol to See that they are Kept Clean also that in future the Natives Shall attend divine Service with they Other Prisoners. 32

May 21 Wednesday: The Sheriff Visited the Gaol Went all over. 33

May 22 Thursday: the Natives King John and King Williamy had Jackets & Trousers put on (we had no Shirts) and the Native in for Murder was washed well and his old Rugs taken away and a New Blanket given to him the Natives was also Removed from No. 6 into No. 5 Cell where the Guard Bed is. Mr. Moorhouse Visited the Natives and Expressed his Satisfaction with their Cloth, Bedding etc he also told King John that his Excellency would discharge him on the Queens Birthday. 32

May 23 Friday: The Rev'd Mr. Farrel Came to the Gaol this Morning the Prisoners was Cleaning the Cells and Windows we did not expect him Not being his day for divine Service I told him they Prisoners would be Ready in 10 Minutes he Said Monday Morning Next he would attend. - The Advocate General Sent for me about the Case of T.N. Mitchell and also when the Sessions ended at the time when King John was tried. 33

May 24 Saturday: Being the Queens Birthday we discharged all the firearms at 12 OC'k Noon His Excellency was pleased this day to Pardon the Native Called Murray King John under Sentence of 10 Years Transportation I took the Native to Government House and was Set at Liberty with a fustian Jacket & Canvass Trousers belonging to the Gaol. 32

The new rules brought in by Governor Grey at his inspection of the gaol meant that the Indigenous man known as 'Murray King John' was clothed at the gaol's expense ready for transportation. He received his clothes then almost immediately was pardoned and released. That Indigenous people were sentenced to transportation in early Adelaide seems particularly cruel. This man expected to be transported until almost the last minute.

The reprieve came only days after the Governor made his visit to the gaol. Confronted with the differences in conditions and expectations for the Aboriginal prisoners compared to the white prisoners, Governor Grey had not consulted Ashton, rather he had summarily directed that, apart from wearing blankets, which was to continue until Moorhouse supplied them with clothes on release, conditions were to be made the same for all the prisoners; they were all to have beds and they were all to go to chapel. His intentions were perhaps admirable, however given the Aboriginal people's preference for sleeping together around a fire and their intolerance to Christian teachings Ashton's first instinct to not separate the Aboriginal prisoners in beds in the dark of night and not insist on them going to chapel is understandable. Whether he was right or wrong he was now overridden.

It is impossible to know what was playing in Governor Grey's mind when he decided to pardon Murray King John. Other prisoners had been pardoned, of course, however in this case he would have been well aware of many of the settlers' ambivalence to any severe punishment of Aboriginal people. It may have been that he thought the local deterrent effect of the sentence of transportation would be lost once the prisoner was physically removed. It may have been time to show his power to reprieve in a grand gesture to coincide with the curious importance of the Queen's Birthday to Aboriginal people; or he may simply have wished to avoid any public debate on the issue.

Moorhouse was of the view that deterrence was already achieved:

> On the 24th of May, [a] native named *Merainmilla*, or *King John*, was pardoned and liberated; he had been in prison two years and five months. He was convicted of sheep stealing. . . . he will not be guilty of a similar crime. His imprisonment appeared to have answered all that was intended; and he will advise his friends and associates to avoid theft for the future.[407]

May 25 Sunday: George Patch a Private in the 96th was discharged at 8 A.M. given Over to the Serg't of the Guards & he has been in Gaol 2 Months for an Assault.   31

May 26 Monday: Saw the Advocate about Mitchells Case Coming on to Morrow in the Supreme Court.   31

On 26 May 1845 the sheriff wrote to the colonial secretary, saying that the wooden fence was rapidly decaying.[408] As the only obstacle separating the 'space between the walls' and freedom, this was a serious concern.

May 27 Tuesday: at the Supreme Court in the Case Mitchell v B.J. Finnis and C. Bonney Esq'rs I Received a written Order to Deliver Over to Police Constable Cre...ry 4 Sailors belonging to the Isabella Watson to be put on board. Their Names are - William Parsons - James Murray - Charles B. Hawkins and Charles Turpin - given over to the Police Accordingly - Thos. Millard (a debtor) was discharged by Order of the Insolvents Court he having found Bail. Divine Service in the Gaol at 11½ A.M. [this last sentence crossed out in the original] 31

May 28 Wednesday: went to the Port and Saw Capt'n Lipson About the Money for the fines & Keep for the above named 4 Sailors etc and left the Amount of the Sum wanted with Mr. Shaw of the Police. The Sheriff - Visiting Magistrate - Mr. Moorhouse - Visited the Gaol Saw they prisoners. 26

The missionary Klose also visited the Aboriginal prisoners that day:

> On the 28th I visited the prison, which I do regularly either on Wednesday or Saturday afternoons ... There are now only three in there: one from the north who was sentenced to 10 years gaol for sheep stealing and has now completed one year; another from Lake Albert for complicity in a murder ... The third is from Rivoli Bay ... Each of these speaks a different language. I can speak only to the first of them. At every opportunity I make him aware of his sinful life, where it has brought him and where it will bring him after his death if he does not take refuge in Jehovah.[409]

Moorhouse made comment on the prisoner from Rivoli Bay:

> On the 26th of May, a boy from that district was charged ... with having stolen 165 sheep ... It has always happened that the natives are subject to attack the flocks in the newly-settled districts; and it

appears a difficult matter to suggest any plan that would prevent them doing so ... accustomed to see animals in a timid and wild state ... astonished at beholding a flock of sheep ... the temptation of having food within reach, and with little trouble, appears too great for them to bear ... The circumstance of one native having been brought to town, will shew the tribes of that district that driving sheep away from shepherds constitutes crime ... deterring them from further offence. I am sorry I am unable to communicate with this boy, as his dialect is entirely different.[410]

In the next part of the journal William Ashton clearly displays his character, attending to the needs of his various prisoners in the very poor weather, and as best as he could, helping all the prisoners feel warm and comfortable. Charlotte was helping out, organising to sew shifts and petticoats for Rosa Hyrdess, still in prison for concealing the birth of her child.

May 29 Thursday: Saw the Sheriff and gave him a Copy of the Gaol Rules. - G.G. Emmett (Debtor) was discharged by Order of the Insolvent Court he having found Bail etc - The Yards in the Gaol have been in a Very Wet State for the last few days Reported to the Sheriff a few days ago that Some Gravel was Much Wanted. - A Pane of Glass was broken in the Kitchen Debtors Yard whilst being cleaned. 26

May 30 Friday: None Ja's Geo. Witt (Debtor) discharged. 25

May 31 Saturday: Received the Pay this day Saw the Sheriff this day Mentioned to that Rosa A.D. Hyrdess was in Much want of Shoes Petticoats Shifts etc he wished Mrs Ashton to See what She did want - and let him know on Monday Next. 24

June 1 Sunday: there being No Debtors in the Yard I directed Morris to let the two Female Lunatics go into the kitchen by the fire during the day and to Sleep in their usual place. 24

June 2 Monday: waited a long time at the Sheriffs Office did Not See him left a list of Articles wanted for Rosa Hyrdess and 5s/- for a debtors discharge (Witt) on his Desk. A Pane of Glass broke in No. 4 Cell felons Yard Caused by the wind. 24

June 3 Tuesday: in Consequence of the Wet I had a large Stone brought in from the front of the Gaol and placed in the lower Cell for the Natives to be in the dry & have a fire. 24

June 4 Wednesday: Saw the Sheriff about the Gravel, Windows & Lamps etc he told Me that we Should Shortly have it etc he had he said written about Rosa Hyrdess's things. - I also Saw the Advocate General Showed him the list of Prisoners for Trial.
Charles Thompson alias Richard Lewis was brought to Gaol as a Runaway Convict from New South Wales This Man was brot to Gaol and Charged the Same about 12 Months ago but was discharged. 25

June 6 Friday: a Native Call'd Billy was Committed for Trial with being Concerned in the Murder of George McGrath the Native Spoke good English and was dressed as a European and had for Some time been a Shepherd with Mr. Scott I therefore treated him the Same as a white prisoner Sleeping with them etc 27

[In margin]
Mr. Farrel attended divine Service at 3 P.M.
Dr. Nash Came at the Same time.

I was with Prisoners. One had his tooth drawn.

June 7 Saturday: Mr. Fisher Came to the Gaol and Saw John Smallacome and demanded a Sight of his Committal which I Allowed him. Took the Calendars to the Governor - Judge - Colonial Secretary - Advocate General - Sheriff - Resident Magistrate - & to the Commissioner of Police. 27

June 8 Sunday: Mr. Gell Visited the Native Prisoners and had them in the TurnKeys lodge Some Time. Dr. Nash Visited the Gaol this day. 27

John Gell had collected a small vocabulary of the 'Adelaide Tribe' and was genuinely interested in their culture and beliefs, a sort of anthropologist of the time. It is from Mr Gell that we know the name of the area that is now the city:

On Tandanya, or South Adelaide [they] laid out a spacious town.[411]

The new experiences of hanging had by now already been incorporated into Aboriginal vocabulary and Gell recorded these. In 1842 he had written:

Last year two natives were hung whose relations are now called Ngarri-warinya, wikandi or willo. Son, father or brother of the rope.[412]

Teichelmann and Schurmann had also noted 'Ngaritya = a person who has been hung'.[413]

June 9 Monday: the Gaol delivery Commenced this Morning at 9½ At the Court all day. 27

June 10 Tuesday: at the Court All day the Native Call'd Wekweki alias Jack was tried and found Guilty of the Murder of George McGrath and Sentenced to be executed on Tuesday the 24th Inst The Other Native Called Koovey Kowminne alias Billy was admitted as evidence against Wekweki and he was discharged by the Court and given over to Mr. Moorhouse after the trial. 23

June 11 Wednesday: A Poor Woman Named Wilkinson Supposed to be Insane was found at 7½ this Morning with 2 Small Children Nearly Dead from wet and Cold at the end of the ditch Near the Gaol the Poor Children were in a Dreadful State their Arms and legs being quite Stiff from the Wet & Cold I had the Woman & Children brot into the TurnKeys lodge by a good fire and Mrs. Ashton and Mr Perry took their Wet Clothes off and put warm Blankets on them and they Soon got better The Court Sat at 11 OC'k this Morning when 7 Prisoners was discharged or held to Bail. The Sessions ended at 2 OC'k - the Sheriff Visited the Gaol Saw the Prisoners and Saw the poor woman & children found in the Water this Morning, wished her to Remain in the Gaol and he would Report the Circumstances to the Government her Husband was for some years in the Government Employ at the port but have left the Colony Since and this Poor woman has no home for herself or Children. 22

June 12 Thursday: Mrs Wilkinson Still in Gaol and her children Supplied from the Gaol Rations by order of the Sheriff. 15

The story above is the one highlighted at the beginning of this book. It is only one of many stories in the journal but on its own says much: much about Ashton, much about Charlotte and also about Perry. It is a story of compassion and of one family's tragedy. Mrs Wilkinson was unfortunately to stay on in the gaol, confined as insane. Her children were taken from the gaol after a time, leaving their mother to its care, to be themselves looked after by a woman in the town. In December 1845 Mrs Wilkinson was taken to live as servant to the sheriff and his lady.[414]

June 13 Friday - Took John Smallacombe before His Honor the Judge on a Habius Corpus granted on the ap'n of Mr. Fisher on the grounds of Informality of the Warrant of Committal - Mr. Bartley in Company with F. Davison Esq'r one of the Committing Magistrates left with me last Night a Second Warrant which the Judge held was good and the Prisoner was Remanded back to Gaol to undergo his Sentence of 42 days imprisonment Dr. Nash Visited the Gaol and Saw Mrs Wilkinson as he Said by the Request of the Government. 15

June 15 Sunday: went to the Port about the Money for fines and Keep of they Sailors belonging to the Isabella Watson - Saw Mr. Shaw who handed over to Me £12-1- in part Stating to Me that Mr. Torrens had the Remainder The Rev'd Mr. Farrel Came to the Gaol at 2 P.M. Divine Service. 14

June 16 Monday: Sent up to the Sheriff this day by Kennedy having Such a dreadful Cold from getting So wet Yesterday in going to the Port and back - Mrs Wilkinson & Children Still in Gaol. 14

June 18 Wednesday: Call'd at the Sheriffs Office did not See him - the Visiting Magistrate Call'd the Gaol See entry in his Book. 13

June 19 Thursday: Saw the Sheriff and handed over to him the £12-1- Which I had Received from Mr. Shaw on Account of they Sailors he wished me to Make inquiries About a Man for the execution of the Poor Native on Tuesday Next Saw the Com'r of the Insolvent Court about giving Mr. H... notice when a Debtor having been Receiving Government Rations before they are Bailed etc - gave Mr. H... the amount for the Keep of Gleeson and Emmitt (Debtors) whilst in Gaol - Men Commenced Whitewashing.   13

June 20 Friday: Sent Perry Round the Reed Beds to find a Man Named Simes to See if he would execute the Native under [Sentence] of Death - Perry Could not See him but left word with a person that Knew him for him to Call at the Gaol. John V. James was brot to Gaol by Borr Sheriffs Officer for Debt - at the Suit of Henry Jickling. - This Debtor was discharged this Evening by order of the Sheriff.   14

June 21 Saturday: Mr. Moorhouse the Protector of Aborigines Came to the Gaol this Afternoon and told Wekiweki the Native under Sentence of Death that His Excellency had been pleased to grant him a Reprieve. - See Mr. Moorhouse's Visiting Book.   13

June 22 Sunday: His Honor the Judge Call'd at the Gaol this Afternoon and told Me that the Native was Reprieved I Mentioned to him that the Protector of the Aborigines had entered in the Gaol Book to the Same effect Yesterday Afternoon - I Saw Dr. Nash yesterday he told me that the Woman Wilkinson was to be detained in the Gaol as a Lunatic the Children was to be taken away but as the person who was to have Charge of them had no bedding they had better Remain in the Gaol untill Monday.   13

June 23 Monday: The Sheriff Visited the Gaol this day Saw the Prisoners the Native Reprieved.
He Saw also the Lunatics and the Woman Named Wilkinson & Children.   18

Moorhouse wrote of Wekweki in his quarterly report:

> I have great pleasure in adding that his Excellency was pleased to reprieve the prisoner.
>
> In my last report I had to state that *Wira Maldira*, or *Peter*, had been hanged for the same offence. He was the chief instigator in the affair; he had lived for nearly two years with Europeans ...

and, in consequence, was more culpable than *Wekweki* and others with him. *Wekweki* knew nothing of Europeans, as no stations had ever been formed in his territory at the time. ... The execution of *Wira Maldira* ... is enough to assure the natives that crime will be punished ... that *Wekweki* is at the mercy of the whites, is sufficient to make his tribe cautious how they again commit similar offences.[415]

June 24 Tuesday: a great Number of People Assembled in front of the Gaol this Morning expecting to See the poor Native executed - Saw Mr. Gilbert this afternoon he Said he would get the bed & blankets and have the Children belonging to Mrs Wilkinson Removed to Mrs Langhams Dr Nash Visited the Gaol.   13

June 25 Wednesday: Mrs Wilkinson's Children was this day taken to Langhams and She herself was placed under the Charge of Morris herself & children have been Receiving the Government Rations Since the 11th Instant 3½ lbs Bread 1 lb Meat per day and 2 oz of Tea & 4 oz Sugar 4 oz Soap per Week Sent the pay Sheets to the Sheriff by Morris.   13

June 26 Thursday: the Rev'd Mr. Farrel Attended divine Service at 11½ A.M. divine Service was held in the Office the Chappel Not being fit in Consequence of the white washers - all they Prisoners attended 13 in No.   13

June 30 Monday: Mr. Henry Gilbert was brot to Gaol as a Lunatic I Received no Order with him either from the Colonial Secretary or Dr. Nash but Mr. Thomas Gilbert (Brother) Colonial Storekeeper told me he had Seen His Excellency about Henry and that he was to Send him here as Soon as he pleased.   13

July 2 Wednesday: The Sheriff Visited the Gaol Saw they Prisoners.   17
July 3 Thursday: The Visiting Magistrate Visited the Gaol etc   18

Moorhouse dated his quarterly report 2 July. On 3 July 1845 the Location at Piltawodli was closed. Klose wrote in his diary:

> 3 July 1845 – The sappers came this morning and removed the roofs of the last 2 houses of the natives. In one of the houses were 7 old

people and 2 small children – they had to leave it and lie down under a tree. I told the soldiers that they should leave at least one house with a roof; that I would hand in a request to the Governor. The answer was: 'No! It is the Governor's order that no longer shall any native remain within the fence.' They climbed up and tore it down. The next day they intended going into the other houses – into the schoolhouse, the attendant's house and Br. Teichelmann's.[416]

The government left Klose his house, however all the huts that had been built for the Kaurna people were gone. The schoolhouse, the attendant's house and Missionary Teichelmann's house, were now to be lived in by sappers and miners. Freeling's 1849 map (see page 34) includes depictions of these remaining houses, labelled 'Sappers and Miners'. The section on the 1849 map labelled 'Aboriginal Location' was not there in 1845. These buildings came later – small brick buildings, a cluster on each side of the river, built in 1846 for adults of children at the new school.[417]

4 July 1845 – Today the sappers moved in, the children cleared the schoolhouse. In the afternoon the Protector Mr Moorhouse, the attendant and the children moved to the new schoolhouse. On the Location only 3 old people and 2 children who were not in a condition to go with the rest, were left.[418]

The new schoolhouse, to be used by both 'Adelaide Tribe' and 'Murray Tribe' children, was a converted part of the old sappers and miners building on Kintore Avenue, next to the earlier gaol.[419]

July 5 Saturday: Ann Bent was this day discharged by Order of the Sheriff His Excellency having been pleased to Remit the Remainder of her Sentence – She had been Sentenced by the Supreme Court to 18 Months Hard Labour and had Served 12 Months on the 3rd Inst.   15

July 7 Monday: left the Gaol at 1 OC'k this day with Henry Dickinson a Prisoner under Sentence of Transportation to 7 Years to V.D. Land

> took him to the Port and handed him over to Capt'n Gwatkin of the Schooner Timbo to be taken to Hobart Town got a Receipt for him and for the Irons on him. 17
>
> **July 8** Tuesday: Reported to the Sheriff my having taken the above Henry Dickinson and put him on board Ship Yesterday. 16
>
> **July 9** Wednesday: the Sheriff Visited the Gaol this day Saw they Prisoners. 16
>
> **July 10** Thursday: Mr. J... Commenced drawing Gravel to the Gaol this day. Mrs Wilkinson (Insane) broke a pane of Glass in the Debtors Yard No. 4. 17

The mention of the pane of glass in the debtors' yard suggests that this yard was now sometimes being used for the female 'lunatics'. The woman who broke it was Mrs Wilkinson, who had been rescued from the ditch. The sheriff was soon to order that she go back to the female yard, however this had limited success. There was clearly not enough room in the gaol.

> **July 11** Friday: Rebecca Somerville (Insane) was taken Ill (fits) Sent for Dr. Nash he Came and Saw her. The Colonial Storekeeper bought us this day and Yesterday 2 Wheel Barrows - 4 Shovels - 1 Spade and 2 Pic Axes - for to do the Yards with. 19
>
> **July 12** Saturday: Saw the Sheriff Mentioned to him about they Prisoners Working Gravelling the Yard to me to let them have ½ lb Meat and a little Sugar Extra whilst at work. - Anthony Best was brot to the Gaol again for 3 Months or to pay a fine of £30- for disobeying Certain Orders Made by the Resident Magistrate Relative to the Support of his Wife. 21
>
> **July 14** Monday: the Sentry from the Guard Room was placed on duty at the Iron Gates during the time that the Gravel was being brot in. I Sent a Note to the Sheriff about Anthony Best whether this was a Case that Should be put into the other Yard as it Appeared he was Sent to Gaol for not Obeying the Resident Magistrates Order the Sheriff was not at his Office. 23

July 15 Tuesday: Saw the Sheriff this Morning he Ordered that Best Should Remain in the Same Yard he was then in. The Sheriff Visited the Gaol Saw the Prisoners and ordered Mrs Wilkinson to be put into the Females Yard - the Visiting Magistrate Visited the Gaol Saw Anthony Best. 22

July 16 Wednesday: Mrs Wilkinson (Insane) Created a great disturbance in the Females Yard all Night and Nearly Made the 2 Female Prisoners as Mad as her Self. I had her put into a Sleeping Room by herself during the Night. 20

July 18 Friday: Prisoners at Work. 19

July 19 Saturday - Not at work Washing their Clothes. 20

July 21 Monday: Several Prisoners brot to Gaol Anthony Best Rather Noisey & Abusive. Julia Caines Committed for Trial a Baby with her. 25

July 22 Tuesday: All They Prisoners Refused to Work at Gravelling the Debtors Yard (No doubt by the Advice of Anthony Best) After My talking to them and Reading the Clause in the Act for the Regulation of Gaols etc - and altho Not Sentenced to Hard Labour yet the Sheriff and Visiting Magistrate had the Power to Order and Make Them Work. They Prisoners all went to Work. - The Sheriff Visited the Gaol Saw they Prisoners etc They Made No Complaint to him Mr. Gilbert was with him. Saw the Adv General this day about Mrs Caines from Port Lincoln. 25

July 23 Wednesday: Prisoners all at work. 25

July 24 Thursday: The Rev'd Mr. Farrel Call this Morning but as all the Prisoners was at work and the Gates all Open to admit the Gravel Said he would attend to Morrow between 10 & 11 A.M. and have divine Service. 24

July 25 Friday: Mr Farrel attempted divine Service. At 10½ all the prisoners attended except Anthony Best and Cruger - Best Stating that he was Reading a Sermon himself - Perry & Kennedy attended with They Prisoners I Could not attend Myself in Consequence of the Gates being Open to Admit the Gravel and Mrs Ashton being Very Ill. 25

July 26 Saturday: Saw the Sheriff this day. Prisoners at work.   23

July 28 Monday: John McHarg was brot to the Gaol for Debt at the Suit of Samual Stocks.   26

July 29 Tuesday: finished Gravelling in Side the Gaol this day.   25

July 30 Wednesday: Mr. John Afford finished drawing the Gravel this day Making 350 Load.   25

July 31 Thursday: The Sheriff Visited the Gaol this day Saw they Prisoners. I wished him to Apply for About 30 Loads More of Gravel to Repair the Walk between the Walls and a few loads for the front of the Gaol.

ND The Sheriff Also took a list of the Articles of Clothing Wanted by they Prisoners (Soldiers) Wilkinson Noone & Brennan.   25

August 2 Saturday: Saw the Sheriff this day at his Office - I Received the Months Pay & Paid the Men.   26

August 3 Sunday: Mr Gell Did Not Visit the Native Prisoners this Day.   25

August 4 Monday: Saw the Sheriff and the Visiting Magistrate They told me that Anthony Best a Prisoner had Sent a Petition to His Excellency I don't know how it was Sent - it did Not go thro Me to the Sheriff in the usual way.   25

August 5 Tuesday - The Sheriff Visited the Gaol in Company with Mr. Newland J.P. He Saw all they Prisoners and went over the Gaol - Mr. Newland Made an entry the Visiting Magistrates Book of his Visit to the Gaol.   26

August 6 Wednesday: Received a load of fire Wood this day from the New Contractor Mess'rs Hamilton King William Street We had no way of Weighing the Wood but we Supposed it to be twenty Six hundred weight - Mistake this load of Wood was brot Yesterday.   26

August 7 Thursday: Brot to Gaol (by Borr Sheriffs Officer) - David Alexander Murray for Debt. 25 Cwt and one quarter of firewood Sent us this day from Mess'rs Hamilton.   27

August 9 Saturday: the Sheriff Visited the Gaol and had the Answer to Anthony Best & to Rosa Hyrdess that His Excellency Could Not interfere Relative to their Petitions.

August 10 Sunday: Anthony Best gave me a Note which he wished to be Sent to the Sheriff. - I told him it Should be Sent to Morrow.

August 11 Monday: Sent Bests Note to the Sheriff and also Reported 2 panes of Glass broken in the felons Yard - one on the 8th Inst in the Native Cell and one on the 10th Inst in No 1 Cell both Accidentally broken by the Wardsman.

August 12 Tuesday: The Sheriff Sent word to Best that he Could Not give him the Governors Answer Nor a Copy.
The Rev'd Mr. Farrel attended divine Service etc at 11 A.M. - I could not go myself - Mr. R...man and Mr. Baynes's Clerk was down at the time about the Debtors Petitions etc and I had to Meet the Advocate General about the Prisoner Julia Caines from Port Lincoln - which I did at 11½ A.M. The Advocate Gen'l gave Me a letter to the Police Magistrate who told Me that he Would Bail the Said Julia Caines at 12 OC'k to Morrow. The Visiting Magistrate Visited the Gaol at 1 OC'k this day None of They Prisoners wanted to See him - All the Prisoners attended divine Service this day Except the debtors who was engaged with their Attorneys etc - and Anthony Best who told me that he was of a different persuasion.

August 13 Wednesday: I took Julia Caines to the Police Magistrates Court at 12 Noon where She was Bailed to Appear at the Next Gaol delivery for the felony Committed by her at Port Lincoln.

August 14 Thursday: Anthony Best gave me his Petition this Afternoon to late to Send it to the Sheriff.

August 15 Friday: took the above Petition to the Sheriffs Office and left it on his desk did not See him.

August 16 Saturday: the Sheriff Sent Anthony Bests Petition back to him Refusing to forward the Same to his Excellency. Anthony Best was Making a Noise in the felons Yard this day as Mr Moorhouse was leaving the Gaol by talking Very loud - I did not Read the Sheriffs Answer to Best this evening thinking that he would be Violent and that I Should have to put him into a Solitary Cell and having Not One empty - the Insane women having a Bed in them. 28

August 17 Sunday: Read the Sheriffs Answer to Best and Returned him the Petition at 9 A.M. I also Cautioned him about Making a Noise by talking So Loud he Said he did not know that he talked Loud but that he was Nearly Mad by being Confined and his Children being Robbed as they was by Selling their property. 27

August 18 Monday: the Visiting Magistrate Visited the Gaol Anthony Best Said he did Not wish to See him. Made Some Remarks which Molineux Could Not hear - The Sheriff Afterwards Visited the Gaol.

His Excellency was his day pleased to Remit the Remainder of the Sentence (one Month Solitary) of Robert Wilkinson a Private belonging to the 96th Reg't and who had been Sentenced to 12 Months hard labour except the Last Month which was to have been in Solitary Confinement The Sheriff brot his discharged down and Wilkinson was handed over to the Military Guard at 3 P.M. 28

August 19 Tuesday: Mr. Playfield Came to the Gaol to See Anthony Best and from the Manner in which Best went on Mr. P. told me that he thought he was Insane. 27

August 20 Wednesday: a Load of Wood was Brot Said to be 29 Cwt & 2 Quarters but we had no way of weighing the Same. 27

August 21 Thursday: A Pane of Glass was broken in the Natives Cell No 6 felons Yard by the Rivoli Bay Native at Locking up time in my Presence by his Accidentally running his Elbow through. 23

August 23 Saturday: Saw the Sheriff Reported to him about the Bell - the Prisoner Brennan to have extra Rations as wardsman in the Debtors Yard with the Lunatics - they Pane of Glass Broken in the Native Cell No 6 - Anthony Best Petition & food etc 22

August 29 Friday: 2 Natives was brot to Gaol One Committed for trial and the other Boy to give evidence against him whilst I was up the Advocate General with the Committals in this Case The Rev'd Mr. Farrel Came to the Gaol and had divine Service - The Sheriff Visited the Gaol Saw they Prisoners and Attended Divine

Service. The Visiting Magistrate Came to the Gaol none of the Prisoners wished to See him I Saw the Sheriff at his Office he Wished the Lunatics (Women) to be Removed from the Debtors Yard to the Outer Cells - which was done on my Return to the Gaol and a Guard bed was taken from the felons Yard put into the Debtors Yard for the Debtors to Sleep on and Burns taken from the felons yard and put into the Debtors Yard to Assist Brennan to take Care of the Lunatics and The Native Boy in Gaol to give Evidence. - And Anthony Best to Sleep by himself in the felons Yard - 7 panes of Glass put in the Windows.   23

September 3 Wednesday: McHarg Debtor was discharged this day by order of the Insolvent Court he having found Bail.   27

September 4 Thursday: a female Named Gurney Wife of Serg't Gurney of the 96th Regiment (Insane) was admitted into the Gaol by Written order from the Sheriff.   27

September 6 Saturday: took the Calendars of Prisoners for Trial to His Excellency the Judge Officers etc - 7 Natives was brot to Gaol this afternoon Under Remand for Sheep Stealing. The 6 males was put into the debtors Yard and to Sleep in the lower Room etc and the Native female with the women in the females Yard Mr. Moorhouse was here and Said that would be the best Plan.   35

[In margin]
A.D. Murray Debtor Discharged.

September 8 Monday: the Gaol delivery Commenced this Morning at 9 - 4 Prisoners tried this day who was out on Bail. - Julia Caines (the Soldiers wife) for the Robbery at Port Lincoln was Sentenced to 3 Months hard Labour except the last Fortnight This woman had a Child with her about 12 Months old (Not at the Breast) which the Sheriff Said She might take to the Gaol with her for the present.   26

September 9 Tuesday: at the Court this day George Welch & David was Tried for the Burglary at Mr. Levi's Gawler Place was Acquitted and as the Advocate General determined to prosecute in the Case of Mr. Sayers Robbery of the £400 - David Hol... and Jane

Ricketts (In Gaol) and Jane Gag (on Bail) was Discharged by the Court. - And the Native Boy Tommy in Gaol to give evidence against a Native Man for felony was discharged and handed over to Mr. Moorhouse. - Ja's Williams Committed for threatening to Shoot Sam'l Reeves - was this day tried on an Indictment for Assaulting his Wife - and was Acquitted as he was in Custody he was Admitted to Bail to Appear to Morrow morning on the Indictment of Sam'l Reeves. 37

September 10 Wednesday: At the Court this Morning Williams as above Appeared The Advocate General did not Prosecute and he found Bail to Keep the Peace Towards Mr. Samuel Reeves etc and he was discharged. - The Sessions ended this day there was no prosecution the Case of a Native Call'd Charley for Sheep Stealing at Rivoli Bay and the Court order him to be discharged and given over to Mr. Moorhouse. Received 24 Blankets from Hamilton & Henderson which was applied for on Saturday last in Consequence of the increase of Prisoners. - Sent word for Mr. Moorhouse to Fetch the Native from the Gaol. 31

September 11 Thursday: Sent a Petition to the Sheriff Addressed to His Excellency from Anthony Best - Kennedy took it to the Sheriff. Robert Rankin was brot to the Gaol for Debt by Borr Sheriffs Officer and James Whyte (at the Same Suit) was brot in on the 9th Inst A Pane of Glass was broken in No 2 Cell felons Yard by a Prisoner named Thomas Kelly by accidentally Running his Elbow through it - the Protector of the Aborigines Came to the Gaol and took the Native Charley Away. 31

September 12 Friday: The Sheriff Visited the Gaol this day Saw the Prisoners and Mr. Rankin (Debtor) Spoke to Anthony Best About his Answer from His Excellency. 31

September 15 Monday: A Pane of Glass was broken in the felons Yard No ... Caused by the wind blowing the Window to during the high winds this evening. 32

September 18 Thursday: the Sheriff Visited the Gaol this day left Me His Excellencys Answer to Read to Anthony Best Relative to his Petition etc which I Read to Best, he wanted a Copy which

I Refused to Give untill I had Seen the Sheriff about it - W. D. Wiltshire (Debtor) was discharged by order of the Sheriff - 13 Prisoners was Discharged this day.   31

September 19 Friday: the Rev'd Mr. Farrel Attended at 11 A.M. Divine Service. - The Visiting Magistrate Came to the Gaol None of the Prisoners wished to See him.   18

September 20 Saturday: Saw the Sheriff he gave me the Answer to Anthony Bests Application to be Supplied With the Answers from His Excellency to his Best Petitions. And as the Sheriff declined to give them to Best he was Rather Noisey as usual about it.   18

September 22 Monday: Henry Gilbert - Lunatic - was Very Violent this evening threatening Hedditch. Took Hedditch out of his Room and let him Sleep in the TurnKeys Lodge.   18

September 23 Tuesday: None
Rankin and Whyte (Debtors) was discharged this day.   18

September 26 Friday: They Lunatics Very worse and worse.   17

September 27 Saturday: the Sheriff Visited the Gaol this day Saw they Prisoners etc - Anthony Best was insulting to him Threatening to take him to the Court for £2-2- for Cart & Horse taking the 2 Natives to the place of execution in 1839.   17

Anthony Best appears to have driven the cart at the first hangings of Aboriginal people in Adelaide, near the Colonial Store in the north parklands. He is here arguing that he was not paid. His behavior is obnoxious and erratic. He has clearly not had a fortunate life in the colony and now, with his marriage over, he was in gaol for refusing to pay support for his wife.

September 29 Monday - Dr. Nash Visited the Gaol he told Me that they Lunatics would in future be on a different Scale of Rations to what they was at present.   17

October 4 Saturday: Saw the Sheriff this day told me to tell Anthony Best that His Honor the Judge had Not an Opportunity to look into his Case but that if brought before him in a Proper Manner he the Judge would Pay every Attention to it: which I told Best and his Answer was that he would See and Make the Judge Pay Attention to his Case when he left the Gaol. 15

October 7 Tuesday: Call'd at the Sheriffs Office did Not See him. 14

October 8 Wednesday: Mr. Mann Came to the Gaol this Morning and took the Statement of John Morris I afterwards Saw the Advocate General about Morris. The Sheriff Visited the Gaol Saw Anthony Best & they other Prisoners. 13

October 10 Friday: the Visiting Magistrate Came to the Gaol. Saw Anthony Best and other Prisoners - Mr. Poulden Came to the Gaol and brought a Habeus Corpus for John Morris to be taken before His Honor the Judge Returnable at 11 OC'k to Morrow Morning. 15

On 10 October Charlotte Ashton gave birth to the family's sixth child, a boy they named George Grey Ashton.[420] His namesake, Governor Grey, was soon to become governor of New Zealand and end his time in Adelaide.

October 11 Saturday: I took John Morris (a Prisoner in Gaol for 60 days for having a flock of Sheep in the Bush the Property of John Hallett Esq'r) on a Habeus Corpus before the Judge and the Prisoner was discharged. 16

[In margin]
Eliz'th Connor was Brot to Gaol as a dangerous Lunatic.

October 12 Sunday: Anthony Best was discharged at 9 A.M. he Said he would not leave the Gaol unless Mr. Wigley the Magistrate who Committed Came and took him out - etc. I told him if he did Not leave quietly he would be forced out and after a Short Consideration he left the Gaol Very quietly. 14

October 13 Monday: John Ryland Gill was brot to Gaol under Remand as a dangerous Lunatic put him into the debtors Yard Brennan & Mansfield was with him All Night Dr Nash was at the Gaol Saw him and they other Lunatics Gill was a little better about 11 OC'k P.M.   15

John Ryland Gill was son of the Reverend Samuel Gill, Baptist minister, and brother to Samuel Gill, early colonial artist. Samual Gill painted several well-known pictures of the gaol.

S.T. Gill, *H.M.S. Gaol 18 – Adelaide*
[National Library of Australia, PIC Solander Box A55 #R374]

This painting is of the half-gaol, before the extension was begun, so pre-September 1846. It shows the two towers and the grand entrance building. Ashton and his family lived upstairs at this end of the building.

October 14 Tuesday: Capt'n Irving Came and paid the fines £5- on Account of Thomas Davis (one of his Sailors) in Gaol for Assaulting the Police. Capt'n Irving took the Man to the Port with him.   15

On 15 October 1845 six girls left the Native School Establishment in the company of a 'native boy' sent by their parents to collect them, and were on their way back to Mount Barker when Moorhouse called for a constable to be sent after them:

> As this is the first decided stand that the adults have made in taking away the girls it is very desirable to resist it.[421]

The protector continued to have trouble keeping the children at school; incentives such as pocket money for the boys and dolls for the girls failed to work.[422] The school finally closed in 1851 and the children were removed from Adelaide, right away from the home territories of any of them, to the Poonindie Mission on Eyre Peninsula.

October 16 Thursday: Edward Alonzo Thomas was brot to Gaol for Debt by Borr Sheriffs Officer - The Sheriff Call'd at the Gaol.   16

October 17 Friday: the Rev'd Mr. Farrel Came divine Service at the Gaol at 11 A.M.   16

October 18 Saturday: Eliz'th Cannon (Lunatic) was taken to Court and was Remanded for another week.   16

October 20 Monday: Saw the Sheriff he gave Me the list of Articles Applied for the Quarter and from whom we was to Receive them.   15

October 22 Wednesday: the Visiting Magistrate Came to the Gaol none of they Prisoners wished to see him.   17

October 23 Thursday - None except 5 Convicts brot to Gaol for Safe Custody they were brot from Bombay in the H.E.I.C Armed Ship Elphinston left here to be Sent to V.D Land.   21

October 25 Saturday: His Excellency George Gray Esq'r went on board the H.E.I.C. Armed Ship the Elphinston as Governor of New Zealand.   23

October 27 Monday: Saw the Sheriff at his Office this day. 26

October 28 Tuesday: Thomas Henry Allen Brot to Gaol fined £100 or to be imprisoned for 3 Calendar Months for distilling without a License. 27

November 1 Saturday His Excellency the Governor Major Robe Visited the Gaol this day at 12½ P.M in Company with His Honor the Judge, Mr. Thomas Private Secretary and the Sheriff The Commissioner of Police was at the Gaol at the Same time His Excellency went over all Parts of the Gaol Saw all they Prisoners etc the Office and all they Book - His Excelly was at the Gaol about an Hour. - The Police Magistrate Came to the Gaol with the Capt'n of the Schooner Timbo for to Show him the 5 Prisoners which he was about take to Hobart Town brot here from Bombay. 24

It was fitting that Governor Robe acquaint himself with the gaol. His predecessors had – Hindmarsh had seen the beginnings of the old gaol; Gawler inherited the old gaol, presided over plans that went much awry for a new gaol, then saw in half the new gaol; and Grey had inherited the new half-gaol.

November 2 Sunday: a Pane of Glass was broken in No 4 Debtors Yard Caused by the high Winds. 22

November 3 Monday: left the Gaol this day with they 5 Prisoners under Sentence of Transportation (from Bombay per Elphinston to Hobart Town) and put them on board the Schooner Timbo at 4 P.M. and left them in Charge of the Capt'n. 22

November 4 Tuesday: Saw the Sheriff and Reported to him having put they Above Prisoners on board the Timbo Yesterday for Hobart Town. 17

November 7 Friday: the Sheriff Visited the Gaol Saw they Prisoners. - A Prisoner this day named McPherson was Committed for trial for attempt at Rape. 18

November 8 Saturday: Mrs Gurny (Lunatic) was taken Very Ill Sent for the Dr. who Came and Saw her. I had Rosa Hyrdess out of the Womens Yard to Sleep with her. She was a little better about 10 OC'k Night. 18

November 9 Sunday: Dr Nash Visited Mrs Gurny She was a little better this day Rosa Still waiting on her. 18

November 10 Monday: Saw the Sheriff this day at his Office Borr Sheriffs Officer brot to Gaol Fred'k Hodding for Debt. 19

November 12 Wednesday: Mr. Fisher Call'd to See Mr. Thomas in Gaol for Debt. Mrs Gurny Still getting better Rosa Still with her. 20

November 14 Friday: The Sheriff & Capt'n Frome Visited the Gaol Saw the Prisoners and etc 20

November 15 Saturday: The Visiting Magistrate Visited the Gaol. Mrs Gurny (Insane) Much better Rosa Hyrdess Still With at Nights. 21

November 17 Monday: Joseph Lewis (Debtor) was discharged by Order of the Insolvent Court he having found Bail. 24

November 18 Tuesday: Saw Mr. Wigley About the Letter Allen (in Gaol under the Act for distilling) had Sent him a few days ago. 24

November 20 Thursday: Edward Alonzo Thomas (Debtor) was discharged this day by Order of the Sheriff. 26

November 24 Monday: delivered the Calendars of Prisoners for Trial to His Excellency, the Judge, Government Officers etc. 26

November 25 Tuesday: The Court of Oyer and Terminer and General Gaol delivery Commenced this Morning at 9½ His Honor Charles Cooper Esq'r Judge
3 Prisoners Tried this day. 26

November 26 Wednesday: At the Court all day The Sheriff Visited the Gaol this day Saw Catherine Wilkinson (that have been in Gaol Some Time as a Lunatic) About going to his home in the Country. 25

The governor's journal 1845

November 27 Thursday: at the Court All Day George Welsh was the last Prisoner Tried for Highway Robbery and was Sentenced to 15 Years Transportation All they prisoners disposed of and the Court Adjourned to 11 OC'k to Morrow morning. 25

November 29 Saturday: Sent the Reports to the Colonial Secretary & to the Sheriff by Kennedy - the Sheriff and his Lady Call'd at the Gaol and Spoke to Mrs Wilkinson about going to live With them as a Servant. 25

December 2 Tuesday: The Sheriff Visited the Gaol. 25

December 4 Thursday: The Sheriff Call'd at the Gaol Saw they Prisoners Cath'ne Wilkinson was this day taken from the Gaol by the Sheriff to live with him in the Country as a Servant - lent her 2 of the Gaol Bed Gowns. 24

December 5 Friday: a Man Named John Wild was Committed to Gaol by the Police Magistrate as a dangerous Lunatic Created a great disturbance with the other Lunatics. 24

December 6 Saturday: a Man Named James Callinan was brot to Gaol under Remand as a Dangerous Lunatic by the Police Magistrate. 24

December 7 Sunday: Dr. Wyatt & Dr. Nash both Visited the Gaol this day. 24

December 8 Monday: Julia Caines and John Rose both Came out of Solitary Confinement and was discharged having Served their time. 25

December 9 Tuesday: His Lordship the Catholic Bishop and the Rev'd Mr. Watkins Visited the Gaol went All over. The Sheriff Also Visited the Gaol Saw they Prisoners. - A Man Named Henry Nye Hosier was Committed to Gaol as a Dangerous Lunatic - His Honor the Judge & Mr. McDonald Visited the Gaol this afternoon His Honor Spoke to J. Wild (Lunatic) and to Walsh under Sentence of Transportation. 25

December 13 Saturday: The Sheriff Visited the Gaol Saw they Prisoners. 26

343

On 14 December 1845 the sheriff wrote to the colonial secretary, pointing out that there were now 12 'lunatics' in the gaol.[423] His concern was with the inexperience of the turnkey appointed to their 'special care' and also that the accommodation was inadequate to allow for proper classification. The eight males were in with the debtors, causing the debtors to complain. The four females were separated from the other women but were in the solitary cells, left open, between the walls.

> I am obliged to allow two or three Sentenced Prisoners to attend to the Lunatics Sleep in the same Cells with them. I am obliged frequently when the Solitary Cells are required for punishment to place two or three of the Insane [females] together, which almost invariably causes violence amongst them.[424]

His letter called for an enquiry into the question of a better way to care for these people and showed considerable understanding of their plight:

> I observe that they feel the incarceration of the Gaol deeply, and immediately on an additional Subject being brought in it causes a disturbance of the System amongst the others which cannot but be injurious.[425]

December 16 Tuesday: Took James Coyle and George Walsh (2 Prisoners Under Sentence of Transportation) to the Port but found the Schooner 'Timbo' was not Ready to Receive them I therefore left them in the Police Station in charge of the Police and Returned home.   26

December 17 Wednesday: P.S. Burford Sent Me Word that The Above 2 prisoners was Put on Board the Schooner Timbo this Afternoon which left Port Adelaide for Hobart Town.   23

December 18 Thursday: Reported to the Sheriff that the 2 Prisoners as above had left for Hobart Town.   23

December 19 Friday: None – divine Service at 11 A.M.   24

December 20 Saturday: Frederick Hodding a debtor was discharged by Order of the Insolvent Court he having found Bail.   23

December 25 Thursday: Christmas Day They Prisoners had as usual on this day Plum Pudding, Beef, Potatoes - Cabbage - and extra Bread - and Tea & Sugar. And all they Prisoners was Thankful and behaved well.   23

December 29 Monday: William B Edmonds was brot to the Gaol this evening by Borr Sheriffs Officer for Debt At the Suit of Mr. Edward Stephens etc and in Consequence of the Debtors Yard having Several Noisey Lunatics in Mr Edmonds was Allowed to be in the Chapel during the day and to Sleep in the Yard at Night.   24

December 30 Tuesday: The Sheriff and Visiting Magistrate Call'd at the Gaol Saw they Prisoners.   24

December 31 Wednesday: The Wind was Very high all this day and Very Dusty one of the window in The Soldiers Guard Tower was blown in and 3 Squares of Glass was blown out of the large Lamps between the walls.   24

This ends the Year 1845 And Also ends the Minute Book And the only one Since the Gaol has been Established.

W.B. Ashton
Gov of the Gaol

It had been a frantic year ending in relative peace with a Christmas to remember – the food was good and 'all they Prisoners was thankful and behaved well'. The last sentence of the year (and of the journal) before Ashton signs off is particularly affecting. Ashton had committed himself thoroughly to this new colony. He had named two of his sons after two of its governors. His home was in the gaol and his work was the gaol. His own family, even the dog, were an integral part of the place, and his charges, the prisoners, were all part of his concern. The tone of this last sentence indicates without a doubt that he was well aware of the importance of this journal as a historical document to be looked back on in the future. His descendants and all of Adelaide can now easily look back.

Postscript

William Baker Ashton died in April 1854. The cause written on his death certificate was 'water on the chest' and his age 51 years, though he may have been older.[426] His illness had been brief but his last days were far from happy. After an unblemished and totally dedicated career he had been accused, as had Kennedy, of all number of things and had had to respond with a public defence. Behind the mischief was a public servant, Mr Hare, who had been given the position of superintendant of convicts by the colonial secretary. His job was to be responsible for the increased number of serious offenders, who could no longer be transported (transportation had ended in 1851), while they worked at the new 'stockade', the Dry Creek Labour Prison (later Yatala), during the day. These same prisoners were the sole responsibility of Ashton at night when they returned to the gaol.

There were now two bosses: Ashton responsible to the sheriff and Hare responsible to the colonial secretary. It is clear from evidence brought out in the enquiry that Mr Hare had long plotted to bring down Ashton so that his own position would be the one in charge. Mr Holmes, late overseer of convicts, previously under Mr Hare, gave evidence after Ashton died:

> Am not in the public service. Have never seen Mr Ashton in a state of intoxication [one of the charges] . . . Mr Hare told me he would get rid of Mr Ashton, and offered me his situation as Governor of the Gaol. I replied that I was not fit. I was not scholar enough . . . Mr Hare told

me I should have a clerk. This did not occur in reference to the Dry Creek Prison but in reference to the Gaol . . . I understood Mr Hare's offer to apply to filling Mr Ashton's place. My impression was that I was to be under Mr Hare.[427]

Mr Hare had provoked tension by moving his office into one of the towers in the gaol and also by employing a prisoner, with a long history and deep grudge, as his personal clerk. It was a letter from this prisoner clerk, Henry Dawson, that sparked the 'bombshell'. In an all too transparent ruse Mr Hare wrote to the colonial secretary:

> Sir – On coming to business this morning, Henry Dawson, a prisoner who acts as my clerk, placed the enclosed letter in my hands. The contents are so remarkable that I think it my duty to place the letter at once into your hands[428]

The letter was a list of accusations – from robbing prisoners of their rations, to stealing money from the possessions brought in by the prisoners, to trafficking with the prisoners, to 'deprecating Divine Service', to intoxication on duty, neglecting to check the cells and bad language. Robbing prisoners of their rations amounted to one incident of Charlotte borrowing salt and replacing it later.[429] Ashton was inclined to dismiss the accusations with the 'contempt they deserved' and only due to respect for the process of investigation, and respect for the panel of enquirers, did he make a reply. He outlined the four times Dawson had had to be incarcerated by him and answered all charges in the negative. He was clearly offended at having to answer such charges. He also explained that

> I have not been down to Mr Hare's office very often. It is repugnant to me to transact business with a convicted felon [the clerk]. I would not like to go further in contradicting the assertion of Mr Hare than to say he mistook indisposition with something else. I have been too long in the service of Government, and know too well what is due to any office to disgrace myself by such an exhibition as Mr Hare speaks of. . . . I shall call the officers of the Gaol, men who have been in the

habit of seeing me at all times of the day or night, to speak as to my capability for duty, and attention to every call.[430]

Ashton died a few minutes after midnight of 27 April 1854. On 28 April the *Adelaide Times* wrote:

The charges brought by the Superintendant of Convicts, Mr C.S. Hare, against Mr Ashton the jailor, and Kennedy the principal turnkey, have been finally investigated ... Until an official decision ... we could not fairly comment ... One circumstance only may be mentioned ... that all information on the facts was carefully bottled up by Messrs Hare and Dawson and only poured out to the Government when it suited the convenience of these persons, notwithstanding that their evident duty was to give the earliest information of the peculation and misconduct they pretended to have judiciously discovered.

However this may be ... one melancholy result has been produced. Poor Ashton, the Governor of the Gaol, has been brought to his deathbed by these proceedings. After a long and faithful service of fifteen years, he felt deeply and bitterly the imputations which Mr Hare, wielding a new broom, possessed with a separate, and to some extent opposing authority, and loudly and roughly exercising both, was pleased to lay to his door. Fully impressed with his own innocence and highly irritated at the proceedings instigated by Mr Hare, his feelings, acting on his impaired constitution, were too much for him. He took to his bed, poor fellow, from which he never arose, having expired last night about midnight.

This closes the first act of the Gaol Drama. Mr C.S. Hare had better look to himself if the public find his charges have been promoted by vindictiveness or by any motive not involving his public duty or the public good.[431]

Ashton was exonerated. The panel investigated the workings of the gaol in every detail and made numerous minor recommendations, for example additional books for recording the visits of officials, weighing of the rice rations and notices in the kitchen. They also recommended that no prisoner again be allowed employment in such a trusted position as a clerk.[432]

Recently, in 2013, a place for offenders found not guilty due to mental incompetence was opened in Oakden, a suburb of Adelaide. It provides transition from a secure locked ward to life in the community. It is the first of its kind in Adelaide and has been named 'Ashton House' in recognition of William Baker Ashton's care of the mentally ill in the early Adelaide gaols.

Notes

1. Keryn Walshe, *Archaeology of the Female Cells, Adelaide Gaol*, The Printing Hub, Victoria, Australia, 2015.
2. State Records, grg54/2/2, sheriff to colonial secretary, 23 January 1850.
3. State Records, grg54/2/2, sheriff to colonial secretary, 12 April 1850.
4. For example, Danvers Architects, Adelaide Gaol Conservation Study, unpublished report to the State Heritage Branch, 1986, and Schwager Brooks James and Partners, unpublished interim report for the Department of Housing and Construction Adelaide Gaol Conservation Plan, 1988.
5. State Records, grg54/2/1, Sheriff's Report, 17 December 1841.
6. 'Early Experiences of Colonial Life', No. XXV (by an arrival of 1838) in *South Australian Chronicle and Weekly Mail*, 27 October 1877, p. 17
7. *Register*, 8 April 1919, p. 4; also the same article in *Observer*, 12 April 1919, p. 13.
8. *Southern Australian*, 7 July 1843, p. 3.
9. *Southern Australian*, 12 May 1840, p. 3.
10. This may be why it was sometimes also referred to as Kingston's 1841 map – it shows the buildings as they were at the end of 1841.
11. *South Australian Register*, 9 October 1876, p. 7; and 'The Torrens, Its Sources, Its Streams, and Its Tributaries' signed 'By a "Loiterer" on its banks', No 2, *South Australian Magazine*, July 1841 to September 1842, p. 96.
12. State Records, grg24/4, colonial secretary to Kingston, 17 May 1842, requesting the gaol plans be delivered to the colonial engineer; and, the same day, grg24/6, colonial engineer to colonial secretary explaining they were not the originals but noting receipt of sketches of the same.
13. Jean Schmaal, article in the *Australian Police Journal*, April–June 1984, pp. 65–69.
14. Malcolm David Johnston, *A Governor, Aye Every Inch a Governor: A biography of William Baker Ashton, the first governor of the Adelaide gaol*, unpublished book, 1990; and Max Slee, *Adelaide's First Gaol (1838–1841) and Its Association with Government House Domain*, Adelaide Gaol Preservation Society, 2010.
15. Meeting with the records manager and FOI officer, 18 February 2014.
16. See Johnston, 1990.
17. Johnston, 1990, p. 15.
18. Johnston, 1990, p. 33.

19 Johnston, 1990, p. 32.
20 Dr Jon Telfer Department for Correctional Services, SA, 'With Greatest Expectations: The Colony, Crime and Corrections in South Australia.' A paper presented at the History of Crime, Policing and Punishment Conference convened by the Australian Institute of Criminology in conjunction with Charles Sturt University and held in Canberra 9–10 December 1999 aic.gov.au.
21 *Advertiser*, 21 November 1936, p. 11.
22 *South Australian Gazette*, 3 June 1837, p. 4.
23 State Records, grg24/1/1837/55, letter to Colonial Secretary, 1 March 1837.
24 *Register*, 'The architect's diary', 26 September 1910, p. 6.
25 'Old Brewing Days', *Register*, 27 January 1920, p. 4.
26 *Southern Australian*, 8 June 1838, p. 4.
27 *South Australian Gazette and Colonial Register*, 14 July 1838, p. 1.
28 *South Australian Gazette and Colonial Register*, 14 July 1838, p. S1.
29 Ibid.
30 Louise Brown, Beatrice de Crespigny, Mary P. Harris, Kathleen Kyffen Thomas and Phoebe N. Watson (eds) 1936, *A Book of South Australia: Women in the first hundred years*, Published for the Women's Centenery Council of SA, Rigby, Adelaide, extract from a letter written 27 November 1838, p. 27.
31 Johnston, 1990, p. 27.
32 State Records, grg24/1, sheriff to colonial secretary, 17 October and 2 November 1838.
33 State Records, grg24/1, sheriff to colonial secretary, 2 November 1838.
34 State Records, grg24/5, colonial secretary to sheriff, 8 November 1838.
35 State Records, Government Notice No 23.
36 *South Australian Gazette and Colonial Register*, 12 January 1839, p. 1.
37 Lutheran Archives Adelaide (LAA), E. Clamor Schurmann letter, S158: and State Records, grg24/1/1837/1A, further instructions to W. Wyatt Esq (protector of the Aboriginal people).
38 State Records, grg24/90/374, list of charges in year ending 1838, Dept of Correctional Services, Adelaide Gaol etc; and grg54/23.
39 *Advertiser*, 21 November 1936, p. 11.
40 'Historic Guests at "Ashton's Hotel"', *Advertiser*, 21 November 1936, p. 11.
41 Malcolm Johnston, *A Governor, Aye Every Inch a Governor: A biography of Wiliam Baker Ashton, the first governor of the Adelaide gaol*, 2nd edition, 2010, p. 50.
42 State Records, grg24/3/3, *Colonial Register*, 12 June 1839.
43 *Register*, 26 September 1910, p. 6.
44 'An Amateur Naturalist', *Advertiser*, 15 July 1886, p. 3.
45 State Records, grg24/1/1841/292, 11 June 1841.
46 Malcolm Johnston 1990, p. 41.
47 *Adelaide Observer*, 'An Old Man Reminiscent', 25 June 1887, p. 21.
48 Tom Gara, 'Adelaide at the time of Koeler's visit', from Peter Mühlhäusler (ed.), *Hermann Koeler's Adelaide: Observations on the language and culture of South Australia by the first German visitor*, Australian Humanities Press, 2006, p. 8, citing Vamplew et al, 1984, p. 14.

49 *South Australian Gazette*, 9 March 1839, p. 7.
50 John Phillip Gell Esq, 'The Vocabulary of the Adelaide Tribe', in the *Tasmanian Journal of Natural Science, Agriculture, Statistics*, 1842, Volume 1, pp. 109–124, p. 16.
51 John Adams, 'My Early Days in the Colony', published posthumously in 1902, reprinted in *Torrens Valley Historical Journal*, Number 33, pp. 43–47, p. 44.
52 William Wyatt Evidence, *1860 Royal Commission*, Minutes of Evidence to Report of Select Committee of the Legislative Council upon 'The Aborigines', Parliamentary Papers South Australia, 16 October 1860, Government Printers, Adelaide, p. 29.
53 'Report of the Protector of Aborigines to 30 June, 1838', *South Australian Gazette and Colonial Register*, 25 August 1838, p. 1.
54 *Southern Australian*, 1 December 1838, p. 3.
55 J. Selby, *Geology and the Adelaide Environment Handbook*, Number 8, Government Printers, 1884, p. 1.
56 Thomas Horton James, *Six Months in South Australia: With some account of Port Philip and Portland Bay, in Australia Felix*, 1838, published 1939, p. 17.
57 *Ibid.*
58 Reverend John Blacket, *History of South Australia: A romantic and successful experiment in colonisation, 1836–1857*, 2nd edition, 1911, p. 78.
59 Recollections of Pastor William Finlayson, unpublished manuscript, 1878, quoted in Stefan Pikusa, *The Adelaide House 1836–1901: The evolution of principal dwelling types*, 1986, p. 6.
60 Adelaide in 1839, recalled by Nathaniel Hailes in the *Register*, 15 January 1878, p. 5.
61 *South Australian Advertiser*, 27 December 1886, p. 6.
62 State Records, grg54/2/1, 18 December 1841; *Government Gazette*, 20 June 1839, reprint of Government Notice 7 June 1839.
63 *South Australian Gazette and Colonial Register*, 26 June 1839, p. 2.
64 Recollections by his son, *Register*, 9 August 1905, p. 6.
65 W. Flavell, 'A Few Recollections of Colonial Life', Proceedings of the Royal Geographical Society, Australasia, SA Branch, volume 5, pp. 103–112, p. 103.
66 Excerpt from the *East India Magazine*, reprinted in *South Australian Colonist*, volume 1, no 20, 4 August 1840, p. 338.
67 'Landing in Pioneer Days', *Register*, 20 July 1907, p. 44.
68 George Morphett, *When Adelaide Was Very Young: Trials and hardships of the pioneers*, undated, p. 9.
69 'Study in Contrasts', reporting on Government Order 3, 1839, in the *Advertiser*, 30 August 1930, p. 7.
70 Government Order No 11, 27 March 1839, printed in *South Australian Gazette and Colonial Register*, 1 April 1839, p. 1.
71 *South Australian Colonist*, Volume 1, No, 17, p. 257 (letter in a British paper, so a time lag, not printed until 30 June 1840).
72 *South Australian Gazette and Colonial Register*, 20 April 1839, p. 3.
73 *South Australian Gazette and Colonial Register*, 30 March 1839, p. 3.
74 Quoted in the *Southern Australian*, 3 April 1839, pp. 3–4.
75 *South Australian Gazette and Colonial Register*, 6 April 1839, p. 4.
76 Notice in *SA Gazette*, 11 August 1838.
77 *Southern Australian*, 8 May 1839, p. 3.

Notes

78 *South Australian Gazette and Colonial Register*, 15 September 1838, p. 3.
79 J. Chittleborough, 'Primitive Adelaide: Recollections and Impressions', *Observer*, 29 December 1906, p. 37.
80 *South Australian Register*, 12 October 1839, p. 6.
81 James Hawker Esq, 1898, *Early Experiences in South Australia*, E.S. Wigg, Adelaide, p. 7.
82 *Ibid.*
83 Letter begun in 14 April 1839, in the *South Australian*, volume 1, no 17, Tuesday 30 June 1840, p. 258.
84 John Adams, 1902, p. 43.
85 'Recollections of Early Days and Old Colonists by Wm Pedler', *Proceedings of the Royal Geographical Society*, SA Branch, 1902–1903, volume 6, pp. 63–65, p. 65.
86 J. Chittleborough, 'Some Recollections of a Buffalo Boy', *Quiz and Lantern*, 21 October 1897, p. 4.
87 *Advertiser*, 17 January 1914, p. 6.
88 *South Australian Gazette and Colonial Register*, 12 January 1939, p. 1.
89 Schurmann correspondence, 1838, LAA, p. S58.
90 Schurmann diary, 1838, LAA, p. S55.
91 Wyatts Evidence 1860, p. 29.
92 MacPherson, 'Our Aborigines', in N.B. Tindale 1935–1939 'Adelaide Tribe Notes', AA 338/1/34, South Australian Museum, undated, loose leaf.
93 Schurmann correspondence, 12 June 1839, LAA, p. S47.
94 An installation including a brass possum sculpture by Silvio Apponyi now marks this important place, in the Par 3 Golf Course near the restaurant at the current weir.
95 Rhondda Harris, 'The "Aboriginal Location" in the Adelaide Parklands (1837–1851) in *Proceedings, The Adelaide Parklands Symposium A Balancing Act: Past-Present-Future*, University of South Australia, Adelaide, 10 November 2006, pp. 56–72, pp. 61–63.
96 *South Australian Register*, 12 October 1839, p. 4.
97 *South Australian Register*, 18 April 1840, p. 3, and 25 April 1840, p. 3.
98 *South Australian Gazette and Colonial Register*, 26 January 1939, p. 3.
99 'A Girl Pioneer', *Advertiser*, 17 January 1914, p. 6.
100 State Records, grg24/4/2, 7 June 1837.
101 *South Australian Gazette and Colonial Register*, 8 July 1837, p. 4.
102 Graham Jaunay, *SA Convicts Sentenced to Transportation 1837–1851*, Adelaide Proformat, 1995, reprinted 1998.
103 Launceston *Advertiser*, 7 June 1838, re-printed in the London-based *South Australian Record*, 8 August 1838, p. 111.
104 *Advertiser*, 21 November 1936, p. 11.
105 'The Torrens, Its Sources, Its Streams, and Its Tributaries', *South Australian Magazine*, July 1841 to September 1842, No I p. 45 and No II pp. 92–96.
106 State Records, grg24/4/11, colonial secretary to colonial engineer, 1845 August 5.
107 Freeling 1849; Penman and Galbraith 1851 (Plan of the City of Adelaide SLSA C229); and the 1865 city surveyors' map, J/42 ACC Archives.
108 James Hawker, *Early Experiences in South Australia*, 1898, p. 9.
109 *Ibid.*

110 *Chronicle*, 16 July 1921, p. 21.
111 Hawker, 1898, p. 9.
112 Both appointed 20 March 1846, State Records, grg24/4/13.
113 Tolmer, *Reminiscences of an Adventurous and Chequered Career at Home and at the Antipodes*, vol 1, London, 1882, pp. 141, 142.
114 *Southern Australian*, 30 January 1839, p. 3.
115 *Southern Australian*, 6 March 1839, p. 6; and *South Australian Gazette and Colonial Register*, 16 March 1939, p. 2.
116 State Records, grg54/20, governor's journal – Adelaide gaol, 1839–1845.
117 Extracts from settlers' letters, *South Australian Colonist and Settler's Weekly Record of Btitish, Foreign and Colonial Intelligence*, 4 August 1840, p. 342.
118 State Records, grg24/4/3, colonial secretary to sheriff, 25 July 1838.
119 *South Australian*, 17 April 1839, quoted in H. Scarborough, *The Rajasthan: The ship, her passengers and voyages to South Australia*, self published, 1998, p. 34.
120 *South Australian Gazette and Colonial Register*, 4 March 1939, p. 3.
121 *South Australian Gazette and Colonial Register*, 6 April 1939, p. 3.
122 *Adelaide Chronicle and South Australian Literary Record*, 8 July 1840, p. 2.
123 Opinion of the editor in article 'What Right Have Englishmen in South Australia', *South Australian*, 8 May 1839, pp. 2–3.
124 State Records, grg24/1/1838/69, Wyatt, Quarterly Report ending 31 May 1838, dated 1 April 1838.
125 *Southern Australian*, 29 May 1839, p. 1.
126 *Ibid*.
127 *Ibid*.
128 Schurmann diary, LAA, 1 November 1839, p. S53.
129 Gawler Papers, Mortlock Library, A805A2 prg50/90/10.
130 'The Queen's Birthday', *South Australian Gazette and Colonial Register*, 25 May 1939, p. 3.
131 *Chronicle*, 3 August 1133, p.15; *Murray Pioneer and Australian River Record* Renmark, 25 July 1919, p. 8.
132 *South Australian Register*, 1 June, 1839, p. 5.
133 *Southern Australian*, 12 June 1839, p. 3.
134 Letter begun 14 April 1839 in the *South Australian*, 30 June 1840, Volume 1, No 17, p. 257.
135 'Report on Coroners Inquest', *South Australian Register*, 7 December 1839, p. 5.
136 *Advertiser*, 17 September 1932, pp. 15–16.
137 *Register*, 9 August 1905, p. 6.
138 *South Australian Advertiser*, 27 December 1886, p. 6.
139 'Primitive Adelaide', *Observer*, 29 December 1906, p. 36.
140 'Seventy Four Years Ago', *Observer*, 7 January 1911, p. 42.
141 'Primitive Adelaide' *Observer*, 29 December, 1906, p. 36.
142 State Records, grg24/1/1837 5B, 8 March 1837.
143 *Adelaide Independent*, 27 October 1841, p. 1.
144 *Southern Australian*, 9 October 1839, p. 3.

145 *South Australian Register*, 9 November 1839, p. 6.
146 'Progress of South Australia up to the Close of December 1840', in *Southern Australian*, 19 January 1841, p. 2.
147 *South Australian Register*, 30 November 1839, p. 5.
148 *South Australian Register*, 7 December 1839, p. 5.
149 State Records, grg24/4/3, colonial secretary to superintendant of the parklands, late 1839.
150 Recorded in 'a faded map of 1838, S.G.O. Plan No 6/5', described in J. B. Cleland and J. McLellan, 'The Forerunnners', chapter in D. Coleman (ed.) *The First Hundred Years: A history of Burnside in South Australia*, Corporation of the City of Burnside, Adelaide, 1956, pp. 49–80, p. 4 (map not located however Cleland and McLelland's description of the map is quoted in Rhondda Harris, 'Archaeology and Post-Contact Indigenous Adelaide', unpublished Honours in Archaeology thesis for Flinders University of South Australia, Appendix A, No 43, January 1999).
151 Elizabeth Warburton, *The Paddocks Beneath: A history of Burnside from the beginning*, Corporation of the City of Burnside, Adelaide, 1981, p. 152; and P. Ifould, 'Rural Beginnings', chapter in Cleland and McLelland, 1956, pp. 23–28.
152 'Peculiar Advantages of South Australia', *South Australian Colonist*, a British paper using reports of returned emigrants, hence time delay, Volume 5, 7 April 1840, p. 65.
153 Extract from the diary of Elizabeth Davidson, in Louise Brown et al, 1936, p. 40.
154 'Proceedings of the Council, expenditure, last quarter 1839, report dated 3 April 1840', in *South Australian Register*, 2 May 1840, p. 7.
155 A report on the criminal statistics in South Australia, requested by Mr Flaxman, Advocate General in London, written by Charles Mann, *SA Colonist*, 24 March 1840, volume 1, p. 34.
156 *Southern Australian*, 23 June 1943, p.3.
157 'Coroner's Courts', *South Australian Register*, 25 January 1840, p. 4.
158 State Records, grg24/4, colonial secretary to sheriff, 14 February 1840.
159 *South Australian Register*, 15 February 1840, p. 5.
160 *South Australian Register*, 15 February 1840, p. 5 and 7 March 1840, p. 5 ; *Chronicle*, 29 November 1934, p. 14.
161 'Old Man Reminiscent', *Adelaide Observer*, 25 June 1887, p. 21.
162 *South Australian Chronicle and Weekly Mail*, 23 June 1897, p. 19.
163 Alexander Tolmer, *Reminiscences of an Adventurous and Chequered Career at Home and at the Antipodes*, volume 1, London, 1882, p. 141.
164 For example the *Adelaide Chronicle and South Australian Advertiser*, 17 March 1840 p. 2.
165 Tolmer, 1882, p. 142.
166 Tolmer Reminiscences, prg 1050 series 1–3, handwritten notes, SLSA, p. 200 original.
167 *South Australian*, 25 March 1845, p. 2.
168 'Old Man Reminiscent', *South Australian Register*, 22 June 1887, pp. 6–7.
169 *Advertiser*, 2 June 1892, p. 4.
170 *Advertiser*, 3 June 1892, p. 5.
171 'North Terrace – Old and New', *Express and Telegraph*, 29 April 1893, p. 6.
172 'North Terrace Reserves and Railway Centres Royal Commission, No. 60,' First Progress Report, August 1916.

173 Note the boundary of Government House domain has recently been altered for the Anzac memorial walk.
174 *Observer*, 28 September 1844, p. 6.
175 'Act for Resolving Master and Servant Disputes', *South Australian Gazette and Colonial Register*, 12 August 1837, p. 3.
176 Robert Foster (ed.), *Sketch of the Aborigines of South Australia, References in the Cawthorne Papers*, unpublished report to the Aboriginal Heritage Branch, SA Department of Environment and Planning, October 1991.
177 Reprinted, courtesy South Australian Museum, in Steve Hemming and Rhondda Harris, *Tarndanyungga Kaurna Yerta, A report on the Indigenous cultural significance of the Adelaide Park Lands*, Adelaide Parklands Management Strategy, unpublished report for Hassell Pty Ltd and the Adelaide City Council for the Kaurna Aboriginal Community Heritage Committee, July 1998, Figure 9.
178 Letter from Reverend Smith, *South Australian Register*, 25 January 1840, p. 4.
179 *Adelaide Chronicle and South Australian Advertiser*, 14 April 1840, p. 3.
180 *South Australian Register*, 18 April 1840, p. 3.
181 *South Australian Register*, 25 April 1840, p. 3.
182 D. Langmead, 'Paranoia, Prisoners & Politics, The contract for the Adelaide Gaol 1839', in *Fabrications: The journal of the Society of Architectural Historians, Australia and New Zealand*, volume 8, pp. 47–62, July 1997, p. 57.
183 State Records, grg/54/2/1, quarter ending March 1840.
184 *Southern Australian*, 19 June 1840, p. 3.
185 *Southern Australian*, 29 May 1840, p. 3; 14 July 1840, p. 2.
186 *South Australian Gazette*, 28 May 1840 p. 1.
187 *South Australian Gazette*, 4 June 1840, p. 8.
188 'Mr Flaxman', *Southern Australian*, 12 May 1840, p. 3.
189 *South Australian Gazette*, 4 June 1840, p. 1.
190 'Town Council Proceedings', Adelaide Chronicle and South Australian Literary Record, 25 November 1840, p. 4.
191 Drafted by Robert Thomas to Colonel Light's instructions, in Tracey Lock-Weir, *Visions of Adelaide 1836–1886*, 2005, p. 25, cited in Rhondda Harris, 'Background Research Paper regarding the proposed site for the Marjorie Jackson-Nelson Hospital', unpublished report to SA Health and the Kaurna Native Title Management Committee, March 2009, p. 17.
192 George Kingston, 'Comments on Colonel Light's Reserves', cited in Rees (compiler), *A Brief History of the Adelaide Parklands*, Printery 174 Angus Street, 1948, p. 3, re-cited in Rhondda Harris, 2009, p. 17.
193 Thomas Horton James, pp. 79–80, cited and discussed in Rhondda Harris, 2009, p. 18.
194 Henry Cleary, 'The Archdiocese of Adelaide', *New Advent*, accessed online 25 October 2016: http://www.newadvent.org/cathen/01140a.htm; Brian Condon, *W. Ullathorne: Impressions of Adelaide*, 1840, accessed online 25 October 2016: www.library.unisa.edu.au/Condon/CatholicLetters.
195 *Adelaide Chronicle and South Australian Literary Record*, 29 July 1840, p. 3.
196 *Southern Australian*, 28 July 1840, p. 3.
197 *Southern Australian*, 28 July 1840, p. 3; *South Australian Register*, 1 August 1840, p. 6.
198 *Adelaide Chronicle and South Australian Literary Record*, 29 July 1840, p. 3.

Notes

199 'Report on the Trial of Stagg', *Southern Australian*, 13 November 1840, pp. 2–3.
200 *Southern Australian*, 31 July 1840, p. 4.
201 *Southern Australian*, 14 August 1840, p. 3.
202 Tolmer, 1882, p. 169.
203 *Adelaide Chronicle and South Australia Literary Record*, 8 July 1840, pp. 2–3; *Southern Australian*, 10 July 1840, p. 3; 7 July 1840, p. 3; 14 July 1840, pp. 2–3; 21 July 1840, p. 3; 4 September 1840, pp. 4; 5 September 1840, pp. 3–4; *South Australian Register*, 11 July 1840, p. 5; 11 July 1840, p. 5; 18 July 1840, p. 6; 5 September 1840, p. 3–4.
204 John Wrathall Bull, *Early Experiences of Colonial Life in South Australia*, printed at the Advertiser, Chronicle and Express Offices, 1878; John Wrathall Bull, *Early experiences of life in South Australia and an extended colonial history*, 1884, E.S. Wigg & Son.
205 'Old Brewing Days', *Register*, 27 January 1920, p. 4; 'Early Experiences of Colonial Life No1V', *South Australian Chronicle and Weekly Mail*, 26 May 1877, p. 17.
206 'Early Experiences of Colonial Life – No. XXV', *South Australian Chronicle and Weekly Mail*, 27 October 1877, p. 17.
207 This information is in a public letter from Borrow and Goodier to Governor Grey, dated 5 November 1841, extracted from a loose, damaged newspaper sheet, date and banner missing, in the Old Adelaide Gaol archives.
208 The writer with the neat hand has a number of oddities in style. Examples are his use of the equal sign to replace a dash and his intermittent decision to place names in quotation marks. Along with tiny, neat writing, these peculiarities of style clearly indicate that in this section it is not Ashton writing.
209 James McLean, undated, 'Police Experiences with the Natives: Reminiscences of the early days of the colony', reprinted in *Journal of the Royal Geographical Society, SA Branch*, 1902–1913, volume 6, pp. 66–92, p. 66.
210 State Records, grg24/4/3, colonial secretary to sheriff, 22 September 1840.
211 State Records, grg24/4/3, colonial secretary to colonial storekeeper, 25 September 1840.
212 State Records, grg54/2/1, various letters, sheriff to colonial secretary, late 1840.
213 State Records, grg54/2/1, sheriff to governor's private secretary, 18 November 1840.
214 Tolmer, 1882, p. 169.
215 *Adelaide Chronicle and South Australian Literary Record*, 18 November 1840, p. 3.
216 State Records, grs 2625/1/P, Corporal Punishment Register of Adelaide Gaol 1838–1975.
217 Journal entry, 27 June 1842, note in margin.
218 Journal entry, 1 August 1843.
219 State Records, grs 2625/1/P, Corporal Punishment Register of Adelaide Gaol 1838–1975.
220 *South Australian Register*, 14 November 1840, p. 3.
221 *South Australian*, 25 December 1840, p. 3.
222 State Records, grg54/2/1, memo, sheriff to colonial secretary circa 1 August 1841.
223 *Register*, 8 April 1919, p. 4; article repeated *Observer*, 12 April 1919, p. 13.
224 *Adelaide Chronicle and South Australian Literary Record*, 27 January 1841, p. 3.
225 Journal entry, 12 March 1841.
226 State Records, grg54/2, sheriff to colonial secretary, 5 January 1841.
227 *South Australian Register*, 6 March 1841, p. 3.

228 State Records, grg54/2, sheriff to governor's private secretary, 13 March 1841.
229 'The Torrens, Its Sources, Its Streams, and Its Tributaries' signed 'By a "Loiterer" on its banks', No 2, *South Australian Magazine*, July 1841 to September 1842, p. 96.
230 *Adelaide Chronicle and South Australian Literary Record*, 12 May 1841, p. 3.
231 State Records, grg54/2/1, sheriff to colonial secretary, 5 April 1841.
232 State Records, grg54/2/1, sheriff to Captain Sturt, 19 June 1841.
233 State Records, grg 24/6/1841, 17 April 1841.
234 State Records, grg24/1, 30 March 1841.
235 State Records, grg24/1, 17 April 1841.
236 *Gazette Extraordinary*, 17 May 1841.
237 State Records, grg24/4/4, 16 July 1841, 3 July 1841, July 1841.
238 State Records, grg24/4/4, 4 June 1841, July 1841, 28 October 1841; *Southern Australian*, 3 August 1841; State Records, grg24/4, 10 March 1841, 8 June 1841.
239 State Records, grg24/4/4, 3 July 1841, 26 October 1841, 8 July 1841, 28 October 1841, 13 July 1841.
240 State Records, grg24/1/1841/292, 11 June 1841.
241 State Records, grg54/2/1, 14 June 1841.
242 *Adelaide Chronicle and South Australian Literary Record*, 2 June 1841, p. 2.
243 *Adelaide Independent*, 16 September 1841, p. 3, illustration not included in SLSA microfilm copy.
244 *South Australian Register*, 20 March 1841, p. 3.
245 *Adelaide Independent*, 9 September 1841, p. 2.
246 *Ibid*.
247 Johnston, 1990, p. 55.
248 *Adelaide Independent*, 2 September 1841, p. 2.
249 *Adelaide Chronicle and South Australian Literary Record*, 4 August 1841, p. 3.
250 *Southern Australian*, 28 September 1841, p. 3.
251 *Adelaide Chronicle and South Australian Literary Record*, 29 September 1841, p. 2 and 3; *South Australian Register*, 2 October 1841, p. 4.
252 *Adelaide Chronicle and South Australian Literary Record*, 29 September 1841, p. 2 and 3.
253 State Records, grg54/2/1, sheriff to colonial secretary, 14 October 1841.
254 *Ibid*.
255 State Records, grg24/4/4, Grey via colonial secretary to sheriff, 16 October 1841.
256 Schwager et al, 1988 diagram p. 35. This shows the chapel upstairs in the governor's house building with a stairway from the space between the walls. It also shows an outline of the perimeter of the gaol as it then was. It doesn't detail the fabric but the wooden fence was the full extent of the western side. The remainder of the perimeter was continuous stone, including the brick-and-stone governor's house, chapel and gaol entrance.
257 *Adelaide Examiner*, 16 December 1841, SLSA microfilm.
258 Minute Book of the Mayor and Corporation of the City of Adelaide, Adelaide City Archives, S 69, 4 February 1841, pp. 67–68.
259 Minutes of Town Council, *Adelaide Examiner*, 23 December 1841, SLSA microfilm.

260 The Kaurna in this area were known to the settlers as the 'Adelaide Tribe'. According to the missionary Klose, those along the river bank were formerly known as 'Wito Meyunna', the 'Reed Men', Klose letter 3 September 1844, LAA.
261 See Mantogani in Darrell Kraehenbuehl, *Pre-European Vegetation of Adelaide: A survey from the Gawler River to Hallett Cove*, Adelaide, Nature Conservation Society of South Australia, 1996, p. 76.
262 *South Australian Register*, 6 February 1841, p. 3.
263 *South Australian Register*, 15 February 1841, p. 5.
264 State Records, grg54/2/1, 17 and 18 December 1841; grg24/4/4, 17 and several on 20 December 1841.
265 State Records, grg54/2/1, 18 December 1841.
266 *Adelaide Chronicle and South Australian Literary Record*, 6 April 1842, p. 4.
267 Entry dates 8 February, 1 April and 8 April 1842.
268 *South Australian Chronicle and Weekly Mail*, 27 October 1877, p. 17.
269 *Chronicle*, 28 September 1933, p. 17.
270 Memorandum on Kingston's 1842 map of Adelaide
271 *Adelaide Independent*, 2 September 1841, p. 3.
272 *Adelaide Examiner*, 25 November 1841, SLSA microfilm.
273 *Southern Australian*, 3 January 1843, p. 2.
274 Letter to Grey, *Adelaide Examiner*, 30 December 1841, SLSA microfilm.
275 *Adelaide Examiner*, 2 December 1841, SLSA microfilm.
276 *Adelaide Examiner*, 20 January 1842, SLSA microfilm.
277 *Southern Australian*, 28 January 1842, p. 3.
278 *Adelaide Chronicle and South Australian Literary Record*, 9 March 1842, p. 4; 16 March 1842, pp. 5–6.
279 *Adelaide Chronicle and Southern Literary Record*, 9 March 1842, p. 4.
280 State Records, grg24/4/7, colonial secretary to sheriff, 15 December 1843.
281 Journal entry, 27 May 1842.
282 *Adelaide Chronicle and South Australian Literary Record*, 20 April 1842, p. 3; *Southern Australian*, 8 July 1842, p. 3; and 12 July 1843, p. 3.
283 State Records, grg24/4, colonial secretary to sheriff, 19 July 1842.
284 Journal entry, 31 May 1843.
285 'Reprieves', *South Australian Register*, 25 August 1894, p. 6.
286 Cawthorne lecture at the Temperance Hall, North Adelaide, 15 April 1864, in Robert Foster (ed.), 1991, p. 91.
287 Klose letters, p. 34, LAA.
288 *Ibid.*
289 *Ibid.*
290 *Ibid.*
291 State Records, grg52/7/1, Moorhouse report to colonial secretary, 6 April 1843.
292 Klose letters, p. 37, LAA.
293 Cawthorne diary, 24 December 1842, Robert Foster (ed.), 1991, p. 5 and a variation on p. 9.
294 See Cawthone diary, 2 November 1843, Robert Foster (ed.), 1991.

295 *Southern Australian*, 8 July 1842, p. 3.
296 Klose letters p. 37, LAA.
297 *South Australian Register*, 6 August 1842, p. 2.
298 *Southern Australian*, 7 October 1842, p. 3.
299 State Records, Report for quarter ending 31 December 1842, grg24/6/1843/132.
300 *Southern Australian*, 15 November 1842, p. 4.
301 *South Australian Register*, 17 January 1844, p. 2.
302 State Records, grg24/4/5, 7 and 13 January 1843.
303 *Southern Australian*, 15 September 1843, p. 2.
304 *Register*, 8 April 1919, p. 4: *Advertiser*, 16 September and 21 November 1836.
305 See Robert Foster (ed.), 1991.
306 Cawthorne diary, 17 December 1842, Robert Foster (ed.), 1991, p. 6.
307 Cawthorne diary, 21 December 1842, Robert Foster (ed.), 1991, p. 4 and 7 (variants of same entry).
308 Cawthorne diary, 22 December 1842, Robert Foster (ed.), 1991, p. 8.
309 Cawthorne diary, 27 January 1843, Robert Foster (ed.), 1991, p. 10.
310 Cawthorne diary, 4 February, 1843, Robert Foster (ed.), 1991, p. 10.
311 State Records, grg 24/4/338, protector's letters, 17 February, 1843.
312 *Southern Australian*, 10 March 1843, p. 2. The term *burka* is not easy to translate. The settlers called Mullawirraburka 'Chief of the Adelaide Tribe' and dubbed him 'King John'. However neither was a good choice of term — the Indigenous culture was not one of leaders and followers. Rather he was an old man, so to be respected without question, and the fact that he had four wives, more than anybody else, was a mark of his influence and sway.
313 *Southern Australian*, 7 February 1843, p. 2.
314 State Records, grg24/6, Moorhouse to colonial secretary, 13 May 1843.
315 Journal entry, 24 May 1844.
316 *Southern Australian*, 10 March 1843, p. 2.
317 *Southern Australian*, 7 February 1843, p. 2.
318 State Records, grg54/2/2, 15 March 1843.
319 State Records, grg24/4/7, 16 March 1843.
320 *South Australian Register*, 25 March 1843, p. 3.
321 *South Australian Register*, 27 March 1843, p. 2 , also 29 March 1843, p. 2.
322 *Southern Australian*, 18 April 1843, p. 2.
323 State Records, grg24/6/1843/495, 12 April 1843.
324 State Records, grg 52/7/1, 25 April, 1843.
325 Klose letters, 1843, p. 44. LAA.
326 Klose letters, 1841, p. 31–33, LAA.
327 Klose letters, 1843, p. 44, LAA.
328 Joyce Graetz (ed.), Klose letter 1843, *Missionary to the Kaurna, The Klose Letters*, published by Friends of the Lutheran Archives, Adelaide, 2002, p. 26.
329 Klose letters 1843, p. 45, LAA.
330 Cawthorne diary, 5 April 1843, Robert Foster (ed.), 1991, p. 11.

Notes

331 Iola Hack with Chris Durrant, *Chequered Lives: John Barton Hack and Stephen Hack and the early years of South Australia*, Wakefield Press, Adelaide, 2013.
332 Family Notices, *Southern Australian*, 20 June 1843, p. 2.
333 *Southern Australian*, 7 July 1843, p. 3.
334 State Records, grg24/7/8, 18 July 1843.
335 Cawthorne diary, 20 July 1843, Robert Foster (ed.), 1991, p. 14.
336 State Records, Moorhouse to Private Secretary, grg52/7/1, 27 July 1843.
337 Cawthorne diary, 20 July 1843, Robert Foster (ed.), 1991, p. 14; *Adelaide Observer*, 22 July 1843, p. 4.
338 Cawthorne diary, 1 August 1843, Robert Foster (ed.), 1991, pp. 14 and 15.
339 *Adelaide Observer*, 14 October 1843, p. 5.
340 *South Australian Register*, 9 August 1843, p. 3.
341 Graham Jaunay, 1885, p. 19.
342 Cawthorne diary, Robert Foster (ed.), 1991, 3 October 1843, p. 24; 21 October 1843, p. 25; 2 November 1843; p. 26; 13 and 16 December 1843, p. 29.
343 *Southern Australian*, 21 November 1843, p. 2; 19 January 1844, p. 2.
344 *Adelaide Chronicle and South Australian Record*, 27 January 1841, p. 3.
345 State Records, grg24/4/9, 20 December 1844; grg24/4/7, 25 April 1845.
346 *South Australian Register*, 8 October 1850, p. 3.
347 *Adelaide Times*, 9 October 1850, p. 4.
348 *Adelaide Independent*, 19 August 1841, SLSA microfilm.
349 *South Australian Register*, 29 April 1848, p. 3.
350 *Adelaide Observer*, 25 April 1846, p. 3.
351 State Records, grg54/2/2, 30 March 1844.
352 State Records, grg24/4/7, 2 April 1844.
353 State Records, grg24/4/7, 15 April 1844.
354 *South Australian Register*, 27 April 1844, p. 3.
355 *South Australian Register*, 1 May 1844, p. 2.
356 Cawthorne diary, 12 and 20 April 1844, Robert Foster (ed.), 1991, p. 45.
357 State Records, grg24/6A/1844/712.
358 Cawthorne diary, 22 April 1844, Robert Foster (ed.), 1991, p. 46.
359 This image is reproduced in colour in *South Australia Illustrated: Colonial painting in the land of promise* by Jane Hylton, 2012, p. 81.
360 Article as repeated in Cawthorne diary, 24 April 1844, Robert Foster (ed.), 1991, p. 46.
361 Interview with Kaurna elder Lewis O'Brien by Rhondda Harris in his home in Adelaide in 1998, cited in Rhondda Harris 1999, p. 51.
362 *South Australian Register*, 27 April 1844, p. 3.
363 *Adelaide Observer*, 22 June 1844, p. 5.
364 *Adelaide Observer*, 6 July 1844, p. 5.
365 Cawthorne diary, 29 July 1844, Robert Foster (ed.), 1991, p. 53.
366 Klose letters, 10 February 1844, LAA., cited Harris, 1999, p. 47.
367 *Register*, 7 December 1844, p. 3.

368 Thomas Horton James, 1839, p. 281.
369 C.F. Folland, 'Our Aborigines', *Observer*, 24 February 1906, p. 48.
370 *South Australian Register*, 1 January 1845, p. 3.
371 'Daring Attempt Of the Prisoners To Escape', *South Australian Register*, 6 November 1844, p. 3.
372 Henry Heath Glover *c*. 1850 Governor and staff at the Adelaide Gaol SLSA B17790 (SLSA notes in the catalogue); also mentioned in an article after Albert Ashton's death at the age of 100, 'Gaol Was His Home', *Adelaide Mail*, 1 February 1941, p. 5.
373 *South Australian Register*, 27 December 1844, p. 2.
374 *Adelaide Observer*, 1 February 1845, pp. 5–6.
375 *Adelaide Observer*, 20 September 1845, p. 4.
376 www.pioneerssa.org.au/early_sa_history.html, accessed online 16 February 2017; and McDougal and Vines, 'The City of Adelaide – A Thematic History', Conservation and Heritage Consultants, Norwood, South Australia, August 2006, pp. 16 and 39. PDF version, adelaidecitycouncil.com.
377 Reprinted in State Records *South Australian Government Gazette*, 10 January 1850.
378 Klose, letter to Dresden 1845, LAA.
379 *South Australian*, 4 February 1845. p. 3.
380 Klose diary, 3 July 1845, LAA.
381 Journal entry, 23 January 1845.
382 Cawthorne diary, 1 January 1845, Robert Foster (ed.), 1991, p. 57.
383 *South Australian Register*, 22 February 1845, p. 3.
384 *South Australian Register*, 15 March 1845, p. 3.
385 *Adelaide Observer*, 22 March 1845, p. 4.
386 *Ibid*.
387 *Ibid*.
388 *South Australian Register*, 19 March 1845, p. 3.
389 *Ibid*.
390 This information is from J.B. Cleland, 'Wright, Edward (1788–1859), *Australian Dictionary of Biography*, Australian National University, htpp://adb.anu.au/bibliography/wright-edward-2818/text/4037, published first in hard copy 1967, accessed online 13 December 2015.
391 *South Australian Register*, 1 March 1845, pp. 4–5.
392 *Observer*, 25 September 1926, p. 59.
393 Supreme Court, Criminal Side, *South Australian*, 17 and 11 March 1845, p. 2.
394 *South Australian Register*, 22 March 1845, p. 3.
395 *South Australian Register*, 19 March 1845, p. 2.
396 State Records, grg24/4/7, colonial secretary to sheriff and to colonial engineer, 25 March 1845.
397 *South Australian Register*, 2 April 1845, p. 3.
398 *Ibid*.
399 Cawthorne diary, 30 March 1845, Robert Foster (ed.), 1991, p. 57.
400 Cawthorne lecture at the Temperance Hall, North Adelaide, 15 April 1864, in Robert Foster (ed.), 1991, p. 91; State Records, grs 2625/1/P, Corporal Punishment Register of Adelaide Gaol 1838–1975.

Notes

401 www.samemory.sa.gov.au/site/page.cfm?c=5264, accessed online 22 December 2015.
402 *South Australian*, 2 May 1845, p. 2.
403 *South Australian Register*, 17 May 1845, p. 3.
404 *Adelaide Observer*, 26 July 1851, p. 8.
405 'Police Commissioners Court 15 May', *South Australian Register*, 17 May 1845 p. 3.
406 *Ibid.*
407 'Aborigines Report, 2 July 1845', *South Australian Gazette and Colonial Register*, 26 July 1845, p. 4.
408 State Records, grg54/2/2, 26 May 1845.
409 Letter to Dresden 1845 referring to 28 May 1845, Joyce Graetz, 2002, p. 42.
410 'Aborigines Report' 2 July 1845, *South Australian Gazette and Colonial Register*, 26 July 1845, p. 4
411 John Gell, 1842, p. 11.
412 John Gell, 1842, p. 121.
413 C.B. Teichelmann and C.W. Schurmann, *Outlines of a Grammar, Vocabulary and Phraseology of the Aboriginal Language of South Australia, Spoken by the Natives in and for Some Distance Around Adelaide*, published by the authors at the Native Location, 1840, Google Public Domain Book, p. 32.
414 Journal entry, 29 November and 4 December 1845.
415 'Aborigines Report, 2 July 1845', *South Australian Gazette and Colonial Register*, 26 July 1845, p. 4.
416 Klose diary, 3 July 1845, LAA.
417 State Records, grg 24/6/1846/907.
418 Klose diary, 4 July 1845, LAA.
419 State Records, grg24/4/11, colonial secretary to colonial engineer, 5 August 1845.
420 Johnston, 1990, p. 8.
421 State Records, grg52,7/1, 15 October 1845.
422 *Ibid.*
423 State Records, grg54/2/2, 14 December 1845.
424 *Ibid.*
425 *Ibid.*
426 Johnstone, 1990, pp. 3 and 55.
427 *Adelaide Times*, 1 May 1854, p. 4.
428 'Investigation at the Gaol', letter dated 7 April 1854, *Adelaide Observer*, 6 May 1854, p. 10.
429 Printed after Ashton's death, 'Mr Ashton's Defence', *South Australian Register*, 1 May 1854, p. 3.
430 *Ibid.*; also *Adelaide Observer*, 6 May 1854, p. 10; see also letter by James Dempster in support of Ashton, 11 May 1854, in 'The Late Mr Ashton', *South Australian Register*, 16 May 1854, p. 3.
431 *Adelaide Times*, 1854, pp. 3–4.
432 'Investigation at the Gaol', *Adelaide Observer*, 6 May 1854, p. 10.

Index

Please note that many of the names listed include aliases, diminutives and alternate spellings. Criminals in 19th-century Australia had many uses for aliases, and nicknames also helped differentiate between common names. Aboriginal people used aliases in different cultural circumstances and also used English names. All listings are at the mercy of Ashton's very unique writing style and are true to the spellings used.

A

Abbott, Mr, Nth Adelaide 72
Abbott, William 125, 130
Aboriginal Location, old Location, new Location, Piltawodli, Piltawodly, 'Native School', 'Native School Establishment' 21, 31–34, 43–44, 58–59, 70, 74, 85, 88, 95, 170, 179, 192–193, 204, 223–225, 273, 283–286, 303, 328–329, 340
Adams Abraham 128, 130
Adams, John 21, 30
Adams, Thomas 189
'Adelaide Tribe', Kaurna 11, 16, 18, 20–22, 30–33, 37–38, 54, 60, 73, 170, 179, 192–194, 216, 218, 223–224, 250–251, 272–273, 283–284, 303–304, 324, 329
Afford, John, gravel supplier 332
Aldridge (152) (157)
Aldridge, Mary 196
Allen, James 139
Allen, Sam'l 140
Allen, Thomas Henry 341–342
Amey, Mrs 35
Anderson, Isabella *aka* Bella, Scotch Bella 133, 137–139, 155, 245, 258–271, 273–275, 277–283, 285–290, 292–293, 303, 317
Anderson, William 189
Armstrong 165, 173, 181

Armstrong, John 227
Arthur, James 136, 143, 154, 159, 166, 185, 203, 214
Ashton, Charlotte 1–4, 8, 13, 132, 149, 178–179, 188, 214–215, 230, 234, 270, 272, 274, 294–295, 323, 325–326, 331, 338, 347
Ashton children, eldest first
    William James alt W.J. 13, 149, 163, 168, 238
    Henry Hamilton 8, 13, 149
    Thomas Mills 13, 149, 168–169
    Albert Gawler 19, 149, 299
    Victoria Hannah Ritchie 149
    Charlotte Maria 230
    George Grey 338
Ashton family dog 299, 345
Atkins, Geo 66–67
Augustus 264, 270, 275, 284
Austin, James 200

B

Bailey, James 110, 117, 118
Bailey, Hamilton 100
Baker 188, 252
Baker, Andrew 135
Baker, Arthur *alias* Hy Baker, Bryce Thompson, Michael Edmonds *alt* Edmond 77, 117–118, 120–121, 133, 135
Baker, Job, debtor 102, 108

Index

Baker, John 140
Barry, John 61
Ballard, John 172–173, 186
Bart 134
Barnett, Joseph 123
Bassett, John, gaol guard 91–92, 120–121, 124, 129, 131
Barrett 317
Barrett, Joseph 181
Bath, Tristram *alt* Tristan, gaol guard 125, 138
Bell, Mr, coffin maker 78
Bella *see* Anderson, Isabella
Bennett, Joseph 115
Bent, Ann 274, 278, 283, 291–292, 300, 308, 329
Benson 221
Benson, Rev'd Mr, gaol catholic priest, numerous 154–247
Berkeley, Alexander *alt* Berkely 260, 296–297, 299, 303–304
Bernard, Mr, advocate general 55
Best, Anthony 281, 291–293, 297, 330–338
Best, Sarah Ann 124, 260
Best, William 93, 102–103, 107, 121–122, 137
Biddle, Rolles, murdered 216, 220, 222, 235
Bigwood, Levi 307
Billy *see* Koovey Kowminne
Bird 189
Birmingham, police constable 52
Birrell, Andrew 236–237
Black, Capt'n, ship's captain 285
Blacket, Reverend 23
Blackford 119
Bland, Thomas, gaol guard 125, 131
Blundell, Joseph 297–298
Bob *see* Tippa Warricha
Bocomola *alt* Boccomola *alias* Karri *alias* Turle Kurree 194, 217, 276–278

Bohr, John *alt* Borr, sheriff's officer, numerous 133–345
Bond, John 183, 188
Boor, James Richard 218–219, 241
Bootes police constable 78
Booth, Henry 314
Borrow and Goodier, builders of the gaol 95, 109, 146, 177, 357
Bower, Charles 283, 287–288
Boyce, James 137–138
Braly, William 134
Brand, Eliza 196
Breaker, Isaac 158, 162
Breeze, Robert Smith 291–292
Brennan 332, 334–335, 339
Breynard 98
Broadrib 89–90, 93
Brodie, Capt'n, ship's captain 239
Bromley, Walter *ad interim* protector of the Aboriginal people 16, 31
Brown, Capt'n, ship's captain 163, 168, 199, 275
Brown, Mary 178, 234, 245
Brown, Thomas 295, 314
Brown, William *alias* William McDonald 70, 72, 77, 80, 86, 171, 226–231
Bryden *see also* Miller & Brydon 180
Buffalo, Buffalo Row 11–12, 21, 24–26, 30, 35–36, 65–66, 85, 145, 235
Bull, John Wrathall 12, 107–109, 124, 129, 131, 174
Bunkin, Elizabeth 61–62
Burford, police sergeant 344
Burns, police constable 92, 335
Bush, Thos 184
Bushrangers 2, 11, 73, 77–78, 81–83, 89
Butler, Capt'n 167, 239, 259

C

Caines, Julia 331, 333, 335, 343
Callinan, James 343

Calton, Henry, preacher 92–93, 95–98, 100–101, 103, 108
Campbell 79, 90, 98, 130
Campbell, Kenneth 102, 109, 111, 116, 125, 136
Cannon, Elizabeth 340
Captain Jack *see* Kadlitpinna
Carson, Mary 216
Carter, John 5, 163, 170–171, 173–174, 179, 182, 185–186
Catchlove 191
Catchlove, Edward and Charles 148, 152
Cawthorne, William 85, 192, 194, 210, 212, 225, 234–236, 250, 271–272, 283, 315
Challenger 196, 213
Chambers, David 67, 70, 72, 77–79, 84
Chanter, police constable 136
Charlesworth, Sarah 310
Charlotte 64
Charley 336
Chase, murdered 313
Chatfield, William Alfred 149, 154, 157
Chittleborough, James 25, 29, 30, 65
Clare, James 311, 319
Clark, Serg't *alt* Clarke, Sarg't, 96th regiment 188, 256, 259, 264, 267, 288, 290
Clarke, W'm *alt* Clark *alias* Brigadier Cross 96–97
Cock, William 240
Cohen, Prisoner Working Party guard 101
Collings, William 134, 141
Collins 135–138, 140–141, 144, 167
Collins, Jeremiah 72, 80, 86, 231
Collins, Mary Ann 158
Conner, Robert 181, 212–213
Connor, Elizabeth 338
Connor, Patrick 181

Convicts 2, 6, 10–11, 13, 16, 36–37, 51, 53–54, 64, 74–75, 91, 100–101, 107, 133–134, 161, 167, 171, 174, 185–186, 226, 231, 233, 258, 246, 264, 266, 269, 290, 294, 301–302, 324, 340, 346
Coltman, constable 12
Conway 129
Cook, William *alt* Cooke 217, 226
Cooper, Charles, judge 53, 75, 80, 160, 212, 216, 226, 234, 241, 254, 281, 342
Cooper, Elisha 140, 185–186
Cooper, John 134, 139
Cope *see* Dowing
Coromandel, Coromandel Row 24–26, 65–66, 145
Cotter, Thos, physician 52, 55, 57, 66
Couzens, William 198–199, 201, 205
Coyle, James 344
Coyle, Michael *see* Smith, Peter
Clare, James 311, 319
Crabb, I.L. 154, 158
Crafter, John, gaol guard 97
Cragon *alt* Cragan, gaol guard 119, 122
Craig, James 270, 274
Craiggie, Robert 243
Crisp 139
Crispe 157, 158
Cruger 331
Christina 101–102, 159
Cullens, John 196
Curren, Henry *alt* Curran 78–83

D

Dalton, Emma 178, 183–184
Daniel Wheeler 164, 167
Dare, George 130, 132
Dark, John 288
Daubiney, William *alt* Dawbiney, gaoler, also Mrs and son 80, 85, 89–91, 98, 100, 103, 105, 107–111, 117, 119, 122–126, 128–129 132, 138, 140, 142, 147, 153–154, 157, 163
Dauntless 100–101

Davies, George 143
Davey, Elizabeth *alt* Davy 229, 234, 214–215, 219, 234
Davey, George *alt* Davy 196
Davey, Mary 136, 229, 234
Davey, Mary Ann *alt* Davy 191–192, 205, 214–215, 234
Davis, Chas, gaol guard 69, 71, 77, 89
Davis, George 140, 265, 282, 288
Davis, John 233, 242
Davis, Robert 260–261
Davis, Thomas 339
Davis, W.B. 288
Davison, F., magistrate 326
Davridge 69
Dawes, William B. 289
Dawson, Henry, prisoner and gaol clerk 347–348
Dean, Matthew 279, 285–286
Dean, police constable 256
Denton, John 190
Deplege, Robert 287
Derke, Capt'n, ship's captain 248
Devnell, John 107
Dickinson, Henry 329–330
Dilby 200
Doherty, Pat'k 87, 99–100
Donovan 110
Dorset 122, 174, 186, 205, 256
Douglas 308–309
Douglas *alias* James Stevenson 195, 200, 203, 205
Douglas, James 311–315
Dowing, John *alias* Cope 314
Downing, David, gaol guard 86, 117, 120–121, 123–124, 154
Downing, John 84–85
Drawbridge, Doubell 138, 153
Drawbridge, Drubill, gaol turnkey 60–61
Driscoll 15
Driver, C.S. 183

Drury, Charles 133–134
Drysdale, Capt'n Alex'r *alt* Drysdall 182–183
Duffield, William *alt* Duffel, shepherd, murdered 17, 57–58
Dumbleton, meat supplier 102
Duncan, physician 168, 311
Dunford, John 190
Dunn, police constable 84
Duthy, Mr 123
Dutton, Sheriff 14–15
Dutton, John 64
Dwyer 163, 171
Dyer, George 207–209, 214, 227, 241–243, 247, 257, 267

E

Edmonds, Michael *alt* Edmond *see* Baker, Arthur
Edmonds, William B. 345
Edwards, meat supplier 116
Edwards, William 118, 128
Edwards, William *alias* John Finnigan *alt* Finigan 100
Edward, police Inspector 72, 79, 87
Edwards, police sergeant 64
Eliza 288, 297
Elphinston 340–341
Elphinstone, Charles Belfour 265, 282
Emma 172, 175, 187, 207, 228–229
Emigration Square *alt* Immigration Square 25–26, 67, 219, 271–272
Emmett, G.G. *alt* Emmit 318, 323, 327
'Encounter Bay Tribe' 32, 193–194, 218, 271, 273
Escape, attempted escape 5, 6, 15–17, 37, 39, 46, 56, 62–63, 67, 69–70, 72, 74, 77, 79, 81, 84–85, 89, 92, 93–94, 96–97, 100, 104, 114, 117–118, 122–125, 128, 130–131, 141–142, 167, 170–171, 173–174, 179, 182, 207–209, 214, 227, 232, 241–242, 257, 293–296, 299, 303, 308
Evans, Jacob 68

Evans, James 63
Evans, William 198
Ewing, Jane *alias* Jane McInstead 274
Eyre, Edward John, magistrate 160, 191, 199, 218, 221, 223

F

Falcon 317
Farrell *alt* Farrel, reverend, numerous 109–340, *see especially* 309–310
Fawcett 159
Fenton 89
Festwell, Chas 52
Fides, Francis 233
Fielder 86, 96
Finke, William *alt* Finks 139, 144, 157
Finlayson 24
Finnis *alt* Finness Capt'n, ship's captain 148, 242, 257, 266–267
Finnis, deputy surveyor, police magistrate and justice of the peace 147, 264–265, 287, 296, 317, 322
Finnigan, John *see* Edwards, William
Finson 137
Fisher, James, supplier 240
Fisher, Robert 138, 147
Fisher, James Hurtle *alt* Fischer, resident commissioner 26, 28, 35
Fisher, lawyer 123, 215, 324, 326, 342
Fitzgerald, Patrick 212
Fitzpatrick 93
Flatt 63
Flannery, Thomas 122
Flavell, Mr 25
Fleming 79, 103, 172
Fleming, religious minister, numerous 130–159
Fleming, Sarah 161–163, 177, 180
Fleming, J. 316
Fleming, W.T. 318, 319
Flett & Linklater, suppliers of tea and sugar 269

Fogarty, Thos 136–137
Flynn 90, 96, 98, 115, 136
Folland 284
Fooks, William Samuel *alt* S. Fooks 157, 162, 166, 184
Forbes, Elizabeth 268, 270–271, 274
Foscett, James, gaol guard 86–87, 93, 96–97
Fox, James 79–82, 86
Freeling, A.H., surveyor general 34, 43–44, 329, 353
Freeman, Thomas 101, 121, 148, 185–186, 221, 225
Frome, Mr *alt* Capt'n Frome, private secretary 40, 122, 154, 158, 164, 182, 186, 245, 276, 342

G

Gag, Jane 336
Gardiner, Matthew, wife Ann *alt* Gardener 103, 181
Garlick, Mr 17–18
Garlick, William 218, 225
Garratt, S.B. 147, 157, 159, 162, 167
Garrett, Emma *alt* Garratt 140–141, 143, 155
Gandy, George, wood supplier 213
Gandy, Maria 35
George Washington 290
Gell, John 21, 324–325, 332
Gibbions, Robert 236
Gibson, Daniel 103, 121–122, 166, 168, 172–173
Gibson, Edward 181
Gilbert Henry 328, 331, 337
Gilbert, Thos, colonial storekeeper 146, 226, 229, 243–244, 253, 263, 266, 268–269, 281, 290, 328
Gilks, George 232, 252, 254–255, 267, 274–275, 294, 307
Gill, John Ryland 339
Gill, Samuel T., artist 339
Gilles, station owner 17, 55–57
Gilmore, Alex'r *alt* Gilmour 137–138

Giraffe 16
Glanville (80, 86–87, 99–100) (252)
Glass, Joseph 141, 143, 206, 209
Gleeson, Edward Burton 73, 78, 316–317, 327
Godwin, Mary 178, 185
Gofton, John 89, 93–94, 98–99, 103–105, 113, 122
Goldfinch 101, 124
Gordon 135–138, 147
Gordon, Mr Insp'r 205
Gordon, Alex'r 133–134
Gordon, James 36
Gouger, Robert, colonial secretary 19, 28, 66, 78–79, 120
Governor Gawler, ship 307
Governors
    Governor Hindmarsh (December 1836 to July 1838) 12–13, 341
    Governor Gawler (October 1838 to May 1841) 3, 5, 10, 13–14, 29, 30, 41, 58, 88, 95, 109, 127, 132, 145, 160, 260, 341, 250
    Governor George Grey (May 1841 to October 1845) 3, 6–7, 145–147, 160, 164, 177, 219, 223, 276, 250, 302, 312, 320–321, 338, 340–341
    Governor Robe *alt* Major Robe (arr. October 1845) 341
Grant, Jane 246
Grant, Helen 311
Green 91, 114, 119, 163, 171
Green, Edward 110, 114, 121–122
Green, George 183
Green, James 67
Green *alias* Williamson 195
Green, Sarah 179, 188, 191, 195, 198, 205, 214–215, 228–229
Gruland, Charles 202, 208, 220–221, 226, 228
Gurny, Mrs *alt* Gurney 335, 342
Gwatkin, Capt'n, ship's captain 330

H

Hack, Stephen and John Barton 229
Hackett, John 205
Hailes, Nathaniel *alias* Timothy Short, newspaper editor 155–156
Halford, police sergeant 62, 72, 76, 182
Hall 96, 98, 181
Hall *alias* T.H. Packman 102, 111–112, 123–124, 135–136, 139–140, 152
Hall, Charles 205
Hall, Geo, Governor's private secretary, acting colonial secretary 55, 63–64, 66, 100, 132
Hall, Geo (prisoner) 101, 116
Hall, Harry 307
Hallack, William 183
Hallett, station owner 17, 56, 58, 338
Halley, Thomas 296
Halloran, George 96, 103, 122
Halse, Edward 98, 120
Hamilton, Mess'rs, firewood and food suppliers 283, 290, 308, 332
Hamilton and Henderson, blanket suppliers 336
Hamilton, Robert 307–308
Hangings 2, 4, 16, 56–57, 59, 82, 56–60, 65, 77, 80–83, 89, 94, 106, 113–114, 210, 220–223, 234–236, 303, 311–313–315, 325, 327–328, 337
Hanna, James 237–238, 244
Harding, Mr 71–72
Hardy, Joseph 246, 253, 263, 267
Hare, C.S., superintendant of convicts 346–348
Hargen, Ernest 290–292, 296, 298
Harriott, food supplier 226, 249
Harry 283
Hart 136
Hart, Jacob 207
Hateley, police constable 52, 55, 63
Hatfield, Joseph 100
Hawk 163, 199

Hawker, G.C., station owner 200, 277, 316
Hawker, James 29–30, 41–42
Hawkins 136
Hawkins, Charles B. 332
Hawkshaw, Joseph 103, 111, 122
Hay, Charlotte 130, 147
Haytor *alt* Hayter 247, 252
Haywood, P. 165
Hedditch, Charles 223, 225, 234, 236, 239, 241, 245, 260, 296, 301, 337
Heinrick, Theodore 235
Helen Thompson 128
Henry 97, 235
Henry, Francis 173, 179, 180
Henry, Isaac 52
Hillier 152
Hoadley, Mrs 187
Hoadley, Henry Thos 186
Hoare, Hannah 197
Hoare, James 36
Horder 165, 167
Hodding, Frederick 342, 344
Hodges, Thomas 194
Holdsworth 157
Holbrook 180
Holloway 98
Hollinsworth, Serg't 274
Holly, Thos 295
Hollyer, W'm 53, 55–56, 60, 64
Hopkins, Charles 137, 141, 155
Hopkins, William, whipper 201
Hornabrook 119–120, 131
Hosier, Henry Nye 343
Howard, colonial chaplain 55, 57, 66, 68, numerous 71–228, 235, 269, 309
Howard, John 254, 263
Howard, Mrs, widow to the Reverend Howard 310
Howey 272
Howie, Patrick 288

Hubbe, Ulrick, Dr 281–282, 286, 288, 290–293, 298
Hugonin, Lieut't *alt* Huganan *alt* Houganon 200, 242, 254–255, 258–259
Hughes 195
Hughes, George 78–83
Hughes, J.A. 183–184
Hughes, Peter 167
Hunt 165
Huon, Charles 187–188
Hutchinson 209
Hyde, Philip 205, 221, 240, 249
Hyrdress *alt* Hyrdess, sisters Rosa Ann Dew, Julia, Marlina *alt* Merlina 280–282, 284, 286–287, 289, 298, 323–324, 333, 342

I

Ilbury *alt* Ilberry *alt* Ilbery 184–185, 209, 221, 227
Inman, superintendent of police 78–79
Iron, James 209, 226, 240
Irving 157
Irving, Captain, ship's captain 339
Isabella Watson 322, 326

J

Jackson, visiting official 158
Jackson, W'm 91
Jack (*alias also used by* Kadlitpinnna, Wekweki) 144
Jacky 286
Jaffray, Elias 318
James, attorney 247–248
James, John V. 327
James, police constable 62
James, Thomas Horton 37
Jeffery, George *alt* Jefferay 200, 204
Jellet 296
Jemmy (*alias also used by* Ngarbi, Warrimirru, Little Jemmy) 125, 217–218
Jenkins 137–138, 140–141, 143

John Pirie 246
John Renwick 24
Johns 157
Johnson 86, 98, 115, 129
Johnson, William 123
Johnson, Alex'r 183–184, 195
Johnston, John Spick *or* John Smith 274, 277, 281
Johnston, William *alt* Jonston 134
Jolley, Francis 182
Jolley, James 230, 235
Jones *see* Littlewood, James
Jones, John 101, 147
Jones, Owen, debtor 130
Jones, Thomas 206, 212–213
Jones, Thos, sheriff's officer numerous 52–198
Joseph Albino 242, 267

K

Kadlitpinna *aka* Captain Jack 84–85
Karri Kudnutya 292
Kate 71
Katherine Stuart Forbes 61
Kavel, Lutheran pastor 106
Kay, William *alias* Yorke the Maniac 89, 91, 98, 165, 205
Keating, John 143
Kell, Smith, police constable 169–170, 240
Kell, Thos Smith 157–158
Kelly 124
Kelly, John (98, 101, 110, 119, 123) (318)
Kelly, Patrick 186
Kelly Thomas 336
Kennedy, John H., gaol guard and principle turnkey, and his wife 61–62, 64, 69, 77, 86, 89, 97, 110, 117, 120, 128, 142, 153, 178, 182–184, 209, 215, 227, 230, 235, 239, 242, 244, 259, 264, 269, 275, 277, 283, 294, 296, 300, 307, 308, 314, 326, 331, 336, 343, 346, 348

Kepuin *alias* Tommy 213, 215
Kerby, police constable 140
Kerr, David 91, 103, 111, 119–121, 137
King 144
King, Benj'n 111
King, Francis 141
King, George 286
King John *see* Mullawirraburka
King John *aka* Murray King John *see* Merrainmalla
King Williamy 320
Kingdom, N.C. 233, 237, 243, 259
Kingston, G.S., surveyor and architect 6–7, 17, 33–34, 40–42, 88, 94–95
Kirby 148
Kitsby, John 182, 185
Klose, missionary 192–194, 223–225, 283, 322, 328–329, 359–363
Knowles, James 72
Koovey Kowminne *alias* Billy 324–325
Kunrilt, police constable 132
Kurti Mukarta *alias* Katamio 200, 204, 249

L

Lady Emma 52, 62, 148, 153
Lalla Rookh 102
Lancaster 98, 102
Lampard, Thos, gaol guard 92, 96, 108–109, 116–117
Langham, Mrs 328
Layton, bread supplier 266
Leamin, gaol guard 134–135
Lean, gaol guard 233, 253, 255
Le Boulangere, Philip 122
Lee, Henry 274, 276, 278
Lennon, gaol guard 72, 76–77, 86–90, 117, 168,-169, 180, 187, 235, 249
Leon, James 200
Leigard, Elise Sophia 100
Lewis, Joseph 342
Lewis, Richard *see* Thompson, Charles

Light, Colonel William, surveyor general 11, 22–23, 34–35, 44, 65, 68, 70, 94–95, 145
Lipson, Capt'n, ship's captain 144, 159, 164, 190, 198, 228, 233, 238, 252, 256, 260, 267, 270, 288, 322
Lister, Edw'd Alf'd 115, 119
Litchfield, Dr 154
Litchfield, Captain, police inspector 122, 137, 167, 171–172, 187, 247, 257, 285, 297
Little, Edward 122, 256
Little Jemmy, hanged for murder *see* Ngarbi
Little Jemmy, child 284, 286
Littlewood, James *alias* Jones 96–97
Lomas, Sergeant 99, 104–105
Long 200
Long, Capt'n, ship's captain 213
Lonsdale, Jos 102
Lorymer, Serg't *alt* Lorimer 86, 317
Lowe, George 186
Lowe, Mary 207, 285, 287
Lyman, James, gaol guard 134
Lynch, Hugh 136–138, 140–141, 144, 154–155

M

MacKie, James 212–213
Macloud, James 226
MacPherson 32
Madras 252
Magee 16, 59, 83, 114
Mahoney, Reverend, Catholic priest 281
Maitland, Will'm 137–138, 140–141, 144
Maitland, Frederick 144, 159
Mamgalle *alt* Mamgela *alt* Mamagelle 137–138
Manifold 92, 94
Manly, Henry 137–138
Mann, master of Supreme Court 79, 286, 338

Marra *alt* Mara, gaol guard 62, 130–131, 165, 233, 253, 255
Marshall, Thomas *alias* Thomas Wood 294, 307
Martin *alt* Marton, meat supplier 243, 309
Martin, Capt'n George 130, 149
Mary Ridgeway 86, 226, 231
Mason, Elizabeth 262, 264, 268, 274–276, 287
Mason, police constable 96
Matthew 190
Maxwell, police constable 78
McBeth 134
McDonald, resident magistrate 181, 296, 343
McDonald 216
McDonald John 290, 294–295, 301
McDonald, William *see alias* Brown, William
McDougal 56
McGouveran, Ja's 186
McGrath, George 311, 313, 324–325
McGrath, Patrick 138
McHarg, John 332, 335
McKenzie 252
McKenzie, Ja's 186
McKinstead, Jane *see* Ewing, Jane
McLean 135, 157
McLean, Sergeant 112
McMann, Patrick 206
McNichols, Gilbert 143, 147
McPherson 341
McPherson, Huntley 148, 260, 298
McSawley, William 122
Medcalfe, Fred'k 230
Meecham, James *alt* Meehan 137–138
Menge, Joseph, geologist and mineralogist 27
Merainmalla *alt* Merrainmilla *alt* Rongist Meraimnalld *aka* King John *alt* Murray King John 216, 320–321
Metcalfe 155

Metcalfe, Harry 254
Miles, Jane 205
Millard, Thos 316, 322
Miller & Brydon, blanket suppliers 286–287
Milner, Robert Lyon *alt* Milne 139, 158, 166–167, 180–181, 185, 187, 190
Mills, John 134
Mitchell, Captain 35
Mitchell, Joseph 186
Mitchell, Thomas Neilson 285, 290–293, 322
Monitya 197
Molineux, Edw'd, gaol guard and turnkey 25, 64–65, 76–77, 86, 89, 103, 118, 120, 165, 170–171, 173, 207–208, 232, 235, 293, 344
Moorhouse JP, visiting magistrate 295
Moorhouse, Matthew, protector of the Aboriginal people 32–33, 67, 77, 87, 135, 179, 189, 197, 199, 201, 204, 213, 215, 217–218, 220–221, 223–224, 231, 234, 247, 249, 271, 279, 282–283, 286–287, 292, 319–322, 325, 327–329, 333, 335–336, 340
Moorpar 194
'Moorunde Tribe' *alt* Moorundie 216, 250
Moran, James 63
More, police constable 140
Morgan 16–17, 163, 168, 171
Morgan, William 114–115, 122
Morris, William, turnkey and 'keeper of the lunatics' 300–301, 303, 323, 328
Morris, Charles 141, 162
Morris, George 196
Morris, John (216–218, 221, 225, 227–228) (338)
Morris, Margaret 128, 138–139
Morris, Mary 139
Moss, Edw'd, gaol turnkey 63–64, 69–70, 115

Moss, Will'm 115
Moullia 216, 220–223, 245
'Mount Barker Tribe' 32, 211, 250, 340
Mulholland 90, 98, 119, 131, 144
Mullawirraburka *aka* King John ('Adelaide Tribe') 216, 304, 360, 273, 304
Mullins, Patrick 86, 96
Munday, A.M., colonial secretary 278
Murdock, John 234
Murphy, Thos 72, 76, 79, 91
Murphy, Prisoner Working Party 87, 90–91
Murray, Andrew 200–201
Murray, David Alexander 332, 335
Murray, James 322
Murray, Thos 148–149
'Murray Tribe' 32, 193–194, 216, 223, 271, 273, 303, 320–321, 329
Myers, Edward 86

N

Nante *alt* Nantes 194, 201
Nash, col'l surgeon 66–67, 69, 72, 78–79, 90, 96–98, 106, 108–111, 114–116, 119–126, 129–130, 134–141, 160, 162, 165–166, 171–173, 179, 187–188, 191, 195–196, 198–199, 202–203, 206, 215–216, 218, 221–222, 226, 229–230, 236, 238–239, 241–242, 245, 247, 251, 260–262, 264, 266, 268–270, 274–275, 279–282, 285–288, 290–293, 300, 316, 324, 326–328, 330, 337, 339, 342–343
Naughton, police constable 114
Ned 245
Neblett, Patience 64
Newcombe, George 178, 181
Newenham, clerk of the Supreme Court 99
Newenham, C.B., sheriff 89, 93, 110, 119, 150, 248, 294, 313

Newenham, W.H. 93, 149, 190, 206
Newington, John 187
Newland, visiting magistrate 332
Newman, William 256
Ngangkiparri *alt* Ngankiparri river, Onkaparinga River 27, 193, 208
Ngarbi *alias* little Jemmy 114, 210, 234–236, 315
Nicholas *alt* Nicolls, coroner 78, 244
Nicholson, Alfred, gaol sentry 232–233
Nixon, visiting official 121, 158, 164
Nonmus, Isaac 188, 241, 245
Norris, police constable 63, 78, 135, 141, 144, 198, 245
Noonan 288, 299
Noonan, John 244–246
Noonan, Patrick 307
Noone 309, 332
Noulan, Patrick *alt* Nowlan 209, 221
Novis, Richard 190
Nultia 216, 220–223, 279
Nunan 159, 181
Nweba 194

O

Oakey, James 257, 267
Oakley, Thomas 36
O'Halloran, Major 99, 159, 169, 185
O'Hea, Dr 162
One Arm Charley 287
Ormrod 93
Owen, Thomas, gaol turnkey 61, 63
Owens, Elizabeth 182–183

P

Packman, Henry 52, 55, 60
Packman, T.H. *see* Hall
Palmer, Edwin *alt* James Edwin Palmer 125, 141, 143
Palmyra 307
Parkinson 157
Parsons, William 322

Patch 180
Patch, George 321
Patton 98
Pavelin, Edward 102
Paxton, chemist 306, 318
Pearce, William 252, 254–257, 261, 263, 270, 279, 280
Pearson 257
Peasley 163, 171
Pegler 16
Pendigras, James 62
Perry, Thomas, gaol turnkey, and his wife 1, 61–62, 72, 76–77, 86, 89–91, 102, 117, 121, 124–126, 131, 147, 153, 172, 180, 203, 207, 213–214, 227, 231, 237–238, 243–244, 254–258, 265, 278, 296–297, 300, 304, 313, 325–327, 331
Perryman, John 190
Peter (*alias also used by* Wera Maldera) 55, 181
Peters 90
Pettman, Henry 167, 182
Pfeiffer, George 53
Pffenders, victims of robbery 81
Pittman, Henry *alt* H'y Pitman, gaol guard 64, 69
Pittman, Henry, debtor 181
Plough, Kezziah *alt* Kaziah 70
Poeverall, Henry 239
Polden *alt* Poulden, attorney 256, 276, 338
Polden 226
Poulden, W.A. 159–160
Pollard, Corp'l, police constable 61, 189, 289
Poonindie mission 340
Porter, colonial engineers department 236, 249, 255, 258, 269–270, 274, 304
Powell, Charles 153, 160, 165
Prettyjohn 157, 159–160
Putland, Thos 137–138, 140–141, 144

Pybers *alt* Pybus *alt* Pybis, supplier of rivets, irons and handcuffs 191, 240, 257
Pye, James 79–80, 86

Q
Quigley 136–137
Quigley, James 185–186
Quinn, Thomas 116, 186

R
Rains, William 167–168
Rankin, Robert 336–337
Rau, Eleanora 99, 103, 105–106, 119, 130
Rajasthan 14, 79, 149
Ram Sham, gravedigger 78
Ratcliffe, John 69
Reading, James 144
Reeves, Samual 336
Regan, William 183, 188
Reynolds, Sarah 167
Rhodes, Mary 128, 132, 144, 259–260, 290–292, 296–301, 305, 309
Ricketts, Jane 336
Riley, James 186
Roach, William 158, 166
Robertson, sailor 239
Robertson, Geo *alt* Robinson, gaol guard 86, 92–93, 96, 100, 118, 126, 134, 163, 165, 171, 175
Robinson, Charles 221, 228
Robinson, James 240
Rogers, Thos *alt* Rodgers, gaol guard 91, 93, 119
Rogers, George 318
Rogers, John (131–132) (185, 209, 212)
Rollands, W'm 96–98, 101
Rollison, Alex'r N. *alt* Rollason 118–121, 125, 129
Rose, John 343
Ross, James 221, 227–228
Ross, undertaker 172–173

Ross, Mr and Mrs, teachers 43, 273
Ryan 91

S
Saddler, Edw'd 196
Sally 90, 98
Sanders, police constable 136
Sans Pareille alt Sans Parielle 239–240
Sayers, R. 130
Scotia 288, 314
Seawood, William D. 122
Selby, Samual, gaol guard 125, 140, 165
Selfs, Thomas 237, 239
Scheibeney 109
Schurmann, Clamor, missionary 31–33, 218, 220, 222–223, 234
Scott (144) (147)
Scott, wardsman 91, 102, 119
Scott, Fred'k Maitland 148, 159–160, 182, 184, 195
Scott, George 116–117, 130
Scott, John 63
Scroggins 16
Shand, John 243–244
Shanks, Peter 115, 129, 147–149, 154
Shaw, police inspector 78–79, 134, 247, 317, 322
Sheard, police inspector 63, 72, 86, 89, 124
Sheibeners, David 108
Shepherd 98, 111–112, 117–118, 120
Sheppard 304, 307
Sherman, physician 296
Short (Bishop) 72
Sidd, Peter 136
Sinclair, Peter 164
Sir Cha's McCarthy 97
Skelton 239
Slackford, Jane 207, 212
Sladden, Isaac 108–109
Slater, doctor's assistant 110, 116, 119–120
Sloggett, Grace 293

Somerville, Rebecca 316, 330
Smallacombe, John 324, 326
Smallacombe, Thomas 166, 168
Smart, sheriff 12, 16, 59, 114, 125
Smith (103) (120–121) (123) (274) (295)
Smith, Peter *alias* Michael Coyle 67, 91, 99–100, 110, 122
Smith, Frederick 304, 307
Smith, James 196
Smith, John (197) (307)
Smith, Mary Ann 201, 275–277
Smith, Mary 158, 283
Smith, Matthew, Port Lincoln magistrate 84, 92, 274
Smith, May 196
Smythe, Capt'n, Port Philip magistrate 91
Somers, William 314
Souter, George 318
Spencer, Harriet 254, 258
Spicer, John William 200
Spicer, George Jefferay 200
Spiers, John William 204
Springbott, Mrs 131
Stagg, Joseph 65, 94, 98–107, 110, 113–114, 122, 179, 191, 236
Staples, Charles 101
Starkey, bread supplier 162
Steel 102, 115–116
Steele 120
Stephen, George Milner *alt* Stephens, advocate general, temporary administrator, then colonial secretary 13, 55–56, 62
Stevens, Charles 240, 244, 248, 258
Stevenson, Geo 199, 231, 233
Stevenson, James *see* Douglas
Stewart, Mrs 207
Stewart, Thomas 202–203, 205
Stone, Cornelius 172, 186
Story 144, 154–155, 157
Story, Mrs 136

Story, Charlotte 158
Story, Joseph 137–138, 140–141, 143
Stratton, John 285
Stuart, police inspector 10, 14–15, 79, 93, 96, 100, 107, 148
Stubbs, Elizabeth 234, 236, 245
Stuckey, bread supplier 52
Stuckey, John 130–131
Sturgess 165
Sturgess, Harriet 234
Sullivan 110
Sutherland 198
Swift, Jeremiah 60–63
Symers Capt'n, prisoner 168
Symonds 79, 85

T

Taglioni 285
Taimy 135
Tamar 64
Tam-O'Shanter, person 55
Tam-O'Shanter, ship 11, 35
Tapley, Capt'n, ship's captain 196
Taylor, Henry 53
Teichelmann, missionary 31, 192, 325, 329
Terror 231
Theakston, John Henry 139, 155
Theile 98
Thickness, Sam 56
Thickstones, J.H. 140
Thirteen 97
Timbo 330, 341, 344
Tippa Warricha *aka* Bob 55, 64, 67–68, 71, 77
Thomas, Mess'rs, printers 149
Thomas, Edward Alonzo 340, 342
Thomas, Samual 181, 186
Thomas, Thos 63
Thomas, private secretary 341
Thomson, James 101–102
Thompson (90, 96) (171)

Index

Thompson, Boyce 154, 157
Thompson, Bryce *see* Baker, Arthur
Thompson, Charles *alias* Richard Lewis 264, 266, 269, 324
Thompson, James *alt* Thomson, shepherd, murdered 17, 55–56, 58, 68
Thompson, James, runaway convict 186
Thompson, Joseph *alt* Thomson 192, 196
Thornton, Thos 226, 228
Tolmer, Alexander, commissioner of police 15, 43, 81–82, 93, 98–100, 104–105, 113, 130, 172–173, 208, 241, 269, 276, 294–296, 301
Tomkins, Thomas 276–277
Tommy 335–336
Tommy Roundhead *see* Wang Nucha
Travers, Arthur, gaol guard 64, 70, 77, 86, 89
Turner, Charles 288, 316
Turner, John 253–254, 258–259, 264, 267
Turpin, Charles 322
Tully 128

U

Ullathorne, Roman Catholic Vicar General of Australia 95–97

V

Vansteine 86, 90, 98, 101, 115, 119
Vauhan, William 121, 131, 134, 138, 154, 157
Victoria 248
Vixon 270, 275, 291, 294–295, 297–298

W

Wainwright, Thos 92
Wainwright *alias* Yorke 201
Walker, John 314
Walker, Capt'n John 147, 149, 153
Walsh, Capt'n, ship's captain 205

Walsh, George 343–344
Wang Nucha *aka* Tommy Roundhead 55–56, 58
Warriaetti *alt* Warriatto *alt* Warriatti *alt* Warrietto 134–136
Warrimirru *alias* Jemmy 246
Wardel, Capt'n, ship's captain 314
Warren, gaol turnkey 56, 60
Waterwitch 233, 238–239, 242
Watkins, reverend 343
Watson, Henry 229–230, 232, 242–243
Watts, Mary 105, 119, 254
Webb, Joseph 110–111
Wekweki *alt* Wekiweki *alias* Jack 325, 327–328
Wells, William 125–126
Welsh, Capt'n, ship's captain 186
Welsh, George 343
Wera Maldera *alt* Wira Maldira *alt* Wera Maldira *alias* Peter 311–315, 327–328
Whippings, lashes 4, 192, 197, 201, 246–247
White, George, debtor 131, 141, 147–148, 152
White, George 299
White, Henry 239–240
White, Thomas 157–158
Whitehouse, John 85, 92
Whyte, James 336–337
Wickham, Thomas 178, 183
Wigley, resident magistrate 55, 61, 92, 115, 169, 213–216, 218, 225, 227, 232, 239, 241, 243, 245, 247, 249, 261, 296, 338, 342
Wild, James *alt* Wilde 254, 263
Wild, John 343
Wilkins, James 313–314
Wilkins, William 260, 299–301, 303–306, 308, 311, 318
Wilkinson, Catherine 1, 325–328, 330–331, 342–343
Wilkinson, Robert 294, 332, 334

Wilmot, David 196
William 157, 163
William *alt* Williamy 168–169
William Fulcher 189
Williams 110
Williams, gaol turnkey 61
Williams, William, government storekeeper 55, 57, 72, 189
Williams, police constable 63
Williams, James (80, 87, 90–91, 98–100) (336)
Williams, John 198–199
Williams, Thos 239–240, 244, 247, 248
Williamson *see* Green
Williamson 188
Williamson, William (226, 230) (241–242)
Williamy (*see also* William *alt* Williamy) (55, 84–85, 87) (144) (214) (227, 231, 287)
Wills, Charles 159, 163
Wilson, Allen 217
Wilson, Henry 262, 277–278
Wilson, John (55, 91, 103) (114, 119, 121–122) (130, 132–134) (198)
Wilson, John Walker 314
Wilson, Rob't 55–56, 64
Wilson, Thos (186) (199, 202–203) (282, 284–285, 287, 290–292)
Wiltshire 337

Winch, William 289
Wright, Capt'n 152
Wright, gaoler 70, 76–77, 79–80, 85, 89, 117, 119, 125, 130, 157–158, 163
Wright, Charles, Dr Edward Wright's son and assistant 305, 306
Wright, Dr Edward 304, 306, 308, 310–311, 318
Wright, John 185, 187
Wright, police constable 131, 137
Wright, William 140, 152
Witt, James George 319, 323
Wood, James 115
Wood, Thomas *see* Marshall, Thomas
Wood, William 236, 238
Worth, Henry 297–298
Worthington, George 131, 138, 140–141, 143, 157
Wyatt, William *ad interim* protector of the Aboriginal people, medical doctor 21, 31–34, 54–55, 57–58, 90, 206, 343
Wylie *alt* Wiley, gaol guard 77, 86–89, 91

Y

Yerr I Cha *alt* Yerr-i-Cha *aka* George 55–56, 58
York, William 125, 140, 160
Yuki Warritya *alias* Jimmy 215

Wakefield Press is an independent publishing and
distribution company based in Adelaide, South Australia.
We love good stories and publish beautiful books.
To see our full range of books, please visit our website at
www.wakefieldpress.com.au
where all titles are available for purchase.

Find us!

Twitter: www.twitter.com/wakefieldpress
Facebook: www.facebook.com/wakefield.press
Instagram: instagram.com/wakefieldpress

www.ingramcontent.com/pod-product-compliance
Lightning Source LLC
Chambersburg PA
CBHW031845220426
43663CB00006B/502